Political Parties
in American Society

POLITICAL PARTIES IN AMERICAN SOCIETY

Samuel J. Eldersveld

Basic Books, Inc., Publishers   New York

Library of Congress Cataloging in Publication Data

Eldersveld, Samuel James.
  Political parties in American society.

  Includes index.
  1. Political parties—United States. I. Title.
JK2261.E425   1982   324.273   81–68790
ISBN 0–465–05935–X   AACR2

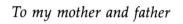

To my mother and father

CONTENTS

PART IV

PARTIES AND THE CAMPAIGN, ELECTORAL,
AND POLICY PROCESSES

PART V

PARTY SYSTEM CHANGE IN AMERICA

PREFACE

THIS BOOK emerged after many years of teaching the "parties course," an intellectual experience that I have continuously enjoyed. The discussions with students, politicians, and colleagues generated by this experience produced the reflections embodied in this volume. Teaching led also to participation in politics and to my own research into the nature of political parties and their activities. This book, then, attempts to embody both my life experiences and scholarly activities. The approach presented here, which is only one of several ways to communicate with others about party politics, has been useful and stimulating for both me and my students. I hope you find it useful too.

The focus of my approach is a concern, both theoretical and practical, for the importance of parties as structures of action in American society. Our parties seem to be on trial today. Their organizational reality and utility are being questioned and debated as they have been often in the past. Scholars and columnists talk about the erosion, the decomposition, and the decline of parties. Reviewing the history of our parties, scholars have argued that after a hesitant beginning parties have played a central role in the development of the American political system as major associations integrating that system and working to solve social problems. Whether this is no longer true is a major query pervading the discussion in this book, as I describe and interpret in detail the nature of party organizations in the United States, their patterns of activity, and their functional consequences for our system, in particular their meaning to American citizens. In this book I am by no means ready to take a pessimistic position. Our parties may be losing some ground. The candidate-centered campaign, the increased role of the media, and the rise of many well-financed Political Action Committees (PACs) have challenged the centrality of political parties. As a result they may be less dominant or relevant today in the performance of certain functions such as in campaigns and in the nominating process. Yet, I am by no means ready to conclude that our party system is being "dismantled" and that our party organizations are ineffectual and impotent. There is much evidence to the contrary, and throughout this book I shall weigh it against the evidence of decline. Parties' contacts with the public, the trends in party identification, the roles of parties in the electoral process, the strengthening of party organizations, the continuing relevance of parties for the behavior of elected officials, and the impact of parties on policy outputs—all these, when analyzed carefully, do not lead cumulatively and exclusively to the conclusion that parties are on their way out. "The party" is definitely not yet "over."

A second, recurrent motif of this book concerns the complex meaning of parties for the lives of American citizens. Parties are actually multifaceted structures that affect people in many ways. Many of us (over 60 percent) call ourselves Republicans or Democrats and are proud of it. One fourth of the public reports having been contacted by party and campaign workers in recent elections. Close to 25 percent have worked for or contributed money to a party, or have engaged in a political campaign on its behalf. Thousands of Americans belong to local party organizations and take on leadership positions as club officers, committee men and women, precinct leaders, ward leaders, and other similar jobs, slogging away during campaigns and often between campaigns on many different tasks. A much smaller number of people run for public office on a party ticket; but even this group is large considering all the partisan positions to be filled in towns, townships, counties, cities, and states. And then there are the administrators appointed to jobs by party leaders on the basis of patronage. The meaning of all this exposure to, and involvement with, parties cannot easily be documented, but clearly for a large part of the American public the parties are relevant. They are reference groups for those who identify with them. They are social groups for those who work in them and who thus through them secure social gratification, social recognition, and friendships. They are policy-relevant groups for those who through parties see the chance to affect policy changes. This complex reality of the party process is what I hope to convey in some small measure in this book.

A third theme I wish to emphasize is the complexity of the American system and, hence, the resulting burden placed on political parties in performing effectively in this political culture. The heterogeneity of our population, its many conflicting social and ideological interests, the federal and fragmented nature of political institutions, and the populist elements in our culture—all these constitute a difficult environment in which parties must work. We elect more people to public office, we hold elections more frequently, and we impose more burdens on citizens for making political choices than any other nation. We confront citizens with more mass media exposure for longer campaign periods than in any other system, and we probably have a more diverse and more heavily financed interest group system soliciting citizen support than elsewhere in the world. The task of the parties to organize effectively, recruit able leaders, run campaigns, mobilize support, reconcile conflicts, and develop creative solutions to domestic problems (and those of the world) in such an environment is a complex and burdensome one. It is this context that must be kept in mind in examining the meaning of parties for our citizens and our system.

While being a very concerned analysis, this is also then a relatively optimistic one. It emphasizes the relevance of parties in the context of a complex system. It reviews the ways in which parties as structures have profound meanings for our society. Hovering over all discussions of political parties are these key questions: How well do parties perform? What impacts do they have? What are their strengths and what are their weaknesses? How important are they to citizens? Do parties really make a difference in the quality of American democracy? And do parties work as well today as in the past? If not, why not? And what can we do about it?

If the aim of this book is to lead students to confident interpretations about our party system, certain requisites are in order. First, the theory (or theories) of party has to be elaborated and discussed in some detail, both at the beginning and throughout so that much of the descriptive and empirical information will be linked to useful interpretations. Next, it is necessary to give the student access to the most important and recent research in the field. Since research on parties has mushroomed greatly, it is a difficult task for any one person. Nevertheless, one must try, if he is really to be confident that he is communicating our knowledge to students. And in this connection it is important to keep in mind the importance of research that is both "longitudinal" and "comparative." That is, at a minimum, the student must have some basis for judging the present American party system both in relation to the past and in relation to other systems. To do this well in one book is difficult, but again, the attempt must be made, if useful interpretations are to emerge. Finally, there is the "normative" requisite; students judging it against various value standards must constantly be urged to question the performance of the party system. The concern of this book is not only how the system works but also *how well* it works and how it can be improved.

In attempting to write a book keeping these objectives and requisites in mind, I may have fallen short. Insofar as this book is at all useful, however, I must credit many others. I am particularly indebted to all the great scholars, old and young, who over the years have engaged in such meticulous and theoretically useful research on parties. The scholarship on political parties in 1982 looks much different, and of higher quality, than that in 1956 when I first got involved in parties research. I am, of course, in great debt to the students with whom I have worked over the years at the University of Michigan, as well as in other universities, many of whom were in the field with me in Detroit at various times from 1956 to 1980. They asked the questions, they did the research work, they provided the insights, they used these materials in class and critiqued them seriously, they provided the incentive. I must note also that the assistance of our able secretaries in the department at Michigan (Carol J. Campbell and Lynne R. Nowak) was indispensable. And, further, the ideas and suggestions of colleagues, such as James Q. Wilson at Harvard, Dwaine Marvick at the University of California at Los Angeles, and Arthur Miller at the University of Michigan, were of great value. Finally I thank my politician friends whom I interviewed in many places, but above all in the United States, India, and the Netherlands. It was through the contacts and discussions with them that I obtained a better feeling for the ubiquity and centrality of party politics and the similarities of party behavior across systems, while I also was beginning to understand the cultural differences as reflected in party systems. This book is a product, then, of the intellectual interactions of scholars, students, and politicians. All three were indispensable for a study that aims at theoretical relevance, empirical evidence, and practical utility.

Part I

INTRODUCTION TO AMERICAN PARTIES

Chapter 1

Parties in Society:

A Theoretical Overview

POLITICAL PARTIES are major structures of politics in modern socie-ies. In developing democracies they are universal phenomena. They are objects of intensive study, primarily because, as apparatuses of po-litical action and social power they engage in activities that may be of great consequence for the individual citizen and for the world in which he or she lives. In order to understand parties and arrive at a useful way of thinking about them, we will discuss parties from three standpoints: their place in the political system, their nature as a special group, and their importance to democracy.

The Place of Parties in the Political System

Modern political systems are highly complex, and the American sys-tem is particularly so. The *institutions* of government in Washington and at the state and local levels consist of huge bureaucracies, large bicameral legislatures with elaborate committee systems, and many layers of courts with different jurisdictions—structures so separated and fragmented as to make coordination of governmental action ex-tremely difficult. In addition to these institutions there is a multiplic-ity of *interest groups* in modern systems, seemingly always increasing in number and diversity, and constantly pressing their conflicting claims and demanding governmental attention, which makes the representation of these interests and the mediation of group conflicts more involved and trying than ever before. And finally there is in modern systems the *mass public*, larger than ever because of the extension of the right to vote and the greater opportunities for participation in politics than in the past. The tasks of political leadership in communicating with this public and mobilizing its support is ever more complicated at the same time that it is ever more important.

If such systems are to survive and to be governed effectively, clearly means have to be developed to bring the scattered parts together, to lubricate the system so that, at least minimally, leaders, groups, and citizens can work toward the achievement of certain goals for the society. Specifically, leaders must be recruited, policy objectives defined, citizens heard, group conflicts negotiated, and elections conducted. Leaders have to mobilize support, competition has to be organized, and the public has to be educated. These activities must be accomplished in such a way as to make sense to citizens as well as to lead to important policy decisions by elites.

What emerges to facilitate government in modern systems under these complex conditions are linkage structures, intermediary organizations that help produce positive action and effective decisions in the face of fragmentation, conflict, and mass involvement. These structures are groups that engage in activities and organize initiatives that make cooperative behavior possible. The political party is one major type of a linkage structure (see figure 1.1); some would say it is the central one. In what ways is such a structure crucial for the system? First, it provides a basis for interaction and cohesion in legislatures, such as the Congress, and often, but not always, between legislative and executive leaders, such as the Congress and the president. Further, a party provides some basis for cooperation between national, state, and local institutions and leadership. Second, the party is a forum within which interest groups can (but not all do) present their views about governmental policies as well as press for particular types of candidates for offices, both elective and appointive. The party is, therefore, an arena for the development of compromises by interest groups as well as the agent in creating interest group coalitions working for particular goals. Third, a party constitutes a medium or channel for communication between citizens, organizational leaders, and governmental officials. Parties bring the citizen into contact with government and, conversely, are used by leaders to communicate with the public. Thus many citizens' involvement with politics occurs through the parties.

Parties, however, are not the only linkage apparatuses in modern systems. Certainly some of the large-scale interest groups, labor unions, business associations, farm organizations, and civic clubs, as well as single issue groups, are important in providing linkages between citi-

Figure 1.1

Parties as Linkage Structures in the Political System

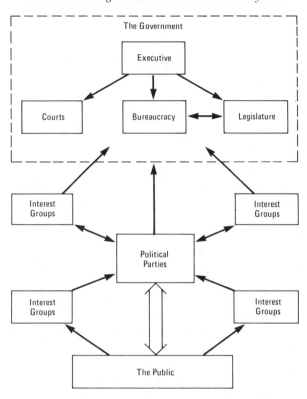

zens and political leaders. In some societies, indeed, such groups play a role as central as that of parties. Further, the linkage contributions of the mass media, particularly of newspapers and television, are considerable in bringing citizens to a continuing awareness of government. Although parties are not the only linkage structures, to many scholars they are more central to the functioning of the American system than are other structures. An early scholar of American parties, Elmer E. Schattschneider, wrote almost forty years ago that "the parties are not ... merely appendages of modern government; *they are in the center of it* and play a determinative and creative role in it."[1] More recently, Samuel Huntington has argued that the party "is the distinctive institution of the modern polity ... the function of the party is to organize participation, to aggregate interests, *to serve as the link* between social forces and the government."[2] Avery Leiserson states the position even more explicitly. "The political party is a strategically critical concept. ... The political party, or party system, *provides the major connective linkage* between people and government...."[3]

There are other scholars who question this emphasis on the centrality of parties for the system. Jeff Fishel argues that "clearly Schatt-schneider and others . . . overestimated the importance of parties . . . it is essential that observers not underestimate the value, role, and contributions of nonparty associations."[4] While recognizing the importance of other political groups and the media in the United States, political parties still play a major linkage role in our system.

A concluding point should be made about parties in their context as linkage structures. We live in a society of considerable conflict between individuals and social groups. And these cleavages are manifest in the nature and workings of our political institutions as well as in other aspects of our society. The disagreements occur at all levels of our system over a variety of immediate political issues: Should property taxes be cut, should the police force be strengthened, should streets be paved, should pollution standards be raised, should a new bomber be built, should welfare programs be cut, and so forth? Our positions on these issues may reflect fundamental philosophical differences concerning the priorities for our society and the proper role of government in solving social problems. It was ever thus. The conflicts among humans about the use of their resources by political leaders and about the proper exercise of political authority have been recurrent and universal.

We also live in a society that is committed to cooperative behavior. That is, we are aware that some resolution of our conflicts must be undertaken if we are to be saved from intolerable turmoil or even civil war. The proper handling of social conflict is crucial for any society. In modern systems we have developed institutions and practices to "manage" conflict. We do this by (1) providing channels for the expression of conflicting viewpoints; (2) providing forums in which cooperative discussions for the resolution of conflict can occur; and (3) a final process of decision making that is responsive to social conflicts and perceived as legitimate and authoritative, even if not happily acceptable to all those involved in a particular controversy.

Parties are groups which are part of this conflict articulation, mediation, and resolution process. Not the only groups or institutions involved with it, but usually very much involved at some stage, if not at all stages in the process. This process, in the large, is what "party politics" is all about—the struggle for power and influence among individuals and groups, which reflects conflicting objectives and viewpoints and leads eventually to the making of policy so that hopefully the particular conflict will be resolved, at least for the time being.

The way parties provide the organization and leadership to participate in the conflict resolution process varies greatly from one society to another. Parties may be centralized power structures in one system or very decentralized in another. They may be very ideological or personalistic and pragmatic. One party may capture majority control of government in one system, while in another system several parties may work in coalition toward social harmony. The parties in one system may be engaged in violent, hostile combat, while in another system the competition may be peaceful. Social groups may work completely within and through the party system; in another society each major interest group may organize its own party. Thus a wide variety of form, style, leadership, and activity may be found. But in all systems where parties exist, they are groups that are deeply involved with the expression and mediation of human conflict.

What Type of Group Is a Party?

It is not enough, however, to visualize the party as a major linkage structure in the system. The key definitional questions that remain are: What kind of group is it? What does it do as a group? What are its distinctive activities?

The search for an acceptable definition of a political party is quite complicated and controversial. The problem is that there are such strange varieties of groups that are called parties or are considered to be parties that to arrive at a universally applicable definition is difficult.

In some democratic systems parties can be very easily formed to promote the interests of a small group of people or to advance a particular cause. Most of these parties have a flash-in-the-pan existence. When should they be taken seriously? Sometimes groups behave as parties are thought to behave but they have different labels, such as appeal, movement, rally, league, congress, or front. Some examples are: the Christian Democratic Appeal (Holland), the Popular Republican Movement (France), the Awami League (Bangladesh), the Indian National Congress, Rally of the French People (Gaullist), and the Popular Front (France before World War II). What makes these groups parties? Sometimes parties exist for a long time but rarely win any elections such as the Prohibition party in the United States. Are they to be considered genuine parties? And what about factions within parties, such as Reagan's Citizens for the Republic—why are they not political parties? The variability in the phenomena taxes our ability at clear conceptualization. We will present here three different images of a party as a group, or three different but complementary ways of describing the major activities of a party. Then we can probably come close to comprehending what is meant by this type of political institution.

The First Image of Party: A Group Seeking Power by Winning Elections

The first image of a party is a group seeking political power by winning elections. The party consists of men and women who either select or endorse candidates for a public office and then work to secure enough votes to put them in office. Thus, one scholar says parties are "organizations that pursue the goal of placing their avowed representatives in government positions."[5] And another writes that a party is "distinguished from other political organizations by its concentration on the contesting of elections."[6]

This view of parties focuses on elections and the struggle for formal public offices. And it is true that most parties, and certainly the American Republican and Democratic parties, engage in this activity. To this definition, however, there are two types of inadequacies. First, scholars in some countries do not accept this conception as identifying the primary role of parties, and hence question the comparative usefulness of the definition. Second, some scholars take exception to this concept by arguing that it does not really explain *the essence* of a party, or it explains only a small part of the essence of the party because parties engage in other important types of activities and pursue other types of goals than just electoral activities and goals of political power. Those who have studied third-world politics have noted that these party leaders, while not uninterested in power, are often inclined to place primary emphasis on developmental economic and social activities: building schools and roads; teaching illiterate peasants to use modern methods of farming; improving health conditions in villages; and educating people in family planning.[7] While elections are not unimportant, what parties actually emphasize more there may differ greatly from what parties emphasize in our society. In many American communities also, however, parties often engage in many activities other than contesting elections. Our local parties can be much preoccupied with social problems in the community, human welfare needs, and providing people with an opportunity for civic involvement. These activities will be discussed in detail later.

A Second Image of Party: A Group That Processes Interest-Group Demands

A second, long-existing image of a party is a group that represents social interests and often is actually a coalition of interests seeking community actions. Some of the earliest scholars saw parties in this light, emphasizing that they were different from other groups because they adjusted interest-group demands in the context of the welfare of the total community. Thus Max Weber, the famous German sociologist, distinguished in an early work between "the communal actions" of parties and those of social classes and status groups, which were concerned, he said, with only one segment of the society.[8] And Charles Merriam, an American scholar, wrote in 1922 that "The broad basis of the party is the interests, individual or group, usually group interests, which struggle to translate themselves into types of social control acting through the political process of government. . . ."[9] The major emphasis of these writers is on the adjustment of group conflicts, or as G. Almond puts it, "interest aggregation" (the converting of demands of groups into major policy alternatives).[10] V. O. Key also saw the party as having "its foundation in sectional, class, or group interests."[11] The party then is unique because it organizes support for governmental leadership from a variety of groups.

Thus this second image sees parties as apparatuses of communal action linked to the groups making up the community, responding to and processing their demands, and thereby translating social reality into political reality. In this conception of a party the acquisition and use of power to contest elections is not inconsequential, but the nature of such a power process is given a broader meaning: Parties are groups which are integrated with the social process.

A Third Image of Party: An Ideological Competitor

There is a third image of what a party as a group does. It is to communicate an ideology to the public and, at least in democratic societies, to compete with other parties on ideological terms. Anthony Downs is a classic exponent of this position; to Downs the most significant aspect about parties is that "they formulate policies in order to win elections." That is, he says, the parties look carefully at the distribution of public opinion among the voters ("the political market") and develop a stance on policy in relation to their calculations of how they can best maximize votes in relation to this political market of public opinion.[12] Figure 1.2 illustrates this conception, both for the United States and for a multiparty system. How parties deal with the political market will vary greatly from one country to the next—in the United States the "market" of opinion and of votes differs in its basic nature from that of other countries. Parties have to adapt to these differences. In a society like the United States, with a "normal" distribution of public opinion, with the majority of the public near the center, parties will crowd that ideological center. In the Netherlands, with a "multimodal" distribution of ideology for the public, parties do not crowd the center but develop clienteles at various points along the ideological continuum.

The essence of this view of a party is ideological competition. Both the parties and the individual voters find ideologies useful. Every party must differentiate its position from other parties in order to attract votes. And voters find party ideologies useful because they help focus attention on the differences between parties. Parties develop ideolo-

FIGURE 1.2

The Downs Model for Two Contrasting Party Systems

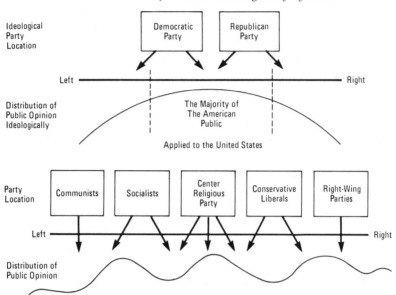

gies and issue positions in relation to voter preference patterns on issues. And the party is a dynamic structure—it adjusts *over time* to changes in mass preferences in order to maintain and maximize its power. If public preference swings left, there will be a perceptible shift in party ideological positions, and, similarly, if the public opinion shifts to the right, the parties will shift. Parties are presumably pragmatic, within reason, in their linkage to mass preferences on policy. V. O. Key called this tendency for the two American parties "dualism in a moving consensus."[13]

Certain key assumptions of the Downs concept may not prevail in the real world. Among these is that all voters have policy positions, that they know the policy positions of the parties, and that they vote on the basis of policy preferences, not on the basis of habitual patterns of behavior such as a long-standing party identification. He assumes also that parties know the political market, develop distinctive ideological positions, communicate these effectively to the public, adhere to them consistently, and, above all, are able to change to left or right to adjust to that market without alienating the hard core of their supporters and activists. Obviously voters and parties do not always behave in these ways.

Despite such reservations it is an ideal-type model of parties and has a real value. In some societies with party systems where ideology is indeed salient, this theory may account for much more than in other societies where ideology is less basic. But parties in any society must compete for power by developing distinctive ideologies and policy positions, whether moderate or extreme, in the minds of the public. Thus weakly in some societies and strongly and effectively in others, parties bring about the intensification and crystallization of ideological conflict or its dilution and deflation. Parties may either clarify and polarize ideological differences or obscure and depolarize them. The relevance of this function for all societies cannot be overstated.

Based on the three images described so far, here is a suggested definition of a party. A party in a democracy is a group that competes for political power by contesting elections, mobilizing social interests, and advocating ideological positions, thus linking citizens to the political system.

Parties in Comparison to Other Groups

To clearly distinguish parties from nonparty groups is not a simple task. Attempts that have focused on the stability of party organizations over time or on their preoccupation with elections are not convincing enough about the special character of parties.

This problem of definition in relation to other groups becomes most difficult, of course, when the attempt is made to distinguish a political party from another kind of group such as a labor union, an inclusive businessman's association, or a general purpose civic group (Common Cause). Max Weber had no difficulty in distinguishing a party from a class or a status group—he saw the latter two as representing only a segment of the community, while a party was communitywide in its orientation. This same context perhaps can distinguish between a party and other political groups in modern societies. Most nonparty groups have a relatively narrow following and a limited, specific interest. Obviously, the Westside Neighborhood Improvement Association, the Catholic Young Men's Club, and the Association of University Professors are groups with limited perspectives. They are not communitywide in their concerns; they do not compete ideologically for people's votes; and they do not have the special patterns of relationships with other interest groups (which parties have). Common Cause, a "peak" or "bridge" association, however, comes somewhat closer to fulfilling the conception of a party elaborated here. Yet there are significant differences between a bridge association and a party—in style, action strategy, and function.

Emphasis must be placed on the special meaning and purpose of parties in modern societies—and the three images outlined here elucidate that meaning. Parties are specialized, community-oriented apparatuses of action distinguished by their special relationships both to other groups in the community and to the public. While seeking formal governmental power they represent and manage group conflict, and at the same time mobilize and compete ideologically for mass support. This in the purest form of a party is its unique goal orientation, its strategy for action, and its community relevance. Parties vary from society to society in the relative importance of their concern with power, their interest-group conflict, and their involvement in ideological competition. But the probabilities are that the further parties diverge from these three differentia, the less likely they are to be considered in empirical terms as party structures. They may be ideological movements or interest groups or flash-in-the-pan ad hoc contenders for governmental office. They are not, then, as likely to be durable, power relevant, and societally functional structures with specialized action strategies and roles in relation to interest groups and the public delimited above. A party is a group which cannot be conceptualized in a power vacuum or a policy vacuum or a social vacuum.

The Relevance of Parties for Democracy

There is a continuing argument over the need for political parties in democracies. Here the differing views of two scholars will illustrate this point. Elmer E. Schattschneider says ". . . political parties created democracy and . . . modern democracy is unthinkable save in terms of the parties."[14] And Leon Epstein counters, "There is . . . a serious question whether parties must perform it (the governing function) in every democratic political system in order for the system to be effective."[15] In trying to resolve this controversy it is necessary to specify what is meant by *democracy*.

Democracy has many different meanings, depending on the particular interests and values of the person explaining it. To Aristotle one major aspect was equality—"the most pure democracy is that which is so called principally from the equality which prevails in it. . . . "[16] Democracy had several meanings including equality to de Tocqueville, but at one point he says that "the very essence of democratic government consists in the absolute sovereignty of the majority."[17] The Russian scholar M. Ostrogorski, observing the American system, stated that "the first postulate of democratic government is the active participation of the great mass of the citizens."[18] To Joseph Schumpeter democracy was a special method, "that institutional arrangement for arriving at political decisions in which individuals acquire the power to decide by means of a competitive struggle for the people's vote."[19] Robert Dahl, advocate of the pluralist thesis, the democratic governmental process that evolved especially in the United States, finds democracy "a political system in which all the active and legitimate groups in the population can make themselves heard at some crucial stage in the process of decision."[20] Leaders, to Dahl, make the decisions in a democracy but they must not only "listen to the noise, but expect to suffer in some significant way if they do not placate the group, its leaders, or its most vociferous members."[21] Peter Bachrach, however, who rejects the emphases of both elitist and pluralist theses, states the essence of democracy differently:

I believe that a theory of democracy should be based upon the following assumptions and principles: the majority of individuals stand to gain in self-esteem and growth toward a fuller affirmation of their personalities by participating more actively in meaningful community decisions; people generally, therefore, have a twofold interest in politics—interest in end results and interest in the process of participation. . . .[22]

This collection of views of democracy illustrates the variety of possible emphases. But upon reflection of these democratic theories a common thread is noticed in the ideas of these theorists with an emphasis on the *citizen public's role in the political process.* Elitist theorists stress the need for political leaders in a democracy to compete for and secure support from the masses in order to stay in office. The pluralistic theorists emphasize the need for elites to be constantly responsive to group demands and to censure. And ultrademocratic theorists place importance on the self-esteem of the ordinary person in a democratic society and the value of participation. Thus *elite competition, elite responsiveness,* and *public participation* (all involving the public in some way) are key elements in any full-bodied theory of democracy. One of these elements may be concentrated on to the neglect of others, but it is difficult to advance a decent and acceptable theory of democracy by ignoring all three. Democracy means conflict among ideas, interests, ideologies, and elites; it means a concern by leaders for public problems and demands and needs. Also democracy means a realistic opportunity for nonelites and the public to be involved in the political process.

Given these conceptions of democracy—including even the most elitist (but democratic) conception—it is necessary to ask what political parties have to do with the functioning of the democratic system. Why is it that parties are central to the system? Historically, when democracies were born, parties came into existence to perform two somewhat contradictory roles: (1) to provide the organizational base by which elites could mobilize resources and compete with each other for votes under the new democratic elections and thus maintain themselves in power; and (2) to provide the organizational base by which new claimants to elite status could mobilize support and thus oppose those in power and eventually dislodge them from power. A later discussion of the origins of the American party system before 1800 will show how parties were functional to both elite power maintenance and to elite displacement. Thus parties historically and today are to be seen as being functional to the acquisition and loss of political power.

In a more specific sense, however, parties are relevant to the functioning of democratic systems (see figure 1.3). First, Huntington finds that the pressure for political participation demands political institutions to cope with and channel such participatory pressure. And parties are one such type of institution, a key type, through which the demands for participation can be handled. "Parties organize political participation, party systems affect the rate at which participation expands."[23] And, according to Huntington, the participation of new groups and their integration into the new democratic order is basic for the stability of the system.

In modernizing society "building the state" means in part the creation of an effective bureaucracy, but, more importantly, the establishment of an effective party system capable of structuring the participation of new groups in politics.[24]

Linked to this role of organizing public participation is a second role, that of providing popular control over elected officials. Many writers have emphasized this for parties. Indeed, it is hard to visualize how elites would be held accountable in a noncoercive state in which there were no parties or similar types of groups. Parties provide the opportunity for such control in at least four ways:

1. They select, encourage, and support individuals who are seeking leadership positions in society.
2. They "structure the competition" among these candidates.
3. They establish an organizational tie to these candidates on the basis of which their performance in office can be judged.
4. They are channels for potential reprisal against, and defeat of, officials whose behavior the public rejects.

FIGURE 1.3

The Roles of Parties in the Democratic Political System

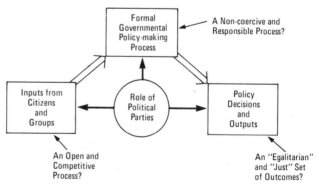

As Robert Dahl says: "One of the strongest claims for political parties is that they assist the electorate in gaining some degree of control over elected officials and, thus, over the decisions of government."[25]

Third, the competition for power in a democracy is closely linked to the party system. Basic cleavages exist in the socioeconomic interests in any society, whether or not one wishes to acknowledge their existence. And these interests collide in seeking governmental power and policy implementation. In authoritarian and totalitarian systems such conflicts are suppressed or ignored, and parties are considered unnecessary or dysfunctional. In democratic societies, however, there are open conflicts and parties are organizational instruments and channels for these conflicting interests. The parties consist of rival cadres of activists and organizational personnel representing policies and programs and making demands to be heard. These conflicts must be managed, compromised, and resolved. As Dahl states it, in a democracy there are "multiple centers of power" and between them "constant negotiations ... are necessary in order to make decisions."[26] Parties provide a major arena for combat among these conflicting interests as well as for bargaining, negotiation, and resolution among the conflicting parties.

It can well be argued that "democracy involves a balance between the forces of conflict and consensus."[27] That parties are structures reflecting and articulating conflict but are also structures that make agreement and consensus possible is their fourth key role in a democracy. Thus parties perform both a competitive and an integrative function in the democratic society. As Lipset points out, Karl Marx saw the modern political system primarily in conflict (class conflict) terms, while theorists like de Tocqueville were the first to see the system in terms of both conflict *and* consensus. And the solidarity or consensus of the system is enhanced by conflict. It is in this perspective that political parties must be visualized in the modern democratic system. So Dahl argues:

Prior to politics, beneath it, enveloping it, restricting it, conditioning it, is the underlying consensus on policy that usually exists in the society among a predominant portion of the politically active members. Without such a consensus no democratic system would long survive the endless irritations and frustrations of elections and party competition.[28]

Huntington, too, sees parties in modernizing societies as a source for stability. "The development of political parties parallels the development of modern government. . . . The Party [in certain developing societies] is not just a supplementary organization, it is instead the source of legitimacy and authority."[29]

From a variety of scholarly perspectives, therefore, political parties are critical for the democratic system. Certainly in the early stages of the formation of the democratic system the beginnings of a party system were necessary. In the later stages of the system, parties developed in a more complex and differentiated way. There are, to be sure, considerable areas of disagreement among scholars who address themselves to this question, but there is strong support and agreement among them as to what democracy means: the enhancement of citizen welfare through political participation; opportunities for citizens to control elites in power; freedom and channels for the articulation of conflict among diverse interests; effective procedures for the accommodation, aggregation, and translation of these conflicts into public policy; the structuring of meaningful competition among rival cadres of activists seeking governmental power; the continuous responsibility of elites for the development of new policies that reflect the claims and needs of new social forces; and the achievement through conflict of an underlying consensus, a commitment to the democratic "rules of the game."

Accepting that these are the characteristics (or meanings) of democracy, then most scholars would argue that parties not only are relevant, but are probably central. For parties are structures for political action which have from the beginning in modern democracies provided constitutional channels for citizen participation, control of elites, interest aggregation, conflict management, competition maximization, policy innovation, and system consensus. Whether political parties *do* effectively constitute institutional channels performing these roles in the American democracy is both the basic and open question in the study of parties and of this book. Lord Bryce said long ago that "party is king."[30] V. O. Key claims, "Political parties constitute a basic element of democratic institutional apparatus."[31] Whether parties are central to the functioning of the democratic state and in what ways is the critical question that will constantly recur in this analysis of the American party system.

Can Only Democracies Have Party Systems?

Some people assume that a party system can exist only in a democratic society because it consists of two or more parties competing freely with each other for influence and power. This position is based on the belief that a certain type and amount of competition between autonomous groups is necessary before there can be a party system. In an authoritarian society like the USSR or China, therefore, it is tempting to conclude that the Communist party is not a party system. Before jumping to this conclusion, care must be taken. The existence of party systems in these countries may be credible because either they do have a certain amount of competitive interaction among subgroups or factions or such groups perform certain key roles in the system. Consider, for example, the one-party system in some southern states in the United States. The Democratic party was often a highly fragmented structure, consisting of several factions. Although there may not have been any viable opposition from the Republican party, there was competition between factions within the Democratic party.

Similarly, Polish scholars argue that there is a three-party system in Poland, consisting of the Polish Communist party, the Polish Peasants party, and the Polish Workers party. Though in reality all three are under the umbrella of the Polish Communist party, distinctive factions exist and compete to a certain extent in the recruitment of people for governmental office. Are the Democratic party of Mississippi and the Communist party of Poland acceptable as party systems? Certainly, if they are structures that perform the kinds of functions described previously. If the single-party structures in authoritarian societies function as intermediaries between government and the public—communicating, representing, and aggregating the interests of the masses— they may indeed be construed as constituting a party system, even though competition may be severely limited.

One-party systems differ from plural-party systems in many respects. Aside from the limited competitiveness of one-party systems, their linkage to the social structure is essentially different. They perform functions other than those manifest in plural-party societies, such as being the arm of the bureaucratic or military operation of the state, but functionally they may be in certain respects similar to party systems elsewhere. Scholars of African societies maintain that the one-party system there reflects the intense tribal division of the society leading to one party, representing one tribal or geographical interest, and gaining control at the expense of all others. Or, they argue, there are no conflicting interests, "the idea of class is something entirely foreign to Africa," and therefore since "there is no fundamental opposition" there is need for only one party to represent a homogeneous society. In either case, the one-party system is linked to the socioeconomic interest-group infrastructure quite differently from that in openly competitive democratic systems. In one-party states interest cleavages are either unrecognized and underrepresented or suppressed. As Huntington states, "a one party system is, in effect, the product of the efforts of a political elite to organize and to legitimate rule by one social force over another in a bifurcated society."[32] Thus one-party systems perform some of the same basic types of functions as democratic party systems, but perform them in a very distinctive, perhaps authoritarian, style.

Are Parties Declining?

Today political scientists and others would argue that parties are not functionally central to modern government, or that they are ineffectual in dealing with our problems, or that they are rivaled by or being replaced by other groups. Some scholars claim that for anyone interested in social change and social progress parties are not of primary relevance. As Walter Dean Burnham says, there has developed an erosion in party loyalty:

The political parties are progressively losing their hold upon the electorate. A new breed of independent seems to be emerging . . . a person whose political cognitions and awareness keep him from making identifications with either old party. . . . This may point toward the progressive dissolution of the parties as action intermediaries in electoral choice and other politically relevant acts. It may also be indicative of the production of a mass base for independent political movements of ideological tone and considerable long-term staying power. . . . It seems fairly evident that if this secular trend toward politics without parties continues to unfold, the policy consequences will be profound. To state the matter with utmost simplicity: political parties . . . are the only devices thus far invented by the wit of Western man which with some effectiveness can generate countervailing collective power on behalf of the many individually powerless against the relatively few who are individually—or organizationally powerful.[33]

Burnham sees parties declining in their importance for the individual because they are not adaptive to the new needs and realities of the American society. This then results in an erosion in loyalty and in a functional irrelevance and sharply poses the question, How important are parties as structures commanding individual loyalty and as instrumentalities for collective social action? Not all scholars will agree with Burnham. Some disagree vehemently, presenting contrary evidence, and arguing strongly that parties are still very important groups, which command the loyalty of well over 50 percent of the public and perform critical functions in the system.

This book will examine closely the idea of party decline: the extent of it in party organization, in participation by citizens in party activities, in party identification, and in the views the American public has about the party system. It is necessary to pinpoint in what ways parties have declined. Then it is necessary to identify what factors and forces are responsible for this decline. If the decline does indeed exist, what is the content of the public's disaffection with parties? Is this due to failures in party performance or in the failure of parties to communicate effectively with the American public or both? Or are there other causes for the malaise—social or economic forces, the rise of new types of groups (with more money to spend on politics), or the roles of the mass media? If party decline is indeed occurring, an endeavor will be made to explain it as carefully as possible.

If party decline is indeed occurring, an explanation must be attempted to explain the roots and causes of that decline, the attacks on parties, and the gloomy forecasts about their future, in conjunction with a consideration of the basic argument of the theories of the "party functionalists." What is their basic position? Essentially they argue that parties have been, and are, important for the political development and thus for the social and economic development of any society which is "modernizing." Historically, these scholars argue, parties came into existence as structures necessary to perform functions of a special nature, particularly as these societies became openly competitive and democratic. The leadership of a new nation then develops a program of policy goals to which it is committed, a set of institutions designed to implement these goals, and a strategy to mobilize public support for these goals. The polity has to be expanded to include sub-elites and citizens, and the role of the political party system in this development process is crucial—cementing a structure of leadership, linking central and local elites, evolving a program of action, and mobilizing public support. It is hard to see how such a development process can occur without a party system. William Chambers in describing the historical origins of the American system argues this position effectively.

As the American founders resolved problem after problem in the shaping of the republic, they not only established the first modern political parties. They were also involved, if most unknowingly, in a general process of political modernization in which parties were at once an element and a catalyst in a broader change from older to newer things.[34]

In the functionalist approach as the system develops, parties perform critical functions for maintenance as well as change in the system. They provide opportunities for citizens to be involved in political group life and to participate in the political process. They recruit individuals and train them for public office. Attempting to resolve differences between conflicting claims, they represent and respond to the demands and needs of interest groups in the society. They socialize the public to the acceptance of the emerging political system and inform it about governmental programs, then they seek to mobilize public support on behalf of these programs. Above all, parties attempt to inject responsibility into the system, by providing integration both between the branches of government and between governmental leaders and their constituencies. In managing government and in providing an opposition to the government, parties provide a focus of responsibility and accountability. Of the role of parties, David Apter says that "the political party is such a critical force for modernization in all contemporary societies that the particular pattern of modernization adopted by each is often determined by its parties."[35]

As we proceed with the description and analysis of the American party system we will not only be concerned with the characteristics of that party system but also with the role that system plays in American society.

Chapter 2

The American Party System:
Origins and Development

THE HISTORY of the American party system is fascinating. It was a complex process of trial and error; some say even today it is incomplete. It was a process characterized by both contradictory, alternating patterns of support and rejection and continuous efforts at reform and revision. In America we have struggled to develop a system acceptable to both the public and the political elites in two respects: We have repeatedly questioned the need and function of parties, and we have periodically questioned our type of party system. At the beginning, before 1800, leaders moved only hesitantly toward a competitive party system, and many people warned against it. In the nineteenth century scholars and political leaders attacked parties, developed new ones when the old seemed ineffective, regulated them rigorously, and seriously questioned their value to our society. In the twentieth century, even while the two-party system was maturing and capturing the public's support, we have attempted to rob parties of crucial functions, such as leadership recruitment, and questioned their superiority compared to interest groups. Throughout our history, therefore, we have wavered between two sentiments and two cultures: pro-party, and anti-party. In the context of persisting ambivalence about parties, this chapter will review the origins of the early parties and then sketch their later developments.

Party systems emerge out of the special historical circumstances and patterns of political, social, and economic conflict attending the development of modern societies. During this gestation period political elites influence greatly the initial character of the system as they struggle with each other for status in the system and seek to organize supporters in behalf of their goals and beliefs. A system then goes through several periods of historical experimentation with one or more party systems. A variety of party groups may come and go, and different types of party systems may be tested before one system crystallizes with a particular form and character. The American party system went through such a development process and has evolved its own special form.

It is useful to remember the events and circumstances at the time of the origin of our system, which culminated eventually in the party system we have today. In a review of this early period one observation stands out: There was not immediately an overwhelming, enthusiastic support for a competitive party system; such support developed only very gradually.

The Early Party Era: 1790–1800

Political parties first appeared sometime between 1790 and 1800. To some scholars this was a pre-party period; to others the evidence of the definite development of parties is stronger.[1] The events of this fascinating period of our history should be recalled in order to understand the way in which political leaders and social groups met the problems of their time and in the process created a type of party system. Before 1790, before and during the battle over the ratification of the Constitution, parties and factions were deplored. James Madison wrote his convincing philippic arguing for the adoption of the Constitution on the grounds, among others, that the principles of that document would effectively prevent a political group like a party, no matter what its size, from acquiring the totality of political power. The doctrines of federalism, bicameralism, and separation of powers, he argued, would blunt the power drive of a party.[2] Also critical of parties, Benjamin Franklin wrote at one time of "the infinite mutual abuse of parties, tearing to pieces the best of characters."[3] Yet, despite these arguments of Madison and Alexander Hamilton and the early antagonism of many of the other Founding Fathers, parties did come into existence early in our country. As Richard Hofstadter says, it was indeed paradoxical that Thomas Jefferson, who played a leading role in "creating the first truly popular party in the history of the western world," was also the leader who initially "had no use for political parties."[4] It was almost grudgingly, then, that leaders like Jefferson took actions which led to the establishment of an opposition party as a counterpoise to the policies and organizational genius of Hamilton.

Political controversy became so profound and conflict among the elites so intense that, despite anti-party sentiment, a party system of sorts was born—perhaps by 1796, probably by 1800.

In 1788 Washington was the virtually unanimous choice for president and, among eleven other candidates, John Adams was chosen as vice-president by the electoral college, consisting of electors elected by the states. People were being called Federalist and Anti-Federalist, as well as Constitutionalist (and ten Anti-Federalists were elected to the first House of Representatives). Parties as groups with any semblance of organization, however, did not yet exist. The maneuvering of leaders such as Alexander Hamilton, Aaron Burr, DeWitt Clinton, James Madison, Patrick Henry, and James Monroe occupied central stage. Their efforts at putting together political coalitions and at the persuasion of others to support particular nominees for the House, Senate, or vice-presidency was the style of our politics. Estimates of popular participation in this early election ranged from 5 percent to 8 percent of the white males.[5] Parties as mass mobilization structures had not yet materialized.

For the first year of the new government there was limited controversy, since the Cabinet and the Congress were preoccupied with implementing the new Constitution and setting up the judiciary and the executive departments. Then, in 1790 Hamilton as the secretary of the Treasury and the dominant figure in the Cabinet presented a series of proposed bills dealing with some critical, economic problems confronting the new government: the funding of state debts, a protective tariff, and the creation of a national bank. When Hamilton pressed for the adoption of these economic legislative measures, differences of opinion became apparent and a debate ensued. In 1790 Hamilton called the first legislative caucus of those identified as Federalists. Dissent from and opposition to his policies became sharper, but it was a highly individualized opposition; no opposition legislative caucus was even held until 1795. In the meantime considerable tensions developed in the Cabinet between Jefferson and Hamilton, and Jefferson began to ally himself with other leaders in the Congress and outside, notably with James Madison. In the election of 1792 the vice-presidency was contested, with the incumbent John Adams pitted against DeWitt Clinton whom the Republican leaders had informally designated as their candidate by means of conferences and correspondence. The resulting vote was concentrated, with Adams receiving 77 and Clinton all but 5 of the 60 opposition electoral votes. Yet, Jefferson remained in the Cabinet until late in 1793.

A variety of party-type activities had been going on since 1790— informal nominations, informal canvassing of electoral votes, the development by oppositionist leaders in Congress of similar policy positions, correspondence of these leaders with other notables in the states, the appearance of an opposition press led by Philip Freneau's establishment of the *National Gazette* in Philadelphia in October 1791, and the founding of Democratic and Republican local societies (which Washington disapprovingly called "self-created societies.")[6] But in the opinion of most scholars these efforts did not congeal into a clearly articulated national party structure. In the congressional election of 1794 the opposition Republicans won the House for the first time; this, however, was primarily the result of both individual efforts and those of particular local societies. Nevertheless, the movement toward the establishment of two political structures at the national level was continued and intensified. The controversial Jay Treaty evoked violent partisan passions, and the appropriations in support of it were only passed by a small margin—48 votes to 51—in April, 1976. (This, in a sense, was an index of the development of party structure—loose, individualized, and informal.) And it was this debate that moved Jefferson to reluctantly agree to be a candidate for the presidency that year. He lost to Adams but again only by the narrowest of margins—71 votes to 68—and thus became vice-president under the electoral college system that then prevailed.

Clearly parties as loose leadership associations were developing. Thus, John Taylor, a planter in Virginia, after consulting with men like Madison and Monroe, wrote a pamphlet in 1793 in which he declared,

... the existence of two parties in Congress, is apparent. The fact is disclosed almost upon every important question ... whether the subject be foreign or domestic—relative to war or peace—navigation or commerce—the magnetism of opposite views draws them wide as the poles asunder.[7]

And on the last day of 1795, Jefferson, who had two years previously stepped down from Washington's Cabinet in opposition to the policies of Hamilton, wrote,

Were parties here divided merely by a greediness for office as in England, to take a part with either would be unworthy of a reasonable or moral man, but where the principle of difference is as substantial and as strongly pronounced as between the republicans & the Monocrats of our country, I hold it as honorable to take a firm and decided part . . . .[8]

These men, as well as others, not only perceived the existence of parties but also were engaged in a pattern of activities and relationships which made parties a reality.

In the latter part of the 1790s, then, it was clear that two leadership structures had emerged differing in basic respects as to the direction of national policy and beginning to articulate the structures from the national level to the local level. Cadres of active followers were beginning to be mobilized and strategies for organizational action were devised, which became more evident in the period leading to the election of 1800. In that presidential election the Federalists and Republicans competed for national and state power as two loose-knit political structures utilizing some of the techniques that today are assumed to be the genius of modern parties. This time Jefferson defeated Adams—73 votes to 65—and the Republicans controlled the House of Representatives—66 votes to 40.

What were the factors most responsible for the emergence of our early parties? First, there was the deepening of controversy over national policy, particularly over the role of the federal government and its program in dealing with the problems of American society before 1800. The issue of critical conflicts over economic and foreign policy raised serious questions concerning what interests and sectors of society should be regulated, protected, and benefited. Too, the issue cleavages then were tied to interest group conflicts. Jefferson saw these alignments clearly in May 1793.

The line is now drawn so clearly as to show on one side:
1. The fashionable circles of Philadelphia, New York, Boston, and Charleston; natural aristocrats
2. Merchants trading on British capital
3. Papermen. All the old Tories are found in some one of these three descriptions.
On the other side are:
1. Merchants trading on their own capital
2. Irish merchants
3. Tradesmen, mechanics, farmers, and every other possible description of our citizens[9]

The original impetus to party conflict provided by Hamilton's economic proposals was followed by the bitter debates over the French Revolution and what American loyalties should be in that war. As Hofstadter has argued,

the French Revolutionary War quickly moved the American party contest . . . into a new phase. From the spring of 1793, when the provocative French Minister Citizen Gênet arrived at Charleston, there came a series of events which rapidly polarized the leaders and their followers and finally inflamed them to the point at which the entire political system was threatened. . . . The war had brought into one common focus three sets of issues: the domestic issues, which mobilized interest against interest, the foreign policy issues . . . and finally, a set of ideological passions of a surprisingly intense kind. . . . Jefferson himself [wrote that] the war "kindled and brought forward the two parties."[10]

Thus the issue cleavages and their linkages to conflicted socioeconomic interests were the seedbed for the origin of these parties.

Two persons with great magnetism, Hamilton and Jefferson, assumed leadership of the two contesting social and political forces. Somewhat reluctantly at first but more self-consciously later, they built their parties, drawing to them a variety of other statesmen, subelites, and mass supporters. Gradually a substructure made up of subelites and the public became more involved in electoral politics. Estimates are that the proportion of turnout for 1792 to 1798 was 24 percent of the white adult male population, which increased to 39 percent by 1800, when Jefferson was elected to the presidency.[11] And while parties were developing local structures that were mobilizing votes at the citizen level, the parties in the government were becoming somewhat more coherent, if not more disciplined. Thus there was a clearer division in party voting in the House of Representatives after 1790. Table 2.1 shows the increase in party voting in the House, according to the calculations of Joseph Charles.

At the elite level the concept of party was indeed taking hold. Generating diverse ideological positions on government, the events of these turbulent years had divided elites and the public. In embryonic form two major parties had emerged as the organizational response to controversy and conflict, parties that were ideological competitors for governmental power and for influence in the society.

Samuel Huntington has suggested that parties in modern societies pass through four stages:[12]

1. Factionalism
2. Polarization of social forces leading to the emergence of initial party structures
3. Expansion of the electorate and perfection of party organization
4. Institutionalization—the establishment of parties that are coherent and complex structures which are adaptive and viable

By 1800 perhaps the country was passing through the second of these stages; between 1800 and the Civil War it had moved into stages three and four.

TABLE 2.1

Percentage of Members Consistently Supporting Either the Federalists or Republican Party Positions

	In the House	
	66⅔ Percent of the Time	*75 Percent of the Time*
1790	58	46
1795	93	86

SOURCE: Joseph Charles, *The Origins of the American Party System* (New York: Harper & Row, 1956), p. 93.

Early Party Culture

In this early period in party history certain norms or beliefs about how the system of partisan politics should function had begun to emerge. Such norms or beliefs, which each country develops on its own and are called its political culture, seem gradually to become accepted by citizens and political leaders, are transmitted to others, are reenforced by experience, and finally greatly influence how politics is conducted in a particular society.[13]

Over the years in the United States there have been two contrasting attitudes toward parties, in a sense, two party cultures. One of these supported the idea of a party, the other was critical of it. Here the concern is with those norms and beliefs that emerged and were connected with the emergence of a pro-party culture. The first such cultural norm in this early period was the acceptance of the idea of, and indeed the necessity of, political opposition. Chambers refers to this as "the legitimacy of opposition and of opposition parties."[14] The republic was born as a result of political opposition, and with minor deviations from this principle (and expectations) it was an orientation that was persistently maintained and exercised in the period up to 1800. Although it was true that Washington was elected unanimously, the principle of uncontested elections never was accepted in the United States. The Alien and Sedition Acts came close to being attempts to suppress the opposition; but this effort failed. Few Federalists actually rejected this concept of the legitimacy of opposition; rather they were deeply concerned by the virulence and bitterness of the opposition to their policies. Certainly we never had as large a body of leadership and public opinion adhering to the concept of unanimity and skeptical of the value of political conflict as is found today in many nations. Robert Dahl points out that as of 1964 of the 113 nations in the United Nations only 30 nations had political systems in which there was significant organized political party opposition.[15] In America, 170 years before, there was a premium on insurgency and protest, and any attempt by government to proscribe organized political action was not to be tolerated. The monopolization of political communication media by the government was rejected, as were serious and sustained efforts to harass the opposition in such a way as to limit its capacity to oppose. This basic orientation was deeply imbedded in the American spirit and in its constitutions. It was a political value and a way of thinking about politics which had tremendous implications for action within our political system. In a way, Watergate tested our commitment to this value. Although today we take it for granted, we must remember that it was the basic cultural norm undergirding the development of a competitive party system.

A second critical element in our early cultural patterns, that *the majority had the prerogative of power*, people have felt somewhat more ambivalent about than they have about the first element. James Madison at the time of the fight over ratification of the new national constitution had taken a contrary position, claiming that no group, even if it had a majority of the population, should be permitted to govern. This view found later exponents in the views of other statesmen, notably John C. Calhoun and his doctrine of the concurrent majority. But, from a practical standpoint, Madison in the 1790s, changed his views as he became a leader of the Republican party and later president. Jefferson saw the need for opposite parties, one of which "must for the most part prevail over the other for a longer or shorter time."[16] Washington had sought to govern with a biparty Cabinet; but with Jefferson's resignation in 1793, the Cabinet was dominated by the Federalists until 1801. The idea that the party that won elections did have the right to use this power in any reasonable, legal, and *legitimate* fashion was a concept that did secure wide currency. And in fact it was practiced. There was no question of this to Hamilton, to Adams, or to Jefferson. When in power they used their power to control the Congress, seeing the Speaker and standing committees as partisan organs. They felt it was their right and responsibility to adopt legislation in accord with their ideologies and campaign programs. And they used the power of patronage to reward their faithful followers and to guarantee support, even if it meant the appointment of their partisans to the Supreme Court, as Adams did just before midnight of his last day in office. The emphasis here should be on legitimacy, for at the time of Watergate when Nixon and his advisors sought to distort this norm, engaging in illegal activities to spy on and harass the opposition, the majority's prerogatives were stretched too far. Unreasonable excesses in the use of this norm were punished.

An important corollary of this norm was the idea that the party that lost an election should withdraw from power. This in a sense was the meaning of the presidential contest in the House after the 1800 election when Burr and Jefferson were tied in electoral votes. In the last analysis the Federalists abstained so that the Republicans in the House could give the presidency to Jefferson, thus ratifying the electorate's choice. This peaceful transfer of power, supplemented by the expectation that the majority party would in fact govern, had significant meaning for American political behavior.

A third general expectation, which developed early, was that *political competition* would be bipolar, but not necessarily extremely polarized. Many people began to expect a duopoly of parties; they supported one of two parties, and over time came to accept a duopoly as proper. From 1790 to 1800 people became accustomed to two ideological, leadership, and political organizational tendencies in politics, constellations of social and political forces that differed in their philosophies and appeals but were not extremely distant from each other. And the parties—at that time the Federalists and Republicans—acted in such a way as to monopolize the political terrain. Often a multiplicity of candidates ran for office, at least nine candidates secured electoral votes in the 1796 election for the presidency and vice-presidency, but there were only two parties. Both of these were open structures, appealing widely for support among diverse sections and social interests. In pivotal states like New York, Pennsylvania, and New Jersey the contest was close and oscillating. But the competition was not shared with any third force. Despite maneuverings for advantage by individual leaders, the party system was developing into a competitive system in which two distinctive parties sought power by their exclusive efforts, and the winning party acceded to power without enduring a bargaining process. No system developed in which parties negotiated over the accession to power.

A fourth expectation, or attitude pattern, in early American political culture was *the tolerance of almost heretical factionalism* within political groups, particularly political parties. In colonial days and in early state politics, as Chambers has pointed out, there were cliques, juntas, social elites, and ad hoc caucuses. And these tendencies continued during the period of Federalist-Republican party development. In 1796 three factions were discernible, perhaps the most notable being the anti-Adams "High Federalists," some of whom had actually connived at displacing Adams as the presidential candidate. During Jefferson's period the most notable faction was the Quids who opposed the party policy in the Yazoo lands controversy and felt that the party was too subservient to northern and business interests. And in 1811 the Young Republicans led by men like Clay and Calhoun became a real threat to the viability of the Republican party. Upon analysis, these factional developments reflected ideological differences, personal power ambitions, and social-interest connections. They were not merely differences between the president and his party in Congress. They apparently had grass-roots popular support and were often extremist and clearly rebellious against party policy and leadership. Significantly each party represented a very broad spectrum of issue positions and socioeconomic interests. These party spectra overlapped considerably, so that the "haves" and the "have-nots" in American society could find a place within one or both of the political parties. Those people clamoring for social status, political rights, or economic betterment in early America did not have to go outside the two major party structures and ideologies.

This openness and breadth of party interests served the cause of the two-party system, and had implications for the goals and tactics of each of the parties. But the factionalism, while extremist and virtually heretical, was contained within the parties. Politicians, concerned about groupism, sought to contain these deviationists and to manipulate them but not to expel them. This tolerance became an important cultural political orientation. Leaders resisted attempts to place them under party discipline. Thus in the first Republican congressional caucus of 1795, Albert Gallatin observed that the members were left "to vote as they pleased." There was no early expectation that America would have a parliamentary party system, with the president and his Cabinet leading a parliamentary group bound to support presidential actions or the majority sentiments of the legislative party group. It was indeed a highly pluralized elite structure, with leaders interacting informally, at times almost surprised to discover like-minded souls, and retaining their independence of judgment. As scholars demonstrate, there was a high degree of party voting. But there were defections— critical ones for both parties. And, more important, this cohesion in voting was not the product of a discipline exercised by the party leadership and accompanied by sanctions. Leadership independence was the accepted pattern of behavior for party elites in early America.

A fifth type of cultural orientation had a localist-populist content and perspective: the expectation that *political leaders would be accessible to the public*, would consult the public, and to a certain extent defer to the public. In reality this is a combination of several attitudes about how politics should be practiced. It emphasized the prerogatives of the local community, the state, and the section. Too, it stressed the responsibility of the representative to the constituency and the potentiality of reprisal by "the home folks." Finally, the feeling that control over groups such as political parties should be local and popular, not in the hands of a centrist cabal of leaders whose actions were clandestine, was markedly important. Early American history is replete with examples of local protest movements, not all as violent as the Whiskey Rebellion in Pennsylvania in 1794 and the Fries Uprising in 1799, or as comprehensive as the Virginia and Kentucky resolutions of 1798. Perhaps more significant than these dramatic populist crises were the developments of indigenous political action movements and party structures at the local level, such as the Democratic and Republican Societies in 1793 and 1794, the Myrmidons of Burr in New York in 1800, and the development in the Middle Atlantic States in the early 1800s of county conventions of delegates to conduct party business and make party nominations. The idea of secret and unrepresentative caucuses of state leaders or of congressmen making decisions for the party was considered undemocratic. Above all, a vote-conscious egalitarianism was the emerging orientation of American politics. Politicians learned to "treat" the voters, as well as to entreat them; those who were not willing to treat the voter as king soon learned the consequences. The story is told of James Madison, who after having lost one election because of his refusal to "treat," campaigned in the subsequent election with great appreciation for individual votes. He traveled in midwinter over frozen roads to state his views at a meeting at a country church. "I then had to ride in the night twelve miles to quarters and got my nose frostbitten, of which I bear the marks now."[17] This vote-conscious and localist-oriented populism became an essential ingredient of American political practice, despite the early contemptuous attitudes of many of the aristocrats for the masses. This cultural orientation required considerable adaptive political ingenuity, and it affected the organization of parties and their strategies of appeal.

These incipient orientations constituted a set of expectations that might be called the developing party subculture. These images of party politics, representing values that were incorporated into practice, gradually became fixed in the minds of American elites and citizens. Though ambiguous and obscure and not unanimously accepted, taken together, they represented a cultural context for party behavior, which if compared to contexts in other societies, reveals both some equivalent characteristics and some striking differences. Thus, the English code was much less localist and populist; the French more pluralist and multipolar; and the Dutch much less vote-deferential, less factionalized, and more ideologically purist. From country to country there are both overlapping cultural patterns and great dissimilarities. These values, orientations, and expectations in each country, however, fundamentally conditioned how the game of party politics was—and is— to be played in that society.

Early Party Organization

Besides cultivating the concept of partisanship, the early party leaders sought to develop a comprehensive organization from the national capital in Philadelphia to the grass roots. Both parties were fully aware of this need, yet developing a neatly-pyramided structure was well-nigh impossible. The twin problems were coordination and cohesion. A variety of expedients was employed to weld a national party together: circular letters, committees of correspondence, use of patronage, legislative and local caucuses, and even purges of the disloyal. In 1796 a remarkable purge of those Republicans who had dissented in the vote on the Jay Treaty appropriations was conducted. Four of the seven were replaced (three by Federalists!), and the behavior of two was subsequently much more republican.[18] Much earlier the device of "inter-visitation" had come into vogue, with travelers going from one local society to another. Finally, in 1808 the Republican congressional caucus set up the first national committee of correspondence consisting of one member from each state. Thus, through informal and formal means the party struggled to articulate a coherent and loyal organization. But geographical diversities of the time, local jealousies, and the sheer problems of communication meant that the early parties were loose aggregations of local groups of leaders and their followings. These local groups showed great independence of spirit, performed with varying degrees of efficiency, and pressured their governmental representatives to conform to local demands.

Whatever their structural defects, in relative terms both early parties opposed each other vigorously and vehemently. Historians of this period have uncovered a great deal of evidence indicating the intensity of party competition. The parties "treated" the voters, helped immigrants to be naturalized quickly (if it was to their advantage), marched their tenants to the polls, held rallies and ox roasts, and hanged their opponents in effigy. They even engaged in the questionable practice of repeating (voting more than once) on election day, and "the Lame, Crippled, diseased and blind were either led, lifted or brought in carriages to the Poll" (in Charleston).[19] In New York City in 1800 Aaron Burr worked out an ingenious method for evading the state's property tax requirement for voters by seeing to it that city workingmen were granted joint land tenancies and thus were qualified to vote.[20] Further, a developing body of volunteer professionals—county committeemen—began to appear at the local level. In addition to mobilizing the vote, their task was to "fight that most formidable enemy of civilized men, political ignorance. . . ."[21]

These were no "mass" parties (those with large followings that could be relied on each election); they were still embryonic party structures. Only white males could vote, depending on their property-tax qualifications, and fewer than 40 percent did so by 1800.[22] But the patterns of parties' activity strongly suggest that they were assuming certain key fundamental responsibilities in American society. Chief among their functions were the determination of public policy, the recruitment of leadership for the top policy-making positions, the mobilization of support for these leaders, and the influencing of public attitudes and preferences. In addition, they saw the administrative and adjudicative processes as proper provinces for party control and activity. Finally, their activities can be construed as having an important socializing function. The party leaders were identified with and believed in the developing American system of democracy. Though intensely partisan, they began to communicate their understandings of that system to the public.

Major Eras in Party History

By 1800 not only did two major political parties exist, they were competing as political structures in fairly systematic fashion for national and local power. But the enduring outlines and characteristics of the party system were by no means irrevocably set. The ebb and flow of American party politics from 1800 to the present is challenging to study in great detail. The objective here, however, is not to deal with the details of each period or each election campaign, but rather to identify the major patterns of change and stability in the party system in form, process, and function. The aim is to describe the alternations in types of party competition and in party system form which occurred—a type of historical experimentation that led eventually to our present party system.

The history of the American party can be divided into five basic periods, called five "party systems" by some scholars.[23] These periods are roughly as follows:

1. From 1788 to 1824

This was the period of the building of the party system. There were three subperiods within it: that of the competition between Federalists and Republicans, that of one-party dominance by the Republicans after the Federalists began to disappear from effective competition after 1808, and that of transitional pluralism and factionalism within the Republican party from 1820 on, between the Jackson, Adams, Crawford, and Clay sub-units within the party.

Under Jefferson, Madison, and Monroe—a period of one-party dominance—the Republicans won from 53 percent to 92 percent of the electoral college votes and from 61 percent to 85 percent of the House seats. By 1824 the Republicans were split, however, and four different presidential candidates received the following electoral college votes: Jackson 37.9 percent, Adams 32.2 percent, Crawford 15.7 percent, and Clay 14.2 percent. The House of Representatives picked Adams.

2. From 1824 to 1854

The masses were mobilized and the parties were democratized during this period due largely to the efforts of Jackson who won in 1828 and 1832. From a 27 percent turnout of adult males in 1824 there was a jump in voting participation to over 50 percent in 1828 and 1832. The delegate convention replaced the legislative caucus (or the mixed caucus) as the basic form of party organization. Sectional and ideological tensions increased in the party system leading to the Kansas-Nebraska Act of 1854 and the breakdown of the two-party competitive system between the Democrats and Whigs (or National Republicans).

From 1854 to 1860 the parties again went through a transitional pluralistic crisis before the two-party system was reestablished. This was the period during which the present Republican party was formed, but no one party could secure a majority. In the 1856 election the vote was distributed as follows: Democrats (Buchanan) received 45.3 percent of the popular vote, Republicans (Fremont) received 33.1 percent, and Whigs (Fillmore) received 21.6 percent. Even in 1860 Lincoln received only 39.9 percent of the popular votes, although he won 59.4 percent of the electoral college vote. This was clearly a period of realignment.

3. From 1860 to 1892

After a period of Republican control to 1874 the two parties alternated control of the presidency and Congress. The major threat to the two-party system was posed by the Populist party in 1892, which secured over a million popular votes and twenty-two electoral college votes. This threat was short-lived, however, and by 1896 the two-party system was clearly the dominant pattern.

The salient events during this period were (1) the development of urban political organizations or machines; (2) the adoption of legislation to protect the integrity of elections (the Australian ballot system, for example), as well as the regulation of party organizations; and (3) the public involvement in the party process both in the strengthening of party loyalties and the participation of people in voting.

4. From 1896 to 1932

There was Republican dominance until 1912, when Roosevelt's Bull-Moose Progressive Movement split the party and led to two national presidential victories for the Democrats with Woodrow Wilson. This was a minor pluralization crisis, but at the time it did split the presidential vote three ways, as follows: Wilson received 435 electoral college votes and 41.8 percent of the popular vote; Taft received 88 electoral college votes and 23.2 percent of the popular vote; and Roosevelt received 8 electoral college votes and 27.5 percent of the popular vote. Republican dominance was restored in 1920 and lasted until Franklin D. Roosevelt's victory in 1932.

Twice, crises or threats to the two-party system occurred, in 1912 (Roosevelt progressives) and in 1924 (La Follette progressives); the former secured 27 percent of the vote, the latter 17 percent. But they, again, were short-lived threats to the system. A major development during this period was the reform movement, designed to take the leadership-nomination function out of the hands of party organization leaders and to put it in the hands of the rank-and-file party members (the direct primary). In addition, there was the movement toward non-partisan elections and the regulation of campaign finance activities of parties. The emphasis during this period was to treat parties as public-interest organizations that should be subjected to legislative control.

5. Since 1932

The New Deal coalition put together by Franklin Roosevelt presumably produced a basic party realignment and ushered in a whole new period of party life, a new party system. The Democrats were well in control until 1952, despite a minor pluralization crisis in 1948 when two factions within the Democratic party nominated their own candidates for the presidency (Henry Wallace and Strom Thurmond). Together, however, they received less than 5 percent of the popular vote. The Eisenhower victories of 1952 and 1956 interrupted Democratic control, and from 1960 on the parties have alternated, sometimes winning in landslides (1964 and 1972), sometimes in very close elections (1960, 1968, and 1976). In 1980 Reagan received 51 percent, Carter 41 percent, and Anderson 6.5 percent of the votes. In this era the most important changes have been the technological developments in campaigning (particularly the use of television), the new awareness of the role of interest groups in party politics and the attempts to regulate their role, and the emergence of ideological conflict in party campaigns. George Wallace's threat to the two-party system in 1968 when he secured over 13 percent of the popular vote was a significant event, but again a short-lived phenomenon. Some scholars argue that 1968 was the year that the fifth party era ended, and that a major realignment in parties began, launching a sixth party era. Others refuse to accept this interpretation. This question of "realignment" will be dealt with later; now, these basic, formative periods of the party system will be evaluated to clarify what historical circumstances molded America's party system.

Three Major Patterns of Party Competition

This glimpse at the historical eras of the American party systems has revealed that in the early days, as well as more recently, *three basic types of party politics* have been experienced: one-party dominance, two-party competition, and transitional pluralism. Since 1800 there have been five periods of one-party control (totaling seventy-six years) when the same party controlled the presidency, the House, and the Senate. There have been four periods of sustained and evenly competitive conflict between two major parties, periods of balanced party competition (eighty-two years in total). And there have been three pluralization periods (totaling twenty-two years) when the popular vote was dispersed among more than two parties or candidates, internal party factionalism and breakup existed, and/or "minority" presidents held office (see table 2.2). Thus the American experience has not been a homogeneous or single-directional experience. In a real sense

TABLE 2.2

The Three Basic Patterns of American Party Politics Since 1800

Years	Number of Years for Each Pattern		
	One-Party Dominance	Pluralized Party Politics	Balanced Two-Party Competition
1800–24	24 (Republican)		
1824–36		12	
1836–54			18
1854–62		8	
1862–74	12 (Republican)		
1874–96			22
1896–1910	14 (Republican)		
1910–12		2	
1912–20			8
1920–32	12 (Republican)		
1932–46	14 (Democratic)		
1946–80			34
Total number of years	76	22	82
Number of "marginal" presidential elections [a]	0	5	14

[a] A marginal election here is one where the winning candidate for president won with less than 52 percent of the vote.

there has been consistent movement in the direction of the basic two-party pattern. But all three patterns have occurred in the twentieth century, just as they did in the nineteenth century. And these historical patterns, reflecting as they must the desires, tolerances, and preferences of the people, constitute the mold and context out of which American party politics have taken and will take shape in the future.

Yet as the grand sweep of parties from 1800 to 1980 is viewed, these patterns have a set of discernible modifications. The periods of one-party control are not as long nor as completely dominant today as they were from 1800 to 1822. Also the pluralization crises are not as deep nor as protracted, nor as recurrent.

The 1912 crisis (and certainly the 1924 and 1948 episodes) in the fragmentation of the party system was mild compared to those before 1864. And finally, the party system has developed a capacity for absorbing and containing threats to the system, whether from the outside or as a result of internal dissension. Thus, while one-party control, duopolistic competition, and pluralization crises are still genuine possibilities today, the two-party system itself appears very viable.

The Party System in Equilibrium

Despite all the variations in American politics since the Civil War, the two major parties, like two giant political corporations, have been pitted against each other, have maintained themselves as the two major parties in spite of all threats, and have generally divided between them the popular vote ("controlled the voter market"), as well as almost all partisan political offices. Thus the American party system for the 120 years since 1860 seems to have been in a state of dynamic equilibrium, as Elmer Schattschneider notes in his 1942 study.[24] That is, it is a system in which change takes place but the basic units in the system maintain themselves, and the basic character of the system does not change essentially over time. Great change takes place in the voting support for the parties, but despite these changes the system does not disintegrate. Donald E. Stokes and G. R. Iverson, analyzing and reporting on this feature of American party history, note a negative correlation of −.55 between the division of the vote at one presidential election and the change of the vote from that election to the next. "In other words," they conclude, "the greater a party's share of the vote at one election, the greater is its share likely to be reduced at the next." Further, their analysis leads them to the conclusion that the probability "that the party division could have stayed within the historic boundaries of the vote for President *without the influence of equilibrium forces* [emphasis added] is less than four in a hundred."[25]

What is the nature of this equilibrium and what are these "equilibrium forces?" Figure 2.1 presents dramatically the nature of the equilibrium since the Civil War, showing a "pendulum" swing in the party vote in presidential elections. The extreme point in major party strength is 65 percent and is usually somewhat less than that, after which the strength of the winning major party recedes. There is a continuous movement toward the 50–50 percent distribution point. When a recession in party fortunes develops it usually continues so that the opposition party gradually reduces the overwhelming support of the winning party. Then the opposition wins with, usually, a victory at the 50.1 percent to 52 percent level, then this victory becomes greater, until its strength reaches an outer limit and also recedes.

Competition for votes is fairly constant. The actual shift in absolute percentages of the two-party presidential vote, as Stokes and Iversen point out, is 5.7 percentage points. Yet significant fluctuations in the vote can indeed occur. Elections such as those of 1912, 1920, 1932, and 1972 might even be called "voting upheavals" or "revolutionary landslides." What is interesting, however, is the celerity of the comeback of a major party that has lost heavily (see table 2.3).

FIGURE 2.1

The Equilibrium of the American Party System

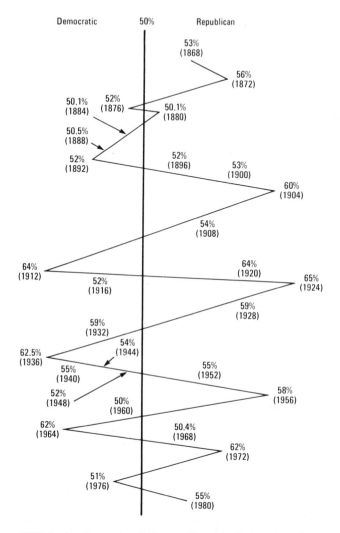

NOTE: Based on the percentage distribution of the vote for the two major parties

These shifts in the strength of the major parties over short eight-year spans are remarkable. They attest to the volatility of the system even though the system remains in a state of equilibrium. The party system since the Civil War has demonstrated a remarkable recuperative capacity—particularly after a staggering defeat of a major party that has often led to dire predictions about the demise of the system. What seems to happen is that the winning party in a landslide election does not continue to cumulate more support but to gradually lose it. Further,

TABLE 2.3
Dramatic Shifts in Party Strength

Election Sequence	Party	Percentage of Increase in Proportion of Two-Party Vote
1904–12	Democrats	24
1912–20	Republicans	28
1924–32	Democrats	24
1956–64	Democrats	20
1964–72	Republicans	24

the landslide election results are not as manifest in the elections to the House of Representatives (the winning party securing a smaller proportion of the vote), and this introduces a balancing factor leading the system to "right" itself and the pendulum to begin a swing back to center.

The key question of course, What are the restoring forces? in a sense contains three questions: (1) Why doesn't the dominant party grow cumulatively and continually stronger until it reaches 70 percent or more of the vote and drives its opposition into oblivion (as happened to the Federalists after 1812)? (2) Why and how does the losing major party maintain its status as the focus of the opposition? and (3) Why has not a third force replaced one of the two major parties in the equilibrium system (as happened in Britain after World War I when the Labour party replaced the Liberal party as the second major party)?

A variety of theories has been advanced to explain this equilibrium. One of them, based on obervations concerning the nature of the coalition of supporters of the winning party, argues that when the party wins overwhelmingly it finds that there are too many interests, many of them contradictory, that have to be served and satisfied. As a party in office has to make hard policy decisions, favoring some interests more than others, discontent sets in among certain sets of supporters who eventually leave the coalition and go over to the opposition.[26] Another theory argues that there is an inevitable "surge and decline" in party support, that a winning party in a presidential election attracts "peripheral voters" (previous nonvoters) and "core voters," supporters who deviate for one election. These supporters drop out or desert the party in the next off-year elections for Congress. Then they either do not turn out to vote, or, more importantly, when they do vote in ensuing elections, they revert to their basic party loyalties.[27] Still other scholars have suggested that there are cycles in the public's attitude toward politics: liberal-conservative reversals in ideology over time, periodic reactions against those in power, and a belief that rotation in office is good for the society. The extent of solid support for such theories is certainly arguable, however. More important, perhaps, is the shift in interest-group support for parties, over time leading to a gradual alteration in the group coalitional character of the parties linked to the specific issue appeals or to personalities of the candidates in a particular campaign. And then, of course, specific circumstances of party competition in particular campaigns should not be ignored. The 1912 election, with the split in the Republican party and the appearance of Wilson as the Democratic party's leader, was very special. So, too, was 1932 because of the Depression, the personality of Roosevelt, and the economic program of the Democratic party. Again, in 1972, George McGovern's candidacy, perceived as too far to the left, and the successes of Richard Nixon in Peking and Moscow were special circumstances influencing the vote.

The equilibrium character of the American system suggests that two major parties have been perceived by the public as sufficient for channeling and representing their divergent demands and interests. This is a proposition, however, that many people will resist. Nevertheless, while third parties have been important, they just have not been able to mobilize committed workers for long periods of time or to secure adequate funds or to attract able candidates for public office at different levels of the system. Above all, they have not secured sustained public support. It is as if there has been a psychological habituation to two-partyism at the mass level, among party elites, among interest-group elites, and in the mass media. This cannot be said for England (with its Liberal party), Canada (with its Canadian Commonwealth Federation or Social Credit party), or any country in Europe. And this is surprising in view of the heterogeneity of the American population, but the evidence is overwhelming. Only sporadically have minor parties got any significant percentage of the popular vote for president (see table 2.4). This is not to say that the minor parties were negligible threats at the time; on the contrary, in four of these presidential elections the vote for a minor party was an important warning for the two-party system. The Populists in 1892 and the Progressives of 1924 were the second-ranking party for one election in as many as eleven states; Roosevelt's break with his party meant the loss of the election for the Republicans; and the 1948 minor parties almost cost Truman the election. But they were only single-election phenomena and fell almost immediately into eclipse. The potential popular base for third-party movements has never been exploited or perhaps never was exploitable.

There seem to be at least three reasons for this acceptance of two-partyism. Both parties have demonstrated a remarkable capacity for reacting positively to threats, whether external or internal, and accommodating themselves to these threats. This might be called the *capacity for absorption of protest*. The new Republican party in 1854 accommodated Whigs, Democrats, Free Soilers, and Abolitionists. In 1896 by in-

TABLE 2.4
Important Third-Party Threats in Presidential Elections Since 1840

Year	Party	Percentage of Total Votes Received
1848	Free soil	10.1
1856	American	21.3
1860	Breckinridge Democrats	18.1
	Constitutional Union	12.7
1892	People's	8.5
1912	Progressive	27.4
	Socialist	6.0
1924	Progressive	16.6
1948	States' Rights	2.4
	Progressive	2.4
1968	American Independent Party	13.5
1980	Anderson (Coalition)	6.6

SOURCE: U.S. Department of Commerce, Bureau of the Census: *Historical Statistics of the United States*; for the earlier years, see the volume *Colonial Times to 1957*, pp. 682–83.

cluding within their platform the "free and unlimited coinage of both silver and gold" the Democrats adopted the major issue and most of the followers of the Populists in 1892. In 1916 the Roosevelt Progressives were already wooed back into the Republican fold. The La Follette family had gone back to the Republicans by 1928, and their followers had opted for one of the major parties. At the 1952 Democratic convention the Dixiecrats were asking to be allowed back into the Democratic fold. Henry Wallace had already resigned in 1950 from his own party of Progressives. Thus, the major parties did not reject the extremists, either within their own ranks or from the outside. They absorbed them. William Jennings Bryan was taken into Wilson's Cabinet, and the La Follettes were again considered Republican leaders.

The ideological eclecticism of the major parties has also been a contributory factor. The Democrats could and did move from left-wing populism in 1896 to reactionary conservatism in 1904, and the Republicans could move from Roosevelt's dynamic progressivism of 1904 to the conservatism of normalcy in 1920. Also parties have been able to modify their positions on particular issues over time—the Democrats on the black question since the Civil War, the Republicans on welfare-state issues since the Depression. But more important is the tolerance in both parties of local and regional ideological deviationism. Conservative Southern states-rights advocates and anti-integrationists can remain within the Democratic party, as can the extreme liberal Americans for Democratic Action or immediate-integration faction. Senator Jacob Javits finds a home in the same party with Senator Barry Goldwater. As W. B. Hesseltine and other scholars have said, there are four ideological traditions in America: liberal (urban and agrarian), and conservative (urban and agrarian). In a sense all four traditions can find a place in each major party. This is not to say that there are not distinguishing central and majority ideological tendencies in each party but rather that there is ideological compatibility within the two major parties. While in the national image the Democrats are more left of center, liberal, and welfare-state oriented, and the Republicans more right of center, conservative, and oriented to a free competitive marketplace, both parties embrace a broad spectrum of ideological positions. The emphasis is not ideological rigidity, but noncomformity. This means that those who crusade for ideological causes have difficulty in claiming that the system rejects their causes.

The coalitional flexibility of the major parties has also been noticeable. That is, neither party has consisted of irrevocable, subordinate social- and economic-interest subgroups whose loyalty to the party is constant and to whom the party in turn is exclusively beholden. Since the Civil War the phenomenon of "the reversibility of coalitional support" has occurred on several occasions. Thus, business interests were not always on the side of the Republican party nor the lower classes and the labor unions always in the Democratic coalition. In 1892 according to A. W. Dunn, "Big Business was behind [Grover Cleveland] and there was no end of campaign money furnished to the national committee."[28] In 1896 the Republican William McKinley, who had supported strikers during his career, "enlisted in their cause large numbers of industrial workers," according to V. O. Key. McKinley carried the ten largest cities in the country. By 1908, however, the working class was moving back to the Democratic party.[29] And by 1924 the American Federation of Labor endorsed the candidacy of Robert La Follette. Thus, in the substructure of the two major-party coalitions there has been considerable and constant movement of subgroups, while the parties themselves have revealed a capacity to win and lose coalitional elements from one election to the next, or from one era to the next. A dramatic illustration of this is the political behavior of the lower and working classes from 1932 to 1952–56. Survey studies reveal that whereas in 1948 less than one-fourth of the unskilled laborers who voted supported the Republicans, by 1956 almost one-half were Republican voters. Of those in the lower-lower class who voted in 1952, 48 percent were Eisenhower supporters. In a real sense the history of American parties is one of the breakup, modification, and reconstruction of socioeconomic coalitions. This limited fidelity of such subgroups to the party as well as the coalitional expansionism of the parties means that the major parties are penetrable by new social forces and amenable to their overtures. Again this does not mean that both parties are but transient aggregations of subcoalitions that desert the party readily, rather it does mean that there is no coalitional rigidity, and continual dynamic renovation of the party takes place as a result of coalitional alliances.

Whenever parties have ceased to be absorptive, eclectic, and flexible, major party-system crises have occurred, for example, in 1824 or in 1854–60. Individual parties have had many other particular crises reflecting the party's incapacity to adapt to threats: the Democrats in 1904, 1924, and 1948; and the Republicans in 1912 and 1932. When a party refuses to be ideologically tolerant, ignores what is happening within its coalitional substructure, and refuses to react to significant voices of protest outside the two parties, apparently it can lose an important proportion of popular support. Ordinarily, however, it loses this support only to the other major party, unless that party too, as in 1854–60, is oblivious to the threats to the system. Usually, one of the two parties is sufficiently adaptive and absorptive to respond to new demands, as in the period 1892–1912 and 1928–36. Our two major parties have generally alternated in their capacity to maintain the two-party system. Seldom has at least one of the two major parties not been sensitive to new social forces and developing protest. No sizeable body of political "have nots" could be mobilized for a new party and persuaded it was a permanent necessity. By alternatively playing the roles of adapter to social change, catalytic broker for new social protest, equilibrator of political conflict, the two parties have preserved each other's place in the system by preserving the two-party system itself. The question, of course, is whether this will continue in the 1980s and the 1990s.

Conclusions

Since 1789 American democracy has gone through a great developmental and maturation process. Despite constant challenges and much anti-party sentiment, the party system was a part of this modification and transformation. Early parties were loose coalitions of social interests, poorly organized, with very little discipline, led by elites with very pragmatic styles. As they became mass-oriented, complex and durable structures, ever more diverse in composition and socially adaptable, parties also assumed responsibility for the performance of a variety of tasks and functions. And over time, particularly from the end of the nineteenth century to the present, the public developed important attachments to the parties.

In the meantime, however, interest groups appeared that also became involved with the political process. Even as the pro-party culture matured, anti-party developments reappeared. Parties began to share with other sectors certain functions, such as the articulation of public opinion, the representation of group demands, political communication with the public, and socialization. Parties concentrated more on the recruitment of leadership for the top policy-making positions in society, and in the mobilization of support for political leaders; they were actively involved in the intergroup bargaining activities that became a very prominent part of the American political scene. Yet parties were constantly harassed by anti-party sentiment. People demanded the regulation and reform of parties, and some atrophying in party functional performance occurred. Yet, despite all these transformations, today the two-party system remains viable and responsive.

Perhaps a basic dilemma developed in the role of parties in the American society as our system matured during the nineteenth and twentieth centuries, a dilemma of organizational cohesion and effective action or lack of discipline and delayed action. Pro-party sentiment pressed for the former; anti-party sentiment resulted in the latter. A two-party equilibrium had developed, after the Civil War, a party system that was relatively integrated with the social order. But the pragmatism and coalitional bargaining that attended the development of this stable party system made it difficult for our parties always to act effectively and expeditiously. And the demand for reform that weakened party organizations may have contributed to a decline in party-system performance. This may indeed be the irony of American parties.[30]

Chapter 3

The American Party System:

Basic Characteristics,

With Cross-National Comparisons

THAT PARTY systems differ is clear to anyone who pays even the most superficial attention to them; that they differ in fundamental respects is clear to anyone who studies them carefully. The number of parties that secures seats in the national legislatures (or parliaments) of countries, for example, varies greatly: two in the United States, three in Canada, six in Britain, ten in Italy, eleven in the Netherlands, and thirteen in Israel. The strength of the largest party in parliament (in percentage of seats) varies also: 57 percent in the United States, but only 42 percent in Italy, and 35 percent or 36 percent in Israel and the Netherlands. Thus even in this numerical sense clearly systems differ in the strength of the dominant party (or parties) and the reality and pluralization of the opposition. Israel has the most pluralized system, followed closely by the Netherlands. On the other hand, the United States, Canada, and Britain have systems that appear to be in a separate class, where one party has a majority and the opposition is much more limited. Yet, the number of small opposition parties in the Canadian Parliament (Social Credit and the New Democratic Party) and in Britain (Liberals, Scottish Nationals, Ulster Unionists, Welsh Nationalists, and the new [1981] Social Democrats) make these two systems clearly distinct from the American system where there is really only one opposition party.

Numerical criteria, however, are only suggestive and scratch the surface of the differences among these systems. They must be combined with other insights in order to specify the ways in which systems differ. The system in the United States has a basic character distinguishing it from other systems, which can be explained by contrasting it with others in terms of six key dimensions.

A Majority-Oriented Party System With Potential for Divided Control

Analysis of party systems must begin with the simple question: Can and does *one* party secure a *majority* of governmental positions such as legislative seats or Cabinet and executive positions, or must parties share power and/or work together in coalitions? This way of distinguishing systems is so obvious that it is often overlooked. It was one of the earliest preoccupations of the Founding Fathers, with Madison believing that the Constitution would frustrate majority control. Jefferson later argued that under the system developing during this early period one of the parties "must for the most part prevail over the other for a longer or shorter time."[1] In a sense the American system emerged with two assumptions: (1) one of two parties would win a majority in any particular branch of government or in any house of the legislature (national or state), but (2) it would be difficult for the same party to control all branches (executive, legislative, and judicial) and all levels (national, state, and local) of government. Thus the system was majority-oriented, but not one-party dominant. While coalition government (several parties sharing power in the Cabinet) never really developed, it was assumed that the two parties might share power *among the branches of government* as well as alternate in power over time. Although it was perfectly possible to conceive of one party controlling the presidency and a majority of seats both in the House of Representatives and in the Senate, as well as a majority of the nine seats on the Supreme Court (to say nothing of the control of state governorships, legislatures, and courts), it was considered unlikely. Even limiting consideration to the president and the Congress, majority control by one party, while culturally acceptable to many, would be difficult to achieve.

In reality, as noted in chapter 2, there have been periods in the United States's history when one party did have a majority in Congress, as well as the presidency, and also periods of divided government—the president of one party, the House and/or Senate controlled by another party. The Jeffersonian Republicans immediately after the election of 1800 had twenty-four years of majority control, and after a brief lull, after the election of 1828, the Democrats had twelve years of majority control. Since the Civil War the United States has fluctuated between one-party majority control and divided party control. The Republicans had majority control of the national government from Lincoln's victory in 1860 to 1874, and again for fourteen years after the 1896 election. Otherwise there was divided party government in the latter part of the nineteenth century. On the other hand, the Democrats were briefly in control from 1912 to 1918 and dominated the presidency and Congress from 1932 to 1946. Again, after John Kennedy's election in 1960, the Democrats controlled both branches up to 1968. With the 1976 election of Jimmy Carter the Democrats again attained strong majority control in the House and the Senate, but it did not last long—1980 produced divided government! It is interesting that the 120 years since 1860 have seen almost equal proportions of Republican or Democratic dominance, and divided party control— forty-two years, thirty-eight years, and forty years, respectively.

To be more precise about the marginality or strength of party control at the national level the *extent* of the party's victory in Congress when it is victorious should be considered. For five political eras since the Civil War, table 3.1 shows the proportionate strength of party legislative dominance by number of years of control. This, then, permits a determination of the amount of time there has been:

1. *divided party control*—no party controls the presidency *and* both houses of Congress
2. *marginal party control*—one party control, but with less than 55 percent of the seats in Congress
3. *moderate party control*—one party control and from 55 percent to 60 percent of the seats in Congress
4. *strong party control*—one party controls with over 60 percent of the seats in Congress.

The data suggest that 53 percent of the time since the Civil War the United States has had either divided party control or marginal control. On the other hand, only 25 percent of the time has there been strong party control. The early period after the Civil War was most marginal. The period from 1960 to 1980 appears to be not the most marginal, but on the other hand it had the most divided party government since 1896—40 percent of the period has been "divided" (primarily the Nixon and Ford years—1968-76) and only 30 percent characterizable as a time of strong one-party majority control.

One factor not entering into this calculation is the margin of victory of the presidential candidate. Carter's marginal victory in 1976 (51 percent of the two-party vote) would raise further questions about whether this is a period of strong party majority control, even though the

TABLE 3.1

The Marginal Majoritarian Nature of the United States Party System,
1860–1980

Strength	1860–1920 (Percentage of 60 years)	1920–1980 (Percentage of 60 years)	Since the Civil War (Percentage of 120 years)
Divided government[a]	36.7	30.0	33.3
Marginal government[b]	23.3	16.7	20.0
Majoritarian government[c] (moderately strong)	20.0	23.3	21.7
Majoritarian government[d] (strong party control)	20.0	30.0	25.0
	100.0	100.0	100.0

[a] No party controls presidency and both houses of Congress.

[b] The party controlling the presidency controls Congress with less than 55 percent of the seats in one or both houses.

[c] One party controls the presidency and up to 60 percent of seats in both houses of Congress.

[d] One party controls the presidency and has a 60 percent or greater majority in both houses of Congress.

Democrats won over 60 percent of the seats in the House and the Senate. The same could be said for Kennedy's slim victory (51 percent) in 1960, even though the Democrats won 60 percent of the House seats and 64 percent of those in the Senate. From 1960 to 1980 30 percent of the time the country had "strong party control" at the national level, but the marginal nature of the presidential victory and the relevance this had for the nature of his popular mandate should be borne in mind. The North-South split among congressional Democrats was a significant factor in this.

The United States party system seems to stand virtually alone as a majority-oriented but often divided party-control system. The British system is certainly majority-oriented since it has only two major parties, the Conservative and Labour parties. But the type of divided party control here between a chief executive and a legislature cannot normally exist in a parliamentary system as in Britain, since there the prime minister is the leader of the largest party, and the House of Lords has only limited power. Similarly, in continental European systems the Cabinet is usually made up of several parties who *collectively* have a majority in Parliament. Further, the American concept of "divided party control" between the executive and the legislature is inoperable elsewhere. The closest parallel perhaps to our system is France, which does have a popularly elected president who could theoretically have a legislative majority, but is more likely to be at odds with Parliament. In 1981, however, the Socialists did win such a majority.

The importance of having unified party control as opposed to divided party control can be considerable. When a party has control of the executive and the two houses of Congress it may be able to accomplish a great deal in innovative policy making, particularly if the president has also received a strong mandate. Roosevelt's election in 1932 and the ensuing years of Democratic control of the executive branch and the Congress illustrate this well. The New Deal legislation was adopted in such a party control context. A similar period was the Republican dominance of the 1920s and in the period from 1896 to 1910. And particularly after critical "realigning" election years (such as 1860, 1896, and 1932) there have been years of strong one-party control that have led to important changes in policy. When there is no one-party majority control, or a weak mandate, the context is not favorable for effective governmental action. Thus, Morris Janowitz expresses well what many students of our system feel, "the outcome of the national election, in one form or another, is such that an effective and stable regime is not created. The result . . . is political fragmentation or disarticulation and a variety of forms of stalemate. . . ."[2] He feels that without clear-cut political majorities political elites have not been able to adopt critically needed reforms in the welfare system. The inability to generate a decisive majority in government has significant consequences for policy outputs, which in turn may have an impact on the public's affiliation with parties and their involvement with the system.

A Party System with a Cohesive Opposition

How are dissent and protest channeled in a party system? This is a key question to answer to comprehend party functioning. In one-party states, of course, protest through separate opposition parties is proscribed, as in many East European systems, the USSR, China, as well as in many African and Latin American states. But where opposition parties are accepted as part of the democratic process, a variety of systems emerges. These systems differ from each other in certain critical respects:

1. The extent to which the opposition is pluralized, or the number of party groups through which protest can be expressed
2. The continuity and durability of these opposition parties over time
3. The effectiveness of these opposition parties in securing governmental positions, particularly in getting seats in the legislature
4. The strength of the opposition parties, that is, their sizes in relationship to the party (or parties) in power

In the United States the opposition is essentially concentrated in one large, major political party that has existed for a long period of time (since the Civil War) and that effectively threatens the party in power by winning a sizable proportion of seats (one-third or more) in the Congress. There are a large number of parties in the United States, and some of them, such as the Prohibition party, the Communist party, and the Socialist party have been in existence for half a century or more. Thus, in 1976, eleven small parties put up candidates for the presidency but as a group secured only 1.9 percent of the vote and no seats in Congress. (In 1980 John Anderson received 6.6 percent, but all the other parties only 1.7 percent.) These parties usually are not important channels for the members of the American public wishing to oppose the Democratic or Republican parties. Or, to put it another way, the two major parties have assimilated almost completely those protesters or dissidents who wish to communicate their opposition.

The American system stands in contrast to most other systems. In Canada three opposition parties have been able for some time to secure seats in Parliament (but only two in 1980). In Britain there is one major opposition party (either Labour or Conservative) plus four smaller parties able to secure thirty to forty seats in Parliament. The diversity of opportunities for effective protest is much greater in continental European parties, in Israel, or in India. Table 3.2 illustrates these distinctions.

The significance of these differences in party systems has not been adequately studied. But it is highly probable that the pluralization of opposition parties in a system, unless these parties coalesce at election time, makes it difficult to dislodge the incumbent party from its control of the system. The convergence of protest forces into a major opposition party or movement maximizes the chances of dislodging the establishment. The recent developments in the Netherlands (the replacement of the Labour party coalition with an opposition coalition

TABLE 3.2

*Differences in Opposition Patterns
in Party Systems*

Number of Opposition Parties	Countries	Percentage of Seats Held by Largest Opposition Party
1	U.S.	44
2–4	Britain	44
5–6	Canada	39
	France	20
More than 6	Italy	36
	Israel	27
	India	8

in which three religious parties combined into one party) and in Israel (the replacement of the Labour Alignment by Menachem Begin's Likud opposition) attest to this probability. On the other hand, if all protest is comprehended into too few opposition parties it may mean the frustration of dissidents and their withdrawal from political involvement. In societies with multiparty oppositionist systems, like Israel and the Netherlands, the opportunities for small protest sections of the population to organize politically and to elect representatives to Parliament are important cathartic aspects of the system. In the United States such pluralized oppositionism is normally difficult to organize, and it may lead to frustration about parties and withdrawal from participation.

The U.S. System Has Parties Whose Strength Is Highly Volatile

Certain systems appear to have the capacity for fairly sudden and frequent change in the electoral strength of the parties, while other systems remain fairly stable with only minimal changes in voting support for individual parties from one election to the next. In recent years in the United States the fortunes of a party have changed quickly in presidential elections. Consider, for example, the Democratic party's variable percentage of the vote since 1956: In 1956 Stevenson received 42 percent; in 1960 Kennedy recouped with 49.7 percent; and in 1964 Johnson had a landslide with 61.1 percent—the extent of change was 19 percent from 1956 to 1964 and 11.4 percent from 1960 to 1964.

The Republican turnabout from 1964 to 1972 was equally dramatic: from 38.5 percent in 1964 and 43.4 percent in 1968 to 60.7 percent in 1972—a jump of 22.2 percent in eight years and almost 17 percent in four years. Our history has been marked continuously with such shifts in party strength, in the vote for Congress as well as for president, although in recent years the Democrats have tended to win a majority of seats in the Congress. At the time of the critical election of 1932, however, the loss of the Republicans in the House and Senate was truly remarkable. Their proportion of seats in the House dropped from 61 percent in 1928 to 29 percent in 1932; in the Senate the Republicans dropped from 58 percent to 37 percent. This paralleled the Republican losses in Congress between 1908 and 1912—they dropped from 56 percent to 30 percent in the House and from 65 percent to 47 percent in the Senate. Similarly, the Democrats dropped from 70 percent control of the House in 1912 to 51 percent in 1916, to 44 percent in 1918, and 31 percent in 1920. There is strong evidence, therefore, that the fortunes of the parties are sharply reversible in the short term, a phenomenon which scholars recently have spent time analyzing.[3]

This volatility of the system (measured in terms of the changes in the voting strength of parties over time from election to election) can be used to compare the American system with other party systems. We have calculated the extent of the volatility of the American system recently by taking the proportions of the vote in the seven presidential elections from 1952 to 1976, noting the percentage shift in each of the two major parties' vote in each election sequence, summing these shifts, and dividing by six (the number of election to election shifts involved) in order to secure the average shift. This is the measure of volatility to be used here (see table 3.3).

Thus, the average shift for each party was almost 10 percentage points during this period from 1952 to the present, or a volatility of 19.3 percentage points. This occurred even though, in a comparison of 1952 to 1976, the Democratic proportion increased only 6.6 percentage points and the Republicans dropped 8.1 percentage points. While both parties retained their long-term status as the bulwarks of the party system, considerable variation in their strength occurred in the short run.

The volatility of the American system can be compared with others by using the same basic measure. Table 3.4 does this for seven other countries. In each case only the major parties in each system are considered (those securing 10 percent or more of the vote in an election during this period), and the time period used is from the early or mid-1950s to the early 1970s. This time span meant more elections for some countries than others, of course, and this number of election shifts was used to arrive at the average shifts occurring from election to election for all the major parties in any given system.

The French and the United States systems are the most volatile, with the British and the Canadian systems following fairly close behind. Systems apparently not susceptible to much short-term electoral change are the Swiss, the Austrian and, perhaps surprisingly, the Italian. The number of parties in the systems is not necessarily the basic

TABLE 3.3
Volatility of American Voting System
(as a percentage)

Party	1952	1956	1960	1964	1968	1972	1976	Total Aggregate Shift	Volatility Measure: Mean for the Six Shifts
Democrats	44.4	42.0	49.7	61.1	42.7	37.5	51.0	58.6	9.8
Republicans	55.1	57.4	49.5	38.5	43.4	60.7	47.0	57.1	9.5
								115.7	19.3

TABLE 3.4

Volatility of the U.S. System Compared to Ten Other Systems (1950s–1970s)
(as a percentage)

Country	Time Period	Number of Electoral Shifts	Number of Parties Involved	Volatility = Average Shift	Largest Shift Occurring for Any Party During This Period
United States	1952–76	6	2	19.3	18.4
France	1956–73	5	6	23.6	14.5
Canada	1957–74	7	4	16.2	16.3
Britain	1955–74	5	3	12.1	12.3
Netherlands	1952–72	5	5	10.1	5.4
Germany	1957–72	4	3	9.7	5.1
Sweden	1956–73	6	4	9.9	6.8
Italy	1958–74	3	4	7.3	5.4
Austria	1956–71	5	2	4.5	5.8
Switzerland	1955–71	4	4	2.9	3.1
India	1952–71	4	4	2.3	3.2

factor, since Austria with really only two major parties (as has the United States) has very low volatility, while multiparty systems reveal both low and high volatility (Switzerland low, France high).[4]

This suggests that there is a certain basic orientation to party-system fluidity that characterizes systems. Citizens apparently shift their votes more readily and in large numbers, relatively, in the United States, even though their defections are only short-lived. This is part of the "surge-and-decline" character of American party life—the surge to a party on the rise and the subsequent drop-off and decline in a subsequent election of those only marginally committed.[5] The relevance of this for the changing nature of American political leadership is great. The challenge it poses to the parties in mobilizing support is also great. The American party system clearly is not stagnant, but rather has continuous potential for change.

A Party System Nonpolarized in Group and Ideological Conflict

The substantive character and intensity of the conflict between parties in a party system is another approach in identifying major differences from one country to the next. Parties in democratic societies represent and mirror the different interests and opinions of the public, and thus a certain asymmetry or difference in viewpoint is bound to exist in individual parties. They are more left or right, more liberal or conservative, more pro-working class or pro-middle class and so forth. The key questions are: (1) How distinctive are parties in their group appeals and group support? (2) How important are issue positions and ideologies of parties in the system? and (3) How *extreme* are the issues and ideological positions of the parties? In some party systems group conflict and ideological differences are important, explicit, and extreme, with a tendency toward party-system dissensus or polarization. In other party systems, such as in the United States, group conflict exists, as well as issue differences between the parties, but it is less salient, less explicit, and more moderate—these systems are more consensual or nonpolarized. As noted in discussing Anthony Downs's theory, parties can be seen as competing for the public's votes by espousing those issue and ideological positions that they think will maximize their success. All parties in a sense do this. But, in their relationship to other parties in the system, where are they located on the ideological continuum, and how intensely in conflict with other parties are they ideologically?

The first point to be made is that ours is not a class-conscious or class-distinct system in which the working class (manual workers, for example) support one party and the middle class (or white-collar workers) the other party. Table 3.5 gives data on 1980 party identification and 1980 voting preferences by occupational groups.[6] While unskilled and blue-collar workers tend to be Democrats more than Republicans, fewer than 50 percent call themselves Democrats, and 40 percent are Independent. And a third of the upper-status professionals are also Democrats while 31 percent call themselves Republicans. In 1980 the blue-collar vote was split between Carter and Reagan, while other occupational groups moved more into the Republican column. Nevertheless, the basic pattern of party loyalty was very balanced.

Table 3.6 presents the extreme differences when the extent of class voting in the United States is compared with that in other systems.

TABLE 3.5
Party Identification and Vote by Occupational Groups
(as a percentage)

Occupation	Democratic	Independent	Republican	1980 Vote	
				Carter	Reagan
Professional	32	37	31	33	56
Clerical/sales	39	36	25	42	48
Blue-collar and unskilled laborer	43	40	17	48	46
Farmer	28	39	33	29	66

SOURCE: University of Michigan CPS, American Election Studies.

TABLE 3.6

*Index of Class Voting in Five
Democracies (based on data from
election surveys in the 1960s)
(as a percentage)*

Country	Index of Class Voting
Norway	51
Britain	43
Australia	28
United States	17
Canada	−4
Italy	−1

SOURCES: Robert Alford, "Class Voting in the Anglo-American Political Systems," in S. M. Lipset and Stein Rokkan, eds., *Party Systems and Voter Alignments* (New York: The Free Press, 1967), p. 85 (for all but the Norwegian and Italian data). The Italian data were based on the findings presented by Mattei Dogan in the same book, p. 174; the Norwegian data are from Stein Rokkan in the same book, p. 413.

NOTE: The Index is arrived at by subtracting the proportion of *manual workers* who supported parties of the center or the right from the proportion who supported the left. Thus if 64 percent supported left parties and 13 percent parties which were not left, the Index would be 51.

The Norwegian and British systems appear to be very class conscious—they have some parties that appeal to, mobilize, and secure the loyalty of large proportions of the working class, while other parties appeal to the middle classes. In the United States there is much less party concentration on the class vote and thus less political party conflict in class terms.

In the United States group conflict is much less explicit and distinctive in the patterns of public behavior in support of parties. Table 3.7 presents data on party identification of various groups in the 1980 presidential election. It is true that some evidence exists of a tendency for certain sectors of the population to give greater support to one of the parties. In the past this has been true of the southern whites (Democrats) as well as the northern Protestants (Republicans). And, the support of blacks for the Democratic party is especially heavy in the North and South. Despite such concentrations of support geographically and racially our system cannot really be called an extremely group-conflicted system. Party identifications in 1980 reveal considerable balance among age groups, religious groups (except for those of Jewish faith), and educational groups. Further, changes in voting behavior are possible. In 1980, 39 percent of the Jews supported Reagan and 45 percent voted for Carter, and those in blue-collar occupations were split evenly between Carter and Reagan. Our parties are socially

TABLE 3.7
*Partisan Loyalties of Particular Groups
of the American Public (1980 Presidential Election)
(as a percentage)*

Group	Democratic Identifiers	Independents	Republican Identifiers
Age			
18–29	31	45	19
30–54	41	35	22
55–69	47	30	22
70 and over	48	22	29
Race–Blacks	72	19	5
Religion			
Catholics	43	37	19
Jewish	73	23	2
Protestants	41	32	25
Education			
Grade school	54	25	17
High school	42	36	19
College	34	36	30

SOURCE: SRC/CPS American National Election Studies (Machine Readable DATA FILE) ICPSR Edition, Ann Arbor, Michigan, 1980. These groups hereafter will be abbreviated throughout as follows: Survey Research Center, SRC, Center for Political Studies, CPS; and National Election Studies, NES.

diverse. The dominance of one party by a particular religious, racial, class, or geographical sector in conflict with another party dominated by another group or set of groups is not characteristic of the American system.

In 1980, as in previous surveys, the Center for Political Studies at the University of Michigan asked a variety of questions of American citizens related to the most prominent political issues of the campaign. Table 3.8 shows how the responses of Democrats and Republicans to those issues in 1980 reveal the extent of the conflict of opinion between the major party supporters.

There are, indeed, differences—this fact should not be overlooked. Thus, Republicans want fewer government services, less aid to minorities, and a decreased role of the government in guaranteeing jobs. But the extent of the differences on many issues—defense spending and women's rights are good examples—was not as great as might have been expected. Further, when people are asked to classify themselves as Liberals, Moderates, or Conservatives there is considerable variation within each party, as table 3.9 shows. The Republicans are clearly more conservative than the Democrats, but one-third do not consider themselves Conservatives. And, only 38 percent of the Democrats call themselves Liberals. Hence, the parties do differ (and did in 1980 more so than previously), but they are not strictly polarized in conflict

TABLE 3.8
Issue Positions of Democrats and Republicans
(as a percentage)

Issue	Democrats	Republicans	Party Difference
Favor aid to minorities	31	11	20
Believe government should guarantee jobs	41	16	25
Believe government services should be increased	60	27	33
Believe defense spending should be increased	65	81	16
Believe in equal rights for women	64	60	4

SOURCE: University of Michigan CPS/NES, 1980.

TABLE 3.9
Ideological Self-Placement of Partisans, 1972–80
(as a percentage)

Self-Classification	Democrats			Republicans		
	1972	1976	1980	1972	1976	1980
Liberals	33	37	38	13	10	10
Moderates	41	39	34	37	30	23
Conservatives	26	24	28	50	60	67

SOURCE: University of Michigan CPS/NES, 1972, 1976, 1980.
NOTE: Respondents were asked to place themselves on a 7-point scale ranging from 1 (most liberal) to 7 (most conservative). For purposes here those at the positions 1 to 3 are combined into the liberal category, number 4 were the moderates, and positions 5 to 7 on the scale were the conservatives.

against each other. The important point to note here is that in contrast to most European systems American parties are not extremist nor are their supporters at extremes of the ideological spectrum.

A Party System with Diverse Patterns of Party Control and Competition by Geographical Region and within Geographical Regions

Party systems are sometimes called centrifugal (if they exhibit tendencies of disunity or incoherence) or centripetal (if they exhibit tendencies of homogeneity and coherence). A system can be centrifugal in several ways—if parties are decentralized organizationally or in their control relationships, for example, or if there is extremism in their ideological conflict patterns. A third centrifugal aspect of the system is diversity of competition patterns.

Upon examination of the patterns of national, state, and local party dominance and competition, the American system certainly appears to be centrifugal. For many years our parties were considered to have sectional bases of support, that is, certain geographical regions where their support was heavily concentrated. To a certain extent this is still true, particularly in elections for the House and Senate. In 1976 and 1980, for example, differences existed in the support for the president and the Congress in various regions of the country. The range in support for presidential candidates by sections in 1980 was 9 percent, with Carter weakest in the West (35 percent) and strongest in the South (44 percent). However, the extent of sectionalism becomes much more apparent upon consideration of the percentage of the *seats* in the House which were won by each party (see table 3.10). For the period from the New Deal to Kennedy, there was great evidence of sectionalism, ranging from an average Republican strength in the House of 2 percent of the southern seats to almost 75 percent or more of New England seats and those from the Plains states. True, the results of the 1976 election reveal less striking contrasts by geographical region, but they still are significant, ranging from 23 percent Republican success for House candidates in the solid South to 52 percent in the Plains states.

The evidence of sectionalism in American politics is also very apparent from the roll-call voting of the members of Congress. The recent voting record of Republicans and Democrats in the Congress of 1976–78 reveals a basic sectional pattern. Using the Committee on Political Education (COPE) scoring of congressmen on twenty-three selected votes in 1977 on legislation favored by the AFL-CIO, the contrasts are

TABLE 3.10

Sectionalism in House Victories
by Republicans and Democrats
(as a percentage)

Region	Number of States	Average Won by Republicans 1932–62	Seats Won by Republicans 1976
South	10	2.1	23.0
Border	7	17.5	26.8
Atlantic	5	56.2	27.2
Midwest	5	61.2	44.2
New England	5	74.6	34.8
Plains	6	78.5	52.0
Far West	3	56.7	27.8

SOURCES: For 1932–62 data: Charles O. Jones, *The Republican Party in American Politics* (New York: Macmillan, 1965), pp. 86–88; for 1976 data: "Electing Congress," *Congressional Quarterly, Inc* (April 1978), 152–210.

as follows:[7] The percentages of congressmen in the area who scored 80 percent or better on the COPE Liberalism Measure were 9 percent for southern Democrats (no Republicans) and 66 percent for northern Democrats, with 2 percent for northern Republicans. Clearly there are major differences in policy orientations within the Democratic party by region.

The patterns of "ticket splitting," which reinforce these observations, in a recent analysis reveal that from one-fourth to two-fifths of the congressional districts are won by the presidential candidate of one party and a congressional candidate of the other party.[8] These data suggest that there is a considerable lack of homogeneity of voting behavior patterns *by office*, as well as *by region*. Detailed study of voting returns within congressional districts and counties would indeed give even further evidence of this diversity in behavior.

We are actually inclined to talk about one hundred state party systems in the United States rather than one national party system. Many scholars have devised classification schemes, perhaps the most popular of which is Austin Ranney's, presented in table 3.11. This classification lists seven "one-party Democratic states," ten states tending to Democratic dominance, five states tending to Republican dominance, and the remaining twenty-eight as genuine two-party competitive states. In Louisiana, for example, the Democratic party ordinarily wins almost all state (and local) offices; however, it is not that overwhelmingly Democratic in presidential elections—Carter won in 1976 and Reagan won in 1980. Vermont, at the other extreme, is strongly Republican and only occasionally do Democrats win state offices: In 1976 Carter received 42.8 percent of the vote and only 39.3 percent in 1980. Between these extremes, in a sense at the middle of the spectrum, there are two-party states like Oregon, New Jersey, Pennsylvania, Colorado, and Michigan, where the parties alternate in power and split control over state offices. Michigan is a good example of this, with a Republican governor and Democratic control of the legislature; but in 1976 Ford won the state with 51.8 percent and in 1980 Reagan won with 49.7 percent (7 percent went to Anderson).

The Ranney classification is useful for purposes of distinguishing the states by party control over the governorship and legislature. It also seems to distinguish groups of states by their partisanship in recent presidential elections. In terms of party control of the elections to Congress, it has less applicability today. As table 3.11 indicates, even in those states classified as "two-party but tending Republican," the Democrats in the 1976 election won 60 percent of the seats for the House of Representatives. Only the extreme group of five "modified one-party Republican states" has a Republican dominance in congressional district elections. But in this group of five states only eleven congressional seats are at stake. This indicates that a classification

TABLE 3.11

Classification of States According to Degree of Interparty Competition

Type of System	States Included in Ranney Taxonomy by Type	Mean Percentage of Democratic Vote for President	Mean Percentage of Total Congressional Seats Won by Democrats	
		1980	Total Seats	Mean % 1976
One-party Democratic	Louisiana, Alabama, Mississippi, South Carolina, Texas, Georgia, Arkansas (7)	48.4	64	84
Modified one-party Democratic	North Carolina, Virginia, Florida, Tennessee, Maryland, Oklahoma, Missouri, Kentucky, West Virginia, New Mexico (10)	43.9	81	69
Two-party states inclined to be more Democratic	Hawaii, Rhode Island, Massachusetts, Alaska, California, Nebraska, Washington, Minnesota, Nevada, Connecticut (10)	37.8	85	71
Two-party states most even in party control	Delaware, Arizona, Montana, Oregon, New Jersey, Pennsylvania, Colorado, Michigan (8)	38.1	75	67
Two-party states inclined to be more Republican	Utah, Indiana, Illinois, Wisconsin, Idaho, Iowa, Ohio, New York, Maine, Wyoming (10)	36.8	119	60
Modified one-party Republican states	North Dakota, Kansas, New Hampshire, South Dakota, Vermont (5)	32.2	11	27

SOURCE: For Ranney Taxonomy: Austin Ranney, "Parties in State Politics," in Herbert Jacob and Kenneth N. Vines, eds., *Politics in the American States: A Comparative Analysis*, 2nd ed. (Boston: Little, Brown, 1971), p. 87. Copyright © 1971 by Little, Brown and Company, Inc. Reprinted by permission. Ranney based his classification on the work of Richard Dawson and James Robinson, "Interparty Competition, Economic Variables, and Welfare Policies in the American States," *Journal of Politics* 25 (1963): 265–89.

NOTE: The Ranney Taxonomy is based on party votes for governor and state legislature, 1956–70.

based on state offices and votes may have limited applicability to national elections.

This characteristic of the American system, which reveals contrasting patterns of party conflict at the local level and the strong influence of both local traditions and party culture, should not be forgotten in the analysis of the American system. There is a great deal of organizational decentralization and diversity in the system, special patterns of leadership recruitment and institutional mechanisms and processes through which parties function in the sections, states, and localities of the United States. Maine is different from California; Michigan conducts its politics quite differently from even its next-door neighbor Illinois; the Republican and Democratic parties of Georgia and Virginia are quite different, and they in turn contrast with other states in the South, such as Florida or Louisiana or Mississippi. To study American party politics, therefore, is a complex undertaking; to generalize about them confidently must be done with extreme caution.

Public Acceptance of the Party System

Countries differ in the extent to which the parties command the support of citizens and maintain that support over a long enough period of time to permit the majority of the public to believe in the party system and feel personally committed to it. Several different types of measures determine whether this is so in any society and include approval of parties, participation in parties, and identification with parties. The latter measure is applicable here; later the attitudinal basis for the public's support of our system and the extent of political participation will be discussed.

The American public's support for parties as evidenced by its identification with them has been extremely high over the years. Since the end of the 1960s, there has been a declining trend in the public's party identification. Although survey research indicates that in the 1920s and 1930s 90 percent of the public was committed, or loyal, to either the Republican or Democratic parties, by the 1970s this trend had declined to below 70 percent and was approaching 60 percent—in 1980 it was 64 percent.

Despite this decline, over 60 percent of the American public does still identify with political parties, and compared to most other nations this is a respectable figure (see table 3.12). Voters in Britain appear to be the most committed to parties—probably at the 90 percent level—while the Dutch and the French electorates are, or were, less committed. Compared to 71 percent in Britain, the Dutch are particularly low, with only 18 percent calling themselves strong adherents of parties and only 45 percent having any firm commitment to parties. In an early study, based on 1958 data, the French were reported to have only 45 percent of the public identifying with parties, while more recently in 1967, an identification with a party or a "political formation" occurred there for almost 65 percent of the public.

In the United States a majority of its public has identified with the

TABLE 3.12

Comparative Party Support by the Public in Selected Nations

Country	Percentage of Public With Strong Party Identification	Rank Order	Percentage of Public With Strong or Weak Party Identification	Rank Order
Britain	71	1	90	1
United States	36	2	64	2
India	35	3	47	6
Norway	25	4	66	5
Germany	20	5	72	4
Netherlands	18	6	45	7
Japan	15	7	74	2
France			45	7

SOURCES: See Samuel J. Eldersveld, "Party Identification in India in Comparative Perspective," *Comparative Political Studies* 6, no. 3 (October 1973) p. 276 for the sources for most of these data. The Dutch data are from the national survey after the 1970 provincial elections. The Japanese source is the national survey of 1967. For the German data used here, see Helmut Norpoth, "Party Identification in West Germany—Tracing an Elusive Concept," *Comparative Political Studies*, vol. 11, no. 1 (April 1978), p. 49. U.S. data come from the University of Michigan CPS/NES, 1980.

Republican and Democratic parties for a long time. At least 90 percent did so as far back as 1920, if the recollections of people interviewed from the 1940s onward are reliable.[9] Since the First World War the British have also presumably had a long period in which a large majority of the public developed and maintained party identification— primarily with the Conservative and the Labour parties since the split of the Liberal party and the adoption by Labour of its socialist program in 1918. In other Western European countries, however, public commitment to parties has been slower to develop and has been interrupted by national crises, periods of fascism and nazism, World War II, and so forth.[10] Thus the Weimar period and World War II resulted in a disintegration of the German party system. The war, de Gaullism, and the appearance of meteoric parties in France during the Fifth Republic did not produce the conditions for stable partisanship in that country. Similar factors may explain the Japanese and Dutch, with their low proportions of strong party identifiers. It is interesting that a new democracy like India, whose independence occurred in 1947, reveals a proportion of its adults as strong identifiers (35 percent in 1971 and 51 percent in 1967), equal to that of the United States in 1971 and exceeded only by Britain.

The two major parties in the United States have a psychological hold on the American public that is probably surpassed only in Britain as to depth of real loyalty.[11] Party identification does fluctuate in the United States, but people do not often wander in the direction of third parties; the wanderers or "floaters" seem always to return to the major parties. This behavior suggests the continuing loyalty, acceptability, and legitimacy of the two major parties in the eyes of the American public.

Types of Party Systems

Systems that are truly competitive (in which parties can and do exist, and can and do compete) are identifiable by six major dimensions, on the basis of which these party systems can be distinguished and the American party system can be characterized. These dimensions are presented in figure 3.1 with the suggested location of the United States and other countries on each continuum. The distinctiveness of the United States is apparent, as well as the similarity of our system in certain respects to other systems. It is perhaps the most majority-oriented of all competitive, democratic party systems, with the most cohesive and nonpluralized system of party opposition. Yet, it is relatively volatile in voting patterns, exceeded only by those of the French. It is also the least polarized in terms of group and ideological conflict, a very centrifugal system in heterogeneity of competitive party patterns, but one that is exceeded only by the British, if just barely, in the durability of public loyalty to parties. Our system seems to be in a class by itself, except other systems are proximate to ours on particular dimensions: majority orientation and opposition cohesion (Britain and perhaps Germany); volatility (France, the Netherlands, Germany, and Britain); and public loyalty (Britain). Thus, we are distinctive but also cross-nationally comparable in certain respects.

In a variety of ways, therefore, the type of party system in a society may be a central key to understanding the basic character of political life in that society. Polarized party systems can pose quite a different set of problems than do essentially nonpolarized systems like ours. Highly pluralized opposition systems create quite different conditions for the power process than those with cohesive oppositions. The capacity for volatility in party systems considerably alters strategic approaches to mobilizing votes, as well as continuity in the nature of public policy, and so forth. Environmental conditions of the party system thus vary greatly; they may be central for understanding the nature of a country's politics and may have a critical set of consequences for what *can* be done and what *is* done by elites and politics in each society.

FIGURE 3.1

Six Dimensions for Classifying Party Systems
(Particular systems are located on the continua only if there is some observational or
empirical evidence to support such a placement)

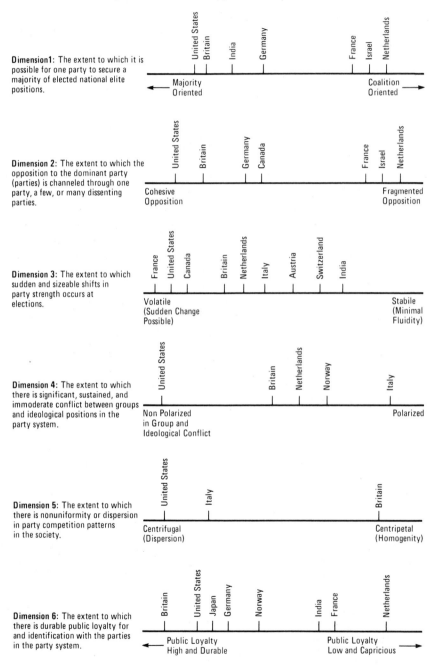

Determinants of Party Systems

Mysteries attend the origins and development of the party system in any society, and they are not easy to unravel. Why did parties come into existence when they did? Why did one type of party system appear? Why did parties with particular characteristics appear, representing particular group interests (for example, working-class or religious parties) and having particular competitive or organizational features? Particular aspects or circumstances of democratic societies made parties both necessary and inevitable, and also molded the emerging nature of the party system. Thomas Jefferson, writing in 1798, very early came to this position, "In every free and deliberating society there must, from the nature of man, be opposite parties and violent dissensions and discords. . . ."[12] As discussed in chapter 1, this is a basic postulate—conflict in the early history of democracy has meant the emergence of parties. Open competition for power, tolerance of opposition, and the expansion of participation in the political system to larger proportions of the public, all make parties necessary and natural. The opportunities for power, as well as the necessities for the performance of certain indispensable system functions (recruiting leaders, formulating policies, and mobilizing support) lead to the appearance of groups called parties.

Given this basic position, however, little has been explained in answer to the question: Why did particular types of party systems appear? The analysis and research of scholars concerned with this question have led them to develop a set of positions that together may constitute an explanation.

Position 1: The Early Patterns of Interest-Group Conflicts

The basic cleavage structures in the formative years of a new democratic society establish the setting within which party conflict develops, and this original cleavage pattern leaves its imprint on a party system as it matures. Thus, Stein Rokkan and S. M. Lipset see for European countries three early cleavage patterns over the role of the Catholic church (a result of the Reformation), the question of secularism (a result of the democratic revolution of 1789), and the primacy of agricultural or industrial interests (a result of the Industrial Revolution of the nineteenth century), to which subsequently was added the conflict between owner and worker in the capitalist system.[13] Parties there presumably were organized in terms of these basic cleavages, each particular form of which varied by society. Representing the interests of the landowners or urban commercial and industrial entrepreneurs, a dominant party emerged in the hands of established elites. And then an opposition party or set of parties emerged that reflected interests in opposition to these established elites, an opposition that could consist of religious or secular dissidents, landowners or urban entrepreneurs, or interests on the periphery opposing central national control.

The early political cleavages in the United States before 1800 conform somewhat to this conception. The differences between Hamilton and the Federalists on the one hand, and Jefferson and the Republicans on the other, were both interest-group oriented and ideological. Led by two magnetic personalities, the dominant elites split into two camps, disagreeing basically over how the power of the new federal government was to be exercised and mobilizing support from different socioeconomic interests. They disagreed over national economic policy, over sympathy for the French Revolution, and finally over the political rights of citizens threatened by the Alien and Sedition Acts. These were ideological concerns of great moment. Above all, the Jefferson Republicans opposed favoritism for the mercantilist class—they opposed government for the privileged few. As Jefferson saw the party conflict it was a dualistic confrontation between different sets of economic interests with distinctive ideologies—"republicans" against the "monocrats"—seeking to impose their will on the people.

Position 2: The Conditions Under Which the Suffrage Was Extended

A major factor in the development of democratic party systems was the timing and circumstances under which the suffrage was extended to all white male adults, at first, and eventually to all adults. As Leon Epstein observes, "There is every reason to believe that modern political parties emerged with the extension of the vote to a fairly large proportion of the populace."[14] He goes on to assert that the United States was "the first to enfranchise fairly large numbers," and "had the first modern parties, . . . in response to the nearly universal white manhood suffrage" by the second quarter of the nineteenth century.[15] It is important to remember that by the mid-nineteenth century America had eliminated religious, tax paying, and property-holding qualifications for voting and had extended the suffrage to all white males. There was a delay in extension of the vote to blacks; the Fifteenth Amendment adopted in 1879 finally forbade abridgment of the right to vote on the basis of "race, color, or previous condition of servitude."

Although the United States extended the suffrage early, in other democracies in Europe there was often considerable delay in the expansion of the right to vote and, therefore, of greater participation in the political process. Following are the dates when universal male suffrage was achieved in European systems and Canada:[16]

Germany	1871
France	1875
Belgium	1893
Canada	1896
Norway	1898
Switzerland	1902
Finland	1906
Denmark	1915
Netherlands	1917
Britain	1918
Sweden	1921

The size of the actual eligible electorate is a major consideration for a party since it is a vote-mobilization structure. As that electorate enlarges, the organizational character and competitive nature of the parties in the system are transformed. From the 1830s parties in the United States had to appeal to rapidly expanding numbers of eligible voters. This made them behave quite differently than they had before in appealing only to the small aristocratic groups of property-holding and tax-paying notables who alone had the vote before 1800.

The most important point here is that the fight over the extension of the suffrage in a sense reinforced the early basic cleavages. In the United States the battle was between an aristocratic group with special status and a "frontier" group demanding inclusion in the electorate. This too became an ideological conflict, just as it did in Europe, where throughout the nineteenth century (in France earlier, at the time of the Revolution) usually there were two sets of elites—liberals and conservatives—divided on this very question: Who should have the voting franchise? The way in which that question was resolved had a considerable impact on the type of party system that emerged.

Position 3: The Treatment by Established Elites of New Claimants for Power

During the nineteenth century in all Western democratic societies new groups made demands for inclusion in the electorate, in a sense claiming admission as full members of the polity. These groups included the urban working class, farm workers, religious nonconformists, Catholics (treated as a minority in certain countries after the Reformation), and particular ethnic, national, or language groups. Several scholars argue that the way these new claimants for power were treated varied greatly from one society to another, and two factors were involved: the rigidity of the status system, and the extent to which the old dominant elites were tolerant of these new claimants. One critical test of the attitude of the established elites, of course, was their willingness to give these new claimants the right to vote. When the old elites were intolerant and the status system rigid, to present the demands of the new claimants new parties formed—religious parties, farmers' parties, workers' parties, as well as ideological splinter parties—which either broke away from the parent liberal and conservative coalitions or mobilized new sectors of the society. New, small parties emerged in all European countries. Britain was spared this development (primarily because in 1867 and 1885 it did move to an expanded suffrage) until World War I when the Liberal party split and the new Labour party organized effectively enough to replace the Liberal party as the second major party.

The United States after its independence never had a rigid social status system of any consequence; it was relatively egalitarian. Very early the established elites accepted the idea of a liberalized suffrage. Because of a variety of pressures, calculations of competitive advantage, as well as arguments on the basis of principle, new claimants did not have to fight their way into the system but were given the right to vote early.[17] As a consequence, urban workers, farmers, Catholics, and other minority groups (with the exception of blacks) did not develop the organizational solidarity, the political consciousness, or the leadership that was necessary for the establishment of the type of minor parties found in Europe.

Position 4: The Political Constitution, Particularly the Election System, as Determinant

Much has been made of the role of the arrangement of political institutions in determining party systems. In the United States the federal system, the presidential office, the bicameral division of legislative power, and the election system itself, it is said, are responsible for our type of party system. Some scholars have suggested that there is virtually an immutable "law" concerning the relationship between election systems and party systems.[18] The simple plurality, single-member district system (United States and Britain) encourages a two-party system; the proportional election system (and the two-ballot system) encourages a multiparty system, it is claimed.

On the surface the arguments that certain basic features of the governmental system determine the nature of the party system seem logical. Indeed, at the time of the campaign for the adoption of the Constitution, the Founding Fathers reasoned similarly. James Madison argued that federalism, bicameralism, and separation of powers would influence the way parties or factions operated. And the election system argument does appear to have a certain rationality. When you can elect only one person from a geographical area a multiplicity of parties is discouraged. The trouble with the argument (whether for election systems or other institutional arrangements) as an explanation for the *emergence* of types of party systems is threefold:

1. *There are too many exceptions to the rule.* Nations with the same institutional features as the United States may have quite a different type of party system. For example, Canada is a federal system but has four durable parties (two major and two somewhat smaller). France has an elected president, but a very fragmented party system. Britain has a single-member district election and a two and one-half- or a three-party system. India has an election system like the United States but a much different party system.

2. *The causal relationship may be reversed.* The parties may be visualized as determining the election system, rather than vice versa. The United States really had established its party system first and then adopted its election system. A good example for a multiparty system is the Netherlands which already had seven parties in Parliament before it adopted a proportional representation system.

3. *Other more basic social and political forces determine the character of a party system.* There may be forces deeply imbedded in the nature of the society, and both the party system and the election system are a reflection of those basic forces. Just as Americans normally would be appalled at the idea of a five- or six- or seven-party system, so the French, Dutch, Norwegians, and Swiss generally would dislike the idea of a two-party system. Why? Because that type of party system would not be perceived as functional to the needs of their societies.

Once, however, a party system is established, the type of institutional framework within which it has to function will affect its operation considerably. And that framework may well work to *maintain* the basic character of that party system over time. The United States is a good example of this.

Federalism, for instance, may have certain effects relevant to the equilibrium of our two-party system. As Madison predicted, federalism makes the assumption of total political power throughout the country well-nigh inconceivable, since no party wins total power at the national and state levels simultaneously. This represents a check on the dominant party coming to national power, and this check is manifest in the actions of state governors and state legislatures in actual opposition to the party in power. This means that federalism provides a sheltering place for the losing party and enables it to use state office as a springboard for restoring the balance in the system. A Woodrow Wilson in New Jersey, a Franklin Roosevelt in New York, or a Nelson Rockefeller in New York can keep attention focused on the activities of the major parties' top leadership potential and keep the losing party a visible political reality throughout the nation. Further, federalism invites minor and third parties to test their wings and to achieve some measure of satisfaction by attempting to capture power in state capitals. In fact, any party that has designs at the national level realizes that it must operate at the state level first. Potential national third parties—the Populists, the Farmer-Labor party, the American Labor and Liberal parties of New York, and even the Dixiecrats—found the federal system with its decentralization of power an outlet for protest. But these third parties expend much of their activities at the state and regional levels, and their impact is rarely felt at the national level. Thus, while the federal system may discourage too much one-party dominance it also severely limits the development of minor parties that are serious national threats. Mounting an effective minor-party organization and campaign in Minnesota or South Carolina or New York is one thing. Doing it nationally is something far more complex. In Canada, however, the success of the Social Credit party may have been assisted by the federal system.

The contention that the presidential system is a deterrent to the development of third parties no doubt has some truth. This is claimed to be so in the American system because the presidency is not divisible, cannot be easily won by a third party, and is so powerful. It can be argued otherwise that the presidency is after all not the entire system of government, that Congress is a very powerful counterbalance to the presidency, and for a minor party to achieve some status in the Congress would in itself be of considerable consequence. In order to constitute threats to the system minor parties need not have the presidency but could serve obstructive or balancing roles in the Congress. The British Liberal party certainly does not expect in the near future to capture the government and provide England with a prime minister; it is but a faint hope. Nevertheless, the British Liberal party contests parliamentary elections in each election, elects some members to Parliament, and sometimes can be successful enough to be a force with which the major parties must reckon. Indeed, recently in order to stay in power the Labour party had to work out an agreement with the Liberals. The presidency, nevertheless, is obviously a chief prize for any United States party; any genuine forces of protest in our society against the system eventually must be interested in capturing the presidency. An example is George Wallace's movement in 1968 that tried but could not capture the presidency and as a movement was short-lived.

Theoretically, the plurality feature of the American system should provide some encouragement and opportunity to minor parties, but it has not, except in certain areas where state third parties have had a limited success, such as New York with its Liberal, Labor, and Conservative parties. The important point is that this election system has not necessarily inhibited the sporadic minor-party movement, but the vote outside the two-party system has not been able to organize into a durable third party. If a significant social need and determined leader-

ship arose, third parties could be organized despite the system of electing legislators from single-member districts. It has been the case in
Canada, England, and India. But the election system is certainly not
facilitative. Third parties, without established clienteles, can easily be
discouraged by the election system unless the conditions of party life
and the problems in the society change radically.

Position 5: The Responsiveness of Established Parties to Social Problems

As parties develop organizationally they become complex structures
both with organs of leadership and decision making at a variety of
levels (from the national to the local), and vertical and horizontal relations articulated in order to make them progressively more coherent
action mechanisms. One characteristic such structures must have is
adaptability; that is, parties must have the capacity for responding to
the needs of society, particularly when crises (social, economic, or
moral) occur which threaten its stability. The extent to which the established parties develop as continuously responsive institutions will
determine whether new parties appear and secure the support of the
voting public. Thus when working-class, Catholic, or farmers' parties
emerged in Europe, it must have been the case that the existing parties
were not adequately sympathetic to the needs and demands of these
groups. The Labour party in Britain became a major party at the time
of World War I because neither the Liberal party, which was badly
split, nor the Conservatives were considered adequately interested in
the problems of the working class. Too, the same can be said for virtually every country in Western Europe.

The Republican and Democratic parties since the Civil War have
been responsive enough to the new problems of American society to
quash the threats of minor parties. However, in the period preceding
the Civil War the Democrats and National Republicans could not solve
the crucial, moral issue of slavery, and, as a result, from 1854 to 1860
America went through a pluralization crisis that led eventually to a
new two-party system. Since that time threats have recurred periodically but the Republicans and Democrats have survived them, so that
no Labor, Catholic, or Farmers' party has lasted for any length of time.
The character of our party system cannot be comprehended without an
awareness of these twin phenomena: the inability of special-interest
parties to take root, and the responsive capability of our major parties.

Position 6: The Psycho-Cultural Socialization of Citizens to the System

Accepted by many scholars, the proposition has been advanced that
long exposure to the same party system without any interruptions
(wars or nondemocratic regimes) will tend to habituate the public to
the acceptance of a party system and the cultural expectations connected to it. Philip Converse argues that exposure for two and one-half

generations is probably necessary for any party system to be firmly imbedded in a society—that is, a system with which people identify for a long enough time and that is transmitted intergenerationally.[19] This may very well have happened in the United States. The period before the Civil War was considerably volatile and too short for firm party loyalties to have developed. After the war the system seems to have stabilized so that even though there still was considerable volatility in party successes, a psychological commitment to the parties that had great durability appeared to emerge. This commitment has declined in recent years; estimates suggest that as much as 90 percent of the public identified with the two major parties at the time of World War I, while only two-thirds or less were party identifiers in 1980. Nevertheless, there is strong indication that the two major parties have retained a hold on the loyalties of the majority of American citizens, a hold that may make a transformation or realignment or significant modification of the party system difficult.

Perhaps this argument should not be taken too far because studies have shown that high proportions of the public identify with parties in other countries that have not had a party system for as long as has the United States. Thus in 1967, in India, 70 percent of the public identified with parties even though India had acquired independence and a new party system as recently as 1947. Similarly, the modern party period in Japan dates from World War II, yet three-fourths of the Japanese public identifies with parties. The evidence is certainly not completely clear on this point and it certainly cannot be assumed that with the passage of time the public becomes so irreversibly committed to the party system that significant change is impossible. Major party-system change is certainly possible, but such change is more difficult and will not be as revolutionary in societies where party systems have survived long enough to evoke sentiments of identification and loyalty from the majority of the public.

Chapter 4

The Public and the Parties

IN STUDYING PARTIES in a democratic society there is a need for a clear understanding of the nature of the public's involvement with, and support of, the party system. This includes attitudinal support, as well as behavioral support. For citizen attitudes toward the parties probably condition citizen behavior and thus provide part of the context within which parties have to function. Citizens' feelings toward parties also constitute a final test of the effectiveness of the party system. If citizens do not want to affiliate with the parties or have only a weak commitment to them, or if citizens do not feel that parties are effective institutions and do not want to participate in them, the task of parties in providing linkages between citizens and government may be extremely difficult. On the other hand, where citizens join parties readily, identify with them confidently, and feel they can achieve objectives through them, the parties' tasks will be easier. Systems may differ considerably in these respects. Before describing party organizations and what they do, mention should be made of what appears to be the state of the American public's attitudes toward parties.

The Public's Evaluation of the Party System

There has always been a tension between the public's acceptance of democracy and its complete support for political parties. As indicated in the discussion of the origins of American parties, there was a great deal of reluctance on the part of both political leaders and the public in approving the need for, and legitimacy of, political parties. While the nation moved toward the institutionalization of a party system, there were at the same time recurrent attacks on "the baneful effects of the spirit of party."

In the public's views about parties this uncertainty or ambivalence is manifest yet today. There seems to be considerable acceptance of the idea of a party, in an abstract sense, as necessary and even important, for a democracy such as ours. In a 1952 study in Detroit, for example, when a sample of adults was asked, "Do you think having parties is good or bad for the country as a whole?" 70 percent of the voters said "good" or "very good," while 54 percent of the nonvoters took the same position. Only 10 percent rated the system bad.[1] Similarly, in 1964, in a Wisconsin study, 68 percent of the public agreed with the statement: "Democracy works best where competition between parties is strong."[2] In 1980 only 32 percent agreed with the statement: "The truth is we probably don't need political parties in America anymore."[3]

While such data suggest strong support for parties, in both of these studies, and in other research, there is considerable evidence that the public is unsure of the role of parties. In Detroit in 1956, for example, a large segment (42 percent in that study) of the public felt that a citizen should do more than just vote, but that the majority would prefer to work outside the party structures.[4] In Wisconsin, Jack Dennis found contradictory attitudes that are similar to the results of the 1980 survey (see table 4.1).

Other types of evidence show that the public's evaluation of parties is often not very positive. When asked whether they would encourage

TABLE 4.1
Public Attitudes Toward Political Parties
(as a percentage)

Attitudes	Wisconsin (1964)	National Sample (1980)
	% agree	
Pro parties		
1. "It would be better if, in all elections, we put no party labels on the ballot."	22	49
2. "People who work for parties during political campaigns do our nation a great service."	68	n.a.
Anti parties		
1. "The best rule in voting is to pick the man regardless of his party label."	82	73
2. "The parties do more to confuse the issues than to provide a clear choice on them."	54	56

SOURCES: For 1964 data: Jack Dennis, "Support for the Party System by the Mass Public," *American Political Science Review* 60 (September 1966) p. 606; for 1980 data: University of Michigan CPS/NES, 1980.

a son to go into politics, only 13 percent of the Detroit sample said yes, while in 1973 in a national Gallup survey, only 23 percent approved the idea.[5] Additional analysis of the public's ratings of parties as compared to other political institutions (Congress, the presidency, and the Supreme Court) in the 1970s shows that parties consistently rank lowest, during this period of low public trust in government.[6] And yet the public's willingness to do volunteer work for parties has remained at the 30 percent to 35 percent level during recent years, while its willingness to contribute money to parties has increased from 30 percent in 1943 to over 40 percent in 1968.[7]

A reasonable conclusion is that although the evidence is mixed when people are pressed with specific questions, the public's support for the party system appears weak. The best description of the state of the public's evaluations is that in abstract terms most Americans accept the probable value of a competitive party system for democracy, but when citizens are asked specifically about the roles of parties in solving conflicts or to choose between "voting for the man" or "voting for the party" or what parties have ever done for people like themselves, many of the reactions are negative. The potential for cynicism and rejection of parties is clearly evident today. The potential for increased support is also there, however. A large segment of the public is "available" for support. To perform in such a way that this abstract and generalized support is translated into more specific acceptance, more active involvement, affiliation, and commitment—this is the challenge to the parties.

Party Identification

When Americans have been asked recently whether they are attached to, or identify with, a political party, between 63 percent and 68 percent indicate they are. These percentages are divided between about 40 percent Democratic and about 23 percent Republican. Another 18 percent to 20 percent approximately, are "leaners" (those who tend to support a party even though not clearly identified with one), and 12 percent to 15 percent stubbornly hold out as Independents. This basic pattern has held up rather well since 1952 (see Table 4.2). In the late 1960s, specifically from 1966 onward, a change occurred that led some scholars to suggest that a major decline in party support, or a dealignment, had taken place.

The dimensions and characteristics of this decline are significant. Its extent and nature can be presented in a variety of ways. First, of course, is the change in the *strength* of party identification, which has

TABLE 4.2
Party Identification, 1952–80
(as a percentage)

Affiliation	*1952*	*1956*	*1960*	*1964*	*1968*	*1972*	*1976*	*1980*
Strong Democrat	22	21	21	26	20	15	15	18
Weak Democrat	25	23	25	25	25	25	25	23
Independent Democrat	10	7	8	9	10	11	12	11
Independent	5	9	8	8	11	13	14	13
Independent Republican	7	8	7	6	9	11	10	10
Weak Republican	14	14	13	13	14	13	14	14
Strong Republican	13	15	14	11	10	10	9	8.5
Apolitical, Don't know	4	3	4	2	1	2	1	2

SOURCE: University of Michigan Survey Research Center/CPS/NES. Survey Research Center hereafter is abbreviated SRC throughout.

TABLE 4.3
Trends in Political Partisanship and Independence
(as a percentage)

Partisanship	*1952*	*1976*	*1980*	*Shift 1952–80*
Strong party identification	35	24	26	− 9
Weak party identification	39	39	37	− 2
Independents—all	22	36	35	+13
—With party leaning	17	22	22	+ 5
—No party leaning	5	14	13	+ 8
Apolitical, don't know	4	1	2	− 2

SOURCE: University of Michigan CPS/NES, 1952, 1976, 1980.

now been commonly accepted (see table 4.3). This change, occurring since 1964, involves two developments: a decline in strong party commitment (about 9 percent) and an increase in Independents of two types—"partisan," who lean to a party, and "pure." The proportion who are weak in party identification has remained the same—about 37 percent to 39 percent. During this same period when asked if their partisan identification had ever changed, few admitted to this in the 1952 study—10 percent for Democrats, as compared to 24 percent for Republicans. In 1972 slightly more admitted such a change—15 percent among Democrats and 31 percent among Republicans.

More evidence of the decline is the disloyalty of identifiers when they vote. This disloyalty is now more readily admitted to by identifiers than previously (see table 4.4). In 1952 only 12 percent of *strong* Democrats said that they had supported the other party at some previous time, but by 1972, 25 percent of the sample said they had defected. The defections of *weak* Democrats were much greater—59 percent by

TABLE 4.4
Comparisons of Consistency in Partisan Voting Behavior

Voting Behavior	Democrats			Republicans		
	1952	1960	1972	1952	1960	1972
Percentage admitting defection in presidential vote sometime						
—Strong identification	12	21	25	27	27	29
—Weak identification	28	56	59	46	44	62
Percentage not voting for own party's presidential candidate in given year						
—Strong identification	16	9	27	2	2	3
—Weak identification	38	28	52	6	13	9
	1958	1966	1974	1958	1966	1974
Percentage not voting for own party's congressional candidate in given year						
—Strong identification	4	6	9	6	12	12
—Weak identification	12	23	22	22	22	32

SOURCE: University of Michigan CPS, American Election Studies.

1972. Except in 1960, the corresponding Republican proportions were higher—rising to 29 percent for strong Republicans in 1972 and a strikingly high 62 percent for weak Republicans. Thus, either it has become more fashionable to claim disloyalty or it is in fact the case or both developments may have occurred together. The net result is that whereas all party identifiers (25 percent) in 1952 admitted disloyalty, in 1972 it was 46 percent. The 1980 surveys reveal that 57 percent say that they have voted for different parties—a significant development.

The actual defections in voting *in particular elections* have not been as sizeable as the above percentages, which refer to disloyalty at some time in the past. Table 4.5 reveals that defections of strong Republicans have been fewer in presidential election years than for strong Democrats; this, however, is not always true in congressional election years. The most striking way to summarize the extent of the decline in loyalty is to use the standard table of the Center for Political Studies on defections by decades. The table presents these data for the president and Congress and adds the result of the recent presidential election.

The basic conclusion from table 4.5 is that the *voting loyalty* of all partisans has tended to decline since the 1950s. This is less apparent for strong Republicans although they also have been more disloyal in

TABLE 4.5

Defection Rates—Average Percentage of Party Identification Group not Voting for Party Candidates

Election Years	Democrats		Republicans	
	Strong	Weak	Strong	Weak
For president				
1950s	4.3	18.2	3.7	16.2
1960s	8.0	22.4	7.2	19.6
1976	9.0	25.0	3.0	22.0
1980	10.8	32.1	4.5	4.6
For Congress in presidential election years				
1950s	10.5	23.0	4.6	8.5
1960s	11.3	21.3	6.3	22.0
1972	11.0	24.0	13.0	20.0
1980	14.8	30.7	22.5	26.4
Off years				
1958–62–66	4.7	18.3	8.3	18.3
1970–74	10.5	24.5	8.0	24.5

SOURCES: University of Michigan SRC/CPS/NES; for congressional vote Bruce Keith et al., "The Myth of the Independent Voter" (a paper presented at the Annual Meeting of the American Political Science Association in Washington, D.C., 1977), p. 31.

their vote for congressional candidates than previously—in the 1950s less than 5 percent defected in the congressional vote, but in the 1970s it was up to 22 percent. The weak partisans, reaching over 25 percent in both parties by 1980, reveal the greatest disloyalty now.

Further evidence that partisanship is declining in overall terms is the phenomenon of split-ticket voting. In the past the classic partisan allegedly voted a straight ticket, from president down to county sheriff, and was proud of this loyalty. Presumably such an attitude simplified voting decisions for the citizen, yet it also reflected considerable confidence in both the party and the candidates the party had picked. To what extent has such loyalty decreased? Recent research reveals a rise in the proportion of congressional districts that were split—won by a presidential candidate of one party and a congressional candidate of another party. The proportion increased from 3.2 percent in 1920 to 44.4 percent in 1972, dropping to 28.5 percent in 1976.[8] While useful, such data do not reveal the extent to which *individuals* split their tickets when voting for the candidates for different parties *in the same election*. This varies from one election to the next. A majority (58 percent) of the Democrats in 1952, for example, split their ballots, many supporting Eisenhower for president. The same was true of more than 40 percent of the Republicans in 1964, and 60 percent of the Democrats in 1972. Overall, there has been a continuing tendency for partisans to split, and if anything this tendency has increased since the 1950s, although 1980 surveys revealed that less than 30 percent of strong and weak partisans split their ballots.[9]

Additional evidence of decline in partisan commitment appears in the voting turnout rates for the partisan identifier groups. Table 4.6 indicates that 1960 was a relatively high point in the last twenty-five years for most of these identifiers and Independents. Strong Republicans in 1952 had an even higher turnout—93 percent. After 1960, a decline set in. The strong Republicans and Democrats maintained their turnout levels rather well in presidential election years, although they dropped considerably in congressional election years. The weak partisans were more inclined to be absent from the polls in recent elections. And, again, the overall impression the data gives is that of irregularity and unreliability among partisans.

The combined information on party identification and voter turnout gives the overall picture of the American public in figure 4.1. It is a bit surprising, perhaps, that only 15 percent of the public consists of strong Democrats who vote, as compared to 8 percent who are strong Republicans who vote. A high proportion of the public consists of Independent voters (23 percent) and Independent nonvoters (13 percent). In aggregate terms, therefore, there is a rather low level of active, voting partisanship in the citizen population.

FIGURE 4.1

Distribution of the American Public by Party
Identification and Voting Turnout, 1980
(Presidential Election Participation)

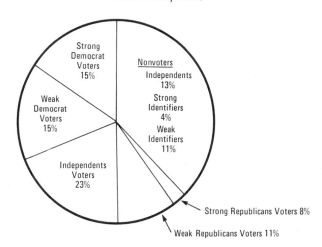

SOURCE: Based on University of Michigan CPS/NES, 1980.
NOTE: Surveys, it should be remembered, always report inflated levels of voting turnout.

TABLE 4.6

Turnout Rates of Partisans and Independents (as a percentage)

Affiliation	Presidential Elections							Congressional Elections	
	1952	1956	1960	1964	1972	1976	1980	1970	1974
Strong Democrat	75	79	85	82	80	79	84	61	58
Weak Democrat	69	68	79	73	71	65	65	49	41
Strong Republican	93	81	89	92	87	88	88	74	69
Weak Republican	77	79	88	85	79	60	77	62	52
Independents									
—Democrat	74	73	72	71	72	60	69	43	46
—Republican	78	74	87	84	76	67	75	54	46
—"Pure"	74	77	77	62	53	45	54	39	25

SOURCE: American National Election Study Series, 1952-1980 [machine readable data files], conducted by the Center for Political Studies, University of Michigan; Herbert Asher, *Presidential Elections and American Politics* (Homewood, Ill.: Dorsey, 1976), p. 80.

The tendency for people to call themselves Independents has prompted a great deal of research to discover their partisan leanings, and this has led to the threefold classification normally used:

TABLE 4.7

Independents' Affiliations
(as a percentage)

Affiliation	1952	1976	1980
Independent Democrats	10	12	11
Independent Republicans	7	9	10
Pure Independents	5	15	13

SOURCE: University of Michigan SRC/CPS/NES.

Researchers argue that some Independents are really "closet partisans" who, when pressed, will usually support the same party. "Leaners" (those who do tend to support a party) have a better voting record than pure Independents. In 1980, the national survey revealed the following turnout rates: for Independent Democrats 69 percent, for Independent Republicans 75 percent, for pure Independents 54 percent.

Thus, the tendencies for these citizens to withdraw from participation vary greatly, and this should be kept in mind when looking at the findings on independence in partisanship. The one-third of the American public labeled as Independents differ considerably in their behavior patterns.

Decline of Party Identification Among the Young

The erosion of party loyalty has become dramatically visible among younger people and new entrants into the electorate. Table 4.8 reveals the long-range shift in Independent affiliation for the twenty-one to twenty-five age group from 25 percent in 1952 to 53 percent in 1974, and 48 percent in 1980. The sharp increase in independent voting after 1964 is particularly noticeable—from 33 percent in 1964 to 53 percent in 1968. At the other extreme are the oldest citizens of whom only 14 percent to 15 percent were Independents from 1964 to 1968, and who increased only 3 percentage points in independence. However, that only the very young new citizens were changing their party loyalties must not be hastily concluded. The data strongly suggest that three phenomena were occurring: young citizens entering the electorate were much more independent; from 1952 on, those in all age cohorts were progressively becoming more independent; and those in the same age cohort were shifting from partisanship to independence.

The first of these trends has already been noted—the youngest were 25 percent Independent, and that was doubled by 1980. The second trend is easily observable in table 4.8—the 41 to 50 age group increased in independence by 11 percentage points between 1952 and 1974, the 51 to 65 age group increased by 13 points, and those 66 years old and over were more independent by 3 percentage points in 1974.

The third phenomenon is revealed from more careful analysis of the Michigan surveys: Of those in 1952 who were in the 18–24 age group, 26 percent considered themselves Independents; in 1974, when they were in the 40 to 46 age group, 39 percent considered themselves Independents. Of those in 1952 in the 25 to 34 age group, 28 percent were Independents, and in 1974 when they were in the 47 to 56 age group, 33 percent considered themselves Independents. This strongly

TABLE 4.8

Extent of Independence from Partisanship, by Age Groups
(as a percentage)

Age	1952	1956	1960	1964	1968	1972	1974	1980
21–25	25	37	39	33	53	51	53	48
26–30	32	31	26	29	41	50	42	41
31–40	23	26	27	26	29	40	39	37
41–50	26	21	25	24	31	30	37	31
51–65	19	24	21	18	24	26	32	29
66 and over	20	13	13	14	15	19	23	23

SOURCES: University of Michigan CPS; also found in Norman H. Nie, Sidney Verba, John Petrocik, *The Changing American Voter* (Cambridge: Harvard University Press, 1976), p. 60.
NOTE: For 1972–1980, age group is 18–25.

suggests that the public is reacting to conditions and events in the political system.

The basic point is that from the early 1970s the situation has been quite different than previously. Since 1968 up to 50 percent of eligible new voters have rejected partisanship, while the old partisans have been dying off. With strong partisans leaving the electorate and Independents entering it, the party-loyalty character of the system may be radically altered for some time to come. An added factor is the relative importance of the younger age groups in the electorate—those under thirty-five are close to 40 percent of the voting population today.

The possible long-range implications of the increased proportion of the younger age cohort should not be underestimated. Depending on the continuance of anti-partisan sentiments and their lack of interest in participating in politics (the voting turnout of the youngest age group has always been the lowest of all age groups), their influence could be considerable both in changing the support structure of the parties and in altering the strategy of the parties in mobilizing votes.

The contrast between those entering the electorate recently and those having entered over sixty years ago is dramatically presented in table 4.9.

TABLE 4.9
First Voter Partisanship, Before 1916, and
1968 or 1972
(as a percentage)

Strength of Partisanship	First Voted in 1968 or 1972	First Voted Before 1916
Strong	14	51
Weak	37	34
Independent leaning	30	11
Pure Independents	19	4
	100	100

SOURCE: Arthur Miller and Warren Miller, "Partisanship and Performance: Rational Choice in the 1976 Presidential Elections" (paper presented to the Annual Meeting of the American Political Science Association, Washington, D.C., September 1977.)

Clearly for first voters a decline in party affiliation has occurred.

There is one final, comparative point: Even though party identification has declined in the United States, a larger proportion of the American public is inclined to say it feels close to parties than in most other countries. Only in Britain do more voters indicate they have a strong attachment to parties.[10] Despite the decline in party identification, therefore, there is a relatively high level of psychological attachment to parties in the United States.

The Public's Affect Toward Parties

In national surveys for a long time researchers have asked people what they "like" and "dislike" about the Republican and Democratic parties. This is different from asking people if they "identify with" or "feel close to" a party. It differs also from probing about their general views concerning the party system. Researchers want to know whether people can express themselves about parties and what types of positive or negative feelings they have. In the early study of voters, these answers were used to determine to what extent there was an "issue content" to voting.[11] Such data on the evaluations of parties indicate that a decline set in probably after the 1960 election for the public generally (see table 4.10). Thus, about 70 percent of the public talked positively (that is, discussed things they liked) about at least one of the major parties. This number declined to 49 percent by 1972, and in 1980 was 50 percent. For new voters there was less positivism already in 1960, and their expressed liking for the parties has declined to about 40 percent.

Further analysis however, of the responses of the people in these studies to the "like-dislike" question, shows two major trends: (1) a decline in the percentage of people who see the parties in confrontationist terms (that is, who feel positive about one party, and negative about another); and (2) the increase in the percentage of people who feel neutral (that is, who have no likes or dislikes to discuss) about both parties. Thus, accompanying the decline in positive feelings an

TABLE 4.10
The Level of Public Affection for the Party
(as a percentage)

Extent of Positive Evaluations of Parties	1952	1960	1964	1968	1972	1976	1980
Public who said it liked one or both parties	74	74	64	59	49	49	50
New voters who said they liked one or both parties	70	65	57	44	35	39	42
Public feeling positive about one party and negative about the other	50	41	38	38	30	31	27
Public feeling neutral about both parties	13	17	20	17	30	31	37

SOURCES: Norman H. Nie, Sidney Verba, John R. Petrocik, *The Changing American Voter* (Cambridge: Harvard University Press, 1976), pp. 58, 69; Martin P. Wattenberg, "The Decline of Political Partisanship in America: Negativity or Neutrality?" *American Political Science Review*, December 1981, based on University of Michigan SRC/CPS, 1952–80.

FIGURE 4.2

Trends in Party as a Reference for Citizens' Political Orientations

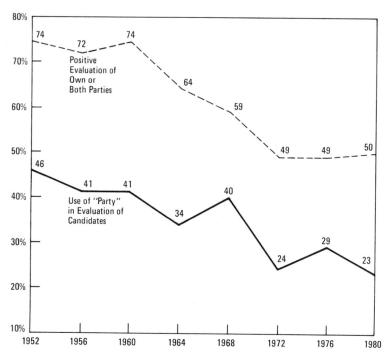

SOURCES: University of Michigan SRC/CPS; Norman H. Nie, Sidney Verba, John P. Petrocik, *The Changing American Voter* (Cambridge: Harvard University Press, 1976), pp. 56, 58, 167; Martin P. Wattenberg, "The Decline of Political Partisanship in America: Negativity or Neutrality?" *American Political Science Review*, (December 1981).

increase in neutrality and indifference has developed, which seems to be at the heart of the trends in public attitudes toward the parties. This phenomenon is particularly noticeable among weak partisans and leaners. By the late 1970s at least one-third of the national public was neutral, about 5 percent was negative about both parties, and less than 50 percent was positive in some way about either party.

This tendency in peoples' feelings toward the major parties also emerges in other research. Over the years the question has been asked "Which of the parties does the best job in solving the problems you consider most important?" In answer to this, the percentage mentioning a party has declined from 62 percent in 1960 to 46 percent in 1976 and 50 percent in 1980. As Merle Black and George Rabinowitz say as a result of their earlier analysis: "The clearest trend . . . is the general rise of the neutrals—individuals who saw neither party as doing what they wanted."[12] It is not that people do not see important differences between the parties—in fact, the percentage who did increased to 58 percent in 1980, as compared to 50 percent previously. Rather, a large proportion of the public feels more than ever that parties are less relevant to their problems. This decline in "problem relevance" combined with indifference and ambivalence seems to be basic to the problem. Why this is, what forces contribute to this development, and what the parties do as organizations help to explain this development and will be analyzed in detail later.

The Public's Participation in Parties

A major test of any system is the *objective* evidence of the public's involvement and participation in that system. A logical surmise would be that if the American public was disenchanted with its system people would withdraw from involvement in it. There are, of course, two basic types of involvement—behavioral and psychological. Psychological commitment has already been discussed. From a look at behavioral evidence, it is difficult to conclude that things are worse today than previously. Table 4.11 presents trend data to suggest that there is no big decline in behavioral participation; the late 1960s and early 1970s do not suggest that a decline took place. Indeed the mean number of campaign acts among citizens has increased since 1952. In some of these measures of participation there has been some decline since 1960, but the picture is by no means one-directional. The 1970s do not generally demonstrate that the activist public has deserted the parties. Warren Miller and Teresa Levitin conclude that "the vast bulk of the electorate worked for their favorite candidates" and engaged in campaign activity "at about the same rate in 1976 as in 1972."[13] And Jack Dennis concludes from his data (on public willingness to give money to parties that has increased in recent years) that these data present "an interesting anomaly . . . could it be that, while the general public displays ever lower support for the parties in most respects, there is nevertheless more willingness to fund the parties than ever before?[14]

TABLE 4.11

Indications of Behavioral Involvement with American Parties by the Public

Public Involvement	1952	1956	1960	1964	1968	1972	1980
A. Percentage who belong to a political club or organization	2.4	2.8	3.2	4.0	3.3	2.8	3.0
B. Percentage who worked for a party or candidate	3	3	6	5	6	5	4

SOURCES: For A: Norman Nie, Sidney Verba, John R. Petrocik, *The Changing American Voter* (Cambridge: Harvard University Press, 1976), p. 271; for B: University of Michigan Survey SRC/CPS/NES.

Comparatively, Americans are more active in politics and in party politics than people in most other countries. A recent study revealed the differences in the degree of conventional political participation for the United States and Europe (see table 4.12). This shows that the American public is, on most measures, more involved in political activity than people in other countries; it is exceeded only by the Germans in their attendance at political meetings. Also much more contacting of governmental officials is done by Americans than is done in Europe—27 percent here compared to 11 percent in Britain and Germany. Finally the analysis of this comparative study points out that in the samples only 12 percent of the Americans were totally inactive, as contrasted to 18 percent in the Netherlands, 27 percent in Germany, 30 percent in Britain, and 35 percent in Austria.[15]

It is very difficult to argue that the American public is less in contact with the parties today than previously. That is, if people are asked whether they have been approached by party or campaign workers, their answers indicate an upward trend over the years. Michael Wolfe's careful analysis of the Center for Political Studies data since 1952 reveals an increase from 13 percent in 1952 to 30 percent in 1976.[16] In 1980 the percentage was 24 percent, slightly favoring the Republicans.

These findings, of course, raise some paradoxes: Why has voting turnout declined if party effort has increased? And what impact does exposure to parties have on people's attitudes? The important fact to keep in mind here is that the American public is being contacted by

TABLE 4.12

Frequency of Conventional Political Participation by the Public
1973–74 (as a percentage)

Participation	United States	Britain	Germany	Austria	Netherlands
Discuss politics					
often	27	16	13	13	17
sometimes	37	30	30	32	35
Total	64	46	43	45	52
Attend political meetings					
often	3	2	5	5	1
sometimes	15	7	17	13	5
Total	18	9	22	18	6
Campaign for a candidate					
often	2	1	2	2	1
sometimes	12	3	6	3	2
Total	14	4	8	5	3

SOURCE: Adapted from Samuel Evans and Kai Hilderbrandt, "Technical Appendix," in Samuel H. Barnes and Max Kaase, eds., *Political Action: Mass Participation in Five Western Democracies,* (Beverly Hills: Sage, 1979), pp. 541–42. © 1979 Sage Publications, Inc., with permission of the publisher and authors.

the parties to a much greater extent than previously. Or stated differently, as far as citizens are concerned, there is more exposure to, and less distance from, the parties now than twenty-five years ago.

Final Observations About the Public and the Parties

The ambivalence of Americans about their parties and party system is clear from the research that has been done. And this is reflected in the controversies among scholars about the meaning of their findings. A gloomy perspective can be taken on the erosion of party loyalty, particularly among young voters and those just having entered the electorate in recent years. Added to this can be the inclination of many voters to see parties as less relevant for the solution of problems, as well as the increasing neutral evaluations of the parties. On the other hand, close to 70 percent of the public still *does* identify with the two major parties; political interest is as high now as it was twenty or thirty years ago; negative evaluations of parties have not really increased; a large proportion of the public still wishes to be in contact with parties; and an undiminished effective minority still is active in party affairs.

Further, comparatively, the levels of the public's identification with, and participation in, parties are high. Except for voter turnout, in these respects Americans rank quite high in level of involvement in comparison to the citizens of other countries.

Generalizations of pessimism about politics in the United States, based on exaggerations of the results of research should be avoided. In fact, the important research findings are these: Only a *minority* of the American public *does not* identify with parties; only a *minority* of Americans feels overtly *negative* about both parties; and only a *minority* says that *no party* can solve America's problems. Despite the decline, then, there is a solid, enduring bedrock of support for parties. This is not to say that the signs of decline in party support are not serious. Indeed they are, and they pose special problems for American parties if the parties are to regain their losses of support and more confidence from the American people.

Part II

PARTY

ORGANIZATION

Chapter 5

The Special Nature of
American Party Organizations

THERE IS much controversy today over what is happening to the structure of American political parties. One writer claims that since 1972 there has been "a trend toward party decomposition" which "has affected both state and national parties, their organizations and their rank and file," due primarily to the unintended effects of efforts at party reform.[1] Another scholar wrote in 1973, "Parties as organizations, have become, if anything, weaker rather than stronger . . . . Parties are more important as labels than as organizations."[2] Others have echoed these evaluations, although there has yet to appear a systematic survey of party organizations in the United States at the local, district, and state levels which would provide evidence for such a statement. It is a speculative hunch, a partial insight—but one shared by a large number of people.

Party organizations should not be prematurely buried. The United States still has one hundred state party organizations (consisting of chairpersons, central committees, conventions, and legislative party caucuses), uncounted district committees (some very alive and active), and an extensive and complicated network of city, ward, precinct, and rural party organizations (not recently enumerated or systematically surveyed). Their effectiveness is a subject for study; their existence cannot be denied.

Party Organization in Modern Democracies

To have a solid perspective for evaluating the state of party organization today it is important to understand the role of party structures in the development of our political system. Indeed, there is a strong basis for arguing that political parties as organizations have become indispensable. According to Huntington, "parties in the sense of organizations are a product of modern politics. Political parties exist in the modern polity because only modern political systems require institutions to organize mass participation in politics."[3] Historically this role worked in two ways. On the one hand leaders needed to mobilize support from nonleaders to maintain their elite position, whether to win elections or to secure a "following" in order to communicate their beliefs about the goals and policies of the system. But the public also needed a party organization to control elites—to become knowledgeable about politics, to concert together to win elections, to express demands to the elites, to make opposition to elite control possible.

Party organizations, therefore, can be seen as structures which come into existence to perform particular functions for both the elites and the mass of citizens. Further, as Huntington and others have pointed out, as modern democracies become more "modern," the performances of these functions becomes more difficult. The body politic, or voting public, becomes much larger. It is spread over a larger geographical area and is more heterogeneous in interests and backgrounds. The electorate also becomes more educated and sophisticated about politics. The tasks of *education, representation, communication, support mobilization*—of sharing the political process with an involved public—are more complex. Thus party organizations must become more complex, as well as more adaptable, structures if they are to function effectively. Beginning as very primitive, embryonic structures, skeletal combinations of political leadership and some followers, party organizations eventually became large-scale organizations with specialized units and subgroups and divisions dealing with particular organizational needs. This is the historical evolutionary ideal of the party as it is transformed from an elementary to a professional organization. Whether in fact this image actually occurs varies greatly from one context to another.

Historical Transformations in American Party Organization

A study of the changing character of American party organizations from the end of the eighteenth century to the present shows certain basic changes. Of course, the size of the electorate increased dramatically in the first forty years so that by the time of Andrew Jackson's elections of 1828 and 1832 the job of voter communication was much greater. The parties (Democrats and Whigs) had to expand their organizations considerably and develop local party units which placed a great deal of emphasis on direct voter contact. In the thirty years before the Civil War the right to vote was given to many more people, the number of elective offices increased (the "long ballot" was adopted), rotation in office was defended, more and more people became interested in party politics.

The twin developments of egalitarianism and populism decentralized the party organizations. In the earlier period the power of the party was in the hands of the legislators at both the national and state levels. The legislative leaders developed the organization, nominated candidates for offices, were the focus for the discussion of policy, and took the initiative to develop and communicate with the local units. After 1800 mass meetings and local caucuses appeared consisting of other than just the legislative party leaders (sometimes called mixed caucuses). The caucus (often a clandestine cabal of an unrepresentative group of party leaders) came under attack. In particular the legislative caucus was attacked by Andrew Jackson who called it "King Caucus" and blamed it for improperly denying him the presidential nomination in 1824.

By the 1830s the decentralization of organization had proceeded to the point where an organizational form, the delegate convention, came into existence. It emphasized the election of delegates from local party units to a representative assembly, the convention, which might or might not include the legislative leaders of the party. At the national level the first such conventions were held in 1831 and 1832, and by 1844 they were well established.

Thus, between 1832 and 1860, there occurred a basic change in two senses in party organization: (1) the power to direct and control the organization was taken from the leaders at the national level and given more and more to leaders with local status; (2) the power of the party organization was taken from the party's legislative leaders and given to those leaders who were largely individuals with no status in either the Congress or the state legislatures. This populist or decentralizing orientation continued in the post-Civil War period and was pushed to its next logical step with the adoption of the direct primary starting in 1900. The primary, in a sense, takes the power of the party (particularly to nominate candidates) out of the hands of the delegate convention (which in the nineteenth century had been criticized as undemocratic and corrupt) and theoretically places that power in the hands of the loyal party supporters. Since 1900 we have moved steadily in the direction of expanding the opportunities for direct popular decision making in party affairs with less emphasis on making decisions through representative party institutions. There are those who today would argue that the expansion of the presidential primary to over thirty states has transformed the national presidential convention into an ineffectual body for party organizational decision making. Figure 5.1 presents a diagram of these organizational changes in the party system.

The contrast between the United States and the British and Continental European party systems in these developments is striking. In the United States legislative and national party leaders gradually have been forced to share control of the party organization with state and local organizations over whom they really have no authority. In England, the members of the party in the House of Commons and national leaders of the party have retained considerable control over party or organizational decisions. The parliamentary party caucus (of Labour or Conservative or Liberal members of Commons) elects the leader of the party, who becomes prime minister when the party wins an election. This leader, then, working with a National Executive Committee, has a great deal of influence over the party apparatus. True, these national

FIGURE 5.1.

Transformations of Party Organizational Control Patterns Since 1790

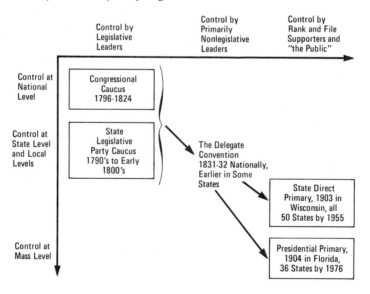

leaders must consult closely with the local constituency organizations (and in the case of the Labour party with the trade union leaders), and they certainly cannot dictate at will to the local units of the party. But there is a strong party structure at the national level, linked closely to the *policy-making leadership* of the party in the legislature.

This is the striking contrast with the development in America since 1800 of an organization primarily focused on the local, nonlegislative units of the party. The British party organizations are focused on the national legislative leaders of the party who share power with the local units. In many Continental party structures organizational patterns emphasize local control as in the United States or have the same contrast with the American system as in Britain. Parties differ radically from Left to Right and from country to country. Central control may be found in some mass membership parties, but not in others. Unions may have a major control in certain Social Democratic parties and not in others. Each party in each system apparently adopts its own organizational style linked to its own ideology, goals, and rank and file support structure.[4]

Major Features of American Party Organization

Each country has a pattern of party organization which embraces particular characteristics and, incidentally, points up the values and preferences of the political participants of those societies. What features stand out in the United States? The first, very elementary characteristic is that in the United States there is a very large number of party organizations, at least on paper; perhaps 200,000 or more precinct, ward, and township units alone, to say nothing of all the units from the local to the national. These groups are organized by geographical or electoral area (by precinct, ward, township, assembly district, congressional district, state)—that is, in units where voters elect persons to public office. Parties in the United States do not organize usually, or primarily, by factory or workplace "cell" as parties of the Left do in Europe, nor by militia units as the fascists used to do, nor by functional interest groups (although business groups and unions may have political organizational arms). In the United States the primary emphasis is to link organization to election-relevant areas, although parties may in fact engage in activities which are not immediately focused on getting out the vote in a particular area.

A second characteristic of American party organization, quite contrary to the practice in foreign countries, is that much of it is regulated by law, by both national and state law but particularly by state law.

Each of the states has accumulated a large volume of state legislation that specifies in detail what the state and local organizations are permitted to do:

How the delegates to the parties' county, district, and state conventions shall be elected

When these conventions shall meet, what their agenda and order of business shall be

How party officers, such as county and district chairmen, shall be selected

What types of committees can and shall be set up at each level (for example, the county executive committee)

How delegates shall be apportioned to wards, counties, and districts in the selection of representatives to party conventions and committees

How those wishing to run as party candidates for organization posts can qualify for placement of their names on the ballot—by posting a filing fee or by submitting petitions with a specified number of signatures

How candidates shall be nominated for public office at the state convention (for example, for lieutenant governor and positions on educational boards of regents or trustees)

How the parties shall select delegates to the national convention once in four years

The amount of money parties and candidates may spend in political campaigns, how candidates can qualify for public funds, how the amount received and expanded shall be reported (before the election, as well as after it) and the penalties for noncompliance

How direct primaries, in which party candidates for public office are nominated, shall be conducted, including who may participate in such party elections

These and a host of other specific regulations, which vary from state to state, force those active in party organizational work to be alert to the constraints of the law. The United States since the latter part of the nineteenth century has sought to regulate how parties organize and do their work. At the national level, in the Pendleton Act of 1883, for example, parties were told they could not solicit money from civil servants on federal government property. In 1907 parties were told that direct contributions from corporations to parties or candidates running for election would not be allowed (in 1947 the same prohibition was applied to labor unions). A variety of other regulations of party finance have been adopted over the years, and today a Federal Election Campaign Act specifies in great detail how candidates for the presidency, Senate, and Congress shall finance their campaigns and report individuals who contribute to their campaigns, and how these funds are spent. All this is supervised and administered by a Federal Election Commission in Washington.

Thus, in legislating how parties shall organize at the local and state levels, select their candidates for office, and finance their campaigns, the United States has treated parties as public groups to be regulated and controlled by legislators, rather than considering internal organizational matters to be private business which each party should decide for itself.

By sharp contrast European systems have a minimum of public regulation of parties. The European attitude is that parties should organize as they see fit and select their candidates for parliaments or local councils by whatever internal process the party prefers—and the public will judge the party at election time. The American attitude is one of distrust of party organization and its leaders; this distrust leads to careful specification of organizational form and process. If the assumptions are that such legal regulation in the United States makes party organizations more democratic, more competent, less corrupt, less elitist, and that the product of such organizational deliberations and processes is superior to the European system, it is highly doubtful that there is evidence to support such positions. European parties without all this regulation are no less democratic or competent or trustworthy than are American parties.

Party structures in the United States function in terms of electoral units and are highly regulated by law. A third general characteristic is that control over, within, or through this organization is limited because power in it is diffused. A description of the American system as centrifugal is a much broader characterization of the party system, meaning variations in state and local party systems (see chapter 3). But, in addition, in our system, it is difficult to achieve integrated control over the party structure, either from below, by the rank and file, or from the top. This means that the system is nonhierarchical. Except in certain big city machines (and there are fewer of them now than previously) there is no central leadership which commands the party organization, is seen as the leadership of the party organization, and is responsible for what the party does. There are many autonomous centers of organizational power—in Congress, state organizations, city machines, county and district units, which go their own way in selecting candidates, running campaigns, and performing other duties irrespective of, or in defiance of, upper level party leadership.

Why is there such a diffuse control system in American parties? The historical development of the system in the United States suggests that over time an organizational norm has gradually been accepted for parties which considered local control paramount (decentralization) and which separated the governmental and nongovernmental wings of the party (separatism). Both the doctrines of federalism and of separation of legislative, executive, and judicial powers strongly contributed to this pattern. Local units and machines developed autonomously and became very jealous of their bailiwicks and prerogatives. ("The Tiger shall not cross the bridge" was the rallying cry of the Brooklyn organization fearful of a Tammany takeover.) Concomitantly, no national or state organization appeared, in the legislature or out, which could direct, control, or pull those autonomous units together into a hierarchy. Thus, this diffuse organization became institutionalized over time, supported by American public attitudes which have never been favorably disposed to discipline from above or to a central control. Among the many consequences of this are parties undisciplined in a formal organizational sense and parties unable to agree on leadership and policies.

This leads to a fourth characteristic: the difficulty in the United States for public, or rank-and file, control of party organization because lines of accountability are often obscure, and indirect, *and* the leadership to be held accountable is often dispersed. Neither the Republican nor the Democratic party has one group as the primary locus of party authority and, therefore, *the* responsible leadership group, whether in the House, the Senate, the party national headquarters, the national committee, or the national executive committee. Similarly, at each state capitol party leadership is dispersed into a variety of locations making it difficult to identify that key leadership group which makes policy, holds power, and is responsible. The same is true at the county level, although there is actually more likelihood of finding a central party leadership group at the city, county, district, and township levels than at the higher governmental levels.

If to this is added the broken lines of control between the public, or the rank and file, and the higher level units and leadership of the party which presumably they should be able to hold accountable, the difficulty in control from the base of the system can be seen. The election system is often not controllable in this way. Many states and localities have a stepladder system, in which, for example, precinct and township representatives are elected to county conventions; these conventions in turn elect delegates to state conventions, which in turn elect delegates to the national convention. Although the time-lag problem in such a system has been reformed by both parties of late (to the best of their ability, that is), a time lag often remains, particularly in the disjunction of the issues confronting the party at the time of the first step in the election process and the third or fourth steps. In addition, the fact that certain party leaders are never, or only remotely, the product of an electoral process in which the rank-and-file party supporter participates only increases the fractured nature of the system. Leaders who are never really subjected to a rank-and-file mandate are the national chairman, the national executive committee, the national committee itself (in only a few states are these leaders directly selected), the state chairman, and the state executive committee and officers (directly elected in only a few states).

Thus, some party organization leaders are not linked to the base of the structure in any meaningful sense, some leaders (state convention delegates, county chairmen, and often county committees) only indirectly, and often tenuously, and some leaders linked directly depending on the "rules of the game" in each state and city. Leaders with a direct electoral link to the party base, if there are any at all, are local leaders from the district and county on down. This suggests, again, the localistic and diffuse character of the American party organizational system. Whether this means the system is not democratic is a complex question, requiring detailed analysis in each case. In appearance at least there is an indirect representative system with very tenuous rank-and-file control over top party officers.

The fifth characteristic of American party structures is that they are *stratarchies*.[5] This is apparent from a look at how the parties are organized from the national to the local level. V. O. Key long ago recognized this, saying, "Although the party organization can be regarded as a hierarchy . . . it may be more accurately described as a system of layers of organization."[6] By a *stratarchy* is meant an organization with layers, or strata, of control rather than one of centralized leadership from the top down. At each stratum, or echelon, of the organization there are specialized organs to perform functions at that level. Each stratum of organization is relatively autonomous in its own sphere, although it does maintain links above and below. There is, thus, the proliferation of power and decision making and a recognition that lower levels are not subordinate to the commands or sanctions of higher strata. The party develops this pattern of relationships—stratarchical rather than hierarchical—because of the necessities of collaborating with and recognizing local echelons for votes, money, personnel. Further, the party must cope with widely varying local conditions. A special component of stratarchy is reciprocal deference. Between layers there is a tolerance of autonomy, of each layer's status and its right to initiative, as well as a tolerance of inertia. This deference stems from the absence of effective sanctions and the fact that the echelons need each other in the drive for votes and its other functions. Mutual need, mutual support, mutual respect, and much interechelon accommodation are the marks of the American party stratarchy.

A close study of party organization at the summit, in Washington, at the state level, and at the district, county, ward, town, and precinct levels makes this stratarchical system apparent, but it may be that in the parties of any democratic system there is always a tendency toward stratarchy because parties must be responsive to social demands and problems while realistically seeking power. When parties are seeking to be adaptive and power-maximizing, the tendency toward stratarchy is present, although varying considerably in degree.

National Parties as Umbrella Structures

A major question which emerges from this description of the American party organization in overall terms is: What holds such a disparate, diffuse, decentralized party organization together? Why don't the Democratic and Republican organizations throughout the country disintegrate since there is no central leadership organ and no hierarchical pattern of relationships? This will be discussed in greater detail later. But here it should be recognized that perhaps *the* Republican and *the* Democratic nationwide organizations really consist of a set of party organs at all levels only loosely held together by a common party name, common symbols of organization, a common history, a sense of identity or loyalty, and, to a certain extent, similar beliefs and philosophies. The Republicans in Racine, Wisconsin, the Republicans in Los Angeles County, California, in Springfield, Illinois, and in Portland, Maine, are not subordinate in any real organizational sense to a Republican party hierarchy. But they recognize most of the same leaders as Republicans, and they think of themselves as Republicans in terms of basic policy orientations, historical traditions, and sense of loyalty. And once in four years they or their representatives get together in a national convention with other Republicans from throughout the country to nominate *their* candidate for president. The Republican organization, therefore (and the same can be said for the Democrats), is a loose-knit set of semiautonomous units at all levels, which may be very efficient or very lax, very liberal or very conservative, very competitive or very subdued—but they are part of an umbrella organization called the Republican party.

There is no power elite directing the Republican and the Democratic parties. Nor is there an ideological straitjacket into which the party units, national and state and local, are forced. There is great diversity in the units in the Republican and Democratic party organizations in terms of their goals, interests, incentives, techniques, ideologies and efficiency, but there is a cement holding them together. They *are* viable structures, however diverse, diffuse, decentralized, and centrifugal they may be. Perhaps this is the reason for their survival. For 120 years the Republican and Democratic organizations have survived. Their longevity is truly remarkable and can only be understood through an analysis of the structure of these diffuse "umbrella organizations" and how they have adapted to the changing American social and political environment.

Chapter 6

National Party Structures: Pluralism, Factionalism, and Co-archy

EVER SINCE the parties in Congress called their first caucuses before 1800 the national organization of the major parties in the United States has vexed us. National conventions appeared in the 1830s to coordinate party activities. The first national committee was set up in 1844 by the Democrats. A Democratic congressional campaign committee appeared in 1842, and the Republicans followed in 1862, in the early part of Lincoln's administration. In 1916, when the direct election of United States senators was adopted, both parties set up campaign committees in the second house of Congress (the Senate). In the latter part of the nineteenth century both parties developed other units for party leadership in both houses. Gradually, therefore, a variety of party organs developed in Washington, whose lack of collaboration has troubled the parties since their inception. A recent example illustrates well the paradoxical conditions of American national party organization.

In the spring of 1981 the Democratic National Committee was wrestling with a question of policy. Sixty-three House Democrats had defected to Reagan to support his budget-cutting proposals. The key House vote was 176 to 253 for Reagan. Mayor Richard Hatcher of Gary, Indiana, who sat on the Democratic National Committee asked, "What is the party's position on those Democrats who voted for the Reagan budget? What are we going to do, forgive and forget?" The committee took no action, prompting one committee member to reflect, "We lacked discipline, we lacked leadership in the House." And Chairman Charles Manatt sidestepped questions as to whether Democrats should be held accountable by the national committee for their votes in the House. As one staff member put it, "I don't believe the Democratic party has taken an official position."[1]

Charles Merriam in 1922 observed that "the relation of the National Committee to the other party committees is not very sharply defined," and "the Committee must make its own way as best it can."[2] The attacks on the national committee and the other components of the national organization often have been more pointed and devastating. Hugh Bone quoted columnist William S. White in 1961 as demanding that the party leaders tell "the national political committees to get out and stay out of foreign policy." "National committees," White claimed, "are strictly political megaphones and bear no iota of responsibility for public policy. . . ."[3] Despite such criticism, the national party organs are functionally important, have important roles, and could potentially have considerably more influence. Before being degraded as relatively useless these national party structures and their place in the system should be examined closely.

A first image of the nature of the national structure is this—it is a segmented and pluralized set of organs. There are five basic elements to this structure for the party out of power, and six (with the addition of the "presidential component") for the party in power (see fig. 6.1). Note that in figure 6.1 there are no lines suggesting the relationships and linkages of these units to each other. This is because it is very difficult to sketch in lines with any confidence that they represent the actual nature of relationships. To draw a line suggesting that the national chairman and his staff are subordinate to the president (a line between 1 and 2) or that the national committee is subordinate to both the president and the national chairman (lines between 1 and 5, as well as between 2 and 5) would indicate questionable relationships in fact; certainly they would not hold consistently over time. It would be much simpler if this organization were pyramidal in structure with the national chairman (or president) or the congressional party at the top directing subordinate substructures and committees. Such a hierarchy would have clear lines of control. The relationships suggested in figure 6.2 illustrate the possibilities.

But reality does not present anything approaching a hierarchy. Rather it can be called a co-archy: "a structure of equal power relationships."[4] It is a set of self-contained organizational subsystems, which are not subordinate to each other but separate power centers. That does not mean that they do not work together nor that the individual leaders in each subsystem do not informally associate together. Nor does it mean that they do not recognize each other's status and role in

FIGURE 6.1
Components of a National Party

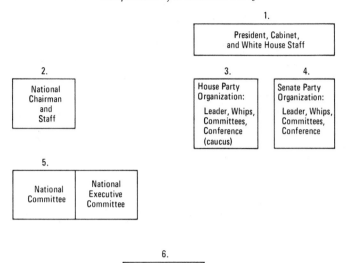

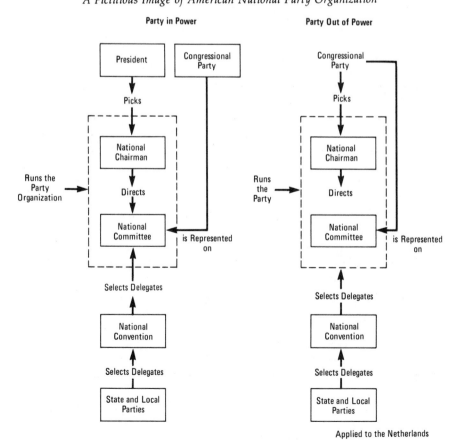

FIGURE 6.2
A Fictitious Image of American National Party Organization

the overall system. Each of these units has a separate organizational life and separate base for its organizational power, performing different organizational functions. The chairman and his staff constitute the management component; the national committee provides the organizational policy making and planning component; the congressional party structures presumably are the policy leadership component; the national convention is the plenary body of the party symbolizing the representative component; and the president and his staff exemplify (ideally) both the official executive decision making and patronage allocation components.

Thus, all the important elements of a successful party are found in these components. The parties have developed specialized organs focusing on particular functions. But these functions are not securely linked to each other in a coherent organizational system. Rather the coordination of functions, if they occur at all, is the product of informal personal contacts and communication.

This then is a co-archy, a multiple-unit power-sharing system, a set of leadership units virtually isolated from each other in a formal sense, minimally collaborative, and jealously guarding their prerogatives. There is no unity of command, of control, of responsibility. This can be illustrated in many different ways. The rules of the Democratic party specify that the congressional campaign committee "has no organic connection with either the Democratic National Convention or the Democratic National Committee."[5] Attempts by one unit to control or coordinate other units usually fail. For example, in 1952 the Taft-dominated National Republican Committee attempted to determine the presidential candidacy decision at the national convention by dictating committee appointments, the chairmanship of the convention, and procedures, but it was defeated by a convention which nominated Dwight D. Eisenhower. When President Franklin D. Roosevelt sought in 1938 to prevent the renomination of prominent anti-New Deal Democrats in the Senate, he lost out in each case. Another illustration of the futility of attempts by one organ over another is the national committee's attempt to take over the policy leadership function from the congressional party in 1956. At the time Paul Butler, chairman of the National Democratic Committee, created the National Democratic Advisory Council which included prominent state and local party leaders and provided place for the top leadership in Congress (Speaker Sam Rayburn and Senate Majority Leader Lyndon Johnson). Rayburn and Johnson refused to join, and the council never was accepted as a policy leadership organ by the Democratic congressional party.

Attempts at centralization of control of the national party have failed. The convention cannot control the congressional party leadership, and vice versa. The national committee cannot preempt the functions of other organs without being rejected and rebuked. The president can sometimes through a loyal national chairman, if he so chooses, influence the management of the party in a general sense, as Franklin Roosevelt did through Jim Farley. But a president is generally hard put to control his congressional party or his national committee. In 1978, for example, President Jimmy Carter appeared before his committee to seek unqualified endorsement for the Panama Canal treaties. Instead, it adopted a watered down resolution which was just too weak to help him much in his drive for Senate votes.

There is, then, no single policy and executive organ, no corporate body of party authority and responsibility at the national level. Rather, it is a system which is many-headed, very pluralized, uncoordinated, with much autonomy. In effect this is a leadership bargaining system. This is the first key image of the American national party structures.

A second way of thinking about the national structures is as collectivities of diverse social, economic, and political interests, all requiring some recognition and mollification. This diversity makes unified policy action by the organization difficult. Scholars have long been aware of this conception of the party. V. O. Key spoke of the "social matrix within which the organization exists—the "groups, classes, and sorts of people that attach themselves to each of the major parties. . . ."[6] The word *collectivities* means aggregations of individuals with different interests. It is possible also to use the word *coalitions* to suggest that a party structure consists of a set of "interest subgroups" (ethnic, racial, ideological, geographical) which provide support for the party and also make demands on it. These subgroups seeking an organization which reflects their interests work through and with the party to achieve their goals. There is a continuing crisis for the party organization as it seeks a compromise on policy acceptable to all or most of these groups. Whether there are in fact purposeful coalitions, or only collectivities of interests, it is clear that the organizational units can be thought of in these terms. Indeed, thinking of them in these terms may explain a great deal about their functioning.

A careful analysis of the national party organs shows that one of their major concerns is the accurate and adequate representation of interest groups. The national convention is a large conclave of local, state, and national party leaders which has grown from a relatively manageable size of 1,000 delegate votes in 1940 to over 2,000 in the 1970s. The 1980 convention delegate votes were: Democrats 3,317 and Republicans 1,994. Although the character and extent of the representativeness have been criticized greatly over the years, special rules have been adopted to make it a representative body. The aim has been to permit more party activists to be involved in the convention and in recent years expressly to give women, minorities, and younger persons a greater participatory role in the party. The emphasis is on representation, diversity of backgrounds and attitudes, interaction in a national party institutional context—to develop a consensus and a coalition, if even in minimal terms, on national party problems.

The national committees also are loose coalitions of diverse interests. The committee is more than a group of representatives from state organizations (the Democrats also include representatives from other components of the party—governors, mayors, congressmen, young Democrats, and so forth). In a broader, more meaningful sense the committees include individuals who come from a variety of social interests. Each national committee seeks to include blacks, women, persons from labor, business, and farm organizations, as well as representatives from different ethnic, socioeconomic, and age groups. Viewed in this light the national committee is a structure with lines out not only to all geographical sections of the country but perhaps more importantly to all key social and economic groups. Presumably these interconnections perform two functions: the representation of many different, often conflicting, points of view and the maintenance of political support, particularly voting support, from these sectors through their leader on the committee. This socioeconomic linkage is crucial for understanding the actual performance of these units, as well as their potential for playing a more effective role in the future.

The congressional and senatorial party organs also reflect a diversity of interests (all geographical zones have to be represented, for example), and the expectation is that they represent the important elements. As a result both the Republican and Democratic policy committees (they vary in size from fifteen to seventeen members) consist of party leaders with different viewpoints. After long years of service these legislative leaders will not surrender their right to oppose policy proposals. They are a collection of different interests which makes effective decision making difficult. The policy committee really doesn't make policy. As Charles O. Jones noted for the Republicans in the House, "If there is considerable division among Republicans on a particular bill, the Committee will not issue a position notice. As one member noted: 'We can't have minority reports from the Policy Committee.'"[7] As for the caucus, or conference, the same observation holds. As Donald Matthews noted about the Senate, "Any effort to obtain a binding commitment [in the Democratic caucus] from members is bound to fail." And for both parties he concludes, "the actual pattern of . . . leadership depends in large measure upon the personalities, prestige and skills of the men who hold the positions of leadership." Senate party leaders "have no major sanctions to employ against party dissidents."[8]

Closely following from this is a third view of the national party—it is a conflict-containing system while attempting to be a conflict-resolving organization. This is particularly true for policy matters of any real consequence. One of the greatest conflict-resolving acts of the party has been the presidential nomination decision. Oftentimes this has been barely accomplished (as for example, John F. Kennedy over Lyndon Johnson in 1960 and Gerald Ford over Ronald Reagan in 1976). However this critical act, it is argued, is now being taken away from the national convention by the extension of the presidential primaries. There are other conflict-resolving actions of the party, of course, such as the selection of the speaker, the party floor leader, and where the national convention will be held. Although of importance, however, these are organizational decisions, and not policy decisions. On the latter the congressional parties are often split by section, by ideology, by socioeconomic interests, and they respect the opinions of major, relevant interest subgroups. They respect them and have great difficulty compromising them. The emphasis is on avoiding confrontation. Conflict resolution has to occur at some points in the system— whether in Congress, the bureaucracy, the presidency, or the courts. The national party structures perform such a resolution painfully, if at all. As Matthews writes: "Debates on policy . . . merely exacerbate personal relations and solidify the conflicting policy stances of different members of the party."[9] Parties, says Gabriel Almond, are supposed to perform the "aggregative function" but if that means more than pulling together the different demands of the social interests, if it means integrating all these diverse demands into a final policy product, that is a function which the party organizational units have to work at but do not easily perform. Walter Lippman discussed this in 1933 in describing the platform-writing process at the national convention. He said,

A platform . . . is concerned with more or less immediate proposals and in a nation split up by class, sectional and racial interests, these proposals are sure to arouse hostility. No definite industrial and political platform, for example, can satisfy rich and poor, black and white, Eastern creditor and Western farmer. A party that tried to answer every conflicting interest would stand still because people were pulling in so many different directions. It would arouse the anger of every group and the approval of its framers. It would have no dynamic power because the forces would neutralize each other.[10]

Of course, platforms require compromise decisions, but ones which are not offensive to critical voting subgroups. This is part of the American political culture.

A fourth basic conception of the national party is that it consists of a set of party organs dispersed and ineffective in the exercise of power but with considerable potential power. When the national chairman and committee want to be a stronger managerial force in party affairs they certainly can, as chairmen like Jim Farley, Roy Bliss, and William

Brock have demonstrated. If the congressional and senatorial party organizations want to assert a more dominant policy leadership role in the party and in the process insist on some influence over the national committee (which up to now it has recoiled from), even though it would be difficult, more could be done. The Republican and Democratic leaderships in the House and Senate tolerate and seem perfectly willing to live for most of the time in a policy leadership vacuum with no one party organ assuming leadership. Even the national convention, indeed particularly the national convention, which has the plenum of party power in the last analysis, could be more effective in restructuring the national committee in its composition and its power role. A study of the history of the party national units shows that on occasion they have haltingly exercised greater authority:

The national convention attempted to reform the national committee (Republicans in 1952, Democrats in 1972), but they proceeded no further than compositional questions.

The national convention attempted to prescribe a loyalty test to describe which state delegation party leaders could be excluded from the convention (Democrats, 1952).

The national committees can refuse to seat (and have done so) any elected committee member "who refuses to support the nominees of the convention." (Republican Rule No. 27, adopted August 21, 1972; the Democrats have a similar rule.)

The party caucus in the House or Senate controls the chairmanship of every standing committee in Congress. (In January 1973, the Democratic caucus in the House did adopt such a rule requiring a secret ballot on the chairmanship of each standing committee, thus abolishing automatic seniority.)

The Democratic party caucus in the House in the sixty-third Congress (1913–15) did bind members to party policy positions, under Majority Leader Oscar Underwood and with the support of President Woodrow Wilson.[11]

The national committee has expelled members who oppose the presidential nominee. (In 1896 the Democratic National Committee expelled the members from Massachusetts and Pennsylvania who opposed William Jennings Bryan, the Democratic presidential nominee. In 1912 the Republican committee could have done the same on authorization from the national convention.)[12]

The representation in the national convention is determined by the national committee, subject to rules adopted by the convention. (The Democratic quota system of representation in the 1972 convention was the product, as was the new apportionment formula, of the actions of the national committee through its subcommittees but on mandate from the national convention of 1968.)

The Senate party conference can and has disciplined members. (In 1924 the Republican Senate conference adopted a resolution to exclude those Republican senators supporting Robert La Follette's presidential candidacy and not to name them to "fill any Republican vacancies on Senate committees.")[13] During Woodrow Wilson's first term 1912–16 the Democratic caucus in the House enforced discipline on his program and was a major factor in pushing this program through Congress.[14]

There is thus a potential for power in the national party organs.

National Party Components

Chairman and Staff

The selection of a national chairman can often be a dramatic event. Theodore White describes the meeting at Miami on July 14, 1972, of the Democratic National Committee convened by George McGovern, who had just been nominated as the Democratic presidential candidate, to announce his choice for national chairman and vice-chairman. The choice was very difficult. He had to decide from among a short list of very able and loyal colleagues—Lawrence O'Brien, Pierre Salinger, and Jean Westwood. O'Brien had been rejected by McGovern's supporters just before this meeting.

At 2:30 in the afternoon, in the crowded Fontaine Room of the Fontainbleau, there walk in, arm in arm, Lawrence O'Brien and George McGovern. O'Brien is white-faced. They stride to the platform and George McGovern makes a speech of fervid praise of O'Brien's performance. Then he says, "I want to tell you ... that he [O'Brien] has reached a judgment that he will not stay on as the chairman of our party. I respect his wishes.". . . There are at least ten people in the room who know this is simply not true . . . McGovern nominates Mrs. Jean Westwood as Chairman of the party. All assent and McGovern now nominates his choice for vice-chairman—Pierre Salinger. . . . The next ten minutes are grotesque. A hand rises from the floor and is acknowledged—Charles Evers of Mississippi. "Madam Chairman," he says . . . "I would like to place in nomination a black man . . . Mr. Basil Paterson of New York." The applause booms out. This new Democratic National Committee is the creation of the new convention—women, blacks, and youth in their beliefs. They know nothing about Basil Paterson of New York . . . . "Who is Basil Paterson?" comes an unidentified voice from the floor . . . now rises George McGovern and says, "I want it understood before this vote takes place that I regard Basil Paterson as one of the most distinguished and capable members of our party and while I have suggested the name of Pierre Salinger, either one of these very able men could be perfectly acceptable to me and a great credit to our party." Loud applause, roaring applause, but the rug has been pulled out from under Pierre Salinger, in public.[15]

Salinger withdraws, Westwood and Paterson are elected!

While often dramatic to those involved, national chairmen are obscure figures to most of the public, with a few exceptions, like Jim

Farley, possibly Joseph Martin, and O'Brien. The 1981 chairmen (Charles Manatt of Los Angeles for the Democrats and Richard Richards of Utah for the Republicans) are fairly typical in that sense. Few people know them; their status as national political leaders is nonexistent. The same can be said for their predecessors, John White and William Brock. Outside Texas, the top echelons of the Democratic party, and the Department of Agriculture where he was an assistant secretary, few people knew of White. Brock was better known perhaps as a congressman from Tennessee, but he too had not been a highly visible political figure nationally.

The national chairman is not selected because of his actual leadership stature. There have been many types—businessmen, managerial types, retired politicians, career politicians, members of Congress—but they are not usually the visible national leaders of the party. Above all, they are usually not individuals who are ideologues pursuing a particular policy or programmatic factional line at all costs. Rather, as one observer put it, they are "minimally offensive," not provoking the antagonism of party subgroups and assuring people they can work with all elements of the party. (Dean Burch for the Republicans, appointed by Goldwater in 1964, and Westwood, may be exceptions to this.)

The jobs of the national chairman are numerous. He, or she, manages a staff which may be as large as six hundred or more, depending on the campaign, or less than one hundred in off years and when resources are low. The organization has a variety of components: research, television and radio, other media, patronage, speakers' bureau, party organization (state and local), field sources, and special personnel concerned with minorities, women, youth, farm, labor, veterans, and business and professional groups. Running this operation efficiently is an important function, whether or not the staff is in charge of the campaign—and it usually is not. Because the chairman also presides over the national committee, he must therefore spend a great deal of time setting up subcommittees and working with these committee members to settle their differences. Planning for the national presidential nominating convention (and in the case of the Democrats, for the mini-conventions every two years) is a major job. He must be able to raise money in order to keep the national headquarters functioning and to defray past debts. He is in a sense the ceremonial head of the party, traveling around the country, making speeches, meeting with state and local groups, and meeting people when they come to Washington. If the party is in power, he may be involved in patronage. On an informal basis he may meet with members of the administration and party leaders in Congress. On occasion he may be asked to state his party's stand on issues or to defend the roll call votes in Congress. He may be a broker who attempts to achieve peace and agreement among contending factions in the party. He may be a public relations man for the party or, as Paul Butler once called him, "about the most unhidden persuader in the political arena."[16] An active practitioner of public relations, he is also a publicity manager using staff publications, mass media, and the speakers bureaus to the best advantage.

The national chairman is well paid and expected to be a full-time leader. He occupies a prestigious position, often fought for, or at least desired, by many. He is picked by the presidential nominee at the convention, and this dictates to a great extent his role in the campaign and thereafter. Linking him to the nominee has been criticized, but the attempt in the Democratic party in 1974 at the Kansas City convention to have him selected by the convention for a four-year term, in off years, and thus not tied to the president, was defeated. When the position falls vacant at other times, the chairman is selected by the national committee; in the majority party the president, again, will usually play an important role. In the minority party, whose presidential candidate was defeated, the national committee has a freer hand. In 1973 McGovern could not keep Jean Westwood in office, in 1965 Goldwater could not keep Dean Burch in office. Although there have been instances of continuity of a chairman despite defeat, the role of the defeated presidential candidate is severely limited.

The powers of the national chairman are contingent powers. Although he has a great deal of operational room and leeway in the job, what he can do is very dependent on his acceptance by others, on his relation to the president, Congress, and state and local leaders. He is really one among many leaders. If the president backs him strongly, he can play a major role. But if his relationship with the president, Congress, state and local leaders does not work out, his position is perilous. Kenneth Curtis said, when asked to step down by Carter, in this sense it is a "lousy job."[17] The chairman has no hierarchical stature in his own right. As a consequence, his role may be very limited and his influence weak outside his managerial functions. But he is available to provide leadership if given the opportunity. With the potential for leadership considerable, and the role specifications ambiguous, much more could be realized through the chairmanship than is normally practiced.

National Committee

Among the labels given the national party committees are the "capstone of the formal party organization," "meetings of state party ambassadors," and "political megaphones." How much power they have has been debated over the years, although most scholars would now agree with the evaluation of the columnist Thomas L. Stokes in 1949: "A national committee never nominated anybody, never elected anybody, never established party policy...."[18] The general goal of the national committee is to strengthen the party, to elect a president, and to make certain organizational decisions to that end. Chief among such decisions is where the national convention will be held, the apportionment procedures for selecting the convention delegates, and all the arrangements for the convention, usually via a set of national committee subcommittees on organization and rules, credentials, and resolutions (or platform).

The organizational policy role of the national committee in planning the presidential convention (and for the Democrats the mid-term mini-convention) is significant and controversial, particularly because the decisions can be seen as benefitting or harming particular aspirants. Thus, the composition of the preconvention credentials committee by the Republicans in 1952 led to decisions seating Taft delegates and not seating Eisenhower delegates, decisions which were subsequently reversed by the convention. Similarly, in 1978–79 proposed changes in the rules discussed in a Democratic national subcommittee (the Winograd Commission) concerning presidential primaries was seen by some as possibly favoring President Carter.

Above all, the role of the national committee in administering the rules of the party for the selection of delegates to the conventions should not be minimized. In the Democratic party the role of the national committee is particularly powerful in this respect. State organizations must conform to the guidelines established by the national committee and submit their procedures for delegate selection to a Compliance Review Commission. The national committee thus tells state organizations how to conduct this selection, and disapproval may lead to a state delegation not being seated at the convention. The Michigan Democrats in 1980 changed their procedure (from an open primary to a caucus system) at the insistence of the national party organization. The Supreme Court has now upheld this power of the national party.

Aside from this role, there are other actions the national committee could engage in but does not—at least on a regular basis. The committee could hold hearings on, or debate, policy matters and issue pronouncements. It sporadically does this but without much authority. It could spell out the conditions of party membership and loyalty and discipline those who are deviant—something it rarely has attempted. It could seek to develop programs strengthening the state and local organizations, which are highly irregular operations. (An exception was the Republican committee's work on organizational renovation in 1980.) Aside from the regular responsibilities for the national convention and selecting a national chairman when the position is vacant, the committee works in a vacuum. As with the national chairmanship, there is much potential, but limited reality.

Why this is so stems from the basic composition and nature of the committees. Selected for the most part by the state organizations, they are large, very diverse representative collectivities, and they meet seldom—usually no more than twice a year. Under these conditions it is difficult for them to be very effective.

As for size, the Republican committee since 1952 has consisted of 3 representatives from each state, including the state chairperson—a body of 162 persons, which includes the representatives from the possessions. The Democratic committee previously consisted of 1 man and 1 woman from each state, but the reforms adopted in the 1972-74 period increased the number from 108 to over 360 (see table 6.1).

TABLE 6.1
Allocation of Democratic National Committee Members

	Number
The state chairperson and highest ranking officer of the opposite sex from each state and territory	110
Representatives apportioned to each state on the basis of party vote and population (or electoral college strength)	200
Representatives picked by the Democratic Governors Conference	3
The speaker and the Democratic floor leader of the House, the floor leader and deputy floor leader of the Senate Democrats	4
Officers of the Democratic National Committee	5
President of the Young Democrats	1
Additional members selected by committee members to represent other groups in the party	(a variable number ranging from 35 to 40)
Total:	approximately 365

This new allocation appears to be a major renovation! There are now voting members from Congress, from city government, from state government, and from a variety of constituent groups within the party. The potential for a new committee with important coordinative roles in party policy and organization at all levels of government is, on the surface, great. But the powers of the committee remain very much the same. The Kansas City mini-convention of the Democrats sought to increase the power of the Democratic National Committee, but the attempt was defeated.

Although the national committee members are selected in a variety of ways, essentially their lines of accountability (if in reality they exist at all) are to the state organizations. States select members in four basic ways (the first of which is the most frequent):

1. By state convention or by district party committees, whose selections may have to be ratified by the conventions
2. By state party committees
3. By state delegations (picked or ratified by state conventions) to the national convention
4. By direct primaries[19]

National committee members owe their election to the local and state organizations. They are usually individuals who have come up through the state party organizations to their present position and, therefore, are loyal to their local constituents, indirect as that line of responsibility may often be. Thus the national committee is a very locally representative body but may also have difficulty acting on national party matters with strong consensus in an innovative fashion.

The national committee was, in theory, to be a campaign committee to elect a president, as when the Democrats set up their first committee in 1844, to elect James K. Polk and George M. Dallas. This conception today is rarely implemented. The national committee is not the institutional focus of the campaign. One of the best descriptions of an efficiently run presidential campaign and the place of the national committee in it is provided by Theodore White writing about Lyndon Johnson's campaign organization in 1964.

The most graphic way to describe the campaign organization of Lyndon Johnson is to say that it was organized—like his White House—on a radial, not a pryamidal, model. First, at the center of the wheel, were the three men with direct access to the President—Jenkins, Moyers, and Valenti.... These three could be styled Team A, or the Household Guard. [He then discusses successive rings in the circle, or teams, as Team B (Oxford, Fortas, and Rowe), Team C (O'Brien and O'Donnell), etc....] Team E was the Democratic National Committee, directed by its Chairman, John Bailey of Connecticut. A hard-bitten and accomplished craftsman of big city politics, Bailey looks upon all officials, elective or appointive, as "pols" like himself.... Bailey described his own operation realistically as "the housekeeping job" [registration, speeches and programs, particularly working on marginal districts held by Republicans, mobilization of minorities, etc.].[20]

Team E, the national chairman and committee staff, therefore, held specific outlying types of responsibilities, linked to national committee staff capabilities. It is this conception of the committee, the chairman, and his staff as performing "service" and "housekeeping" roles which is probably most accurate today in understanding its place in presidential campaigns.

Nevertheless, the national committee is not an unimportant body. It performs important organizational policy-making decisions. It has considerable prestige among the party supporters. It contributes to the representative apparatus. It could be a major arena for party leadership and policy conflict. But this in the larger sense it has never been.

The Congressional and Senatorial Party Structures

There is a set of party organizational units which exists in both houses of Congress for both parties, operating alongside the formal legislative organization and yet intermixed with that formal organization.[21] The specific units are included in the diagram of figure 6.3, which illustrates the organization and the relationship of the units to each other. Here again there is no hierarchy. Rather it is a hybrid structure with a dispersion of power and responsibility and no centralized leadership control system. The caucus of all party members in the House or Senate is theoretically the body of greatest plenary power; it can create other organizational units, select personnel, and make policy decisions. On occasion the caucus has asserted policy leadership. Indeed, at the beginning of each new Congress the conference makes the critical decisions on organizational leadership. For the Democrats in the House, with the reform beginning in January 1973, the caucus by secret vote decides standing committee chairmanships, and since 1975 all appropriations subcommittee chairmanships. Despite this fundamental power base, the caucus today is not a body which articulates party leadership positions, disciplines members, or binds the party together. The Democratic party bylaws themselves permit members to ignore caucus policy decisions (on the rare occasion when the caucus tries to formulate policy) if the decision conflicts with a mandate from the constituency, with campaign promises, or with the members' feeling that a "constitutional question" is at stake.[22] Thus, caucus positions on substantive policy are not binding, in contrast to the party caucus decisions in the British House of Commons, for example.

In addition to the caucus other organs of the legislative party perform important diverse functions but no one of them represents the center of the party leadership system.

The Floor Leader. He is selected by the caucus and plays a major role in legislative planning. In the party perspective he is a parliamentary tactician, noted for his skill and shrewdness in furthering the party advantage in the arrangements of the legislative schedule. He is a person of lengthy experience, commands considerable respect, but does not command others. In the last analysis he is one outstanding leader among many such leaders.

The Whipping System. Working with the floor leader is a senior member of the House or Senate known as the Whip (or Assistant Floor Leader). He in turn has assistant whips, varying from a few in number in the Senate to fifteen to eighteen in the House. There are geographical zones of delegations in the House, and each zone has its whip. These party leaders perform the function of communication with party

FIGURE 6.3
Party Organization in Congress, 1981

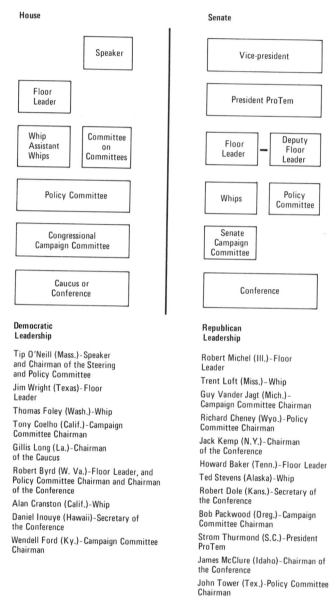

Democratic Leadership

Tip O'Neill (Mass.)-Speaker and Chairman of the Steering and Policy Committee

Jim Wright (Texas)-Floor Leader

Thomas Foley (Wash.)-Whip

Tony Coelho (Calif.)-Campaign Committee Chairman

Gillis Long (La.)-Chairman of the Caucus

Robert Byrd (W. Va.)-Floor Leader, and Policy Committee Chairman and Chairman of the Conference

Alan Cranston (Calif.)-Whip

Daniel Inouye (Hawaii)-Secretary of the Conference

Wendell Ford (Ky.)-Campaign Committee Chairman

Republican Leadership

Robert Michel (Ill.)-Floor Leader

Trent Loft (Miss.)-Whip

Guy Vander Jagt (Mich.)-Campaign Committee Chairman

Richard Cheney (Wyo.)-Policy Committee Chairman

Jack Kemp (N.Y.)-Chairman of the Conference

Howard Baker (Tenn.)-Floor Leader

Ted Stevens (Alaska)-Whip

Robert Dole (Kans.)-Secretary of the Conference

Bob Packwood (Oreg.)-Campaign Committee Chairman

Strom Thurmond (S.C.)-President ProTem

James McClure (Idaho)-Chairman of the Conference

John Tower (Tex.)-Policy Committee Chairman

members, informing them of legislative scheduling plans, the importance of the bills as they come to the floor, and on occasion, the leader's view on the proposed legislation. Again in contrast to the British system, American whips communicate, they do not whip.

The Policy (or Steering) Committee. This body varies in size by House and party, with the Senate committees smaller and the House committees (from fifteen to seventeen persons) being selected by zonal aggregations of delegations. These committees are partisan strategy groups in which policy is discussed, and often issues may be formulated to embarrass the opposition, but in no sense are they policy leadership groups which arrive at policy and commit the party to a position. Under a dynamic floor leader like Johnson or Robert A. Taft or Alben W. Barkley, they may be a focal point of discussing policy alternatives and seeking some unity in support of, or opposition to, a president's program. But usually the members have considerable tenure in Congress, are powerful standing committee chairmen in their own right, and disagree considerably on policy so that issue consensus on the committee is difficult to come by. They are often prima donnas who will not surrender their own autonomous policy leadership roles.

The Campaign Committees. These are committees which came into existence in the House in 1866 (Republicans) and 1882 (Democrats) to help with the reelection of members of the House. When the Senate became popularly elected in 1916, such committees were set up in that body also. They are essentially committees mobilizing funds and developing assistance (in publicity, media usage, and speech writing) for incumbents and for nonincumbents who are considered to have a chance at election. Their function, therefore, while extremely important (and no other organ fulfills it) is highly specialized. The existence of three separate committees—the national committee, the senatorial committee, and the congressional committee—in a sense devoted to this function suggests again the power dispersion of national organization.

The Committee on Committees. In the House each party has a group who assigns members to committees when vacancies due to retirements, deaths, and defeats arise. For the freshman member this committee may make crucial decisions affecting his career. In 1973 the Democrats, who have traditionally done this job through their members on the Ways and Means Standing Committee, added to this committee the speaker, the floor leader, and the caucus chairman with the speaker as chairman, attesting to the significance of this committee in party affairs in the House. The Republican committee whose function is the same—personnel recruitment, screening, and allocation to the standing committees—consists of a representative from each state in the House where Republicans are represented.

An evaluation of the congressional party structures points up their obvious importance as instruments in the legislative process, their necessity for the performance of leadership tasks, yet their undistinguished role as authoritative decisional entities. There are indeed recognizable leaders like Tip O'Neill and Jim Wright, or Jack Kemp and Robert Michel in the House. In the Senate there are important figures like Robert Byrd and Alan Cranston or Daniel Inouye and Howard Baker or Ted Stevens or John Tower. Nonetheless, the question is, Where is *the* leadership, who *are* the responsible Democratic leaders, who *has authority* in the congressional and senatorial parties? There is really no single corporate body of party power, only an abstract concept of party discipline, unity, and loyalty with no leadership unit having the right to speak for the party.

Why this is so is answerable only in terms of the nature of American political culture and the realities of the American legislative process which does not seem to develop political leaders who believe in centralized party control, authoritative party decision making on policy questions, and party discipline. And this in turn is related to an awareness of the priorities in the political relationships of our legislators (see fig. 6.4). Their first loyalty is to the voters back home who will have to be called on to reelect them. The next loyalty is to the social interest groups who supported them and with whom they feel congenial. Next their loyalty is to their congressional committee associates of both parties, which is related to a heavy commitment to their career in the committee system. Following that are their loyalties to ideological associates and their own friendship circle. Finally, they are loyal to their party and its leaders in the House or Senate. Hopefully the conflict between loyalty to party organization and other commitments is not too irreconcilable. Usually it is not. On the other hand, it is clear that loyalty to the congressional party caucus is not primary. This pattern of conflicting loyalties produces the minimally effective party leadership emerging in the American system.

The National Convention as a Party Structure

Despite the criticisms and the changes which reforms have produced, the national convention remains a body of critical significance for the party. It may be in the process of losing some of its importance in connection with the nomination of the presidential candidate, but it remains an important integrative structure with the potential to act if it so wishes. V. O. Key said long ago, "It is the basic element of national party apparatus."[23] An attempt at evaluation of it as a part of the apparatus will be made here. In chapter 12 its role in presidential nominations will be discussed.

As an organization the national convention has developed considerably since it first appeared in the 1830s. First, the number of delegates has increased from a small number from each state to between 5,000 and 6,000 delegates and alternates today. In 1976 the Republicans had

FIGURE 6.4.

Congressman's Linkages with His Party Organization and Other Reference Groups

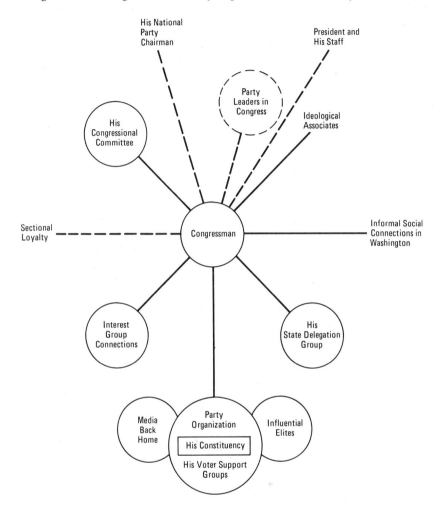

2,259 delegate votes; the Democrats 3,008. In 1980 the Republicans had 1,994, the Democrats 3,317. In addition there are the official alternates as well as other officials and party activists accompanying the delegates. For 1980 the Democratic National Committee announced a convention of 3,317 delegate votes plus 2,042 alternates, a total of 5,404. A body of that size can make deliberation difficult, and the mobilization of votes requires careful organization before and during the convention.

Second, the manner in which delegates are selected for the convention has changed. Originally representatives of the state party were chosen by state party committees or conventions; now major use is made of a third selection method—direct election by the rank-and-file party supporters who, in many states, may be only marginally affiliated with the parties. The great move to using primaries occurred from 1912, when fourteen states used them, to 1976, when the number increased to thirty,[24] and then in 1980 to thirty-six states plus Puerto Rico and the District of Columbia. Today over 70 percent of all delegates to the convention are selected directly. Thus the nature of the convention as an organization has been radically altered because of the representative orientations of convention delegates and their varying lines of responsibility.

Third, the convention as an organization has been modified over time in its internal structural patterns. There are four internal subgroups: (1) the formal, or official, convention committees and leadership, which includes the presiding officer of the convention and other officers and the three or four committees (credentials, rules and organization, resolutions); (2) the various presidential candidate organizations which seek to communicate with delegates and mobilize support for the vote on the nomination; (3) the interest group caucuses, such as delegates with labor union affiliation, the black caucus, the women's caucus, et cetera; and (4) the state delegations, where many of the votes are taken before they are reported on the convention floor.

In the past the convention basically consisted of fifty autonomous subgroups of state delegation with each delegation housed in a particular hotel for its own headquarters and meetings. Particularly true before the onset of the presidential primaries ten years ago, to a certain extent this structure is still true today, depending, of course, on the convention situation. Individual delegations have a chairman, vice-chairman, other officers, a set of bylaws to proceed by, and definite meeting times. Before 1976 it was in these delegations' meetings that the debates and decisions initially took place. The delegations decided, after debate, on which presidential candidate to support and debated the platform. They also selected their representatives to the convention's formal committees although this was done often before they arrived at the convention, and some state delegations chose their representatives to the national committee. The state delegation was a powerful subgroup at the convention and still can be for certain purposes, even though it no longer acts as a unit as it did in both parties to a great extent as recently as ten to fifteen years ago. It is in a sense both the key representational and decisional substructure of the conventions. But the old image of the convention as organized through fifty state delegation blocs led by powerful leaders is not as accurate today. Conventions are structurally less coherent and may operate less as power brokerage arenas than in years past.

In recent years there have been two major attacks on the convention—that it is not an efficient deliberative body and that it is unrepresentative and undemocratic. Anyone who has observed these national conventions is aware of their time-consuming inefficiency and carnival-like atmosphere.[25] Since they are accepted generally as political spectacles for launching presidential campaigns, they cannot be made into completely rational, efficient bodies. There has been an attempt to cut down on the demonstrations, the polling of each delegation member on the floor in a dispute over a vote, the length and number of seconding speeches, et cetera, but there is no possibility of eliminating the convention's celebrative aspects. Despite appearances, a great deal of thoughtful deliberation over programs and analysis of strategic alternatives goes on in the convention.

It is for the second criticism of the convention, that it is unrepresentative, that remedies have been sought in recent years, in at least five ways:

1. By changing the apportionment formula which determines the *number* of delegate votes for each state.
2. By requiring proportional representation in the primary states and, thus, giving each aspirant for the presidential nomination the proportion of delegates he or she is entitled to in terms of the primary vote received. The aim is *equity* to candidates in allocating delegates.
3. By requiring the selection of delegates in nonprimary states to begin in the same year as the presidential election. Previously, in some states, selection of local convention representatives to county conventions began one or two years earlier. Eliminating the time lag would make the convention more representative in a temporal sense.
4. By specifying that the state delegations include an adequate, fair, or proportionate representation of racial minorities, women, and all age groups. The proper representation of significant social groups is obviously the purpose here.
5. By requiring that the selection process of delegates, from the grass-roots base of the organization to the top, be open and democratic with a clear understanding of who may participate, adequate advance notice for meetings, adequate meeting room facilities, and clear and fair rules of procedure.

In the last ten years the Democratic party has sought to improve the representative character of its national conventions, and to a certain extent the Republicans have attempted to do the same. A brief discussion of these complicated issues may help clarify the changes which have been made.

The apportionment question, the number of delegates permitted to each state, has plagued both parties. The issue is whether the electoral college principle should control these allocations (each state receives a number of delegates proportionate to the number of its congressmen and United States senators), or the party strength principle. The electoral college principle was used exclusively until 1916 when the Republicans first began to reward states for electing Republicans. By 1940 the Democrats began using the party strength principle. Both parties now use formulas utilizing both principles. The formulas for 1976 and 1980 are shown in table 6.2.

The differences in the party formulas are quite clear. The Democrats award bonus delegates to the states proportional to the party *vote*, the Republicans do not attempt to do so. Since 1972 these formulas have been widely debated. Critics in both parties wish to see the parties go much further in awarding bonus delegates relative to the party vote. The Republicans in 1972 had a large state (the Steiger) proposal and a small state (the Tower) proposal. The former plan of Congressman William A. Steiger was similar to the final Democratic plan, but the plan of Senator John Tower prevailed, giving small states, it was argued, a convention influence greatly disproportional to their contribution to the Republican presidential vote.

Proportional representation (PR) is now the law in the Democratic party but is left up to the states by the Republican party. This issue came to a head in 1972 when the McGovern forces demanded all 271 California delegate votes even though they had received only 44.3 percent of the California primary vote. According to winner-take-all principles of California state law McGovern was entitled to all 271. By the new reform rules of the 1972 convention the Democratic party had indicated it opposed the unit rule and winner-take-all primaries.[26] In the Credentials Committee McGovern lost and was deprived of 151

TABLE 6.2
Formulas for Allocating Delegates, 1976, 1980

Democrats	Republicans
1. Electoral college principle: 3 delegate votes for each congressman and senator Total: 1,614 delegate votes	1. The same as the Democrats
2. Party bonus delegates awarded states on the basis of the *Democratic vote* in the last three presidential elections Total: 1,386 delegate votes	2. Party bonus to a state on the basis of the *number of Republican officials* previously elected:
3. Votes allocated to the territories: Puerto Rico, Virgin Islands Total: 8 delegate votes	a. 4½ votes if the state went Republican in the previous election (plus 60 percent of the state's electoral college vote)
4. Added in 1980: a 10 percent "add-on" to permit each state to send its senior party and elected officials	b. 1 vote if a Republican was elected governor or senator
Total: 3,008 delegate votes (1976) 3,317 delegate votes (1980)	c. 1 vote if one-half of its congressional delegation was Republican Total: 613 delegate votes
	3. Representation of territories: 32 votes Total: 2,259 (1976) 1,994 (1980)

delegates. But convention Chairman Larry O'Brien ruled that only the 120 McGovern delegates were certified and could vote in the battle on the floor over this issue. Under a favorable chairman's rulings and gavel, McGovern won. But the Democratic party then made the rule explicit—PR was mandatory. In fact the principle is even more general. Each state must now fairly reflect in its delegation the presidential preferences of those participating in the selection process. The variations by states in the application of the principle are considerable, and there are implementing regulations of states which deviate from strict PR, such as the loophole primaries where the winner-take-all principle still operates at the district level. These deviations will be discussed in more detail later in connection with the role of presidential primaries in the nomination process. But progress toward proportional democracy has been made by both parties. It will be difficult now to return to doctrines of acquiescence, let the voters decide, unit rules, slate making and winner-take-all.

The time-lag change has been made now by both parties. Previously in certain states precinct and township delegates were elected to county conventions two years before a presidential election year. These same county convention delegates would select their representatives to a state convention in the election year; they in turn elected delegates to the national convention. The delegate constituent base was two years old and theoretically behind the times. To remedy this problem all states were required to commence the delegate selection process in the presidential election year.

The most dramatic representative issue which has preoccupied the Democrats is the representation of minorities. It really all began in 1964 in the Democratic convention at Atlantic City when Lyndon Johnson, while sweeping unopposed to the nomination, was briefly disturbed by the protests of the Mississippi Freedom Democratic Party that there were no blacks in the Mississippi delegation. Johnson not only seated two honorary members of the Freedom party, but the convention adopted a resolution that in the future any state delegation which excluded blacks could not be seated. Then, at the wild and violent convention in Chicago in 1968, the entire all-white Mississippi delegation was ejected, as well as half of the Georgia delegation's whites, who were replaced by blacks.[27] More important, the 1968 Democratic convention adopted a credentials committee resolution and a minority report of the rules committee (by a vote of 1,350 to 1,206) recommending the establishment of two special committees, on rules and party structure reform.

The two new party commissions were set up in 1969 by national Chairman Fred Harris (who had been picked by Hubert Humphrey, the losing presidential candidate). James G. O'Hara headed the Rules Commission which produced the new apportionment rules. McGovern was selected to run the Commission on Party Structure and Delegate Selection (later known as the Reform Commission). With Senator Harold E. Hughes of Iowa as the able and liberal vice-chairman and a staff of equally dedicated and liberal young assistants the commission held hearings throughout the country, collected information on the peculiar and discriminatory ways in which many state and local organizations conducted the delegate selection process, raised the basic questions of what a party was (a private club or a public institution), who should determine party operations (the national party, the state or local party, or the state legislature), and who had the right to participate in party affairs. It was this commission which first developed a position on winner-take-all selection procedures, finally urging, but not requiring, states to protect political minorities from winner-take-all systems. Ironically, this came back to haunt McGovern in the 1972 convention on the California issue. Though other matters were discussed, the critical question was that of quotas. After much heated controversy the Reform Commission, on November 18, 1969, adopted the key resolution requiring states to include women, blacks, and youth (ages eighteen to thirty) so their number in the delegation should be conceived as "bearing a reasonable relation to the presence of the group in the population." Subsequently, in a letter to all state chairmen on November 29, 1971, from the Democratic National Committee, the directive was clearly stated,

We believe that state parties should be on notice that whenever the proportion of women, minorities, and young people in a delegation offered for seating in Miami is less than the proportions of these groups in the total population, and the delegation is challenged . . . such a challenge will constitute a prima facie showing of violation of the Guidelines, and the state Democratic party along with the challenged delegation has the burden of showing that the state party took full and affirmative action. . . .

As a result the composition of the delegation at the Democratic convention in 1972 markedly changed over 1968 (see table 6.3).[28]

TABLE 6.3
Minorities' Delegates to National Conventions
1968, 1972, 1976
(as a percentage)

	Democratic Convention Delegate Composition			Republican Convention Delegate Composition		
Group	1968	1972	1976	1968	1972	1976
Women	13	39	33	17	30	31
Blacks	5	15	11	2	3	3
Under age 30	3	22	14	1	8	7

There was a considerable difference of opinion over whether the changes in the numbers from these minorities vitally influenced the McGovern nomination. Certainly those voting at the convention were less white, less male, and younger. And in decisions over credentials fights, such as over the seating of the California and Illinois delegates, these numbers may have turned the tide.

After the 1972 convention there was a hue and cry from certain quarters that the party had gone too far with quotas and as a consequence many party regulars were unseated, the party's image had changed, and its chances of winning elections diminished. Consequently, after considerable further debate in a subcommittee of the national committee, the mini-convention at Kansas City, in early December 1974, adopted a revision of the quota rule of 1972. Mandatory quotas were rejected, and affirmative action was required of states in the selection of delegates so that the minorities would be represented in each state delegation "as indicated by their presence in the Democratic electorate." The language change was significant as was the whole tone of the resolution. Each state was required to prepare plans for selecting its delegates and submit these plans to the national committee well in advance of the convention in 1976. If these plans were approved, then the burden of proof on a charge of unrepresentativeness would be placed on the challenger, not on the state party or its delegation. These were indeed significant changes, softening the language and eliminating the presumption of guilt. After the 1974 convention the Democratic National Committee set up a Compliance Review Commission to which all states did, indeed, submit their delegation selection plans. There was controversy and criticism, particularly over the attempted centralization of control and the red tape (Leonard Woodcock, for example, of the United Automobile Workers blasted those "awful new rules"). But eventually this new system worked smoothly for the 1976 convention, where the proportion of these minorities declined slightly.[29] The changes and the standardization of the criteria for affirmative action are now accepted and well established in the Democratic party.

The Republicans in certain states have moved also in this direction. The Michigan Republican party rules in 1976 stated,

The Congressional District Caucuses when electing their three National Convention Delegates and the State Convention when electing its 27 at-large delegates to the Republican National Convention shall make every effort to insure that the Michigan delegation . . . is a representative delegation so that the Michigan delegation includes representation of minority groups, young persons, women and persons 65 years old and older in *reasonable relation to their presence* and activity in the *Republican Party*. . . . Neither the District Caucuses . . . nor the state convention . . . shall discriminate on the basis of race, creed, color, sex, age, national origin or economic status (when electing delegates). . . .

The Michigan Republican Party shall endeavor to have equal representation of men and women in its delegation . . . [emphasis added].

Note the identical phraseology to that adopted by the Democratic mini-convention of Kansas City in 1974.

Many questions remain concerning the representativeness of the national conventions. It is clear, however, that some of the most archaic and undemocratic forms of delegate selection and the processes underlying that selection have been scrutinized and to a large extent changed. The conventions today are likely to be more representative structures and therein lies the irony—and perhaps a basic dilemma. The task of the convention has been to nominate a presidential candidate. In America's diverse, centrifugal politics that has been for the two parties a herculean task: once in four years to somehow bring together the disparate elements in the party and in the space of five days achieve a consensus on the top office in the land. This requires a concentrating of efforts, bargaining and compromise for a majority somehow to coalesce. Today, because of the party reforms, the presidential nomination decision may not reach the convention but is settled by the primaries. We have reformed the conventions which may no longer select the candidates. Furthermore, the reforms may have so fragmented and individualized the convention and produced blocs of delegates so irrevocably committed to a plurality of candidates that a majority at the convention may have become more difficult to achieve, immobilizing the convention for a long time. Thus, protest leads to reform, which leads to more representation, which may lead to greater difficulty in arriving at effective decisions. It may also lead to less party unity. Careful observation and analysis of the conventions of 1984 and 1988 will be necessary to see whether the national convention, one of the most crucial structural units of the political parties up to now, has had its powerful role in the party sapped by the cumulative consequences of reform.

An Evaluation of the National Organizations

Historically, the power of the national party organizations has been decreased. The structure is very fragmented with little centralized authority, more dependent than independent. Yet it is capable of making important organizational policy decisions. The question remains: What is the cement that permits it to maintain its legitimacy and acceptability, if not its effectiveness? At one time patronage distribution kept the organization attractive to leaders, persons seeking governmental careers, but in reality this has never been the major function of this structure. Nor are there other material rewards dispersed frequently enough and to a large enough body of the faithful by these national party organs to explain their continued viability. Ideology or the opportunity for participants in the national organization to be involved in decisions over the policy and programs of the party is certainly not the cement of those involved at the national level. Policy leadership is too erratic and dispersed to command the loyalty of many supporters for the national organization.

Rather, the national organization continues to act as it does because of its status and function in the system. Despite all its weakness in decision making it has tremendous prestige. Through these organs comes whatever national leadership there is—national chairman, national committee, House and Senate committees, leaders of delegations to the national convention. These leadership positions are prestigious and are fought over by many party activists. The sense of being involved in important party decisions, of having some organizational power, is satisfaction enough for the participants, many of whom have developed a career in party organization politics, the capstone of which is the national organization. Thus the structure is attractive, partly because decisions are made at the national level in the United States for the party, partly because it satisfies ambitions. All this plus a love of party politics keeps most participants involved, even though their power is limited.

What are the critical powers of a party organization in a democratic society like the United States and where are they exercised? Particularly, are they exercised at the national level? This is the key query to keep in mind. The critical powers of the party include at least the following:

1. Determining the policy positions on which the party will compete in an election
2. Selecting the candidates who will carry the party label in the election
3. Deciding on the strategy to be employed in appealing to the public
4. Raising and dispensing the money needed to finance the campaign and interelection party activities
5. Enforcing discipline over elected members disloyal to the party and over organizational leaders who do not support the party in practice
6. Distributing patronage—"discovering" and participating in screening and certifying individuals considered for appointive positions in the government, particularly attesting to their party loyalty and service
7. Recruiting and training party activists for the thousands of organizational posts at the local level, the cadre of precinct, ward, and township party workers who contact voters

8. Monitoring the operations and actions of government at all levels, the legislatures, bureaucracies, and courts of cities, counties, states, and the District of Columbia, to insure efficiency, honesty, and equity of governmental performance.

A basic question is, Are these powers exercised with authority by the national party organs, on behalf of the entire Republican and Democratic parties? The answer is, The exercise of power is partial, intermittent, and often not decisive. Rather, the national organizations often perform at a minimal level doing what is necessary to maintain themselves. They leave to the state and local organizations much of the power, authority, and activity. The presidential campaign is run primarily by the candidate and his organization, not by the national committee. Other campaigns are considerably dependent on local conditions, where the strategy is planned and support mobilized. For finances a variety of fund-raising centers and operations exist. The national committee has its financial committee, as do the House and Senate party groups. But much of this operation is decentralized and again dependent on state and local activities. Patronage is handled differently by presidents, but the party organization as such cannot demand a role. The traditional rights of senators and congressmen to be consulted on (and to virtually veto) appointments are rarely violated, and these people are very aware of local interests back home in their recommendations on patronage. Again, the party organization itself is not in control.

As for the other critical powers on the list the answer is fairly clear. National organs normally do not have a major share in the exercise of these powers. Party activists are recruited at the local level. Policy leadership is dispersed and not authoritative. The national convention adopts a platform, but its policy resolutions cannot be enforced on anyone and may be ignored by presidential candidates (as well as presidents), to say nothing of elected congressmen and senators. The amount of monitoring of government done in Washington by the party organizations is minimal; individual congressmen and senators may do much more. Discipline to a certain extent could be exercised but, as indicated earlier, national organs are afraid to use sanctions.

It used to be said that at least one critical power was in the hands of a national party organ—the nomination of presidential and vice-presidential candidates. It is an extremely important power, without which the party as a national entity would disappear. But now even that power is being whittled away by the increasing use of presidential primaries which may make the nomination a foregone conclusion by convention time (as in 1980). As for selecting candidates for other elective offices, the House and Senate, the national organization is virtually uninvolved. Unlike the British system, where the national committee and central office in London do exert some influence in consultation with the local party organizations, the American system is decentralized in this respect. On careful scrutiny, then, it appears that the national party structures are only minimally relevant in this sense: They may act on their own behalf, but they do not act *authoritatively on behalf of the entire national party.*

Is the national party organization (or rather the variety of organizations) useful? The mobility aspirations of power seekers are helped. These organs are also the symbols of national legitimacy for the Republican and Democratic parties. They do represent the diverse elements in the party, the special interests of California versus those of Florida, the different types of activists in Manhattan and Chicago, of Mississippi and Montana. When these diverse elements of the party get together they may not resolve any great policy conflicts authoritatively, but they do share their contrasting experiences and perspectives about American politics. And in this sense the national organs, particularly the national committees and the national convention, are important integrative institutions. They bring people together, to share views about politics, to argue controversial positions, to plan for the party together. Conflicts are articulated, disagreement softened, tolerance of diverse viewpoints enhanced. While the national organs perform service functions, provide symbolic legitimacy, represent the incredible heterogeneity of the parties, occasionally make important organizational decisions, and provide maintenance for the parties, these national organs also give the parties a minimal national character.

There are those who argue that a new nationalization is taking place in the parties, that national party organs have been displacing local and state structures for a long time and that this process has been accelerated. There are others who see a deinstitutionalization taking place, that parties as national structures still have no capability to respond expeditiously to new social and economic problems, and that the public has lost confidence in national party leadership in these institutions. Finally, there are those who see an individualization in party action throughout the country, that politics has been turned over to individual decision making, to ad hoc groups, to candidates and their coteries of supporters. The greatest danger allegedly is the presidential primary. Gerald Pomper says,

There is a different character to the new party system, particularly evident among Democrats. It has an individualist base and plebiscitarian tone. The extension of the primaries, the emphasis on "making each vote count" through proportional representation, and the allocation of delegates are alike in their focus on the individual voter ... the plebiscite is replacing political organization.[30]

This may be a bit overdone and alarmist. The decline of national organization due to the spread of presidential primaries is not that apparent, although the threat to the convention is, indeed, there. National party organizations still exist, perform certain functions, and provide a national focus for political conflict. Though they are limited in power we cannot get along without them. We may well want more policy leadership, discipline, and organizational control. But if such goals are to be achieved, there must be a change in at least a century of progressive dispersion of party power and the institutionalization of a type of party organization at the national level which preserves pluralism, contains conflict, and fragments power.

Chapter 7

State and Local Party Structures: Variations in Form, Activity, and Power

IMPLICIT in a discussion of the national party organizations was the significance of the state and local levels of the party. Since the bulk of the powers of a party are only partially exercised at the national level, and then only on a contingency basis, with heavy emphasis on local representation and support, it is necessary to study party organization below the national level to discover what an American party really is. True, attempts have been made recently to strengthen the national organizations, but it is clear that they remain limited in authority, fragmented, and very dependent on other elements of the party. In any party system the crucial questions are, Who has the power? and Who has the responsibility? In vote mobilization terms, the answer for the American system is the state and local units of the parties.

There has been considerable controversy recently over the question of the actual effectiveness of state and local structures. There are those who argue that a disintegration of lower level party organization has taken place. David S. Broder of the *Washington Post* writes,

The condition of the political parties at the state and local level is so varied as to defy safe generalization. For the most part, however, they are plagued by inadequate finances and the lack of a trained, stable cadre of personnel to man the headquarters and provide essential services for the party's office holders and candidates. . . . Someone has said that the political parties may well be the worst-managed large enterprises in America.[1]

Broder goes on to argue that some states from time to time have strong organizations and this is tied to strong executive leadership in the mayor's and governor's offices. However, the bulk of the "task [of reform] is still ahead of us," he says. Frank Sorauf also is inclined to this view, claiming that "the average local party organization comes closer to the pole of disorganization than to the pole of maximum organization."[2]

Along with this theory of deinstitutionalization is the view of displacement of the local organizations by other institutions, forces, and groups. Many scholars maintain that the new techniques of mass persuasion in campaigns have replaced the local party organizational efforts at communication. The voting public presumably now secures its campaign information and stimuli from the specialized media campaigns. Others argue that state and local organizations are being displaced by other forms of group action. Single-issue groups, often representing new interests and causes, have appeared. It is argued that, on one hand, people participate much more in politics through such groups and, on the other hand, the public listens to the appeals of these groups today more than to the parties.

There certainly is some evidence to support such a position. Howard Jarvis in California was successful in organizing his Proposition 13 tax reduction drive, spurring the tax-cutting fever in other states. Similarly, the Equal Rights Amendment and Right to Life groups have at times dominated much of the political action in certain states. The environmentalists often organize effectively, as have such groups as the gun lobby, the National Organization of Women (NOW), the consumer groups of Ralph Nader, Common Cause, as well as groups of the New Right, such as the American Conservative Union. The significance of the new PAC's (political action committees) which have mushroomed since 1974 will be discussed in the chapter on party campaigning and finance. But there is no doubt that there are, indeed, new groups with particular goals and special interests, and in the process they do drain off talent, money, and interest from the regular party organizations.

The argument that these developments have led to the demise of party organization should be accepted cautiously. There is considerable evidence from recent research on state party organizations, for example, that they have become larger, more professionally structured, and better financed. Indeed such research does "challenge the widely held impression that state party organizations are insubstantial."[3] State and local parties in many ways are important infrastructures undergirding the electoral process.

Theories about the decay of state and local party organizations assume without substantiation that they were once powerful, active units, engaging in a great deal more activity than now, more efficiently and with many more trained activists, having a tremendous impact on the public. It will be difficult to investigate the realities to validate or refute these assumptions convincingly.

Basic Form of the State and Local Organization: A Stratarchy

To understand parties within the states it is necessary to comprehend the basic structural form and the essential nature of organizational relationships. It is like a series of layers of organization, or strata, superimposed figuratively one on the other but with no indication that it is a neat pyramid of authority. Figure 7.1 attempts to represent the strata in this nonhierarchical sense. There are no dependency connections between these layers nor any indication that one layer has a more dominant role to play in the total structure than any other, which is the essence of this structural pattern—it is not usually a hierarchy of command from the state chair to the district chair to the county chair and on down to the precinct chair. That does not mean that there are no formal connections whatsoever, because surely there are. Lower level conventions select delegates to upper level conventions, for example, and some city chairmen may appoint ward chairmen. But the key elements in a stratarchy in the states are:

1. No command from the state level down to the base of the organization
2. Limited control (if any) by intermediate echelons of authority over another
3. Autonomy in decision making at each stratum and, thus, dispersion of decision-making centers
4. Reciprocal deference, or the tolerance by each level of authority of other levels and a recognition of the independent status of each level in the system

This means, in addition, that (1) there is limited interference in the operations of each level from above or below and thus freedom to develop indigenous approaches to party work; (2) the clear lines of communication found in a hierarchy are not found here, and leaders rely on informal associations and persuasion, rather than directives; and (3) to hold leaders and committees accountable for the functioning of the total structure is virtually impossible, although individual chairmen and committee members are, indeed, periodically elected. There is no centralized leadership locus for the entire state party organization in such a stratarchy.

Now, to say the system tends to stratarchy is to suggest a model with certain characteristics. Not all of these elements of the model may be equally true in each of the fifty states, however. Two alternative mod-

FIGURE 7.1.
Party Stratarchy

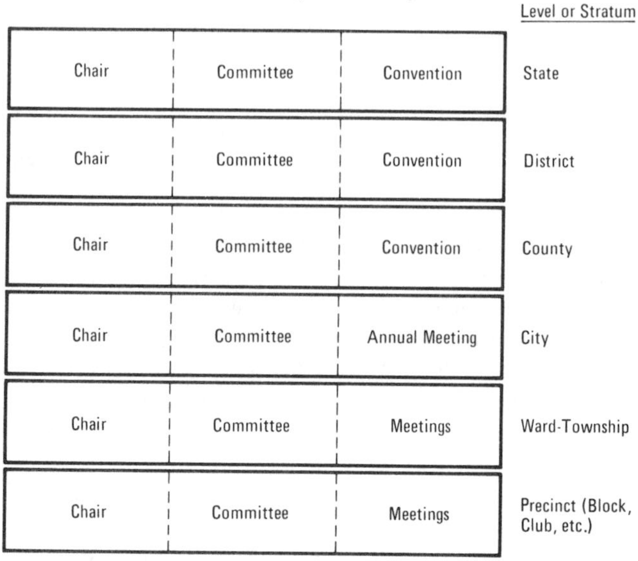

			Level or Stratum
Chair	Committee	Convention	State
Chair	Committee	Convention	District
Chair	Committee	Convention	County
Chair	Committee	Annual Meeting	City
Chair	Committee	Meetings	Ward-Township
Chair	Committee	Meetings	Precinct (Block, Club, etc.)

els emphasize other characteristics of the state and local parties. In figure 7.2 the two alternative models highlight the striking contrasts which theoretically could exist in state structures. The command model emphasizes a chain of command and a flow of directions from the state chairperson on down through the five levels. Committees are subordinate to the chairmen, who if controllable at all are controlled through the election and reelection by the state convention. The echelons are certainly not autonomous under this model, and the deference is strictly upward!

In the accountability model, there are a variety of possibilities. But its essence is that those at the base of the organization have opportunities to elect, control, and hold accountable their own local chairpersons and committees, as well as, through indirect or direct electoral processes, district, county, and state chairpersons and committees. There may still be considerable autonomy in each stratum, but the deference in the organization is certainly downward.

While the state organization is usually more of a stratarchy than conforming to either of the other two models, from time to time in certain state and local party structures there is a tendency away from stratarchy to either of these other two models. Certainly the city boss and his machine, exemplified by former Mayor Richard J. Daley and his party in Chicago, came close to the command model, although studies of his organization revealed much evidence of reciprocal deference.[4] On the other hand, in some states attempts have been made at least to implement the accountability model. Thus in about one-fourth

FIGURE 7.2.
Two Alternative Ideal Party Structure Models

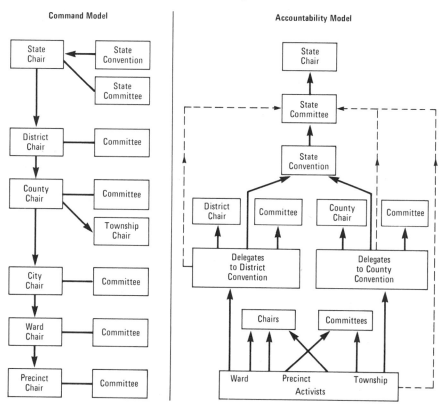

Command Model

Accountability Model

of the states there is direct election of state level committees by party supporters at the base of the system.[5] Caution, therefore, should be taken before jumping to the conclusion that all state and local party structures are complete stratarchies. Obviously this is not so. However, if parties are to respond to changing social problems, be adaptive to the needs of citizens, and maximize their power in elections by mobilizing votes effectively, there must be considerable tolerance by upper echelon party leaders of the lower level activists, diffusion of control, and much autonomy in decisions. There must be respect for local initiatives, local strategic improvisation, and recognition of the need for adaptation at the base of the organization. In organization relationships parties must accommodate to actors at all levels of the organization. There must be deference by the local leaders to those at the top also and respect for their leadership prerogatives; but certainly there must be respect by the leaders at the top for the local organization activists, for the latter theoretically have the power to mobilize the vote. As Elmer E. Schattschneider said long ago, noting the decentralization of power in American parties, "The strongest and most stable organization within a city may be a ward organization rather than a city-wide machine."[6]

Other Major Features of State Organizations

There are other important characteristics of American state party organizations. First, the indirect method of election and representation from one level to the next is found in many states. Precincts, wards, and townships (or clubs, assembly districts, et cetera) elect delegates once in two years to county or district conventions, which in turn elect delegates to the state convention. Therefore, if an interested and attentive voter wishes to influence the party organization, he must be certain to vote in that one election opportunity, the party primary election when local delegates are selected. In terms of party control that is the crucial election.

Second, in most state party structures there is separatism or dualism, which is the tendency for the legislative party organization to exist pretty much by itself. Some states do give seats on the state central committee to legislative party leaders, or legislators may seek control over the state organization, but often they are separate party leadership systems. This is true also at the county level, where often the party representatives on the county board or commission keep organizationally separate although they may maintain informal relationships with the county party chairman and the county committee. This separation tendency parallels identically the national party level, with Senate and House party organizations generally keeping aloof from involvement with the national committees.

Third, in most state organizations there is a preoccupation with organizational specialization. Thus, many states set up a professional financial organization specializing in fund raising. Similarly, there are other specialized organizational subunits and divisions dealing with such matters as patronage, race and ethnic relations, women's affairs, and coordination of publicity. In many states these party organizations are considered important political action apparatuses, set up carefully to get things done. Today they seem to be stronger and more professional structures than ever before.[7]

State Level Party Units

The same types of party organs are at the state level as at the national: state chairman, state central committee, state convention, and party organizations in the state House and Senate. The state chairperson is usually selected by the state convention to a full-time position, and he or she is often well paid. The tenure is, however, rather brief, about two years.[8] The job of the state chairperson is variable from state to state but generally it is a relatively important position in the state organization. The tasks and prerogatives include membership on the national committee, presiding officer of the state central committee, manager of the stage party headquarters, patronage clearance if the party is in power, spokesperson for the party in the state, and above all, if the chairperson wishes to assume the roles, factional broker and organizational liaison with the critical groups in the party. Of all the tasks, research reveals that state chairpersons consider the following as very important: building the party organization, fund raising, campaign activity, and candidate recruitment. Less emphasis is accorded to such tasks as providing a link between the local and national organizations. State chairpersons often maintain that they participate in primaries and are actively in contact with county party organizations. What this means, however, in terms of type of activities and the extent to which county organizations can be influenced is another matter.

The role of the state chairperson is, again, often highly contingent on the extent of support from the governor. One study identifies a particular type of chairperson as the "political agent" of the governor, contrasted to the one who is independent of, and possibly in conflict with, the governor, as well as the chairperson of the party out of power who has to act more on his own authority. The state chairperson thus has to act in the context of powerful other people—governor, House and Senate leaders, big city leaders, interest group leaders, and powerful entrenched county bosses. His role is to take care of the organization, encourage party workers, and resolve conflicts. He is probably better financed today (an estimated median budget of $100,000 a year in off years[9]) and has a larger permanent staff (on the average of ten in election years) than before, but he still is not a powerful figure. He works through a state central committee varying in size from fifty to five hundred and is usually accountable to a state convention which reviews his mandate at least every two years.

The other state party organs vary in form in each state, but there are similarities. The state central committee seems to be a buffer group. It is strictly representative of the district and county parties, often on a proportional basis of representation, and is a prestigious position for an upwardly mobile party activist. But aside from these functions, it is often not important except for making certain organizational policy decisions, such as planning for state conventions. It is not a key policy leadership body although it may debate policy and thus provide a certain catharsis for those party activists who are ideologues. In most states it usually makes no critical policy decisions for the party.

The state convention is the analogue of the national convention with one important exception—its nominating function is usually, except for a few states, much more atrophied. The state convention used to be of great importance in selecting the party's candidates for governor, lieutenant governor, and a host of other state officers. Today it is still used in some states for that purpose. In Michigan, for example, it selects the lieutenant governor, attorney general, secretary of state, state treasurer, superintendent of public instruction, members of the board of regents of the three main universities, as well as state supreme court justices. In several states the convention is a pre-primary endorsement forum. In Colorado any candidate who gets 20 percent of the convention vote automatically qualifies for the primary. In New York a candidate needs 25 percent of the convention vote to get into the primary. In Utah a convention endorsement is necessary to get into the primary. Thus, the convention is still relevant to the nominating process in several states, but it does not have the final authority. The emphasis in the state convention, as in the national, is on the representation of lower units of the party, the opportunity to discuss mutual experiences and problems, involvement in discussion (usually off the convention floor) of party policy, and, periodically, participation in the selection of (1) the state chairperson; (2) state committee; (3) the delegates to the national convention; and (4) the selection of members of the national committee. As an important intermediate personnel selection body, as a buffer group, and as a symbolically important representative assembly, therefore, the state convention has a significant role. Theoretically it is the plenary body in the state party organization; actually it does not often assert its authority. It must be seen as a key integrative party institution bringing people of heterogeneous backgrounds and interests together to share a feeling of likemindedness while performing organizational tasks.

Although state party units are not powerful in a hierarchical control sense, they are important nevertheless. They are indispensable for the maintenance of a viable Republican and Democratic party. They operate collaboratively with district and local organizations below and with the national structures above them. They are infrastructures of coordination, accommodation, and liaison, working on state problems with state leaders to resolve conflicts and promote party harmony.

Variations in State Parties and Their Political Environments

It has been said that the United States has one hundred different state party systems, and a study of state organizations indicates this characterization may be true. State organizations live in different social and political environments and thus seem to develop differently. To begin with, state parties reveal great differences in the extent of organizational unity. The analysis of contests within the parties for state office reveals this. In some states party factions fight regularly for leadership positions; in others there are rarely such primary contests. For example, relatively few primaries are contested in Connecticut, but all of them are contested in both parties in Missouri, Washington, Kentucky, and in the Democratic or Republican party in thirteen other states.[10] At national conventions the state party delegations may be very unified in their voting (such as the California and Wisconsin Republicans, and the Illinois and New Jersey Democrats) while other states seem very divided (such as Iowa for the Republicans and California for the Democrats).

Further, state parties differ in their liberalness or conservativeness. Frank Munger and James Blackhurst studied state party voting patterns for presidential candidates in national conventions from the 1940s to the 1960s and found certain Democratic and Republican states remarkably consistent and unified over the years. There are about eight consistently liberal Democratic states (California, Michigan, Oregon, for example) and about fifteen which are consistently conservative. There are also about fourteen consistently conservative Republican state organizations (Illinois, Ohio, Nebraska, plus several in the South), but twelve Republican state organizations which seem much more liberal in presidential candidate voting preferences. The remaining states are moderate in their voting tendencies at national conventions.[11]

Thus, two pictures emerge—one of considerable factionalism and disunity; the other of variations, within the parties, in terms of ideological differences. The effect of these conditions on the way politics is conducted in a state may be very great. In a state like Michigan where there is a low level of organizational cohesion in both parties, and both parties reveal fairly consistent liberal orientations, the nature of party combat, the type of leadership, and the direction of policy is of a different cast than in Illinois, where both parties rank high on organizational unity and also are conservative (very conservative for the Republicans, rather conservative for the Democrats). Contrast these two situations, however, with California politics, where there is high Republican party unity and relative conservatism, but low Democratic party unity and very consistent liberalism. The conditions of state party competition as parties square off against each other in each state, thus, vary a great deal.

Further, the political turnout environment in each state within which the parties have to compete varies greatly. As table 7.1 reveals, the proportion of voters going to the polls ranges from an average of 72 percent in Utah to 32 percent in Georgia. The relevance of such a fact to the nature of party competition in a state is great. Parties will function quite differently in a situation of voter apathy than of greater voter involvement. In one-party areas it makes the task of the opposition party to persuade candidates to run much more difficult in areas of low voter turnout. In 1976, for example, there were twenty-five uncontested House seats, and seventeen in the South, where the average voter turnout is lowest.

No doubt other environmental conditions under which state and

TABLE 7.1
Mean Percentage of Turnout, 1962–72
(President, Governor, Senator, Representative)

State		State	
Utah	71.9	Nebraska	57.4
South Dakota	67.7	California	57.3
Idaho	67.1	Kansas	57.1
Montana	67.1	New Jersey	56.9
North Dakota	66.8	New Mexico	56.2
Minnesota	66.2	New York	55.3
Indiana	65.7	Ohio	55.2
Wyoming	65.1	Oklahoma	51.5
Illinois	63.9	Hawaii	51.3
Connecticut	63.4	Nevada	49.5
West Virginia	63.3	Arizona	47.1
Rhode Island	63.1	Maryland	45.0
New Hampshire	62.3	Alaska	44.7
Delaware	62.2	North Carolina	44.0
Washington	62.0	Kentucky	43.9
Massachusetts	61.55	Tennessee	42.8
Vermont	61.5	Florida	41.5
Iowa	60.9	Arkansas	39.9
Oregon	60.1	Louisiana	38.3
Wisconsin	60.0	Alabama	38.1
Pennsylvania	59.4	Texas	37.9
Maine	58.43	Mississippi	37.7
Colorado	58.4	Virginia	34.1
Michigan	58.3	South Carolina	34.0
Missouri	57.5	Georgia	31.8

SOURCES: Austin Ranney, "Parties in State Politics," in Jacob and Vines, eds., *Politics in the American States: A Comparative Analysis*, 3rd ed., (New York: Little, Brown, 1976), p. 54. *Copyright © 1976 by Little, Brown and Company, Inc. Reprinted by permission.* See also *The American Almanac, 1974* (New York: Grosset & Dunlap, 1974); R. Scammon, ed., *America Votes* (Washington, D.C.: Governmental Affairs Institute and Congressional Quarterly Inc., 1962–72).

local parties have to function—such as the type of direct primaries states have, the nature of the ballot, and similar legal regulatory conditions—limit the party organization's effectiveness or at least require extra efforts by the party to mobilize support.

V. O. Key said that the strength of the state party organizations and their competitiveness determined the type of policies the citizens in a state would see adopted and hence determined their social and economic welfare. The organization interacts with its political environment, reflected in the level of voter interest and the nature of its opposition. Strong organizations in a healthy political environment should mean more effective governmental action. In the last analysis this is the critical linkage.

District and County Levels of Organization

District and county units may be, depending on the locality, key cogs in the state party structure. The obvious reason for this is that they are the geographical electoral areas from which congressmen, state legislative personnel, and county governmental personnel are selected. Theoretically, therefore, the party organization at these levels would have an important role to play in electing these individuals. This may be the case, depending on the type of campaign organization the party candidates for Congress, state Senate, county sheriff, et cetera, wish to put together. Often they will indeed depend on the district and county organizations; often they prefer to set up their own ad hoc organizations.

The county, or district, chairperson is traditionally considered to have a powerful position. In earlier days, before the primary, the recruitment and nomination of candidates was an important task, but this has declined, although county and district chairmen may in certain areas still spend a great deal of time persuading party regulars or outsiders to run for office—or not to run. Although this function may be of less importance today, the county or district chairman can still have a major power role. If the party is in power in the state and/or county, there may be considerable patronage to dispense, and this is ordinarily funneled through the county or district chairman's office. As the coordinator and planner of party activities in the area (not only the planning of the county convention) the chairperson has a major responsibility. He can build the organization from the precinct and township on up, particularly if there is no strong city organization in the area. Building a strong party machine in the area is a goal which may either be satisfying in itself or may be a stepping-stone to a higher career. The county and district chairpersons are often kingpins in the state organization, playing major roles at the state convention, being consulted by the state leaders before any critical decisions are made. While the potential for a significant role is there, the county and district chairpersons often operate in dangerous conditions. They have to maintain harmony among the many warring factions in the organization, some of whose leaders may aspire to the very position the leader is seeking to preserve. A study of Detroit congressional district party leaders found that dealing with factions was the overwhelming priority. Here are quotations from two chairmen,

The district chairman has to be a Sherlock Holmes in the Republican party. We have, as you know, many splits in our party, and there is a constant battle of wits as to who is for whom.

Let's take this district here. There are two major racial groups, the Negroes and the Jews. But it is not only nationality groups, but also political groups— for example, we have the Young Democrats and the CIO. We do not have a right wing faction, but we have small businessmen's interests and labor interests. Our trade unions are split into two separate units, even though they are externally united. The AFL is conservative, the CIO is the liberal group. . . . [12]

Clearly these leaders are aware of the linkage of the organization to socioeconomic interest groups. They also are realists and know how fragile their hold on power is!

County and district committees can be important adjuncts of the chairperson's activities, as well as important representatives of all the diverse activists in the area. They also can be merely social get-togethers, relatively quiet, and performing only intermittently. Yet to get on a county or district committee, may be an important goal for the party worker. The county or district convention, which used to hold the all-important nominating function (now taken over by the direct primary), is still usually the basic representative link of the party with the local activists. It is the first stepping-stone upward in a party career, and from this convention the aspiring careerist can go to the state convention as a delegate or assume other responsibilities in the party. But the heavy emphasis in the county and district arenas is *organizational* influence.

How active county organizations are in the United States is hard to say. One recent study which asked state chairpersons to provide an estimate (which is highly dependent on the accuracy of their knowledge) concluded that 14 percent of the counties were not active while at the other extreme 23 percent were very active, and the balance in various degrees of activity. [13] Activity, of course, can mean many different things. Nevertheless these limited data do not suggest that party organization at the county level is a great void.

The City, Ward, and Precinct Organizational Levels

This in many respects is the most fascinating level of the party. However, to generalize about party organization at the local level is well-nigh impossible. Local party organization varies by region, state, and by communities within states. In some states there may only be town committees or clubs and no wards or precincts. The form of organization and the functions performed by these lower units can vary greatly. Such differences are linked to political traditions which influence party practices.

The style of local party organization is actually bewildering in its variety. Although the day of the city boss and his party machine is allegedly behind us, the signs of machine politics of the old style can still be found in certain areas. On the other hand, a majority (73 percent in 1975) of cities with a population of 25,000 and over has *nonpartisan* elections, which doesn't mean the party organization is completely quiescent but does contribute to a different type of party environment. Another special condition is found in states with voluntary clubs at the base of the organization—such as the Wisconsin and California clubs which were set up before World War II. More recently there have been club movements in the borough of Manhattan in New York (the City Reform Democrats, for example), the California Democratic and Republican clubs, and volunteer clubs in Illinois, Pennsylvania, Ohio, and Missouri.[14] Partisan politics differs at the local level and leads to great diversity in party organizational form. At the risk of oversimplification, all that can be done here is to summarize from the available literature some of the major characteristics of American local party organization.

It must be realized first, that local party organization is very voluntaristic. The organization is usually wide open to anyone who is interested in participating. Positions are usually not rewarded by pay or by patronage or other material rewards. Individuals are not trained but often learn on the job and eventually do achieve some real competence for party work. Self-starters and those who are not recruited by the party leadership make up a large proportion of the workers and those who hold precinct and ward positions. Turnover is considerable each year. Studies reveal that even for a majority party up to a third of the lower level positions (such as precinct positions) in an area may be unfilled, and many more are filled by untrained personnel.[15] Further, many lower level leaders are brought into the organization by friends, family members, and working associates, or join by themselves. Thus, the need for workers is continuous, recruitment is haphazard, with no careful screening of available personnel, and people are appointed often by default, because there is no one else for the position.

In certain big city machines, however, even very recently, there was much more control over the selection of party personnel than the above description would indicate. Patronage was (and, to some extent in some areas, still is) important as the incentive and reward for local party personnel. Mayor Daley is reputed to have had thirty thousand to thirty-five thousand jobs to give out through the Cook County Democratic organization.[16] A 1970 study claimed that three-fourths of Pittsburgh's Democratic committeemen held public jobs. During John Lindsay's administration in New York, there were thirteen thousand personnel on "temporary" appointments and another seventy-five thousand noncompetitive jobs not under civil service.[17] There are no systematic studies to indicate how much patronage is still available as payment to party personnel, but the above illustrations are exceptions rather than the rule. In many large cities no more than 10 percent of precinct leaders are on the public payroll. For the large majority of local party personnel, therefore, it is basically a voluntaristic and avocational role.

A second characteristic is the diversity in the backgrounds, interests, expertise, and incentives of people who work at the local level. It is obvious that with such little control over entry in party activism and into precinct and ward positions it is inevitable that the workers will not be a homogeneous, like-minded group. Again, local organizations will vary a great deal in the class, racial, ethnic, and other demographic characteristics of their activists. In some areas there is a tendency toward more middle-class backgrounds; in others, more working-class. Some wards may be almost entirely lower-class blacks, others may be middle-class Polish Catholics, others upper-class professional Protestant whites. Although there will be these clusters of socially homogeneous neighborhoods with their socially homogeneous party activists, the local party organization for the entire community will be a great mixture. And the potential for differences in perspective, for controversy over ideology and policy, and, hence, for disruptive factionalism is considerable. Above all, such heterogeneity makes it difficult to achieve party harmony.

A third characteristic of the local party organizations is its improvising mode of operation: there is a looseness, flexibility, and informality in how local party cadres operate. They are not very much controlled and resort to their own ingenuity. Since there is much autonomy at the local level, the local ward and precinct leader and his coterie of supporters and workers (often family and friends) can decide by themselves how much to do and what to do. Communication is often poor, either from the city level downward or from ward to ward and precinct to precinct laterally. Thus, leaders often define their own tasks and roles. This may mean that nothing is done or the precinct work is done poorly, but it may also mean that it is done well and done in a way adapted to the conditions of the people living in a particular neighborhood. In a sense the local level of party operations is a small army or company of party activists who have somehow wandered into the party operations and then are left very often to themselves to improvise as best they can in order to maximize the party's goals, however they conceive these goals. This, again, is to a great extent the derivative of a centrifugal and stratarchical system.

A fourth characteristic of the local structures is that they often thrive on and reflect apathy about politics. Few citizens take an active and continuous interest in local elections. The median percentage of eligible voters turning out for city elections in 1975 was 29 percent. Fewer of them will take the time to vote for precinct delegates to county conventions or participate in the election of precinct, ward, and city leaders at annual meetings. As a consequence, local party elections can often be controlled by a small number of votes, precinct leadership and delegate positions are won by default, and reform of the local party organization usually does not occur. When attempted, however, it can be easier than originally predicted. The local party establishment survives often because of inert opposition. Except for occasional reform movements, there is infrequently an interest in ideology and in policy innovation. The organization is in the hands of activists whose interest is fleeting or careerists who are not innovators in policy, indeed who may not be very well informed on policy matters. The pressure for policy leadership so badly needed at the city, county, state, and national levels of the party organizations is minimal and infrequent. Status quo politics flourishes under these conditions, for state and national leaders hesitate to risk policy innovation in the absence of pressure from below.

A fifth and final basic characteristic of local parties is organizational slack, that is, a tendency for the local activists to perform at a minimal level of efficiency, without too much system, in a rather hit-and-miss mode of operation. In an efficiently functioning local organization able personnel man the key posts in the wards and precincts with sufficient workers who have been adequately trained and know their jobs. In a well-run local party organization there is a plan of operation, a campaign strategy, an effective communication system. However, rarely does the local organization function at full capacity. The absolutely critical tasks to be performed in a precinct are:

A. Organizational Tasks
   1. Up-to-date, complete records on all registered voters (at minimum, on all registered voters who have been classified as probably supportive of the party). These records should be cross-referenced by name and street.
   2. Adequate number of workers who are trained or in the process of being trained and who are reliable.
   3. Meetings with the activist personnel in which the plan for the campaign

is discussed and the procedure for the deployment of personnel explained in detail. Follow up communication by precinct leader is necessary throughout the campaign—by phone, personal contact, or other meetings.

B. Groundwork Activities—Before and Between Elections
1. Registration drives. Periodically it is necessary to see that new people coming into the area and those who have not been registered before and who may be own party supporters are registered to vote. This should be selectively done if possible and linked to the local strategy for the party.
2. Fund-raising drives. The precinct party has to participate in the statewide or countywide money-raising efforts, as well as see that its own treasury is adequate for planned local efforts.
3. Public rallies, coffee hours, and social events. Periodically between elections, as well as in campaigns, the local party should invite the public to rallies and events, to inform them of the activities of the party, to encourage them to be involved, and to try to make politics exciting and interesting to them.

C. Vote Mobilization Activities. A great variety of alternative techniques can be utilized.
1. House-to-house canvassing. The aim should be the 100 percent canvass—or the contact of every registered voter, at his or her home, who might possibly support the party. Careful records should be kept of the nature and results of each such contact.
2. Telephone canvassing. This can either substitute for the house-to-house canvass or be used in the last few days before the election to remind those who were contacted earlier.
3. Distribution of literature. A certain amount of written material can be sent to each voter in the precinct (there is a sharp disagreement on how much of this is worthwhile) in order to inform the voter of the candidates, the issues, and the existence of a party to which they can be affiliated in the precinct if they want to.
4. Election day round-up. The critical payoff of all this effort is, of course, on election day. And a precise schedule of activities must be planned and tasks assigned for all workers—challengers at the voting places who check off from the precinct lists those who have voted, runners who transmit this information to precinct headquarters, telephoners who call those who by midafternoon and later have not yet voted, chauffeurs who can take voters to the polls, and baby-sitters for mothers who need one in order to vote. Without a system on election day much of the effort may not reach its fruition.

Admittedly, these are rigorous criteria for efficiency and many precinct or ward operations should not be expected to measure up to this. Nevertheless, it is enlightening to look at a party organization to see to what extent it does approach this ideal. A study of the Republican and Democratic party organizations in Detroit and Wayne County, Michigan, was made in 1956. The results are revealing (see table 7.2).[18]

In 1980 Detroit precinct leaders were interviewed again. When 1956 is compared with 1980, a higher level of activity is found for Democrats and about the same level for Republicans.

TABLE 7.2

Efficiency of Political Organizations, Wayne County, Michigan, 1956

Task	Percentage of Precinct Leaders Performing Specific Tasks	
	Democrats	*Republicans*
Records adequate	48	44
Workers (at least three)	42	18
Meetings (at least two in the campaign)	34	10
Registration	93	80
House-to-house canvassing or telephoning	46	32
Election day roundup	68	80

SOURCE: Samuel J. Eldersveld, *Political Parties: A Behavioral Analysis* (Chicago: Rand McNally, 1964) pp. 74–75.

Two major observations emerge from these data: there are very efficient operations in some precincts; this is true, however, in only a small minority of precincts—less than 25 percent are operating at a peak level of efficiency, performing the critical tasks of registration, canvassing, and election day roundup of the voters. In Detroit there is inadequate organization in more than one-half of the precincts. The Democrats had a better record than the Republicans on balance, but one-half of the Democrats did not canvass house-to-house and one-third did not engage in election day work. Above all, the impression is left of a great deal of autonomy and improvisation. Forty-seven percent of the Republican precinct captains were classified as lone operators (and 26 percent of the Democrats), persons who were running the precinct alone without help and few contacts.[19] Finally, these data do not really support the contention that there has been a decline in local party activities in the past twenty-five years. Only a minority of local leaders are meeting the requisites for efficiency in 1956 and 1980.

TABLE 7.3

Percentage of Precinct Leaders Who Performed the Critical Tasks

	Democrats		Republicans	
	1956	*1980*	*1956*	*1980*
Three critical tasks: registration, house-to-house canvassing, election day roundup	17	30	25	16
Two critical tasks	38	35	22	34
	55	65	47	50

Studies reveal also that precinct leaders are relatively active in party work between elections—holding rallies, social events, giving advice to and aiding constituents. Further, over half usually are joiners and involved in the community life by belonging to social groups. These contacts may be of considerable value in vote mobilization work.

The local party has tremendous potential organizational power. This is obvious from the evidence of this great organizational slack. If the local party is activated and mobilized properly it can be extremely effective.[20] Why isn't the potential mobilizational power of the ward and precinct realized more frequently? A combination of factors is responsible: activists are often ignorant of what to do, and are poorly trained, advised, and led. The motivation to put a great deal of time into the precinct work doesn't exist often, either because the candidates are not attractive or the issues not clear-cut. Conflicts among factions destroy the sense of organizational unity and purpose and also result in the loss of a tremendous amount of time spent in promoting harmony. Local leaders may be engaged in a holding operation, feeling no need to exert themselves in order to hold to their position and its prerogatives. The turnover rate is high and thus the local effort is too sporadic and not a continuous operation, hence start-up costs for each campaign are considerable. The system of rewards for local activists may be inadequate to keep them performing at a high level of efficiency— little patronage, limited chances for upward mobility, inadequate recognition. All these are important reasons but there is a more basic condition. What will activate a local political party is an organization which is exciting to be a part of, which is working effectively for community projects, which involves people with the party in a social, as well as a political, sense. If this element of excitement and involvement in worthwhile projects is present and the local party has able, dedicated leadership, the local organization can be dynamically involved, produce the vote, demonstrate its organizational power, and in the process have a great effect on the community.

Bosses and Political Machines: Are They Withering Away?

In March 1979, an event occurred which some considered impossible. Jane Byrne defeated Mayor Michael Bilandic and the Chicago Democratic machine in the primary, thus being virtually assured of election as the next Chicago mayor. *Time* magazine quoted Alderman Vito Marzullo before the election as saying, "The Machine may not be well oiled but it will never break down. Mayor Bilandic is going to swamp them."[21] But the Daley-Bilandic machine did break down to the surprise of many. The question raised by many now is, Have we seen the last of the political boss and his machine?

American party politics is often considered by foreigners to be unique because of the phenomenon of big city bosses with their machines. James Bryce in the *American Commonwealth* described bosses and rings at the turn of the century and while cautioning his European readers not to take too dim a view of "the Boss," said, "He is a leader to whom certain peculiar social and political conditions have given a character dissimilar from the party leaders whom Europe knows."[22] It may be argued that this was not so in Europe in Bryce's time nor today, but the machine is still considered one of our unique contributions to government. To think of machine politics is to think of organizations led by such bosses as Tom Platt and William Tweed of New York, Frank Hague of Jersey City, Edward Crump of Memphis, Tennessee, Huey Long of Louisiana, J. Henry Roraback of Connecticut, Anton Cermak of Chicago, Tom Pendergast of Kansas City, Missouri, Jim Curley of Boston. What was comprehended in the conception of these earlier, classic machines? Essentially they were considered to be authoritarian structures dominated by a boss, carefully organized as command structures with authority exercised from the top down and responsibility from the bottom up, and a cohesive group of individuals which systematically and efficiently (like a machine) performed the tasks of the party (in particular electing leaders and mobilizing votes and distributing patronage) while exploiting the political system for private purposes. In the classic type the emphasis was on:

1. Hierarchical control of the organization, and usually also centralization of authority over the entire urban political community
2. Vote mobilization linked to the provision of a great range of services to the public
3. A material reward system with patronage and financial success coming to those who performed efficiently in the hierarchy
4. Iron discipline and use of a variety of sanctions in maintaining the highest level of efficiency and in replacing those who were not continuously productive
5. Very little emphasis on ideology although the machine often did promote particular programs of action
6. Manipulation, through the use of the public power of the machine, of other groups and sectors of the community, including the media, labor, business, et cetera
7. Utilization of threats, intimidation, surveillance, violence, and harassment to make organization of an opposition difficult
8. Tolerance of illicit and corrupt actions and relationships as the rewards of power
9. Fraud on election day in vote-getting activities and election administration
10. A very limited ethic of day-to-day responsibility of the machine to the public, except in the special sense of providing services to maximize votes

These were the attributes of the old-style machines, most of which in this extreme form had disappeared by the 1960s. A conception of political organization which was considered peculiarly American, it came into existence in the latter part of the nineteenth century and thrived in the early twentieth century as the response to the needs of the immigrants who were swarming into our cities, the needs of the poor which were not ministered to properly by government, the dissatisfaction of citizens with the poor government they were getting, and the emergence of a type of personal leader who saw the possibility of accumulating personal power by building a special type of political organization combining vote-getting with social welfare. Because it performed critical political functions, fulfilled many human needs, and, as most studies of this early period show, because voters were satisfied with the kind of government they got, these machines survived. The machine was a cohesive structure which, whatever else its shortcomings might have been, provided leadership.

There are still many machines with somewhat different characteristics in the United States (and in Europe) today. But this old-style machine has been disappearing for some time. Perhaps the only one which survived into the 1970s in large cities in this classic form is the Chicago machine, which was created by Mayor Anton Cermak in 1931 and was continued by Mayor Edward Kelly and Patrick Nash from 1933 to 1947, by Mayor Martin Kennelly (despite his attempts at reforms) from 1947 to 1955, and then flourished in classic form under Mayor Richard Daley until he died in late 1976. Mayor Bilandic carried on after him until his defeat by Jane Byrne in March 1979. Mayor Byrne, it is now alleged, is attempting to control the machine which she formerly served.

That the Daley machine was a classic cannot be denied. The journalistic accounts and analyses of writers like Mike Royko of the *Chicago Sun-Times* and Professor Milton L. Rakove have described its recent nature in detail. The 3,500 precincts in Chicago in the 50 wards each have a captain and most have an assistant captain, making upwards of $15,000 a year on patronage jobs.[23] Below them there are those who have lower jobs in government (swinging mops at the county hospital, digging ditches, et cetera) and who help out at election time, contribute part of their salaries (estimated at 2 percent), and engage in other party activities such as attending political fund-raising dinners. Above these personnel are the ward committeemen (of which there are fifty)—"the clout," "the chinaman," "the guy," and "our beloved leader."[24] It is a well-articulated structure with power delegated and responsibility specified. Power is delegated from the Cook County central committee of the party to the fifty ward committeemen and from them to the precinct captains. "The entire system operates on the principle of autonomy of authority at each level in the political pyramid."[25] Daley was at the top of this pyramid. Vote production is a responsibility and failure means discipline, loss of a job. Daley personally took an interest in the disciplining action. "The leverage a political boss can exert on his lieutenants is directly in ratio to the patronage and other benefits that he can grant or withhold from them. Daley absolutely controlled all such matters in Chicago."[26]

The description of the actual functioning of the Daley machine is fascinating reading, as Rakove describes it. The patronage clearance system was precise. For example, a young Chicago attorney in the Democratic party (a precinct captain of Daley's machine) being considered in Washington for an appointment to a federal regulatory commission had to get Daley's approval, but this was not possible without the ward committeeman's approval, who in turn checked with his other precinct captains before endorsing him and informing Daley of his approval.[27] An estimated thirty thousand jobs locally were distributed through this system. Precinct captains usually held down these patronge jobs as long as they produced. Before elections they must estimate what their precinct's vote will be. If they cannot do this fairly accurately (being too low is as bad as too high in one's estimates) their reputations suffer and it is assumed they are not in touch with the public.[28] A captain who had lost his precinct and abjectly reported to his superior was asked by his ward committeeman bluntly, "What kind of a job are you going to look for now?" The ward committeeman has considerable power in such a system. The famous leader of the Twenty-fifth Ward Vito Marzullo at one election said, "The mayor don't run the twenty-fifth ward. Neither does the news media or the do-gooders. Me, Vito Marzullo. That's who runs the twenty-fifth ward, and on election day everybody does what Vito Marzullo tells them."[29]

Marzullo is an Italian immigrant, seventy-seven years old, who came to Chicago at the age of twelve, and spent over fifty-five years in politics there after only a fourth-grade education.

The services performed by precinct captains are extremely diverse— legal service for the poor, repair of broken street lights, more police squad patrols in a neighborhood, special antirodent cleanups, new garbage cans for tenants provided by landlords, and talks with probation officers for youngsters in trouble. In middle-class neighborhoods precinct captains can help get tax bills appealed, curbs and gutters repaired, scholarships for students to the University of Illinois, summer jobs for students, and help with the bureaucracy. Marzullo says he has

the most cosmopolitan ward in Chicago—30% blacks, 20% Polish, 12 to 15% Mexican, 5% Italian, Slovenians, Lithuanians, Bohemians . . . but I take care of all my people . . . . My home is open 24 hours a day. . . . I'll go to a wake, a wedding, whatever. I never ask anything in return. On election day, I tell my people, "Let your conscience be your guide."[30]

Marzullo tells his captains, "Mingle with the people. Learn their way of life. Work and give service to your people." According to Rakove, on election day every captain gets between $50 and $200 for expenses in his precinct. What the precinct leader does is adapted to the individual needs of people. A top Democratic leader in Cook County maintained that there has been a considerable change in the types of services provided: "The political organization today [in the 1970s] is a service organization, an ombudsman, and an inquiry department. I consider my ward has fifty-seven community organizations doing public service [by his fifty-seven precinct captains—his 'community representatives']."[31]

Another leader agreed, saying, "To a great extent the service we offer now is referral." Daley's language, in March 1975, to describe his precinct captain's services and work is interesting:

He never gets in the newspapers unless he is criticized. He's as honest as the rest of us and he's a better neighbor than most of us . . . . He has solicitude for the welfare of the family in his block . . . . He gets your broken-down uncle into the county hospital, if he lives in the slums. He's always available when you're in trouble. . . . The people who make up the Democratic party of the city of Chicago are always and will always be a reflection of the people in their respective neighborhoods. Until someone devises a better method of Democratic political organization that has a broad base of precinct captains who punch doorbells and recite the virtues of their party and candidates, we ought to be more careful in our moral judgment about a political party. . . . As long as we have the kind of organization we have in the city of Chicago, we will time and time again be victorious.[32]

Rakove's overall image of the classic Chicago machine is worth keeping in mind:

As an organism, the Chicago machine is a hydra-headed monster. It encompasses elements of every major political, economic, racial, ethnic, religious, governmental, and paramilitary power group within the city. It recognizes the reality of all forms of power . . . and it understands the need to subordinate all . . . forms of power to the political. . . . The machine believes with Machiavelli that men in politics are greedy, emotional, and passionate and are not governed by reason, morality, or concern for their fellowman. It believes that men can be coopted, bought, persuaded or frightened into subservience to or cooperation with the machine. Every man has his price, according to the machine. . . .[33]

This then is the image of the classic machine. Its decline has long been celebrated by many scholars. The old-style machine has been disappearing because, it is argued, the adoption of the merit system has led to the decline of patronage. Further, it is claimed that the absence for some time of the conditions which produced this type of organization originally have led to its demise: the need to take care of immigrants, ignorant of living conditions in the big city, has disappeared as has the need for social welfare services since presumably these are now taken care of through governmental and other private agencies. It is also argued that the public is not willing to tolerate the machine today because of its manipulative and illicit activities and techniques.

Has the political machine really disappeared from American politics? Those who take this position are thinking only of the old-style boss and his very specialized authoritarian structure. Other types of party machines are conceivable. And there certainly is still a need for political organizations in American cities (and in cities everywhere) to provide certain services and fill certain human needs. Raymond Wolfinger has raised the question in his article entitled, "Why Political Machines Have Not Withered Away" and concludes both that the need for machines continues to exist and that although these needs may be left unfulfilled in certain areas, certain types of machines still do exist, but that the types of constituent services they perform now are different. Direct material assistance to the poor is still necessary, but new types of welfare assistance are required (such as helping people get into public housing units), while new types of help (for small businessmen, for example) and for those dealing with the bureaucracy may be necessary. There are basic social conditions in most American cities of medium and large size which require and will reward (with votes) a political organization with some of the characteristics of a machine.[34]

The basic point is that political machines can be of many different types. The Daley machine with its emphasis on discipline, payoffs, patronage, and loyalty to a leader is not the only type. Other types of machines can be suggested by utilizing two of the key dimensions of the classical machine and conceiving of organizations which have opposite characteristics (see fig. 7.3).

The Daley machine was an authoritarian, materialist-oriented structure. But theoretically there can be authoritarian, ideological structures (as the fascist type of organization), decentralized materialist structures, and nonmaterialist, decentralized structures. In fact, some of the local party organizations today tend to be either decentralized and materialist, or decentralized and nonmaterialist, or hybrid structures with a mixture of these characteristics. Yet, they may still be machines in the sense of being relatively efficient organizations for the performance of particular types of political functions. The workings of the party in American municipalities show that many of the conditions of the classic political machine no longer exist—the intimidation, the bla-

FIGURE 7.3

A Two-Dimensional Classification of Party Machine Types

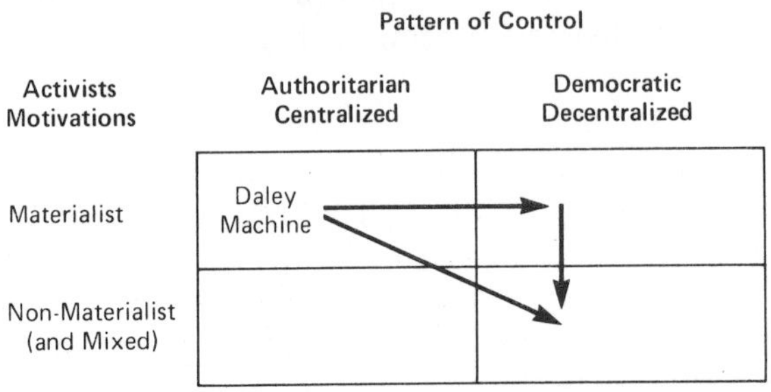

Pattern of Control

Activists Motivations	Authoritarian Centralized	Democratic Decentralized
Materialist	Daley Machine	
Non-Materialist (and Mixed)		

NOTE: Arrows suggest possible trends.

tant manipulation, the fraudulent control of votes, the use of the payroll to reward all party personnel, the unquestioning loyalty to a leader. But machines, in the sense of a rather cohesive group of committed partisans, inside and outside the formal organization of the party, doggedly and tirelessly performing the tasks of the party (screening candidates, raising money, recruiting workers, registering voters, getting out the vote) and being rewarded on other than purely materialistic grounds—are often a reality. It is easy for people to shout at Chicago on election night as they did when Jane Byrne defeated Mayor Bilandic, "There is no more machine. There will never be a machine again,"[35] but surely this is a misconception. Where there is politics there will be machines, otherwise the work of politics at the local level would never be completed.

Evaluation of the Local Organizations

What basic images should there be of the parties as local structures? First they are the structures which maintain the closest personal relationships to the public and, therefore, can be repositories of important powers of the party: power to select candidates, to produce the vote, to raise money, to recruit personnel, to determine issue positions (at least at the local level), to reward the activists, to seek to control elected candidates, to develop party membership, even to discipline their members. They can be influential and powerful if they are well organized and wish to assert their powers. Here is where the bulk of the party's power can lie. The concerting together or coordination of a large number of effective local precinct and ward operations can mean a successful county, district, state, and national party.

The problem with most local party structures is, again, the looseness and diffuseness of control (aside from the few boss-run machines today). At the local party level are the same maladies found as at state and national levels—fragmentation in authority, no centralized leadership, no clear lines of responsibility. The local organizations are not undemocratic oligarchies basically, but they are also not strongly democratic structures where members have rights and duties and participate effectively and regularly in making party decisions. A key problem is that there is no membership concept as most European parties have, the idea of the card-carrying, dues-paying member who has voting and other participatory rights and roles in the organization. The closed direct primary states attempted to move in that direction but very ineffectually. The idea of a mass membership-based party is something rarely found in the United States at the local level.

Another problem with most local party structures is that they are preoccupied with organizational tasks more than with deliberation on policy and utilization of the organization to achieve policy goals. Local party politics is often just not very issue-oriented, partly because in over 70 percent of the cities the local elections are nonpartisan but also because there is no local tradition to see the party as basically a policy instrument. The idea is to elect candidates to office and then give them free rein unless their behavior is so outrageous as to require opposition in the succeeding party primary. Strengthening the policy deliberative role of the local party would make involvement with the local party infinitely more attractive. When the local party has been activated, it is usually due to policy controversies.

All local organizations are not of one type, however. They differ in several basic dimensions:

1. They can tend to be hierarchies, or stratarchy systems with much autonomy and democratic control.
2. They can be wide open systems which anyone can join, with great diversity of personnel, or they can be relatively closed membership systems.
3. They can be voluntaristic structures with a haphazard incentive system, or one which has developed a reward system based on recognition of work done, patronage, or other material rewards.
4. They can place considerable emphasis on the role of ideology in recruiting members, selecting candidates, and running campaigns, or they can ignore the role of ideology.
5. They can be highly efficient structures with well-trained cadres performing the critical tasks of maintaining contact with the public and getting out the vote, or they can be quiescent and utterly inefficient and status quo structures.

Local parties in a democratic society such as ours, if they are to maximize their power and role, are inclined to be nonhierarchical, open, voluntaristic, nonideological, and inefficient given the conditions of American society and political culture. There are, however, community differences and the possibility, indeed the capability, of local parties to move in other directions.

Despite the problems of American parties at the local level, local parties do exist, are active from time to time, and do perform important functions. They are the entry point for the member of the public who wishes to do more than just vote and wants to act through the instrument of party. They are usually his or her initial contact with the party system. Local parties are often structures through which other social interest groups work or with which they work in order to influence local governmental decision making. They are the important link between the national and state party organs and the public. They can represent the public's concerns (or that segment of the public which they see as their constituent group) upward when their delegates attend county, state, and national conventions or sit on county, state, or national party committees. The local party also links the elected candidate to the public and to his electoral constituency. In all this the local party organization can play a vital integrative role in the political system. Local parties are much more than merely symbolic. Even in their relatively ineffectual organizational condition, they can perform vital functions as critical links between the public and the government. When activated they can make the difference between stagnant consensus and policy innovation.

American local parties do much more than European parties usually do at the local level, except in Great Britain. On the Continent rarely do parties engage in any house-to-house canvassing because it is considered contrary to their political traditions, is believed to be resented by the public, and an invasion of the privacy of the home.[36] Telephone canvassing is equally unheard of in Europe. Of course, many European parties are organized as mass membership parties, may have professional agents directing party work (as in England), and may have different types of units at the base of the organization than in the United States. Without the payment of membership dues these parties would not be able to function. Parties in Europe are organized differently, and their role and techniques in getting out the vote are quite different than for American parties. There is much more reliance on the large rally, the sound truck, the distribution of literature, and candidate speeches and appearances. The local organization mobilizes votes differently. It usually has a reliable clientele who votes regularly. In the United States the task of the local organization to get out the vote is more demanding.

Finally, in evaluating local party structures it must be remembered that the local party is a social group as much as it is a political group. Fulfilling social as well as political functions for those whom it attracts and to whom it appeals, the party penetrates deeply into the social structure. To many, politics at the local level is social fun, and provides opportunities for social interaction as well as chances for social mobility. The party is thus a critical social institution for many Americans. The meaning of the local party for the activists will be discussed in a later chapter.

Chapter 8

Theories of Party

Organization

MANY SCHOLARS have addressed themselves to the question, What type of group is a party organization? In essence they want to know what are the major characteristics of a party as a human association. This has intrigued writers because it is assumed that the common interests and goals of parties have resulted in common structural tendencies. But there is much disagreement as to which characteristics are most important and what the organizational meaning and reality is. The most prominent of these theories will be described briefly here.

The Party Structure as an Inevitable Oligarchy

In 1911 a German who had been active in the radical syndicalist wing of the German Social Democratic party, a young scholar trained in sociology and frustrated with what he saw in the development of that party, wrote a book called *Political Parties: A Sociological Study of the Oligarchical Tendencies of Modern Democracy*. The man was Robert Michels. His book has had a profound influence on students of political groups and democracy throughout the world, presenting as it does a theory which is widely quoted, praised, tested, and denounced. There are those who say, "Michels was right, all is oligarchy." There are also those who say, "The theory of oligarchy is an inaccurate and gross misrepresentation of reality." Whatever one's reaction, it is necessary to understand the key elements of this seminal theory.

Michels begins with two basic premises: parties must be studied as organizations which exist for themselves (the party has its own soul); and parties must be understood in the power context, as struggling for power. He then describes the party:

> It is [an] organization which gives birth to the dominion of the elected over the electors, of the mandatories over the mandators, of the delegates over the delegators. Who says organization, says oligarchy. . . .
>
> As a result of organization, every party . . . becomes divided into a minority of directors and a majority of directed. . . .
>
> It is indisputable that the oligarchical and bureaucratic tendency of party organizations is a matter of technical and practical necessity. It is the inevitable product of the very principle of organization.[1]

Michels's theory explains step by step what happens to a political party from the time of its early origins. It begins as a small group of individuals who have certain goals, principles, objectives (in the case of the German Social Democratic party, these original founders had a set of revolutionary ideals). As the organization increases in size, it becomes necessary to have certain individuals perform the elementary managerial tasks. Gradually a leadership develops in the group, individuals with organizational skills, and these become more important as the organization increases in size and as differentiation and specialization of structure take place. The need for leadership, the learning of tasks, the satisfaction with the expertise acquired, and the willingness of the ordinary members to have such leadership means that the original spontaneous type of leadership becomes more professional. And with this goes power. The leadership then becomes entrenched. They assert their right to leadership, having convinced themselves not only that this is what the masses want, but also of their own superiority in the leadership function.

While this is going on at the apex of the organization, an increasing distance develops between the leadership and the rank-and-file. Leaders are preoccupied with their own tasks, the size of the organization interferes with the intimacy of relationships, the rank-and-file acquiesce in leadership being distant, an apathy develops at the base of the structure, and gradually the organization is transformed into a set of leaders and a mass base, with considerable space intervening between the two.

In the next phase of the dynamics of party organizational change, Michels pictures the leaders as developing into a cohesive elite group. They have acquired a taste for power and a desire to remain in power. Their incentives now are directed to the preservation of their leader-

FIGURE 8.1

Michels's Theory of Party Oligarchy

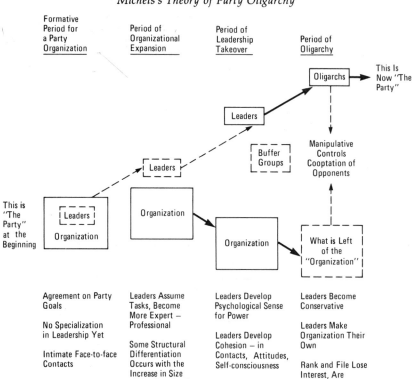

Formative Period for a Party Organization	Period of Organizational Expansion	Period of Leadership Takeover	Period of Oligarchy
Agreement on Party Goals	Leaders Assume Tasks, Become More Expert – Professional	Leaders Develop Psychological Sense for Power	Leaders Become Conservative
No Specialization in Leadership Yet	Some Structural Differentiation Occurs with the Increase in Size of the Organization	Leaders Develop Cohesion – in Contacts, Attitudes, Self-consciousness	Leaders Make Organization Their Own
Intimate Face-to-face Contacts		Increasing Distance Develops Between Leaders and Masses	Rank and File Lose Interest, Are Controlled

ship positions. They develop similar attitudes and orientations toward power and toward the party, attitudes congruent for the entire leadership group. In short, they become a like-minded elite, characterized by what Meisel calls the Three C's: "group consciousness, coherence, and conspiracy."[2] It follows from this also that they become conservative. "Power is always conservative," says Michels. As the organization develops, "the struggle for great principles becomes impossible."[3] The original (revolutionary) goals of the organization are forgotten by the oligarchs who conceive of the party now in terms of quite different goals, primarily personal goals.

In order to deal with the rank-and-file membership of the organization, and remain in power, the leadership utilizes a variety of techniques. They, of course, have control of the communication channels and thus can use these to inform, propagandize, rationalize their actions. They seek to control the intraorganizational electoral process through manipulation. They create buffer groups to protect the elite from the masses, committees which debate issues *in camera* and which therefore contain the conflict in the organization while providing for some catharsis. They coopt or amalgamate those members who challenge the leaders, bringing them into the elite group and socializing them properly. Thus, through a variety of techniques, the rank and file are manipulated and their control over the leadership is diminished until it becomes essentially inconsequential.

The consequences of these successive phases of party organizational development are striking. The leaders become a new political class, and *they* are the party. The party in its original organizational form has been emasculated. The few have taken it over, for their own purposes. Yet, this elite, since it is a party elite in a democratic society, must still win elections. So, Michels says, it periodically steps down to win votes. But since they cannot rely exclusively on their followers, they must appeal more broadly, to solicit openly the votes of all citizens.

Thus, over time the party has changed in its structural relationships, in its ideological goals, and in its coalitional character. Indeed the party has been conquered by its oligarchs.

There are, of course, many criticisms of this model despite the tendency of many scholars and students to agree with this conception of the party.[4]

1. The basic assumption is that political elites in modern societies are always exploitative of the masses, that political leaders only follow their self-interest. This has certainly not always been true. Many party leaders have been advocates of changes in society in order to improve the social and economic conditions of the masses.
2. It is claimed that leadership becomes conservative and *then* deviates from and destroys the progressive purposes of the organization. But conservative leadership is often a *response* to rank-and-file conservatism.
3. Democratic revolution and replacement of elites and oligarchs is much more possible than Michels will accept, and such replacement is often more than just a formal one. It can lead to basic changes in leadership policy initiatives.
4. The cohesiveness, cooptation, and manipulative control by leaders of the organization is overdone by Michels. In parties in democratic societies, there is much more mutual dependence and interaction than he recognizes.
5. Michels sees the party organization in a social vacuum. Parties are transformed in their leadership because they have to be responsive to social forces if they are to stay in power and win elections.

Despite these criticisms of Michels there are those who will argue that Michels's model of oligarchy is operative in parties in certain areas, under certain conditions, or that certain elements in Michels' model come very close to reality. The problem is to muster the evidence necessary to confirm or disprove Michels.

Party Organization as an Instrument of Revolution

"Give us an organization of revolutionaries and we shall overturn the whole of Russia." Thus wrote V. I. Lenin in his 1902 treatise laying out the plans for developing his organization to achieve the Russian revolution. He called his treatise "What Is to Be Done?" In it he elaborated the concept of the political party which he felt was necessary to overthrow the czar and establish the dictatorship of the proletariat.[5] His concept is worth studying for his prophetic insight and clarity in defining the nature of the party for his purposes. The party he planned was "the magnificent organization," the essence of which was "a small, compact core, consisting of the most reliable, experienced, and hardened workers, with responsible agents in the principal districts and connected by all the rules of strict secrecy with the organization of revolutionaries."

Lenin had seen what happened to the earlier clandestine revolutionary organizational efforts of the 1870s and 1880s, their vulnerability to the secret police and their weaknesses as effective structures. He was against relying merely on trade unions as the organizational base for improving the welfare of the working class. He wanted a party organization which was:

1. an elite cadre of trained professionals
2. controlled from the top down and disciplined
3. committed without question to the Revolution and "not [just for] their free evening but their whole life"[6]
4. a closed, secret leading cadre of members who were carefully screened
5. a mass base for the party of persons who will work for the party, will be deployed by the leading cadres wherever they are needed, but who will not constitute the hard core of the organization

Thus, Lenin said in 1902,

I assert (1) that no revolutionary movement can endure without a stable organization of leaders that maintains continuity; (2) that the wider the masses spontaneously are drawn into the struggle, forming the basis of the movement and participating in it, the more urgent the need of such an organization, and the more solid this organization must be. . . . (3) that such an organization must consist chiefly of people professionally engaged in revolutionary activity; (4) that in an autocratic state the more we *confine* the membership of such an organization to people who are professionally engaged in revolutionary activity and who have been professionally trained in the art of combating the political police the more difficult will it be to wipe out such an organization; and (5) the *greater* will be the number of people of the working class and of other classes of society who will be able to join the movement and perform active work in it.[7]

Trotsky, at the Second Party Congress of the Russian Social Democratic party which met in Brussels and then in London in the summer of 1903, said that in Lenin's view, "the organization of the Party takes the place of the Party itself; the Central Committee takes the place of the organizer, and finally the dictator takes the place of the Central Committee."[8]

This concept of party differs basically from that of Robert Michels. Whereas his theory of oligarchy conceived of the leadership as wresting the party from the hands of the membership, Lenin sees the party as created by the leaders and an organization in which the "ordinary cadres" and activists never have a controlling role. As in Michels's conception, Lenin's party structure is in the hands of a cohesive elite. But contrary to Michels, this elite nucleus runs the party for its idealistic revolutionary purposes, not for private gain. The function of ideology in the development of the party organization, thus, is considerably different, and in Lenin's image at least the final end of the party is ideology. Further, in Lenin's view there is no emphasis on the party in democratic, competitive terms.

The year 1917 brought to fruition Lenin's concept of party. There was, however, much disagreement on what the character of the party should be, particularly on how much internal factionalism and dissent would be tolerated. Lenin wanted a unified structure and successfully overcame the opposition. Subsequently, Stalin, after cleverly maneuvering the dissidents into the opposition, was able to become the head of a monolithic, elite party organization devoid—after the purges—of all dissent.

Party Organization as a Mass-Membership Structure

In 1951 the French scholar Maurice Duverger published a book in which he attempted to identify the basic characteristics of the mass party (as distinct from the cadre party, as well as what he called the devotee party). To him there had emerged a type of party organization in Western Europe which had a special "social and political substructure." This was the mass-membership party. The key characteristic of this type of party was a base of a large number of individuals in the citizen public who were "adherents" or "members" of the party, rather than just "supporters."[9] The party consisted thus of more than a set of leaders or notables (as a cadre party did); it consisted of leaders together with a set of adherents, who constituted the organizational group called "party." It should be noted that the "mass party" was distinct from the "devotee party," which included for Duverger Lenin's party, as well as fascist parties—elite parties based on devotion.

To Duverger the adherent had a special status in the mass party—he or she was a dues-paying member (thus solving the financial needs of the party) but also a person with certain responsibilities, opportunities, and equities, although this was emphasized less, in the organization. The leaders in a mass party interacted with the members, recruiting and training them for party duties, educating them to party goals, and selecting from the members those "capable of leadership and administration." Duverger was not arguing that the mass party was a democratic structure but rather that the existence at the base of the structure of a mass of adherents paying dues and committed to party work radically altered the meaning of the party. It was a structure of leaders interacting with members, often exploiting them, but nevertheless maintaining a continuing relationship with them in the pursuit of common goals.

This conception of the party is obviously distinct from both Michels' and Lenin's formulations, placing much more emphasis, as it does, on the role of rank-and-file adherents, on a mass base, and on the party as a leader-nonleader joint enterprise.

The concept of the mass party has existed for a long time. Duverger discussed the early forms and manifestations of such parties. The critical requirement for a mass party is the existence of a large body of members. Using Duverger's figures and those of other scholars, many parties in Britain and Western Europe, as well as in non-Western parts of the world, have been mass parties in this sense. The French Communists have had as many as 1 million dues-paying members; the British Conservatives almost 3 million; the British Labour Party 800,000 individual members; the German Social Democrats have been over the half-million mark for some time; the Italian Christian Democrats had 1.6 million in 1964. In India the Congress party which enrolled 17 million in 1949 had almost 9 million primary members in 1952, and declined to under 5 million in 1964.

Duverger suggested that the mass-based party was a working class phenomenon and was founded in Europe, but not in the United States. He felt that center, conservative, and right-wing parties were not the best examplars of the true mass-based party. The ideological orientation of the mass party to him was socialist. In this respect he was incorrect, for surely there are many instances of nonsocialist parties which are (or were) mass-membership structures. As for the observation that American parties are cadre parties and not mass-membership parties, basically Duverger is correct, although in some states and localities the Democratic and Republican parties have moved in the direction of mass memberships. Duverger himself recognized the possibility of this, suggesting that in the closed primary states (with more or less rigorous tests of party affiliation) the parties approach the mass-membership party concept—he called them semi-mass parties.

Party Organization of the American Boss (the Machine)

The classic American big city machine provides another model of party organization. The Daley machine in Chicago is an illustration of this concept of party organization, with its emphasis on hierarchical control, performance of services for constituents in exchange for votes, use of patronage and other types of public plunder in order to provide rewards for the faithful ward and precinct leaders, and penetration of the party into most aspects of the social and political life of the community. Some have called this the professional model of party organization; others the rational-efficient model. Studies have revealed that material incentives were heavily emphasized. The machine was above all a disciplined command structure.

In contrast to Michels's theory of oligarchy, Lenin's view of the party as an elite instrument of revolution, and Duverger's concept of the mass-membership party, the American boss and machine model has other special characteristics. First, its emphasis on ideology in the origin of the political organization or as a factor in subsequent functioning was negligible. Although it was, in a sense, a social welfare society, its strategies were pragmatic with its emphasis on social service as a means of getting out the vote. Second, the machine placed great emphasis on the relationship of interdependency and mutual support between the elite and those activists and supporters at the base of the structure. This distinguishes the machine from Michels's conception of oligarchy with its cadre party of elites distant from its rank and file. Third, the machine was not a mass-membership structure in the European sense. It financed its operations in other, more immediately lucrative ways and was not interested in the same types of political education as Duverger specified for European mass parties. The American machine, as an empirical model of a party structure, was distinct although in many ways as much an oligarchy.

The Party as an Amateur Association of Idealists

In contrast to the models discussed above, which place emphasis on the elitist element in party organizations, an alternative operation is variously called the amateur model or the party democracy model.

Several studies have appeared detailing the characteristics of the amateur organization, particularly in New York and California.[10] The important elements in this amateur model are:

1. For the activists committed to the amateur organization their interest in politics is ideological or at least not materialistic (as in the machine).
2. The activists differ in their social backgrounds from those in the professional model—they have more education, higher socioeconomic status, and many more women tend to be involved.
3. The control of the party is less elitist and the processes for decision making in the organization tend to be democratic.
4. The basic conception and meaning of the party are different for those in the amateur organization than for those in the professional machine. The party is seen as concerned with the broadly conceived problems in society, not in the narrow sense with providing services and social welfare in exchange for votes.

Thus, the amateur, as contrasted to the professional, is motivated by and sees political activity as linked to issues, is concerned that internal organizational procedures are democratic, emphasizes commitment to principles, and believes in contesting elections on the basis of clear-cut issue positions. Elected officials should be held strictly accountable, political convictions should not be compromised for victory at election time (or in the nomination process), and party loyalty may be less important than ideological causes. The professional, who places much more emphasis on length of party service and rewarding faithful party workers, theoretically takes positions which are at odds with those listed above. Victory, party loyalty, and organizational control are the primary values, which presumably distinguish him from the amateur.[11]

The theory of the amateur party organization posits a different type of motivation, different organizational dynamics, and a different linkage of the party to the society for those involved with party politics. What such a party means to people is best illustrated by a quote from those who have been involved. James Q. Wilson includes a colorful vignette from a leader of the New York West Side Democratic Club:

The West Side Democratic Club was composed of young people who couldn't get anywhere in the regular organization. . . . I think most of the young people in the club . . . felt that they wanted to get something out of politics. . . . The new generation . . . is very rebellious. . . . Politics is a good outlet for their general frustrations and they are fully aware of it. . . . They can get a good job on their own, but they're still interested in politics—politics for a different reason: because it is a way of expressing, what? Something, something that is eating them. They're young and very idealistic.[12]

The excitement about politics and the motivations for being active which emerge from this comment stands in striking contrast to the meaning of the party in the Chicago machine. For example, here is Alderman Marzullo of the Twenty-fifth Chicago Ward again: "I ain't got no axes to grind. You can take all your news media and all the do-gooders in town and move them into my Twenty-fifth Ward, and do you know what would happen? On election day we'd beat them fifteen to one." And later: "I'm not an intellectual, but I love people. I'm not elected by the media, the intellectuals or do-gooders. I'm elected by my people. Service and communication. That's how my ward is run."[13] The contrast with the amateur model is, indeed, striking!

Party Organization as a Candidate-Centered Aggregation

Another conception of the party organization is that of the party as a candidate-centered organization. Joseph Schlesinger has developed this model, particularly in his 1966 book *Ambition and Politics*.[14] The focus of his theory is the candidate and his political ambitions, which can be of three types: static (desire to hold one particular office for some time); discrete (desire for a particular office for only a specified term); and progressive (desire to develop a political career by aspiring to more important offices). Each candidate has a nucleus of supporters and adherents who are involved in politics, and their aim is seeking or retaining control of a particular office (whether sheriff, state legislator, governor, or United States congressman, et cetera). Thus, the party consists of an ad hoc set of candidate-oriented nuclei. These nuclei may be linked to each other in a variety of ways: sharing resources or competing for them, working together to win votes or competing at cross purposes. The model is a complex one, but the heart of the party organization is this group of workers tied to a candidate with his ambitions. To anyone who has been active in an American campaign in the fall of even-numbered years (when United States senators, governors, congressmen, plus a host of state and local officers are elected), the Schlesinger model will often appear realistic. For some activists (a small minority, as the data from studies has demonstrated), this is what party politics is all about. In some localities this may indeed be the party. But party organization generally is more than this, structurally and functionally. The party is more than a set of candidates and workers, nuclei who are relevant only at campaign time. It has a durable character which supersedes individual candidacies and campaigns.

Party Organization as a Hybrid Type

An attempt can be made to contrast the oligarchical or professional machine model and the amateur model on certain key dimensions. William Wright has suggested there are two extreme or "polar types" of party organizations—the "party democracy" type, which is close to the amateur organization, and the "rational efficient" type, which is close to the boss and machine model (see table 8.1).[15]

It is important to remember that the "pure" party organization, one which fulfills perfectly all the particular characteristics of a type, is rarely found. Thus these dimensions are continua with party organizations ranging between one extreme and another, and most likely tending not to be extreme in all its characteristics. Any party organization consists of a heterogeneous group of activists who will have a variety of motivations, social backgrounds, and orientations to politics. Rarely is an organization made up of activists, precinct leaders, and ward leaders who are completely ideological about politics and about their motivations for party work, as the amateur model suggests. On the other hand, rarely is the party organization populated exclusively by those seeking to plunder the public treasury for private gain. The world of reality differs considerably from the world suggested by these models of party organization. It is not a question of whether the local organization matches either this or that model. The world of ac-

TABLE 8.1
Comparison of Amateur and Professional Party Organizations

Dimensions	*Party Democracy* (Amateur) Model	*Rational Efficient* (Professional Machine) Model
Motivations for being active	Ideological and social ends and rewards	Material gain
Social profile	Middle-class, younger, more women, good education (many college-educated)	Lower-class, older, male, limited education
Internal organization	Democratic process, membership rights, decentralized control	Disciplined, hierarchical, integrated
Place of ideology	Primary	Minimal
Party functions	Broad concern for community, diverse policy interests, goal-setting a major focus	Narrow, electoral, no goal-setting in broad terms
Style of politics	Idealistic	Pragmatic, opportunistic

tual party politics is too complex for such simplistic formulations. A close look at the world of the activists is necessary to understand party organizational life at the grass roots.

What kind of structure is the party? This question has intrigued and baffled scholars for a long time. In 1887 a German scholar, Ferdinand Tonnies, said that parties are similar to social movements, societylike "collectives," and they parallel or correspond to the class system in society. Although he was aware of different types of parties, he saw the normal party in this sense:

A party is a group which one joins, an object which one takes, an opinion which one chooses—all this insofar as it occurs with the consciousness that it is advantageous for one's own purposes. . . . The party is thus a collective through rational will which is 'taken' as a means for specific or indeterminate ends. . . .
That parties will become organized is a natural law in the sociological sense. For essentially merely a union of those who strive for a certain aim, the party becomes, through organization, a corporation fit to fight.[16]

"A corporation fit to fight!" The question for scholars, since Tonnies, has been what type of corporation, what type of organization?

Chapter 9

Party Activists: The Working Elites at the Base of the Political System

TO UNDERSTAND the reality of party organizational life, particularly at the grass roots, it is necessary to study the research that has been done on the subject. What is the nature of local party organizational activism? Who are these activists and what is known about their backgrounds, motivations, attitudes, and activities?

Social Background of Party Activists

American parties are thought to be open groups, that anyone can get into party work and, indeed, move quite rapidly upward without impediment in the structure if he or she wants to. How true is this actually? How undiscriminatory are parties in encouraging people from diverse social backgrounds to participate? Parties might be open because of their wide appeals for support, or closed because of a desire for solidarity and efficiency.

The social-class status of activists, based on educational and occupational data, can give some idea of the openness of local organizations. In an early study of Chicago, Harold Gosnell found the precinct captains to include a large proportion from the lower class. In 1928, 58 percent of them had only a grade-school education, and only 20 percent went beyond high school.[1] They were also from lower-class occupational backgrounds. In studies done since then in other cities, it was found that the activists were usually better educated, but that communities differed in the proportion of party activists from the blue-collar class (see table 9.1).

A comparison of Detroit and Los Angeles shows an increase in the number of activists with at least a high school education in 1980, in relation to earlier years. Los Angeles particularly has a high proportion of college-educated party leaders.

The attraction of the working class, the blue-collar workers, into party positions also varied by community. In the early years in Detroit, Los Angeles, and Massachusetts cities, the Democrats particularly were able to attract blue-collar workers; in recent years this seems to have declined. Yet, close to one-fifth of these party posts are manned by the working class. What is interesting is that the Republicans compete

TABLE 9.1

Educational and Occupational Status of Lower-Level Party Activists in Selected Communities

(as a percentage)

Status	Detroit		Los Angeles			New York City	Massachusetts Cities	Rural Illinois
	1956	1980	1956	1972	1980	1960	1966	1960
No more than a high school education								
Democrats	65	20	34	6	6	29	39	83
Republicans	47	14	27	12	5	37	28	91
Blue-collar workers								
Democrats	57	26	49[a]	28	22	32	50	25
Republicans	31	16	34[a]	33	19	28	13	35

SOURCES: For Massachusetts: Lewis Bowman and G. R. Boynton, "Recruitment Patterns Among Local Party Officials," *The American Political Science Review* 60, no. 3 (September 1966): 667–76; for rural Illinois: Philip Althoff and S. Patterson, "Political Activism in a Rural County," *Midwest Journal of Political Science* 10, no. 1 (February 1966): 39–51; for Detroit: Samuel Eldersveld, *Political Parties: A Behavioral Analysis* (Chicago: Rand McNally, 1964), ch. 3; for Los Angeles: D. Marvick and C. Nixon, "Recruitment Contrasts in Rival Campaign Groups," in D. Marvick, ed., *Political Decisionmakers: Recruitment and Performance* (Glencoe, Ill.: Free Press, 1961), pp. 193–217; also "Party Organizational Personnel and Electoral Democracy in Los Angeles, 1963–1972," in W. J. Crotty, ed., *The Party Symbol* (San Francisco: W. H. Freeman, 1980), pp. 63–86; for New York: R. Hirschfield et al., "A Profile of Political Activists in Manhattan," *Western Political Quarterly* 15 (1962): 489–506, used with permission of the University of Utah, copyright holder. See also M. Margaret Conway and Frank B. Feigert, "Motivation, Incentive Systems, and the Political Party Organization," *American Political Science Review* 62, no. 4 (December 1968): 1159–73. We use here data from two studies in 1980, one in Detroit and one in Los Angeles (Eldersveld and Marvick were the investigators). Both studies asked the same questions of base personnel in these cities—223 precinct delegates in Detroit and 474 club presidents and county committee members in Los Angeles (a paper presented at the Annual Meeting of the American Political Science Association in New York City, September 1981).

[a] Not based strictly on occupation but on the "lowest level of socioeconomic status."

with the Democrats for activists from the working class although they usually do not attract as many as the Democrats. Hence, there is an imbalance in the social class character of the parties in most communities.

Those from the lower social classes can get into the base units of the party organization, although they are outnumbered by those with white-collar, professional, business, and managerial occupations. This openness is in contrast to opportunities for lower-class persons at the state level of the party, as well as for national political elites. A look at the educational backgrounds of political leaders at different levels of the system illustrates the contrasts. Table 9.2 suggests the importance of a university education for upward political mobility. The social-class *origins* of America's political elites illustrates this point even better, particularly when contrasted with countries such as Britain and West Germany (see table 9.3). Apparently American parties do not mobilize those with lower-class origins as well as do the parties on the Left in Europe. To move upward in the political system to top policy positions is very difficult for those with lower-class status.

The great diversity in the social background characteristics of local party leaders is shown in table 9.4. The lower echelons of the parties seem to be moderately open to the young, women, blacks, union members, and religious groups (depending on the city). A kind of rivalry in the attraction and competitive recruitment of the parties can be sensed as they seem to invade the social territory of the opposition.

This is not a recent phenomenon. The Detroit research reveals clearly that the Republicans have for years recruited from Catholics, blacks, union members, and the poor—60 percent of the leaders from such groups joined the party before 1952. The Democrats recruited many from the professional-managerial group, those with high incomes,

TABLE 9.2
Educational Background of Party Politicians
(as a percentage)

Education	Population	Local Party Activists Detroit	U.S. House of Representatives	U.S. Senate	U.S. Civil Service (GS and Above)
Less than college	69	18	7	4	1
Some college, no degree	18	30	14	13	3
College/university degree, or higher	13	52	79	83	96

SOURCE: Randall B. Ripley and Grace A. Franklin, *Congress, the Bureaucracy, and Public Policy* (Homewood, Ill.: Dorsey, 1980), p. 32.

TABLE 9.3

Social Origins of National Legislative Elites
(as a percentage)

Father's Social Class	United States		Britain		Germany	
	Democrat	Republican	Labour	Conservative	Social Democratic Party	Christian Democratic Union/ Christian Social Union
Middle and upper middle	86	75	54	96	48	70
Lower middle and working	14	25	46	4	52	30
N=[a]	22	28	50	52	44	43

SOURCE: Joel D. Aberbach, Robert D. Putnam, and Bert A. Rockman, *Bureaucrats and Politicians in Western Democracies* (Cambridge: Harvard University Press, 1981), p. 60.

[a] N is the number of cases in the sample.

TABLE 9.4
Social Diversity in Party Cadres
(as a percentage)

Characteristic	Republicans		Democrats	
	1980		1980	
	Detroit	Los Angeles	Detroit	Los Angeles
Black	35	2	59	10
Jewish	5	7	3.5	19
Union member	32	15	60	47
Protestant	41	65	44	40
Graduate or professional education	37	48	36	47
To age 40	35	27	32	36
Female	38	37	42	37

SOURCES: The 1980 Detroit study was directed by Samuel J. Eldersveld; the 1980 Los Angeles study was directed by Dwaine Marvick; and the data used here are by his permission.

those with German and English backgrounds, into party work long ago—47 percent before 1952.

It is interesting to discover also that there is often evidence of economic advancement of party activists at the local level. Table 9.5 shows the percentages of the leadership group which moved from blue-collar to white-collar occupations, if the father's occupation is compared with that of the respondent.

Thus party career mobility seems to be linked to the improvement of the economic status of leaders in both parties.

Pathways into Party Work

How people become involved in party organization work is difficult to summarize. There are so many different stimuli and circumstances. Interviews with precinct activists reveal a multiplicity of conditions for involvement in party work.

"My father was a saloon keeper in Detroit and quite a politician. A lot of politics went on in the back room of the saloon. I heard a lot as a child. I was brought up in a political atmosphere and having had a taste of politics I wanted to know something about what went on in the inside. So I started to work for the party when I was first able to vote. I then ran for precinct delegate."

"When I was a kid I carried papers and worked for [James M.] Cox, the Democratic presidential candidate. Cox was a newspaperman and I always

TABLE 9.5
Upward Mobility in Detroit, 1956
(as a percentage)

Position	Democrats	Republicans
Congressional district chairmen	40	40
Congressional district executive boards	33	9
Precinct leaders	18	19

SOURCE: S. J. Eldersveld, *Political Parties: A Behavioral Analysis* (Chicago: Rand McNally, 1964), p. 61.

liked him. I also believed in the League of Nations. My family have always been Democratic and interested in politics."

"We were the only Republican family in our block and one day a ward chairman who was a friend of mine asked me whether I would like to be a precinct worker. He told me the job of the precinct worker was simple—to sell the candidate and get out the votes—not so simple! My parents were immigrants . . . and they came over to escape tyranny and build a new life. Therefore they were what you might call rugged individualists."

"I was active in the UAW as a shop steward. One night at a local educational meeting I heard Governor [Mennen] Williams speak. I don't remember what he said, but a state senator pointed out to me the position of the parties in Lansing. . . . I wanted to find someone else to run, but couldn't. The usual candidate was associated with the Communists so everybody was for me when I said I would run."[2]

Often the role of the family in discussing politics and in interesting family members in the possibility of party work is very important. Studies reveal that 30 percent to 40 percent of those who become active in politics did so through their families. There are additional conditions which, after this early introduction, lead to actual entrance into party activism:

1. The party leadership itself may play an important active role in recruiting (38 percent in Detroit, but as high as 54 percent in North Carolina and 69 percent in Massachusetts).
2. Other groups such as unions, business groups, or civic, racial, and ethnic groups may play a decisive role in recruitment (10 percent in Detroit, but usually less than 10 percent in other communities in which studies have been done).
3. Friends and relatives not in politics may also be the stimulus for getting people into the party apparatus (13 percent in Detroit, higher elsewhere).
4. Self-recruitment occurs for many of these activists, because of their interest in issues or causes and their independent decision to seek a career in politics (up to 32 percent in the Detroit, North Carolina, and Massachusetts studies).

5. Desire to work for a particular candidate (12 percent in Detroit—there is evidence that in other communities it is higher).
6. Accidental involvement—individuals who just happen into the party group even though they have never had much interest in party politics—a haphazard, unpremeditated social involvement.

Getting involved with the party, thus, is the result of quite different events in the life of a party activist and several different routes into party careers. There are three basic routes—the recruitment, self-starter, and accidental models (see fig. 9.1). The party organization by itself recruits only one-third or two-fifths of its activists; the remainder comes in through other routes, with a fifth actually becoming accidentally involved. A minority gets involved because of an interest in a particular candidate. Persons arrive in the local party organization, therefore, after having traversed quite different paths, and the particular path they have traversed will probably have considerable influence on how they look at party work. Those from the labor unions will

FIGURE 9.1
Alternative Pathways to Party Activism

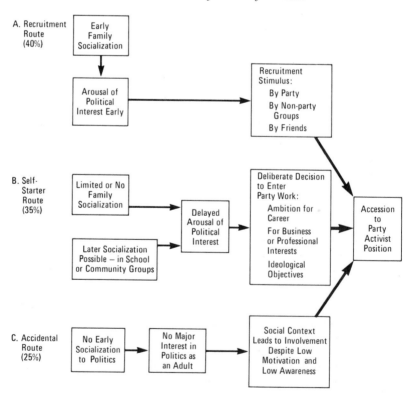

have a quite different perspective than those who became interested as a result of their work in an ethnic, racial, or business organization or who decided on their own volition to enter party work because of their beliefs and preferences concerning governmental policy.

Motivations for Party Organizational Activity

The motivations of those who become active partisans, and why they enter the party and seek to develop a career there, rather than in other groups, are intriguing. Over the years scholars have noticed three basic reasons: a desire for personal ambition or material gain, personal satisfaction from affiliation with a party group, and ideological-philosophical (impersonal) satisfaction. Table 9.6 shows the results of the Detroit studies of 1956 and 1980 which elucidate the frequencies of personal motivations for initial entry into party work.

TABLE 9.6
Personal Motivation for Organizational Activity
(as a percentage)

Reasons	1956	1980
Personal friendship for a candidate	12	5
Desire for social contacts and friendships	5	5
Fun and excitement of politics	7	6
Seeking a personal position in politics	2	2
Like being close to influential people	3	3
Gives a feeling of recognition in the community	2	2
Total personalized motivations for becoming active	31	23

Table 9.7 shows the more impersonalized reasons for precinct leaders' becoming active.

TABLE 9.7
Impersonal Motivations for Precinct Leaders
(as a percentage)

Reasons	1956	1980
Political work is part of way of life	11	13
Strong attachment to the party	13	5
Desire to influence governmental policy	21	36
Helps fulfill sense of community obligation	20	23
Total impersonal motivations	65	77

Other studies which have probed for the major reasons explaining entrance into party work revealed similar findings. The level of ideological involvement by itself is not high (about 20 percent to 35 percent). Yet, the majority of activists explain their entry into party work in rather idealistic, impersonal terms. There is considerable emphasis on civic duty and the obligation to work in the community. The significant thing to note is that while ideology per se is not explicitly mentioned as the major reason, neither does personal ambition and self-gratification emerge as the major reason for entrance into the party cadre. A complex set of other reasons is also very important.

Motivational Change During the Party Career

On entering party work the majority of activists are rather idealistic in their interests and expectations. What happens to them after they become active—do they retain their idealistic fervor or do they develop other satisfactions from party work? From the few studies which have looked into this matter, it appears that the experience in the party has a resocializing effect, that is, it orients the activist to seek more personalized satisfactions while continuing in active party work (see table 9.8). Thus, in Detroit in 1956, 65 percent began with ideological-philo-

TABLE 9.8

*Party Activists' Shift to Personalized Motivations
(as a percentage)*

Motivations	Detroit 1956	Detroit 1980	Maryland 1966	Rural Illinois 1967
Began with personalized motivations when entered party work	31	23	19	44
Held personalized motivations at time of interview	67	61	78	61
Balance in the direction of more personalized motivations	+36	+38	+59	+17

SOURCES: For rural Illinois: Philip Althoff and Samuel C. Patterson, "Political Activism in a Rural County," *Midwest Journal of Political Science*, vol. 10, no. 1 (1966): 39–51; Detroit: Samuel Eldersveld, *Political Parties: A Behavioral Analysis* (Chicago: Rand McNally 1964), ch. 3; for Maryland: M. Margaret Conway and Frank B. Feigert, "Motivation, Incentive Systems, and the Political Party Organization," *American Political Science Review*, vol. 62, no. 4 (December 1968): 1159–73.

sophical reasons for being involved (67 percent in 1980), but at the time of the interview, when asked what were their real satisfactions *now*, only 14 percent in 1956 (and 28 percent in 1980) talked in terms of such impersonal incentives. In Maryland the same attrition in impersonal motivations was found. In rural Illinois there was less impersonal motivation to begin with and thus the loss was not as great, but the same tendency was discovered. It appears that working in the party is very likely to reduce philosophical incentives and substitute as a reason for being active other personalized rationales—the fun of politics, social recognition and interaction, career ambitions.

To many people the party is a social group providing social rewards and opportunities. For 55 percent of the Detroit precinct leaders in 1956 and 41 percent in 1980 this is what the party meant—social contacts and friendships while doing party work. This was also the highest satisfaction in the Conway and Feigert study of Maryland and also rural Illinois—from 40 percent to 50 percent said that if they had to drop out of party organization work, they would miss social contacts more than anything else. This social reality of the party to these precinct activists must be kept in mind. In their day-to-day work, for many activists, it is social gratifications, not ideology, political ambition, patronage, or philosophic commitment which keeps them working for the party.

Ideological Distinctiveness of the Parties' Activists

In a two-party system such as is found in the United States, according to at least some of the theorists, two things should be expected in the attitudes of party leaders toward governmental issues: the two parties would develop platforms with some distinctive positions, and the differences between the two parties should be moderate since they are converging toward the center in the search for votes. The parties must be responsive to public opinion, yet they do not want to lose their hard core of supporters as a result of apathy or cynicism in the move to the center. But how distinctive, how moderate, are activists?

Several studies have been done of local party activists which reveal both the distinctiveness and moderateness of their views (see table 9.9). In all three of the major cities in which such studies were completed the party differences are apparent. The Democratic activists are without exception more liberal than the Republican and were only outbid in New York City by the Liberal party for the vote on the Left. The difference in Detroit and New York is considerable; however, in Los Angeles the contrast between the two parties is greater. On eight

TABLE 9.9

Ideological Contrasts for Democratic and Republican Party Activists
(as a percentage)

Liberal Position	Detroit 1956		Detroit 1980		New York City 1960			Los Angeles 1968		Los Angeles 1980	
	Dem.	Rep.	Dem.	Rep.	Dem.	Rep.	Lib.	Dem.	Rep.	Dem.	Rep.
Civil rights	67	50	62	27	65	43	85	74	19	60	8
Medicare (or aid to the poor)	75	34	82	41	68	36	83	91	50	71	27
Average Difference	29		38		27			48		48	

SOURCES: For Detroit: Samuel Eldersveld, *Political Parties: A Behavioral Analysis* (Chicago: Rand McNally, 1964), ch. 3; for Los Angeles: D. Marvick and C. Nixon, "Recruitment Contrasts in Rival Campaign Groups," in D. Marvick, ed., *Political Decisionmakers: Recruitment and Performance*, pp. 193–217; also "Party Organizational Personnel and Electoral Democracy in Los Angeles, 1963–1972," in W. J. Crotty, ed., *The Party Symbol* (San Francisco: W. H. Freeman, 1980), pp. 63–86; *(New York):* R. Hirschfield et al., "A Profile of Political Activists in Manhattan," *Western Political Quarterly* 15 (1962), pp. 489–506, used with permission of the University of Utah, copyright holder. See also M. Margaret Conway and Frank B. Feigert, "Motivation, Incentive Systems, and the Political Party Organization," *American Political Science Review* 62, no. 4 (December 1968): 1159–73. Further data from two studies in 1980, one in Detroit and one in Los Angeles, used.

NOTE: Civil rights issues were different in the communities, so the results are not strictly comparable. They dealt with helping blacks get fair treatment in jobs, housing, and in education. The medicare question was used in Detroit and New York (low cost hospital care and medical assistance provided by government programs). In Los Angeles a more general question was used concerned with the government's role in expanding the opportunities for the poor.

TABLE 9.10
Ideological Positions of Detroit Local
Leaders (1980)
(as a percentage)

Position	Democrats	Republicans
Liberal	60	14
Moderate	25	46
Conservative	3	29
Other (or no response)	12	11

SOURCE: See sources for Table 9.1.

key issues in 1980 the following "average liberalism" in Detroit and Los Angeles among local party activists was found: in Detroit 69 percent for Democrats, 46 percent for Republicans; in Los Angeles 67 percent for Democrats and 24 percent for Republicans. Table 9.10 shows how these local leaders in Detroit classified themselves on their ideological position.

Normally there is a considerable range of opinions within each party's activist group, reflecting the haphazard and eclectic nature of the recruitment process, the great diversity of people working within the parties, as well as the absence of a clear party line. Thus in the New York and Detroit Republican parties 40 percent are liberal on these issues and even 27 percent in the Los Angeles Republican party supported more aid for the poor. A good illustration of this diversity of opinion within the party organization can be found in Detroit in 1980 on the medicaid issue. Leaders were asked whether they agreed or disagreed, strongly or not strongly, with the statement "The government ought to help people get doctors and hospital care at low cost" (see table 9.11).

Clearly neither party is homogeneous; contrasting tendencies certainly exist.

TABLE 9.11
Precinct Leaders

Party	Position on Medicaid Issue (Detroit, 1980)				
	Very Liberal	Moderately Liberal	Unsure	Moderately Conservative	Very Conservative
Democratic	62	25	7	4	2
Republican	17	23	21	34	5

SOURCE: See sources for Table 9.1.

The ideological pluralism within the parties suggests some basic disagreements on policy for subgroups. The Detroit 1956 study reveals that, indeed, this is the case. On civil rights issues, for example, over 70 percent of the black precinct leaders in both parties were very liberal, as might be expected, but the proportions of liberals among white precinct leaders were 36 percent for Republicans and 52 percent for Democrats. In 1980 on the issue of housing desegregation the proportion who felt the government should do more to alleviate this problem were as follows: among blacks, 92 percent for the Democrats, 70 percent for the Republicans; among whites, 52 percent for the Democrats, 12 percent for the Republicans.

Such data indicate that there is considerable tension and ideological factionalism within the parties; and that the party organizations are alliances of interest groups who may have different policy preferences. The task of the party to somehow hold these groups together could be a difficult one. Fortunately, in most communities the party activists are not motivated primarily by ideology, nor is ideological conflict overt and salient most of the time.[3] If it were, the party organization could never be held together.

Activities and Roles of Party Activists

Ask precinct or ward leaders what their most important task is and their answers will vary by community, by party, and by the individual leader's image of his place in the organization. Research revealed this distribution of role perceptions in Detroit in 1956:[4]

Vote Mobilizers (Major emphasis on getting out the vote)	45 percent
Ideological Mentors (See job as communicating with the public about issues)	24 percent
Social-Economic Welfare Promoters (See self as representative of a particular group, as the union, business, blacks, and so forth)	18 percent
Unclear as to Role	13 percent

What this means is that in a community like Detroit getting out the vote may be the critical task, but less than half of the local party activists wish to define their role immediately in those terms. Other ways of describing their tasks are used—educating the public, instigating neighborhood action, fighting for particular legislation, or servicing their constituents and interest group supporters. They may feel responsible for vote mobilization, but this is secondary to other roles, although their performance in other roles may be very efficacious in getting out the vote. The stereotype of the American party as consisting mainly of a group of activists only interested in votes must, therefore, be modified.

Harold Gosnell in his massive study of Chicago politics (with nine hundred interviews of precinct and ward leaders) long ago documented the great variety of activities which local party leaders can engage in. Table 9.12 gives examples of these activities for two separate years in Chicago.

TABLE 9.12
Activities of Chicago Precinct Captains
(as a percentage)

Activity	Those Engaged in Activity 1928	1936
Benevolent: distributed food	49	70
Christmas or Passover baskets	56	39
Advisory: to juveniles	40	35
to adults on domestic problems	30	25
Government agencies help: helped secure jobs	55	51
adjusted taxes	70	36
social agency contacts	33	67
medical aid	59	57
Courts: legal aid	65	62
traffic violations	53	27
naturalization help	71	69
"Deference" activities: funerals	77	62
weddings	51	52

SOURCE: Harold F. Gosnell, *Machine Politics: Chicago Model*, 2nd ed. (Chicago: University of Chicago Press, 1968), p. 71.

The range of activities in an organization like the Chicago machine was fantastically broad. In the 1970s under the Daley machine the same service conception of role prevailed. In other communities, also, more goes on than merely getting out the vote.

Not many intensive studies of the activities of precinct or ward leaders have been done since Gosnell, in the 1930s. However, one was done in Gary, Indiana, in 1957. The summary of the activities of the precinct captains from that study is valuable.[5]

On the average the Republican precinct committeemen in Gary see 8 persons each day, while the average is closer to 13 for the Democrats. Black leaders have a better record of personal contact in both parties. The frequency of business contacts is highest for the blacks ... Roughly one person every two days asked a favor of some kind from each member of the (Negro) Democratic organization. By comparison, requests directed toward Negro Republicans seemed small indeed. The kinds of aid requested by blacks are different than white requests: (1) jobs, (2) relief money, (3) aid in dealing with law enforcement agencies. In a majority of white precincts the requests are for (1) a summer job with the park district for a high-school age son, (2) information about how to contact city government agencies.

As the campaign approaches, the tempo increases, and "the contacts become more specific in objective." Each precinct committeeman is supposed to finish a poll of his precinct 30 days before the primary election. This is done by 80 percent of the White Democrats and 90 percent of the Negro Democrats who are precinct leaders. Republicans do not bother before the primary but they claim to do some of this before the general election. After the registration task is completed, the job is to persuade the voters to support the candidate—which was done as follows:

Leaders	Percentage of precinct leaders who tried to persuade voters in primary	
	Democrats	*Republicans*
Blacks	88	72
Whites	51	24

This detailed description of activities attests to the intensity of involvement with the mobilization of voters by local party personnel. It also reveals a variety of activities.

Other studies reveal similar patterns of precinct leader activity. In New Jersey counties in the early 1960s it was reported that the local party leaders engaged in door-to-door canvassing (94 percent), telephone canvassing (78 percent), helping the poor get jobs (72 percent), and legal assistance (62 percent).[6]

In the fall of 1980 parallel studies were done in Detroit and Los Angeles, asking in detail what activities the lower level activists engaged in. Table 9.13 presents details on three critical tasks and indicates a rather high level of activity. These data indicate that voter registration activity was low in Detroit in 1980 compared to Los Angeles, but the house-to-house canvassing efforts were rather high. Further, there did not seem to be a great decline in 1980 in precinct leader activity.

One of the major problems, of course, is activation of the organization. It is obvious from these data there is a great deal of such "organi-

TABLE 9.13

*ortion of Activists Personally Engaged in Performance of Critical Tasks—Detroit and Los Angeles
(as a percentage)

| | 1956 | | 1980 | | | |
| | Detroit | | Detroit | | Los Angeles | |
ty	Democrat	Republican	Democrat	Republican	Democrat	Republican
registration	93	80	42	19	60	72
e-to-house canvassing	46	32	60	61	53	48
on day round-up of votes	68	80	69	62	68	77
		281		223		474

RCES: 1956 and 1980 Studies of Detroit precinct leaders (conducted by Samuel J. Eldersveld) and 1980 study of Los Angeles committee-
d club presidents (conducted by Dwaine Marvick).

zational slack." No more than a third of these lower level activists are performing at peak efficiency. Aside from the Daley machine operation, this level of performance is probably not uncommon.

The problem of precinct activity and performance often is complicated by the fact that there is a high turnover in precinct leadership. In the Detroit study it was found that there were no Democratic leaders who could be interviewed in 11 percent of the sample precincts and no Republicans in 5 percent. Further, there were no helpers (for the leader) in 19 percent of the precincts for the Democrats and in 40 percent of the cases for the Republicans.[7] Twenty-two percent of the precinct leaders had just taken over their positions in 1956 when the interviews were done. This incompleteness of organization also emerged from William Crotty's study of North Carolina, where he found that the proportion of counties in which all precincts were organized by the Democrats was 76 percent, and for the Republicans 35 percent.[8] In 1980, at least one-third of the precincts were unmanned for the Democrats and an even higher number had no active Republicans.

Vacant precinct posts, an inadequate working force to assist, high turnover in personnel, and only partial performance of duties are the conditions under which the parties seem to perform at the local level, except where there is a strong leadership, a long tradition of efficiency in party activity, and an incipient movement to elect new elites to office on the basis of new and dramatic issues. When these conditions are fulfilled performance is incredible by the local organization. The local party cadres have tremendous potential organization and mobilization power, but the activists have to be trained, stimulated, and activated.

Amateurism and Professionalism Among Activists

Most research is inconclusive as to this question. The amateur orientation is an important phenomenon in party life. But what patterns of attitudes are linked in this syndrome, *for the individual,* and how large the proportion of amateur activists exist, *in the party,* has not been clearly documented.[9] Thus, in a study of a sample of delegates to the Democratic National Convention in 1968 the investigators found 42 of the 180 delegates to be amateurs, 52 semiprofessionals, and 82 professionals. But it is unclear to what extent delegates manifested the particular attitudes on the basis of classifications made.[10] Similarly in the Detroit and Los Angeles studies in 1980 the extent of amateurism was probed with a variety of items to which party activists were asked to respond. The results were very mixed (see table 9.14).

Such data underscore both the difficulty of measuring the extent of amateurism or professionalism, as well as the hybrid nature of the local party cadres. It appears that there may be a very strong hard core of amateurs—at least one-fourth, possibly more. It appears also that there is a hard core of professionals—again perhaps 30 percent at minimum. (The range in responses is between 26 percent and 79 percent for all groups in both cities.) No consistent set of orientations emerges from these responses. While ambiguity in campaign appeals is opposed (by about 60 percent), a good many of these same activists do not oppose party compromise and the reconciliation of conflicting viewpoints, *even if this means not taking controversial stands.* Most activists are amateurs in the sense of wanting internal procedural democracy (about two-thirds), but only a minority are amateurs in the sense of leaving the party if its issue positions are unacceptable. Most would stay in the

TABLE 9.14
Party Activists Giving "Amateur" Responses, 1980
(as a percentage)

Statement		Detroit	Los Angeles
If you disagree with a major stand of your party, stop working for it (agreeing)	Democrat	27	26
	Republican	29	30
Campaign appeals should be vague enough to attract a broad spectrum of voters (disagreeing)	Democrat	59	54
	Republican	65	58
Parties should try to reconcile conflicting views rather than take controversial stands (disagreeing)	Democrat	35	72
	Republican	45	75
Only party organizations run by a few leaders are really effective (disagreeing)	Democrat	72	64
	Republican	70	60

party even if disagreeing with a major stand of their party. Perhaps this suggests again that activists may begin party work as idealists and amateurs, but that gradually they become professionals attitudinally, in terms of their relationship to the party. Yet, they cling to certain beliefs about party work which still can be considered amateur. Only a small group, in the last analysis, are consistent, bona fide amateurs adhering stubbornly to a set of idealistic and ideological orientations toward politics and working only for such goals. In this sense, again, the complexity of the party organization is manifested. It is indeed a multi-motivated and attitudinally diverse structure.

Organizational Viability

What holds these party structures together? It is clear from the vast amount of research that they are highly complex, differentiated, pluralized structures. They comprehend a wide variety of human actors differing from each other by social background, motivations, ideological orientations, role perceptions, and activity patterns. How do they continue as minimally integrated systems of action? Previously, different theories might have been advanced to explain their survival: One theory was that patronage and disciplinary control held them together; but in most American communities this is no longer the case—they are more often than not volunteer structures. A second is that ideology binds them together into a group of like-minded individuals; but the diversity in views about policy is too great, and ideology is too negligible as a primary motivation to be a strong unifying force. Similar social backgrounds could also be suggested as a possible force for cohesion, with lower- and working-class persons seeing the party as their channel and instrument for political action against the upper and middle class; but America has never really had this type of class politics. What then is the explanation for the viability of these heterogeneous structures?

The key question here is, Why do local party activists not only stay on in the organization but continue to work hard, feel loyal to the party group, and reflect relatively high satisfaction at their place in the organization? What are the conditions which are linked to efficiency, loyalty, and morale? And, conversely, what are the conditions which are linked to disillusionment, dissatisfaction, and withdrawal from party work?

Based on the Detroit study, three factors seem most relevant for explaining organizational coherence. The first factor which was helpful was decisional involvement, or the extent to which the activist felt that he or she had adequate input into the party's decision-making process at the local level. Those who felt involved were much more likely to be more integrated.

A second factor of importance was the communication contact pattern of the activist—whether he or she was a cosmopolitan (in contact with party leaders at all levels), a localist (only in contact with other local level workers), or an isolate (rather withdrawn from party contacts). This factor was important for explaining both loyalty and efficiency. Thus, among conservative Republican leaders only 13 percent of the cosmopolitans approved ticket splitting (as a test of party loyalty) while 75 percent of the conservative Republicans who were isolates or localists approved of ticket splitting. Apparently extensive contacts in the organization are functional to the reinforcement of loyalty norms among the orthodox.

A third, and perhaps the most basic, factor explaining morale, loyalty, and efficiency is what may be called the political aspiration of the activist, that is, whether he or she is interested in continuing in party work and taking on a more responsible position.[11] In explaining the efficiency level of activists this was a most useful variable. We found as follows:

| | Percentage in the Highest Efficiency Levels of Party Work | |
	Democrats	*Republicans*
Aspire to a party career	90	67
Do not aspire to a party career	48	34

Aspiration seems to be particularly important for increasing the level of efficiency in the organization. Yet, extensive communication and decisional "say" also contribute. Thus, for those with no career aspirations the efficiency levels were as follows: with no decisional involvement, 33 percent for the Democrats and the Republicans; with higher involvement 68 percent for the Democrats and 47 percent for the Republicans. When communication contacts were poor the efficiency level was 33 percent for the Democrats and 9 percent for the Republicans; and where it was good the level was 62 percent for the Democrats and 89 percent for the Republicans. Thus, clearly the development of organizational conditions which make the activist feel involved are critical for improving the efficiency level of the parties.

The party is indeed a paradoxical structure, but the mystery of its minimal cohesion can be partially explained in these terms. It is remarkable to find such a high proportion of activists fascinated enough by party work to want to stay in and move upward—from 50 percent to 60 percent of all those in the cadre. If the organization gives them a sense of belonging and of potential achievement, the challenge is apparently great enough to maintain their morale, loyalty, and efficiency—at least at a high enough level to hold the structure together.

Contrasts with the Wallace Activists of 1968

The personnel working for America's major political parties at the local level in many respects differs significantly from those in a third party movement. Empirical studies of the latter are virtually nonexistent. In one study of the Wallace American Independent party activists in a Detroit district (the fifteenth congressional) in 1968, a sharp contrast was found between the Wallace workers and the activist cadres of the Republican and Democratic parties.[12] James Canfield found that the Wallace campaigners were a rather special group of blue-collar workers (72 percent) who had stopped their education with high school (81 percent) but who had respectable incomes (66 percent over $10,000). One-half were Southern migrants. They came overwhelmingly from working-class families (81 percent), and only 20 percent had moved into middle-class status. They thus were a much more homogeneous group in social-class characteristics than either the Republicans or Democrats.

These Wallace activists were, above all, in politics for different reasons. They were problem and issue oriented. The most important issue was law and order (referred to by 55 percent) with the "no win" strategy in Vietnam running second (20 percent mentioned it). They were also concerned about Communism—77 percent and 89 percent respectively feeling there was Communist "influence" in both the Republican and Democratic parties, and 43 percent feeling Martin Luther King was "Communist inspired." Further, 69 percent opposed integration of blacks.

Their avowed motivations for party activity differed from the major party activists dramatically. Two-thirds said the most important reasons for their activity was to influence governmental policy. Social contacts and political fun, therefore, were only marginally of motivational significance (mentioned by 9 percent and 5 percent respectively). The comparisons with the other parties in Detroit in 1956 are striking (see table 9.15).

These findings thus throw into bold relief the distinctions at the local level between the major parties and a charismatic, issue-conscious minor party. The Democrats and Republicans are, in Downsian terms, struggling for power and votes but are not as self-conscious about ideology. A minor party like that of the Wallace movement in

TABLE 9.15

Comparison of Motivations for Party Activists

Reasons	Percentage Mentioning Current Satisfaction in Party Work		
	Wallace American Independent Party	Democrats	Republicans
Social contacts	9	63	47
Fun and excitement of the campaign	5	12	8
Ideology, moral, and philosophical	52	7	10

SOURCE: James Canfield, "The Wallace Campaign Worker in Wayne County." Ph.D. dissertation, University of Michigan, 1971.

1968 involved people, who had been out of politics previously, by attracting them to work for particular issues. The former two survived on the American scene; the latter has disappeared. This fact says much about the conditions for survival of parties with ideologically committed and distinctive activist cadres. The limited social base of the Wallace party and its narrow, somewhat extremist ideological appeal, which distinguished it from both the Democratic and Republican parties, spelled its doom in a two-party duopolistic environment.

Conclusions

The empirical data on party activism in America speak to a variety of theoretical concerns. In a sense they test the validity of the models of party organization. Do these data suggest that our parties at the grassroots level are oligarchies, mass-based machines? Or are they ad hoc candidate structures committed to furthering particular candidate fortunes? Or are they "party democracy" amateur structures? Or are they some type of hybrid model?

The real tests of the professional model, however conceived, are the existence of a cohesive and like-minded elite at the apex of the party structure motivated by personal power and economic mobility drives. Careful recruitment by elites presumably controls entrance into the system. A hierarchic authority structure exists subordinating the rank and file to the oligarchs. An exploitative relationship develops between the elites and the rank and file—political activity in exchange for material rewards. Different theories emphasize different aspects of the professional model. The data from most of the studies at the local level of party organizations in American cities and rural areas dispute the existence of these conditions. In a few cities there is still considerable patronage, and in the Chicago machine there may still be a hierarchy and emphasis on material rewards. But normally the leadership in local party organizations is not a cohesive power elite.

Second, for the party democracy model the key tests are the centrality of ideology for party activism, the broader functional perspective toward party work, and the emphasis on the individual actor as a free participant in a meaningful party democratic process. But by and large it is very difficult to demonstrate that there is ideological motivation for the majority of party activists. Party activism may be interesting because of a philosophy of citizen involvement, or as a game which is interesting in its own right, or because of an interest in (achieving) a particular policy goal. But party structures reveal great ideological diversity and are not monolithic ideological communities.

Perhaps a party in the United States is a mixed association, a hybrid group, or something similar to, but not identical with, the Duverger idea of a semimass structure. It is not a cadre party in the Leninist or Duverger senses, nor is it strictly a mass party structure. It consists of party operatives and campaign workers who are involved in party work for a multiplicity of motives, holding to a variety of role perceptions, manifesting highly divergent ideological orientations and who work at their precinct and campaign tasks with minimal direction and control. They have considerable autonomy in defining their tasks and implementing them. They do have a relationship with upper level leaders, but this relationship is one of mutual tolerance, limited control from the top down, and great permissiveness. It is thus a very open system depending on improvisation at the base, and therefore an inefficient and slack system in task performance. It is also a system which can be activated from time to time to produce results. The parties are highly pluralized, autonomous associations of minimal efficiency. If American local party structures can be described in general terms at all this may be the closest to reality.

Part III

PARTIES AND RECRUITMENT

Chapter 10

Parties and

Leadership Recruitment

in Democratic Societies

IN ALL SOCIETIES the process by which the few leaders are selected, or emerge, from the many who might be considered eligible has been of vital concern. This is the recruitment process—the discovery, screening, and designation (or certification) of leaders for governmental positions. It is during this process that the credentials (or eligibility criteria) for elite status are determined, that particular mechanisms for arriving at agreement about preferred candidates are utilized, that political support groups for particular candidates are formed, and presumably the relationships between elites and their support groups are cemented. Much goes on, therefore, in the process of recruiting persons for governing positions in the society, and theoretically the circumstances and conditions of what goes on have a considerable effect on how these leaders behave when they get into office. To understand the behavior and performance of the elite in any society it is extremely important to understand the process by which it arrived at elite status.

In modern democratic societies a set of procedures, channels, and pathways have developed for the recruitment of leadership which is *in theory at least* more open, inclusive, and egalitarian than in nondemocratic societies and a process in which the interested public plays a decisive role. In traditional and authoritarian societies, by contrast, the recruitment of leadership is the prerogative of a family, or a small ruling group, which determines the credentials for leadership, does the screening of eligibles, and makes the final decisions. It is a system which is closed, exclusive, and nonegalitarian. The accessibility of the elite and its permeability by nonelites is one of the major differentiating characteristics of a democratic society. The second feature is the role of the public in the final selection of leadership. This is not to say that in a democratic society the elite group is completely open, nor that its composition is completely determined by elections. Any observer of American political leadership is aware of the difficulty for lower-class and less-educated individuals in seeking public office or in getting administrative posts. The same is true for women, blacks, and certain nationality minorities. Furthermore, it is very difficult to get rid of certain incumbents in elite positions—the system seems often to favor those who are entrenched in power. Nevertheless, in a democratic society, in contrast to a closed authoritarian or traditional society, the channels for achieving a leadership position are more diverse, the opportunities for someone who seeks political elite status are much greater and exist particularly for those who are nonelites, for those out of power. Finally, the interested citizenry has a role to play in the selection of the ruling group.

The complex process of leadership recruitment in democratic societies involves political parties. One reason political parties came into existence in such societies was the need for specialized structures to bring people together who would evaluate, screen, and sponsor potential leaders, and mobilize support on their behalf in relationship to particular group goals. Parties are modern democratic structures developed for this purpose. They are not the only type of structure to engage in recruitment, but they are often the major one, and if they did not exist in a true democracy they would soon be created. It is natural and inevitable in a democratic community for individuals to band together to promote their political interests, and in the process they will do the following: (1) *identify* individuals, from the large pool of possibles, who have the qualifications for public office and who would promote the group's interests; (2) *test the electability* of such individuals and begin to build a preliminary political coalition in support of such individuals; and (3) *sponsor* these individuals, and give them the group's endorsement, so that the voting public will be able to evaluate and identify with these individuals in terms of the group interests represented.

The recruitment of leaders is, therefore, *a search process,* which can be broken down into certain stages (see fig. 10.1) Part of this process is going on in groups, part of it in the public more generally. Of course, at the same time that groups (parties) are screening and exploring the qualifications and support of particular would-be candidates, individuals (self-starters) may also be considering the possibility of candidacy, without particular group support. In most such cases, however, even-

FIGURE 10.1

Party and Group Recruitment as a Search Process in Democracies

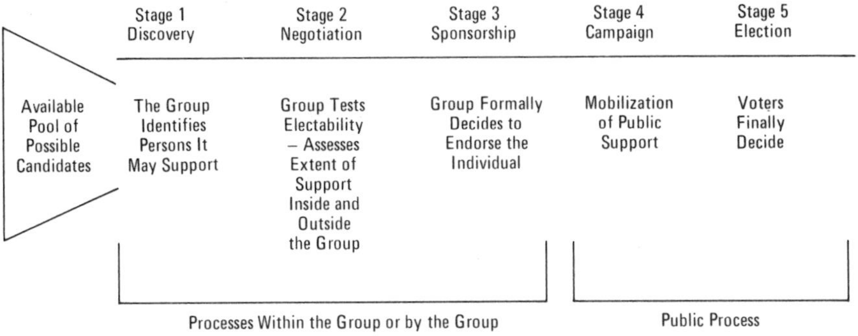

	Stage 1 Discovery	Stage 2 Negotiation	Stage 3 Sponsorship	Stage 4 Campaign	Stage 5 Election
Available Pool of Possible Candidates	The Group Identifies Persons It May Support	Group Tests Electability — Assesses Extent of Support Inside and Outside the Group	Group Formally Decides to Endorse the Individual	Mobilization of Public Support	Voters Finally Decide

Processes Within the Group or by the Group   Public Process

tually the individual seeks group support and hopefully will get group sponsorship. The entire recruitment process has two critical ending points—first, when the group formally designates and sponsors a candidate, and second when the public decides among a variety of candidates, endorsed or not endorsed. The first of these critical decision points is often called the nomination and the second the election.

Democratic societies differ in their elite recruitment patterns, and particularly in the role that parties play in this process.[1] First, countries differ in *eligibility requirements,* or in the qualifications necessary to be considered for public office. There are, of course, formal requirements—citizenship, age limits, and in certain systems residence in the area. More important are the informal expectations, which are difficult to prove as *requirements* but which are assumed, and those who do not meet them may seek office but will rarely be selected. Educational achievement of a certain level is expected for elite status, and white males in our society have a much better record of acceptance than blacks, those from minorities, or women. Particular skills are often considered advantageous, as attested by the high proportion of lawyers in the bureaucracies and legislative bodies of certain countries. It is sometimes argued that the ideological conformists have a much better chance to be selected than the unorthodox.

Second, the *channels* through which persons move in the recruitment process may vary considerably. Civic groups, labor unions, business societies, the church—these and other channels may be important. Political parties are certainly a major channel in both Communist and non-Communist systems. In Great Britain, after education at Oxford or Cambridge, promotion through the party to the Parliament is the major route. In Western European democracies sometimes education at prestigious universities is also very helpful. In the United States sometimes nonparty groups are as important as parties, or work through parties. And in some communities, indeed, such groups take over the recruitment functions. Finally, there is always the self-starter who does not follow any prescribed channel but decides to mobilize by himself the political coalition he needs in order to seek high office. This is a phenomenon found much more in the United States than in Great Britain or in Western European countries. Figure 10.2 suggests the channels found in democratic (and to a certain nondemocratic) societies. From this one sees that:

1. The party *is but one* major route to legislative, political executive, and administrative position.
2. In certain systems alternative channels may be just as successful or even more so. Those who develop public careers through civic associations, labor unions, et cetera, may in some systems, like that of the United States, be designated as candidates for office without any experience in party organization.
3. The party is usually the final mechanism for the formal designation of candidates for elective public office (certainly for national office). Even though individuals may follow a nonparty and self-starter channel, normally in order to be candidates for elective office they must be designated as such by parties. (The major exception to this in the United States is nonpartisan systems such as are found in the majority of middle-sized American cities, where anyone can get on the ballot without party nomination.)
4. To secure a top position in the administrative system is more often the result of different backgrounds, as well as recruitment through different channels, than is the case for elective public office. University education may lead immediately to the administrative system, and mobility within that system may lead to a top-level administrative elite position. But other paths are also possible, depending on the society—through particular occupations in business and industry or through the party or even via a transfer from political elite positions in the legislature. Party career may be an important stepping-stone for administrators (in the United States it is more important than in most other countries) but is usually less important than for the achievement of elite positions of a political nature.

A third basic observation is that societies also differ in the *mechanisms* and *procedures* which parties employ for final certification and formal nomination of individuals for elite positions. The party may use different types of group decision processes, as a convention or a caucus, or as in the United States a special election participated in by others than merely private members of the party.

The way in which leaders are recruited in modern societies is critical for the performance of the system. As V. O. Key said, "Perhaps the most important function that party leadership needs to perform is the development, grooming, and promotion of candidates for [public office]."[2] This process of recruitment is critical because in it decisions are made concerning the types of leaders needed—the skills, personal

FIGURE 10.2

Alternative Channels for Elite Recruitment to Administrative and Political Positions

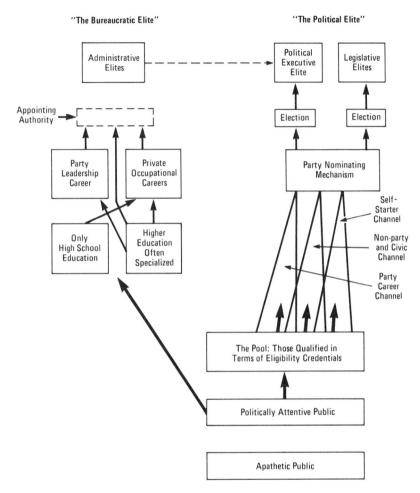

qualities, group characteristics, and orientations toward the political process which are necessary for effective government. If the elite recruitment process is done poorly not only will inept leadership emerge, but the policy output will be inadequate or defective, and the public will lose confidence in the system. Therefore, recruitment is very important for the *political system,* just as it is very important to the *party as a group* which has particular goals and which hopes to compete successfully for political power. For the party to remain credible and to stay in political business, recruitment of able leaders is critical.

The importance of the leadership nomination process is underscored by the practice in nondemocratic societies of the state controlling the way in which candidates are finally designated for candidacy for public office. In a society like the Soviet Union, by way of illustration, although quite a few groups may be permitted to suggest possible candidates for office, the final list of candidates is determined by *one party*, the Communist party, and its final slate is the one which appears on the printed ballot. There may indeed be a large number of proposed candidates, and it may appear that a real choice exists for the voter. But the key decisional point in the whole process is in the preparation of the final list, and this reveals what basically distinguishes a democratic and undemocratic system. Who controls the final decisions in the makeup of the list which goes to the voters is a crucial decisional point in the process. In the Soviet Union there is one group, the Communist party, which prepares this final list. In the United States the Republican party prepares its list, the Democrats another list, the Socialist Workers party a third list, the Prohibitionists a fourth list, and so forth. And no one has the power to collapse all these lists into one.

Who makes a party nomination? and *how?* are the basic questions. Is it to be made by a small claque of unrepresentative leaders or by a larger but indirectly representative body or by the loyal party supporters or by the public generally or should all levels of the party be involved? And, if there are stages in the process, whose decision is to be final? Further, is it to be an open process of true deliberation, or closed, with deliberation a facade? These are the questions which have plagued the American people since 1789.

Major Characteristics of Political Elite Recruitment in the United States

The political leadership in the United States emerges as the result of a continuous and highly varied set of recruitment circumstances and conditions. It is important, first, to remember that the system of government influences this recruitment. We have a federal system and a presidential system, and therefore must select leaders from a nationwide constituency for president, as well as, at the other extreme, officials who run the fifty states, the local mayors, city councils and county boards. And because of the belief in the separation of powers between the legislative, executive, and judicial branches, as well as in the public's right to participate, there is a complex set of opportunities for public involvement. This includes the recruitment of different types of leaders—judges, state governors, other state administrative and executive personnel and, at the local level, county sheriffs and other administrators, city mayors, as well as legislators at the national, state, city, county, and rural township level of governments. Thus thousands of elite positions at all levels are screened and certified each year on the basis of considerations which may be primarily local.

Second, this nation is a relatively decentralized and autonomous system, so that every state has the right to adopt its own procedures for the recruitment of officials at the state and local levels of government. There is no uniform system. In Virginia the state party committee may play a major role in the selection of candidates for state office; in Iowa a major role may be exercised by a convention of delegates; in California the decision may be in the hands of a fairly exclusive set of party supporters who decide in a special election; and in Michigan there may be such an election also, but one which is open to anyone who wants to participate, independents as well as partisans. This variation in procedures is a result of political culture differences in the states—some state parties wish to be (or are required by state law to be) much more disciplined and exclusive than parties in other states.

Third, the American elite recruitment system provides for multiple opportunities for candidacy. Lester Seligman has described five types of party candidacies in the United States:

1. Promotion—the selection of a person who has worked in the organization, seeks the support of the party, and is awarded the nomination on this basis
2. Conscription—the persuasion of someone in the party organization to be a candidate, on the basis of his/her work in the party, even though the person has no desire to run for office
3. Cooptation—the persuasion of someone *outside* the party to become the party's candidate
4. Agency—the selection of a candidate who is the representative of a major nonparty group (such as a labor union leader, business leader, black leader, and so forth)
5. Self-starter—a candidate who did not come up through the party ranks or other groups and who decides on his own initiative to run for office, despite the initial absence of group support[3]

All of these types of candidates are possible in the United States, particularly the last type—the self-starter. This contrasts with, for example, the British and Continental systems, where without party endorsement the likelihood of a successful bid for elite status is rare. Under our system the maverick and the insurgent have an opportunity to oppose the establishment candidates by declaring their intention to appeal to the public for support in the primary election of the party. Similarly, other groups may decide to present their representatives as candidates for office. On occasion union leaders, for example, run for office in the party primary.

Fourth, as a consequence of these possibilities it is a recruitment system where the party organization often does not have exclusive responsibility for decisions on the certification of candidates. The organization may seek out possible recruits, may encourage people to seek public office, may actually work to mobilize a coalition of support behind possible candidates, but the decision at the final certification stage may be made by a voting public, many of whom may not be strongly involved with the organization. This again is in striking contrast to European and British systems, where the final decision on candidacy is made by the organization, and one which the organization will stand behind. The crucial element of party organization responsibility is often missing in the American system. And, consequently, the voters may blame the party for leadership behavior, but in actuality the party as an organization may not have approved the candidacy selection or may not really have been involved in the final decision.

Fifth, American recruitment decisions often are not majority decisions—by the party or by the public. Rather, they may be decisions made by a plurality of participants in a primary election where there is a multiplicity of candidates. In certain parts of the United States, notably the South, there is an effort to create a majority decision by the use of run-off primaries, in which the two highest winners in the first primary confront each other. But in actuality in the South and in other states, there is a strong possibility that a person will be certified as a candidate who secures the backing of only one-fourth or one-third of the party supporters. This raises serious questions concerning the legitimacy of the decision and the extent to which it will enlist the wholehearted support of the party rank and file. Plurality nominations are often not genuinely authoritative and thus they weaken the role of the party, as well as result in nominations of persons who are not well qualified.

Finally, the American system is a conflict and protest-maximizing approach to elite recruitment. A great deal of emphasis is placed on giving all members of the public a right to participate, whether or not they are and have been genuinely involved in party politics previously. Further, insurgent groups are encouraged to present candidates for office and thus to challenge the established leadership in the parties. And all of this dissension and protest is done in public, in campaigns preceding party recruitment elections, the primaries. This may well exacerbate factionalism within the parties and make it difficult for the development of organizational cohesion, harmony, and efficiency. The American emphasis is on populism and protest, not on organizational coherence and responsibility.

The American political culture as it has developed over the years is linked to these special characteristics of our elite recruitment process. Disciplined party systems are inclined to attempt to control the procedures more tightly than we do. Unitary (non-federal) systems will not reveal such a great variety of mechanisms and techniques for doing the job. Where interest group politics is associated more closely with party politics, elite recruitment may be much more simply the certification of interest group leaders by the parties. Where conflict is frowned upon there may be less opportunity for self-starters and challenges to the established leadership. Political systems differ in their cultural norms, and these in turn are reflected in how the system goes about the elite recruitment task.

Ours is a diffuse, decentralized, populist-oriented recruitment system. Yet, despite the special opportunities for candidacy in the United States, political leadership is no more open than in other countries. Our national leadership is high in social status, in education, and in occupational level. In this respect we are no different than other countries. Members of the United States Congress come from middle- and upper middle-class families, as high as British MPs and higher than their opposite numbers in Germany or the Netherlands. In addition, no more than 1 percent of them had manual occupations. Similarly, of all United States presidents since 1789 only 2 percent were manual workers or small farmers by occupation (and only 25 percent had fathers with such occupations).[4] And, a look at the class origins of our Cabinet members shows that from 1950 to 1972 only 8 percent came from the lower class and 13 percent from lower middle-class backgrounds, not much different than the period from 1789 to 1809![5] Opportunities are there for persons from the lower classes to reach top level political leadership positions, but individuals with middle and upper social status have at least five times as good a chance of entering the political elite.

The Importance of Parties in Influencing Political Recruitment

In the complex and decentralized politics of the United States the role of parties in leadership selection is difficult. And it is also controversial. It can be a very central and controlling influence; it can also play a negligible role. When the party organization does assert itself, studies reveal that there are significant consequences. Thus, Seligman, after his Oregon study, concluded that if the party did instigate the candidate selection, the party could influence the candidate's behavior considerably. The conclusion from this study was that "recruitment influences the distribution of power, the representativeness of elites, elite competence, policy outputs, and the collective norms of elites."[6]

In a landmark study of congressional party recruitment in 1966 in

Chicago and its environs, Leo M. Snowiss analyzed the key differences in the party organizations and their candidate selection processes in five inner-city districts, three in the suburbs, and five in the outer city.[7] The inner city was controlled by the Daley machine, the classic type of machine organization. Here recruitment was an internal affair with absolute control in the organization's leadership. In the suburban districts (with safe Republican control) the Republican organization relied on volunteers and issue-oriented activists since it had no patronage. The Democratic suburban organization was very similar to, and tied to, the inner-city organization, with one basic difference: since the Republicans usually won, the Democrats had to recruit others than party stalwarts. In the outer city districts, much more competitive and balanced in party strength, the party organizations function still differently. The conclusion reached in the study was that the degree of the party organization's involvement with the recruitment process has an impact on the type of leadership which contests public offices. Party organization control can be centralized and dominant in the selection of candidates, or it can be weak and ineffectual, factionalized and pluralized, highly dependent on support from other groups in the electorate if it is to be successful. In the former case there is greater likelihood that the elected officials will follow the party organizational line, in a sense, mandated by the machine. In the latter case, the elected officials may well be agents of other groups, such as interest groups, or entrepreneurs who do not feel beholden to the party organization, mavericks who work out their own personal strategies of decision making in office and for successful reelection.

This leads to a key question for American scholars of parties: To what extent do parties *in fact* play a role in the recruitment of candidates to public office? This question may appear anomalous since much of the preceding discussion assumes that parties have a major role, and because parties are thought of as recruiting political leadership, if they do anything at all! And certainly in Britain one is not likely to ask this question, since British parties are deeply involved with leadership selection, above all. In the United States there are a variety of channels by which one can seek public office. The party channel is only one, and therefore the question is pertinent. And of course the advent of the direct primary and its increased usage has restricted the role of the party organization.

Several studies have provided information on the extent to which parties are involved in recruitment. Studies of the selection of candidates to state legislatures reveal that there are great variations by states. In six states the proportions of state legislators running because of "instigation" by party organizations are: New Jersey 69 percent, Pennsylvania 43 percent, California 20 percent, Wisconsin 21 percent, Ohio 31 percent, and Tennessee 17 percent.[8] This suggests that local conditions may influence considerably the extent of the party's involvement.

One must be careful not to jump to conclusions, however, from these data. In these same states where the candidates claimed that the party did not instigate their candidacy, there is evidence that the candidate had been involved in party work and had held party office. In California, for example, 48 percent of the candidates had been active in the party at the local or state level, or both levels. In Ohio the same is true for up to 40 percent of the legislators. Nevertheless, a majority of legislators in these states (except New Jersey) did not see the party as the *primary sponsor* of their candidacies—perhaps 10 percent were sponsored by interest groups, 20 percent to 30 percent were sponsored by friends, many were simply self-starters.

More recent studies of the role of district or county party organizations suggest that under certain conditions candidates for Congress can be quite dependent on, or strongly supported by, the local party. These studies will be analyzed in detail in chapter 16. One of them was the Greenberg study of New York congressmen which revealed that close to 60 percent of those candidates worked fairly closely with county party leaders and campaign workers.[9]

In another study of the relationship between congressmen and their district party organizations (for thirty-six Congressmen in 1964 in seven states) David Olson found that where the party organization was well organized 60 percent of the congressmen relied on the party for both the nomination and election. But since the party often was weak almost half of all congressmen in this study developed their own organization.[10] There is strong evidence therefore that the party organization can be very involved, and can be very relevant, in the leadership recruitment process. Often it appears that the organization is too weak to take an interest or to be effectual.

Conclusions

Although the evidence is not all in or crystal clear, there *is* evidence that the party organization can, and does, have a considerable role in the recruitment of leadership. Where it does have influence, it appears that the type of leadership which seeks office may be different, and the type of leadership behavior in legislative bodies may also be different. Members of Congress are very likely to come from families where the parents, and other relatives, were concerned about partisan issues, discussed them in the home, and took an active part often in party affairs. Up to 40 percent of congressmen in a recent study said they had relatives who had held jobs in politics or the civil service.[11] Then, too, congressmen themselves were often exposed to the party organization in early adulthood (or even late adolescence). Finally, many of them were deeply involved with the party organization at the time of their candidacy, and since being elected they have had to maintain close relationships with those constituency party elites who could help them with reelection, or who might make life difficult for them by opposing them. Thus, at four different career points the party has been visible to them, in contact with them, helping (or opposing them), and a significant reference group with which they must reckon. The cumulative socialization impact of this must be considerable.

There is a strong possibility that the authority and role of the party organization has been corroded because of the place of the direct primary in the system. If parties are to be effective they must be united and strong. Otherwise their leadership will not be cohesive and responsive.

Chapter 11

Leadership Recruitment at State and Local Levels: The Parties and the Primaries

THE GREAT NUMBER of public offices to be filled in the United States at the state and local levels suggests the considerable recruitment burden on parties. Aside from the 100 United States senators, 438 congressional seats, and the 50 governorships, there are approximately 7,800 state legislative posts which have to be filled fairly frequently, in addition to state judicial positions, administrative posts, and the educational leadership of the major state universities for which candidates must be sought. Added to this is the responsibility of selecting candidates for thousands of county legislative, administrative, and judicial positions, and the positions of mayor, and councilman in those cities with partisan elections, to say nothing of township elective positions. What becomes obvious is the continuous burden facing a political group which sees its task as the recruitment of public leadership.

A political party has the dual role of persuading able persons to seek these offices and to screen out those who are ill fitted. The former task is not easy. While one-fourth to one-third of the citizen public is willing to engage in some type of campaign activity through parties or other action groups,[1] it is quite another matter to convince able people to run for office, to take on the new occupation of a governmental career. Studies have underscored the unwillingness of those with established positions who are successful in business, labor, or other types of employment to choose such a public career.[2] Politics attracts many types, but it is often difficult to persuade the most able citizens to leave their private careers for public office. Serving the public by holding a governmental position may be a noble profession, but not many people see it that way. Only a small proportion will encourage their sons or daughters to enter politics.[3]

The task of the parties, then, is to discover, sponsor, and develop support for individuals to run as candidates for office or, alternatively, to decide among several prospective candidates who seek office on their own. The final pre-election act of nomination—endorsing or designating a person as the party candidate for sheriff, governor, state senator, or congressman—is the result of much testing, screening, and consultation. If that job is done well, the public will be presented at the general election with able persons to choose from; if the job is poorly done, the public will be ill served.[4] How is that job to be done? In the history of the United States different party nomination procedures have been tried, changing from the legislative caucus to the delegate convention (after 1800) and then to the direct primary (after 1900). In each case it has been a change in the answer to the basic question of *who* should make the nomination decisions.

The decision which evolved over the years to decentralize and popularize the nomination function—to take it out of the hands of party leaders and to put it in the hands of the public in a separate election— is unique. It stands in contrast to the British system of nominations where the decision on candidacy remains to this day in the hands of the party, whose leaders and supporters at both the local and central levels make the nomination decision. The American emphasis is on mass involvement in the nomination decision by persons not necessarily loyal to, and active within, the party organization. Today there is one *general* answer to that question with the fairly universal adoption of the direct primary at the state and local level. But each state has its own *specific* answer to that question.

Major Types of State and Local Nomination Procedures

All nomination procedures can be classified into nonpartisan and partisan procedures, each containing various subdivisions.

A. Nonpartisan Procedures.
  1. Independent filing. In many states a person can get his name on the general election ballot by filing a petition with a specified number of signatures (usually very large and sometimes requiring a geographical

diversity). He may create his own new group for this purpose (as the Progressive-Conservatives for Jones, or, in 1980 in Michigan, the John Anderson Coalition).

2. Nonpartisan primary. In at least two-thirds of the cities, all with non-partisan elections, the designation of candidates takes place in a special primary election in which party labels do not appear on the ballot. Theoretically parties are not involved in leadership recruitment and designation, but often they are active behind the scenes. If, for example, 10 persons are to be finally elected to the city council, the primary election will narrow the field of would-be candidates (as many as 100 perhaps) to 20, who then compete in the general election.

B. Partisan Procedures

1. The caucus. In rural areas often a township meeting of partisans is held (such as the Democrats of Superior Township or the Republicans of Superior Township) to directly choose their candidates for township clerk, supervisor, treasurer, et cetera. This direct democracy approach is still used in certain areas every year.

2. The delegate convention. Representatives (delegates) from county or other local party organizations assemble in a plenary body called a convention to select the nominees. It was the widely used procedure at both the state and county levels of government until 1900 when it began to give way to the primary. In some states it still is used, however, as a nominating device, although supplemented by the primary. In Connecticut, for example, party conventions are still required to nominate candidates, but such convention decisions can be challenged by anyone who received at least 20 percent of the convention's votes. (This is the challenge primary law.) In Colorado and Massachusetts the parties must meet in state conventions before the primaries and ballot on nominees, and those who receive 20 percent or more of the vote are then listed on the primary ballot. In New York, the state party convention meets to designate candidates and anyone getting 25 percent of the convention's votes may demand a primary (as may anyone securing 100,000 signatures on a petition). There are other states which hold conventions to make extralegal endorsements before the primary—California and Wisconsin are notable in this respect. Finally in some states, such as Michigan and Delaware, certain state offices are still filled by convention nomination (lieutenant governor, secretary of state, attorney general, state treasurer, superintendent of public instruction, regents of the state universities, and justices of the state supreme court).

3. The direct primary. This is a partisan nomination method with direct mass participation and decision making. In a separate election, usually at public expense, the loyal party supporters (but in some states any citizen regardless of party loyalty) go to the polls to select the party candidate from among two or more aspirants who were placed on the ballot by convention decision, by the petition method, or by filing a fee.

The primary has become the most widely used method at the state and local level and is used in all 50 states in some form. What these primaries have in common is *direct voting* (rather than indirect representation through a convention), *mandatory* character (since they are required in almost all states for both parties) and their *public* operation (administered by state and local officials, financed by public funds). There are several types of primaries.

a. *Open primaries.* Anyone can usually participate in these, there being no tests of party loyalty. Party preferences usually do not have to be declared in order to secure a ballot; however, the voter cannot vote in the primary of more than one party. Seven states use this type.

In the wide open, or blanket, primary the voter may vote in the primary of more than one party, but may not indicate two preferences for one office. (Thus he may help the Republicans pick a candidate for sheriff, the Democrats a candidate for governor, and the Socialist-Labor party a candidate for Congress.) Three states, Alaska, Washington, and Louisiana, use this method.

b. *Closed primaries. Theoretically* only those citizens who meet some test of party loyalty or commitment are permitted to vote. They are usually required to register for a party before the election although some states permit a declaration of party affiliation at the time of voting as sufficient. There are three types of tests: *previous allegiance* or support, *future intention* to support the nominees of the party, and *present affiliation*, or current declaration of support. The voter under this system may be asked to declare and make public a party preference before being permitted to vote. Actually, the applications of these tests may be so loose that often it is possible to participate in a party's primary without too much evidence of prior commitment. Certain states, however, have deadlines for shifting from one party to the next, usually from one to three months before the primary. Six states require six months.[5]

There is one more basic distinction to be made among state primaries—whether or not they are majority oriented or not. Ten southern states, plus Oklahoma and the District of Columbia, use the run-off primary, that is, a second primary election if no one in the first primary secures 50 percent of the vote. In the South this is usually necessary only in the Democratic party. In the run-off the two top contenders oppose each other. Similarly, in two states, Iowa and South Dakota, a postprimary convention makes the nomination if no one get 35 percent or more of the vote in the primary. This is to assure a majority winner (no matter how superficial the majority decision really is) in states where one party is so dominant (historically, the Democrats in the South and the Republicans in South Dakota and Iowa) that the person who wins in the primary is the probable winner in the final election. The run-off primary and the postprimary convention then are devices to legitimize the party decision.

A survey of this bewildering array of nominating procedures seems to indicate that each state has developed its own special approach to the task of leadership designation. In actuality there are two basic distinctions in these procedures and thus in how state nominations can be classified: (1) the accessibility of the nomination decisions to the general public—that is, the extent to which the citizenry generally has the opportunity to participate, irrespective of party loyalty or activity; and (2) the encouragement and tolerance of party organizational attempts to influence if not control the nomination decision.

Although other distinctions can also be made (for instance, majority-plurality), the two principles of accessibility and encouragement help to differentiate best among these systems. On the one hand is the question, Does the procedure adopted by a state assume that any citizen has the right to help decide what candidate the party should nominate, or should this be the exclusive right of a more limited set of party leaders and party faithful? On the other hand, how involved should the party organization be and does it have the prerogative of *structuring* the nomination decision, if not actually making it? These two basic questions may appear to be the obverse of each other, but in actuality they are not because it is conceivable a state could have a direct primary which is accessible to all but which also permits (or even requires) the party organization to make a preliminary designation before the primary or a postprimary decision if the primary results are inconclusive. In a sense this is exactly what some of the states have done. The two-fold issues involve *organizational responsibility* and *citizen involvement*. Both are desiderata of those designing a nomination system although one might seem more important than the other.

If the state systems are classified on these dimensions, we can see how both principles are in fact manifest in the procedures adopted. Table 11.1 uses the two dimensions to characterize the system in 50 states, and table 11.2 gives the distribution of states by these classifications.[6] Thus, in approximately one-fourth of the states the primary is used in conjunction with a requirement for, or tolerance of, the party organization's involvement in the process. In another 56 percent the primary is theoretically closed to party supporters, but the party organization's role is not specified. In only 16 percent of the states does it appear that the nomination is thrown completely open to the public with apparently minimal party organizational influence. From this it appears that the states have given quite different answers to the question, Who should make the nomination decision? and often the answer is ambiguous.

Since 1900 the United States has experimented with various approaches to the nomination problem at the state level. The delegate convention method was viciously attacked in the latter part of the nineteenth century for being unrepresentative, corrupt, and manipulative. The charges were often made that the delegates were bought and that the will of the party rank and file was ignored by the bosses controlling the conventions. That was the basis for the attack on the convention in Wisconsin by the Progressive wing of the Republican

TABLE 11.1

A Classification of State Nominations Using Two Dimensions

Influence Role of the Party Organization	Dimension of Public Accessibility to Nomination Decision				
	Most Closed (6 months' requirement)	Closed (less than 6 months' requirement)	Open (but voter must declare party preference at polls)	Open (no declaration of preference)	Wide Open (can vote in more than one party's primary)
Party convention used before primary—required to endorse candidates		Delaware (no primary at state level—conventions nominate)		Utah, North Dakota	
Party endorsements legally permitted	Rhode Island	Connecticut Colorado New York Massachusetts		Idaho	
Party endorsements of an informal nature occur and are tolerated	Pennsylvania	California	Illinois	Wisconsin (Republican), Minnesota	
No evidence of party organizational endorsements publicly before primary	Kentucky, Maine, Maryland, New Jersey	Iowa, South Dakota, West Virginia, Wyoming, Oklahoma, Oregon, Nevada, New Mexico, Nebraska, New Hampshire, Kansas, Arizona, Hawaii, Indiana, plus ten Southern states	Missouri, Vermont, Ohio	Montana, Michigan	Alaska, Washington, Louisiana
Total	6	30	4	7	3

SOURCE: Adapted from Malcolm E. Jewell and David M. Olson, *American State Political Parties and Elections* (Homewood, Ill.: Dorsey Press, 1978), p. 120.

TABLE 11.2

Distribution of States by Primary Classification

System	Number of States	Percentage
Closed primaries with considerable evidence of party organization involvement	8	16
Closed primaries with no evidence of party organizational role publicly	28	56
Open primaries but with evidence of party organizational influence	6	12
Open primaries with no evidence of party organizational involvement publicly	8	16
Total	50	100

SOURCE: Malcolm E. Jewell and David M. Olson, *American State Political Parties and Elections* (Homewood, Ill.: Dorsey Press, 1978), p. 130.

party under Robert M. LaFollette, which led to the adoption of a mandatory, statewide primary there in 1903. It was the result of a protest against establishment forces within the party and the way in which the leadership manipulated and controlled conventions. Thus, the attack on the conventions by those who were left out—by the have-not activists in the parties—convinced people that a change was necessary. Had there been an effective, acceptable, democratic convention method of nomination by 1900, or some acceptable intraparty procedures which were considered democratic, such as the British had, for example, the primary might not have been necessary. But people were angry at the abuses of the system. They demanded regulation. They got the primary, which quickly swept most of the states. The American political culture with its emphasis on populism and mass participation, its concern about bosses, its extreme belief in the right of protest and the protection of insurgency, particularly in areas of one party dominance—these elements aided and supported the reform movement. Forced to accept a reform of the system, the parties have had to adapt to the new conditions of leadership recruitment which these reforms imposed. The basic idea of the direct primary caught on, but its specific implementation varied from state to state. But what is its impact on the system, on public involvement, and on party organization?

The Effects and Consequences of the Direct Primary

The controversy over the primary has been heated. A variety of strong arguments was made for the primary in the era of its widespread adoption, and since that time an equally articulate set of arguments has been made against its adoption. Many of these arguments are summarized in table 11.3. Essentially, of course, the primary adherents emphasize the virtues of mass involvement and the need for protest and competition. The opponents at heart feel that if we want responsible parties nominations should be left to the organization, and that interlopers should not interfere with the organization's performance. As one scholar has put it, "You wouldn't let General Motors stockholders in to vote at a Ford stockholders meeting merely because there is some possibility of their purchasing a Ford!" Similarly, it is argued that Republicans should not be allowed to enter a Democratic primary to help the Democrats pick their standard bearers, because then the Democrats as an organization could not be held responsible. Nor should independents who are not committed to any party be permitted to tell the parties whom they should nominate.

Open primary advocates say, however, that since the candidates who emerge from the party designation procedures may be elected and affect their lives profoundly, there should really be considerable opportunity for everyone to be involved. Closed primary advocates say, "Let's limit participation to bona fide partisans (although let's not be too rigid in defining who these are and let's allow them to make up their minds shortly before primary election day or on that day), but let's really give these people a guaranteed voice in the decision." Anti-primary enthusiasts say, "We already do that through the representative democratic procedures by which delegates are elected to conventions." And so the debate rages, with very little evidence that the United States public is ready to backtrack from its increasing support for the direct primary system.

The Primaries and Public Involvement

Do primaries attract a high proportion of citizens? Is there a relatively high turnout? Analyses reveal a wide range in public interest, as table 11.4 indicates.[7] In a few states *outside the South* the participation is quite high (Washington and West Virginia are examples) and almost as high as in the general election (in Alaska and Nevada, for example). In other states primaries usually do not attract many citizens (New Jersey

TABLE 11.3
A Summary of Arguments in the Direct Primary Controversy

Pro-Primary	Anti-Primary
1. It permits direct popular participation in nominations decisions.	1. Primary participants are unrepresentative of the party supporters—in commitment to the party, in attitudes and beliefs, in social and political characteristics.
2. It provides opportunity for protest against the established party leadership which controls the party organization.	2. The conflict produced by primaries pluralizes the party, leaving scars that are not easily healed.
3. It may contribute to the development of a membership idea through its tests of party affiliation.	3. It takes the nominating function out of the party organization, thus rendering the organization less relevant and making participation and membership in it less meaningful.
4. It enhances the competitiveness of the political process by giving many more would-be candidates an arena to compete for offices.	4. The competition that develops in the primary is not where the party needs it the most—in areas where the party is strongest.
5. It provides a pretest of the election strength and popularity of candidates.	5. The primary makes party success more difficult because it does not permit the party to put together a slate of candidates representing different geographical, ethnic, and ideological, factions in the organization.
6. In one-party dominant areas it assures that leadership selection will be a diverse and competitive process in that party.	6. The party's ability to integrate candidate selection with its program is impossible under the primary since the platform is adopted by the convention but the candidates run by themselves and can ignore the platform.
7. It may encourage independents to become involved in party politics.	7. Cross voting in the primary can be either irresponsible or mischievous—that is, supporters of Party A may vote in the primary of Party B and may never expect to support Party B's candidate in the final election; indeed they may try to nominate B's weakest candidate.
8. It results in different types of candidates than under the convention method, and, therefore, it will lead to different types of politics emanating from this elected leadership.	8. Primaries often produce minority nominations that are not considered truly legitimate and authoritative, and will not be backed by the entire corps of party supporters.

TABLE 11.4

Comparison of Participation in Primary and General
Elections in Selected States, 1946–76

State	Average Primary Vote as Percentage of Voting Age Population	Average General Election Vote as Percentage of Voting Age Population
New Jersey	16.9	50.0
Iowa	21.0	65.8
Minnesota	32.2	64.0
Alaska	37.8	48.7
Nevada	35.8	47.7
Illinois	28.0	66.4
California	38.7	50.7
Washington	40.2	64.0
West Virginia	46.7	71.0

and Iowa are examples, as well as Colorado, Ohio, Maryland, Maine, and Wisconsin—all of whom attract 25 percent or less of the eligible voters). On the average, outside the South the turnout is estimated as 27.5 percent.[8] In *Southern* states the participation in primaries is not always high in relation to the voting age population (30.1 percent average participation in the Democratic primaries from 1946 to 1956 in eleven Southern states). But it is high relative to the general election turnout, as Ranney's analysis reveals (see table 11.5).[9] Three observations stand out from these data: (1) The turnout is low in one-party Democratic states of the South, much lower than might be expected for primaries which are in actuality the final elections; (2) the turnout in other states is even lower, and much lower than in the general elections (a 30 percentage point difference); and (3) to get 27.5 percent of the Americans of voting age to participate in party primaries could be considered quite an achievement; in terms of sheer numbers it is a

TABLE 11.5

Comparative Participation in Primaries and General Elections
for Northern and Southern States
(as a percentage)

	Voting Turnout in Governor Elections, 1962–72		
	Primary Election	General Election	Difference
One-party Democratic states in South	36.7	37.7	+1.0
All other states	27.5	57.5	+30.0

SOURCE: Richard Scammon, ed., *American Votes*, 4th ed. (Washington, D.C.: Governmental Affairs Institute and Congressional Quarterly, 1962–72), p. 415.

greater involvement than occurs in the election of convention delegates, although no systematic study of such a comparison has been made.

Factors for a Higher Turnout in Primaries

The variations in the number of citizens who participate in primaries is no doubt linked to different factors in each state's political traditions, the particular campaigns in a given year, the types of primaries, and perceptions by the public of the importance of the primary battle to state politics. The intensity of conflict among candidates theoretically should result in higher turnout, that is, the public should see contested primaries as attention demanding. There is some evidence to support this hypothesis, but it certainly is not overwhelming (see table 11.6). States where the primaries, are almost invariably contested have a higher turnout on the average. But there does not seem to be a great surge in voting participation in such primaries, in contrast to states where primaries are less frequently contested. Missouri, where all the primaries are contested, has a turnout rate of 30 percent, in contrast to Montana or Wyoming, where primaries are not contested as frequently, with turnout rates of 45 percent.

There is also no overwhelming evidence that the number of candidates in the primary produces a great surge of votes, although the

TABLE 11.6

Association Between Turnout and Primary Contests
(as a percentage)

Region	% of Primaries for Governor Contested 1946–76	Turnout of Population of Voting Age
South		
Eight southern states	100 (Democratic primaries only)	33.3
Three southern states (Texas, South Carolina, Virginia)	81 (Democratic primaries only)	21.5
Non-South		
Ten states outside South	95 (both parties)	35.8
Fifteen states outside South	78 (both parties)	31.7
Ten states outside South	45 (both parties)	25.7

SOURCE: Malcolm E. Jewell and David M. Olson, *American State Political Parties and Elections* (Homewood, Ill.: Dorsey, 1978), p. 143.

TABLE 11.7

Turnout Rate for Gubernatorial Primaries, Non-Southern States Only, 1946–76

Category	Number of States	Median Number of Candidates	Mean Turnout (Based on Population of Voting Age, as a Percentage)
States with high median number of candidates	6	5–7	36.2
States with moderately high number of candidates	5	4	32.4
States with moderately low number of candidates	10	3	32.4
States with only two candidates in the primary	7	2	30.9

SOURCE: Malcolm E. Jewell and David M. Olson, *American State Political Parties and Elections* (Homewood, Ill.: Dorsey, 1978).

turnout is slightly higher in multiple candidacy situations. Table 11.7 presents a summary for gubernatorial primaries based on the Jewell and Olson data for the years 1946 through 1976.

Another hypothesis which might be advanced is that the *open* primary would attract more voters. An analysis of the extremes of types of primaries does indeed present some evidence in support of this, but a study of the variations in types of primaries in terms of their accessibility to the public shows no monotonic increase in turnout as the primary becomes more open. The *mean* turnout for states outside the South can be summarized as follows:[10]

	Most Closed (6 month time limit) 6 states	Normally Closed (Shorter Time Limit) 15 states	Closed (Declare Preference at Time of Election) 3 states	Regular Open Primary 7 states	Wide Open Primary (Alaska and Washington) 2 states
Mean Turnout	23.8%	32.5%	24.8%	33.8%	39.0%

The difference between the extremes (23.8 percent and 39 percent) is suggestive here, but on the other hand the normally open primary does not necessarily attract many more voters than the normally closed primary (33.8 percent and 32.5 percent).

A supplementary question is whether primaries in which the party organization endorses candidates discourages public participation. Again the evidence is ambiguous although it tends to marginally confirm the proposition. Thus we find average turnout by types of states as follows:

	Percentage of Voting Age Public Participating	
	Party Organization Has a Legal or Public Role	Party Organization Has No Legal or Public Role
Closed Primary	30.7(3)	32.0(18)
Open Primary	32.9(4)	35.1(5)

NOTE: Number of states is in parenthesis.

Four factors are, thus, slightly linked to primary turnout: whether there is a pattern of contested primaries, the number of candidates, the openness of the primary, and the involvement of the party organization. But these findings must be used with caution, for there is certainly no striking contrast here between high and low turnout states.[11]

One final consideration must be kept in mind in explaining primary turnout—the pattern of party competition and of turnout in these states. Jewell and Olson found that those states which were inclined to have the highest turnout in general elections were also inclined to have the highest turnout in primary elections (see table 11.8).

The striking contrasts are West Virginia (71 percent general election turnout and 47 percent turnout in primaries), and, on the other hand, Maryland (only 39 percent in general elections and 25 percent in primaries). Obviously, there are many exceptions to this pattern, including the geographical differences—western and border states have the highest turnout averages (close to 37 percent), while the midwest and northeast states are low (28 percent and 24 percent, respectively). These differences suggest regional political cultural patterns which may influence voter interest in primaries more than the type of primary or the particular circumstances of the primary.

TABLE 11.8

Comparison of Turnout Rate for General Elections and Primary Elections Outside South, 1946–76 (as a percentage)

General Election Turnout Average	States Outside the South	
	Primary Turnout	Number of States
60–73	35.1	12
50–59	29.7	13
under 50	28.7	10

SOURCE: Malcolm E. Jewell and David M. Olson, *American State Political Parties and Elections* (Homewood, Ill.: Dorsey, 1978) Press

TABLE 11.9

United States Senate Primaries When No Incumbent Was Running,
1920–60

States Where Democratic Strength Was:	Number of Primaries	Number of Close Primaries	Percentage of Close Primaries
Very low—less than 30 percent of vote in general election	27	3	11
Medium low—30–39 percent	49	12	24
Marginal with Republicans —40–59 percent	197	86	44
Strong—60 percent and more	43	22	51

SOURCE: V. O. Key, Jr., *Politics, Parties and Pressure Groups*, 5th ed. (New York: T. Y. Crowell, 1958), p. 438.

NOTE: Data are recalculated. He also attempted an analysis of House seats, 1952–58. Data are incomplete but seemed to confirm competition was less where party was weak.

Primaries and Political Competition

How competitive are primaries? Where is this competition most likely to occur? What are its apparent consequences? In his classic work on parties, V. O. Key argued that there was a "tendency for the frequency of primary competition to increase with the general election strength of the party."[12] That is, when the party became progressively more successful in an area there was more primary competition. He illustrated this principle at both the state level and in contests for the United States Senate and House nominations. The basic proposition advanced was that where the party was strong and virtually assured of the election there were more hotly contested primaries—in terms of the likelihood of contests, the number of candidates, and the close division of the vote.

V. O. Key's analysis demonstrated also that although the Democrats had more contests in states where they were strong, there were still no more than 50 percent of the primaries for the United States Senate which were close, that is, won with less than 60 percent of the primary vote (see table 11.9).

Thus although V. O. Key's analysis revealed greater competition in the strongest party in one-party areas, he also discovered that "not all nominations for sure seats are contested."[13] The electoral strength of the party is one criterion for evaluating the effectiveness of the primaries. Among other factors Key noted as determining primary competition were incumbency and the bargaining among leaders in the party organization. The research suggests that primary competition will be greatest when:

1. One party dominates the politics of a state (but the competition *only* will occur primarily in this party).
2. Both parties sense a chance of victory (both parties' primaries will be contested).
3. The party organization is weak or not involved in the nomination process.
4. There is no incumbent running for reelection.

The extent to which primaries are contested varies greatly from state to state. Using gubernatorial primaries as a test, research has revealed that in the last thirty years in the South almost every Democratic primary was contested, but outside the South only 51 percent of all primaries were contested if an incumbent was running, compared to 78 percent when there was no incumbent.[14] State legislative primaries are much less contested.[15]

A central question is whether the strength of the party is still, as V. O. Key claimed, a major factor in explaining the incidence of contested primaries. Research suggests that in recent years Key's observation is marginally confirmed but not as convincingly as he suggested (see table 11.10). In the past thirty years in competitive states both parties have had primaries with an equal and relatively high frequency of contests (72 percent and 74 percent). And it is true that when the Democrats are in the majority, the Republicans are somewhat less likely to have contested primaries, although it is still rather high (68 percent). But in Republican controlled areas the Democrats are much less likely to have contested primaries (42 percent). Ironically, then, competition is depressed more in Republican controlled areas than in areas where there is a strong Democratic majority. Generally, in the South contested Republican primaries have been rare. Exceptions are Florida, Arkansas, North Carolina, and Texas where over 40 percent of the Republican gubernatorial primaries have been contested from 1946 to 1976.[16]

The argument was advanced over twenty-five years ago that primaries might be a competitive antidote to one-partyism, that primaries gave voters a true choice between candidates in districts dominated by one party. Julius Turner's research demonstrated that this was generally not true. He concluded that primaries did not provide "realistic" alternatives in over three-quarters of the safe congressional districts of the country. . . . [17] His data were for the period from 1944 to 1950 for seats in the U.S. House of Representatives. Harvey Schantz has repeated Turner's analysis for the period 1964 to 1974 and found even less support for the argument.[18] There is strong evidence here that today

TABLE 11.10
Linkage Between Party Electoral Strength and Primary Competition

Electoral Strength of Parties	Percentage of Contested Democratic Contests	Percentage of Contested Republican Contests	Median Number of Candidates	
			Democrats	Republicans
States with a Democratic majority	86	68	4.0	2.7
States with a Republican majority	42	69	2.4	3.0
Competitive two-party states	74	72	3.1	2.7

SOURCE: Adapted from data in Malcolm E. Jewell and David M. Olson, *American State Political Parties and Elections* (Homewood, Ill.: Dorsey, 1978), pp. 134–35.

NOTE: Based on gubernatorial primaries outside the South, 1946–76.

TABLE 11.11

Comparison of Research on Primary Competitions in Safe Congressional Seats

Competition	1944–50 (Turner)	1964–74 (Schantz)
Percentage of safe seats, won with 60 percent or more of vote	55.6	64.8
Percentage of safe districts with real challenger, defeated by less than 2 to 1	22.2	9.1

SOURCES: Julius Turner, "Primary Elections as the Alternative to Party Competition in 'Safe' Districts," *Journal of Politics*, (May 1953); no. 15 p. 198; Harvey L. Schantz, "Julius Turner Revisited: Primary Elections as the Alternative to Party Competition in 'Safe' Districts" (Communications) *American Political Science Review* 90, no. 2 (1976):541-45.

primaries are even less a way to assure competitive politics in one-party areas. Less than 10 percent in the 1964–74 period were really close contests in safe districts. In a period when competition at the general election is also declining (in this same recent period the percentage of house seats won with 60 percent or less of the vote was 35 percent, compared to 44 percent in the earlier period),[19] primaries can not be considered the saving grace of the system.

As the party organization becomes involved in nomination activities, theoretically contests should decline, because of bargains reached among leaders and an awareness that the power of the organization will be used to promote a particular candidacy. This, in theory, explains the ability of strong machines, such as that in Chicago, to discourage candidacies. And no doubt there are many instances when this indeed is the case. In actuality the limited evidence on this point does not support the theory.[20] It appears that party organizational roles in the recruitment process do not reduce competition. Thus, despite a legal requirement of pre-primary endorsement in Utah, six out of eight Democratic primaries and eight out of eight Republican primaries were contested. In Pennsylvania and California, where informal party endorsements are permitted and occur, 94 percent of gubernatorial primaries are contested. In Illinois the number is 69 percent.

Another interesting question raised long ago is whether in areas of one-party strength the opposition party gradually loses votes, as well as the interest of the public in its candidates, so that the focus of political attention is on the majority party. Thus the majority party may gradually increase its support and strength in the community to the eventual discouragement of the opposition. This suggests an incremental trend to one-party domination. To prove that this indeed happens over time is difficult, but the data do suggest that the strongest party does tend to monopolize the vote cast in the primary even when there are contests in both parties. Thus we find as follows for the period 1946 to 1976:[21]

	States Where Both Parties Have Contested Primaries
Ranney Index of Party Strength	(Percentage of the two party primary vote which on the average goes to the Democratic party)
Democratic majority states	76
Competitive states	53
Republican majority states	39

Even in those Democratic states where the Republicans regularly have contests in their primaries, 76 percent of the primary vote is cast in the Democratic primary. Thus it is not merely a matter of whether there are contests in the weak opposition party but also a matter of whether the public sees the opposition party as the place where the basic battle for power and leadership is being fought in the community. Opposition party primaries may be contested, but in areas of one-party strength the public's interest is in the primary of the strongest party. This does not conduce to two-party competitiveness in the long run.

A final concern is that competitiveness in primaries, signalling intraparty factionalism and conflict, will lead to party defeat in the general election, and hence detract from the party's capability to maintain its status against the opposition party. Research on this question is inconclusive. There seems to be no systematic relationship between divisive primaries and general election results.[22]

However, the data presented by Jewell and Olson shows that among states with a striking contrast in competitiveness of the two parties (by the Ranney Index), there was a definite tendency for the party with fewer contested primaries to be successful in the general election. The data are as follows:[23]

In Competitive States (Ranney Index)	Percentage of general election gubernatorial contests won (1946–76)	
	By Democrats	By Republicans
Four states with a high frequency of Democratic contests and a low frequency of Republican contests	47	53
Four states with a low frequency of Democratic contests and a high frequency of Republican contests	54	46

Where both parties had similar proportions of primaries contested, it was not possible to link primaries to general election results. Only when there was a decided imbalance—when there was much more divisiveness in one party than in the other—did there seem to be an impact on general election results. And in states where the competition is very close, this tendency to intraparty divisiveness may be the key factor explaining defeat.

Primaries and Public Opinion and Partisan Preferences

Who are the persons participating in these primaries (representing on the average only 27.5 percent of the population of voting age) and who make these critical leadership decisions? Extended in-depth research of this matter has not been attempted. Key's thesis of over twenty years still stands for the most part: "In states with a modicum of interparty competition primary participants are often by no means representative of the party. . . . The effective primary constituency may often be a caricature of the entire party following."[24] To what extent this is true is difficult to determine, even in these days of a great deal of survey research data. A few studies have been done, particularly in Wisconsin in 1964, 1966, and 1976, and from these we gain some idea of what the primary electorate looks like. However, it must be remembered that Wisconsin has an open primary permitting voters greater freedom in the primaries.

The first question concerns the involvement of the party faithful in primaries, and there are two ways to summarize the Wisconsin findings (see table 11.12).[25]

TABLE 11.12
Party Identification and the Primary Vote
(Wisconsin Study, 1964)

	Percentage of Each Group Voting in Own Party Primary			Percentage of Total Primary Vote from Each Identification Group*		
imary	Strong Identification	Weak Identification	Independent Leaners	Strong Identification	Weak Identification	Independent Identification
?mocratic	41	43	40	32	47	21
?publican	63	36	39	46	39	15

SOURCE: Austin Ranney and Leon D. Epstein, "The Two Electorates: Voters and Non-Voters in a Wisconsin Primary," *The Journal of* ?tics, vol. 28, no. 3 (August 1966), p. 602.
NOTE: In the first section of the table the percentages should read: 41 percent of the strong Democrats voted in the Democratic ?mary.
?ut of 100 percent.

First, the parties vary in the proportion of strong identifiers who may be attracted to a primary—in a state like Wisconsin a high percentage of primary participants are weak partisans or Independents. In fact, 29 percent of those without any party identification participated in the Wisconsin primaries in 1964. This is a finding similar to that of 1972, from national survey data—34 percent of those in the sample who were Independents had voted in a party primary in 1972.[26]

Associated with this is a second finding: The party activists do not make up the bulk of the primary participants. Only 22 percent of the Wisconsin primary electorate for both parties had done campaign work for the Republican or Democratic parties. The activists represent a larger proportion among primary voters than among voters in the general election (15 percent of the latter had done campaign work for the party). Yet, the overwhelming number of voters in primaries haven't been involved in party work, don't consider themselves party members, and have not given money to the party.[27]

A third finding to note is that the sociodemographic characteristics of primary voters may be distinctive. The 1964 Wisconsin study was particularly interesting in this regard. Two such characteristics to indicate the contrasts between the participants in primaries and in general elections—age categories and income categories—will be used here (see table 11.13). It is quite clear that in Wisconsin at least the older and higher income status individuals in the population dominate primary voting. The discrepancy in age is particularly noticeable in the Republican party, and on income it is particularly noticeable in the Democratic party. There is a strong suggestion here of unrepresentativeness. The 1966 Wisconsin study (although the voter turnout was much lower for that year) suggested the same discrepancy for age and income groups.[28]

A fourth point concerns the issue orientations and ideology of primary participants. There is no very strong evidence that primary par-

TABLE 11.13

*Social Characteristics of Primary and General Election
Participants (Wisconsin Study, 1964)
(as a percentage)*

| | Type of Election | | | |
| | Democrats | | Republicans | |
Characteristic	Primary	General	Primary	General
Age group				
21–29	22	84	21	72
60 and over	43	89	60	85
Income group				
Low—under $4,000	38	80	42	65
High—$8,000 and over	60	94	55	93

SOURCE: Austin Ranney and Leon D. Epstein, "The Two Electorates: Voters and Non-Voters in a Wisconsin Primary," *The Journal of Politics*, vol. 28, no. 3 (August 1966), p. 610.

ticipants are of a special type or hold particular attitudes. It is true that Ranney found in 1966 that among the sample of Wisconsin Democrats 35 percent classified themselves as liberals, while 46 percent of the primary participants were liberal. But the Republicans showed no difference—58 percent in the total sample were self-classified conservatives and 59 percent of the voters in the Republican primary were conservatives. The evidence is limited and uncertain on this point, but it does not point to great attitudinal unrepresentativeness.

A fifth and final concern is the loyalty of the persons voting in a party primary. Are they reliable partisans? Will they support the party in the ensuing election, or, to think of them in the worst light, are they actually invading, or raiding, the other party's primary in order to do mischief? Again, there are only fragments of information. In the 1964 Wisconsin study there was a subsequent defection—22 percent of those voting in the Democratic primary supported the Republican candidate for governor, and 15–16 percent of those voting in the Republican primary supported the Democratic candidate for either United States Senate or for president.[29] In addition, 22 percent of those voting in the Republican primary later voted for Lyndon Johnson in 1964.[30] Caution must be exercised, however, in interpeting such findings as defections. Such crossovers between the primary and general election may represent partisans "raiding" a primary and returning to the party fold!

To this can be added the information derived from Ronald Hedlund's analysis of the presidential primary in Wisconsin in 1976 (to be analyzed in more detail in chapter 12).[31] Hedlund's results suggest that in a primary where there is no exclusion of voters by tests of affiliation (legally true in several states and actually true in many states because of lax administration), the party identifiers are not making the primary decisions. They are "helped" by Independents and opposition party crossovers who may have decidedly different candidate preferences. Some of these may be raiders, maliciously or capriciously entering the opposition party's primary to vote for a candidate *they really do not believe in.* David Adamany claims that the extent of crossovers in Wisconsin primaries in recent years has ranged from 23 percent to 27 percent, most of which is not exclusively to raid, but which nevertheless might dilute the votes of the regular party supporters. He, too, presents data to suggest that "the candidate preferences of crossover voters are quite different from those of (in this case) Democratic voters" (see table 11.14).[32]

Clearly, when a primary is opened up, the consequence can be serious in the sense that it can change the composition of the voters and make the party nomination process permeable by citizens who may be serious—or mischievous—participants in the political process. Even though raiding is infrequent, the nominee who secures the label of

TABLE 11.14

Candidate Preferences of Democratic and Crossover Votes
(as a percentage)

Preferences	1964 Presidential Primary		1968 Presidential Primary		1972 Presidential Primary	
	John Reynolds	George Wallace	Eugene McCarthy	Lyndon Johnson	George McGovern	George Wallace
Democrats	93.2	6.8	47.9	39.4	51.5	7.4
Crossover						
Republicans and Independents	37.5	62.5	69.6	14.3	33.3	29.0

SOURCE: David Adamany, "Crossover Voting and the Democratic Party's Reform Rules" (Communications), *American Political Science Review* 70, no. 2 (June 1976).

the party may indeed be selected by a heterogeneous collection of persons, many of whom are not committed to the party.

The extent to which primary participation by crossover voters is defensible because it results in conversion to the opposite party, is highly questionable. This is Adamany's conclusion on the basis of very limited evidence from the 1964 and 1972 Wisconsin primaries. Thus, in 1972, of the Republican crossovers in the Democratic primary, 39 percent voted for McGovern, but only 18 percent of these Republican crossovers voted for McGovern in the general election.[33] It is on the basis of such findings that it is argued that primaries should be closed and restricted to bona fide partisans.

Conclusions

Throughout the many years of our party history we have been seeking an answer to the question "Who should have the power to nominate candidates for public office?" At the state level we have experimented with a variety of procedures and even today, after adopting the direct primary, in many states we still are uncertain. We have "open" primaries but are not sure how "open" we really want them to be. We have "closed" primaries but permit people to shift easily to the opposite party just before election. We allow the party organization in certain states to endorse candidates prior to the primary, even though the primary is designated to replace the convention. The United States seems to be torn between the two principles of wide open accessibility of nominations to the public generally, and some role for the organization in assuming responsibility for leadership selection. If we were to specify what type of nomination system we should have *ideally*, most people would agree that we want nominations arrived at through a process which is

- *competitive,* so that real choices are available to those who participate in the selection process;
- *representative,* in the sense of reflecting accurately the desires and opinions of the people who are most attentive to politics and concerned about the nature of our political leadership;
- *structured,* in the sense that those organizations under whose label and program candidates run can be held responsible for the leadership recruited;
- *majoritarian,* so that the decision in the selection of leadership is not the act of a factional minority to which the majority dissents.

Serious doubts emerge from the research done that the primaries approximate these requirements. Participation of the voting age population in primaries is relatively low, very uneven from state to state, and certainly below the expectations of the reformers. No particular type of primary seems to be able to maximize voter turnout greatly, even in the most contested primaries. Competition has been declining and is low in precisely those areas where the reformers said it was needed, in "safe" areas for a party. In certain respects the primaries are unrepresentative of the party followers. In the accessible primaries persons may secure primary support which differs from the preferences of the party faithful who have to promote them in the subsequent campaign.

The "side effects" of the primary appear to be potentially serious. The heavy public support for the dominant party in a safe area, while not a monopoly, could lead to atrophy of the opposition. There is also some indication that the divisiveness of hotly contested primaries may lead to bitterness and the withdrawal from politics of those activists on the losing side in the primary.[34] In two-party competitive areas the party with a hotly contested primary may hurt itself so badly that its chances of success in the general election are impaired. Finally, strong arguments can be made that the divisive nature of the nominating process may have an impact on the subsequent process of policy making at the state level. Governors elected in bitterly contested primaries may find it difficult to work with opponents in the legislature.[35] These research findings raise some serious questions about the consequences of the primary for our system.

In the last analysis the proponents of the primary must argue, and demonstrate, that the primary is a more democratic mechanism than a representative delegate convention—that it is a sound participant mechanism, that it performs the nomination job effectively, and that it doesn't have side effects which limit the functioning of parties. For the line is sharply drawn between primary and convention advocates. The latter feel the reformers have done a disservice. They say that strong, cohesive, programmatically responsible party structures are needed and that this goal can be facilitated by having the parties nominate through some intraparty screening and designating process which puts a premium on two things: restricting the nomination function to those loyal and active in the organization, and conducting the deliberations in a forum which will permit the development of a consensus among the many factions in the party support structure. This is in the British and European tradition of responsible parties. For the primary advocates this is unacceptable, particularly because it is contrary to their conceptions of what most enhances democracy. After much historical experimentation, American culture, with its emphasis on populism, its paranoia about party leadership, and its antipathy for organizational discipline, seems to have led to the direct primary. But it is still an open question as to whether its costs for the system, and particularly for a responsible party system, are not greater than its contributions to the democratic spirit.

Chapter 12

Presidential Nominations: Have the Reforms Produced a New Process?

ON March 18, 1980, Illinois citizens went to the polls to vote in their presidential primaries. When it was over the press said the presidential nomination races had, for all practical purposes, been decided. Ronald Reagan, although getting only 48 percent of the vote, received 50 delegates while Anderson, in his home state, received only 26 (Bush's delegates numbered 2). On the Democratic side Jimmy Carter was given 65 percent of the vote, but because of the nonproportional Illinois system, he received 163 delegates; Kennedy received 16. The press concluded the races were over, so far as it could tell, and the Carter and Reagan staffs relaxed. Yet the nominating conventions were still more than three months away. From this situation, many students of American politics have concluded that the presidential selection process has now been fundamentally altered. The question is, How and to what extent?

The manner in which American political parties select their presidential candidates is unique in the Western world. In fact, to many scholars of other countries the system provokes wonder, disbelief, and criticism. In most parliamentary systems, the process is much different. A candidate for the chief executive position (or prime minister) is nominated by a caucus of the legislative representatives of the party, and then becomes the head of the party, as well as eligible to become head of the government when the party is successful in the election and is asked to form a government. There are some deviations from this practice, in France and in Canada (where from time to time party conventions are held to select party leaders). But basically the process for the selection of chief executives is linked to the parliamentary system.

The unique nature of American practice derives from several features. First, there is no established leadership succession system. Therefore, there is a long, drawn-out process which may begin soon (within a year) after the preceding presidential election, with potential candidates coming forward on their own or being encouraged by others. These would-be candidates then test the extent of their support by making many personal appearances, consulting with party leaders, and watching the public opinion polls. The organization and strategy have to be planned carefully for the preconvention operation. It is a time-consuming and wearing process. Jimmy Carter began his campaign right after the George McGovern defeat in 1972. Ronald Reagan began his campaign after Gerald Ford's defeat in 1976.

Second, it is an open and accessible process, at least relatively more accessible to newcomers to national politics than is normally found in other societies. There is ample encouragement for self-starters—a Jimmy Carter, a George Wallace, a Shirley Chisholm. As Theodore White wrote, "Nowhere can men gather together on their own initiative and self-election . . . and then rush the bridge of state with greater chance of success."[1] Third, in direct contrast to what transpires in a parliamentary system, the United States gave up the legislative caucus system of nominating presidential candidates in the 1830s. This took the power from the legislators and turned it over to a more diffuse set of actors at the state and local levels of government; national party leaders sometimes play an important part in the process, sometimes not.

Fourth, it is a decentralized process and has been since the 1830s. The emphasis for would-be candidates has been on appeals to local party leaders and followers, because these are the people who control the selection of delegates at the local level. In recent years with the addition of the relatively open presidential preference primaries there has been an even greater emphasis on the need for candidates to demonstrate their mass appeal throughout the country and hopefully thereby to generate strong support in the press and in public opinion polls. Obviously candidates must appeal at several levels: state party leaders, big city politicians, local convention delegates, financial supporters, interest-group elites, those controlling the mass media, and potential supporters in the public.

It has become, thus, a diffuse, decentralized process. The task of candidates is formidable—putting together an organization which is an expanding coalition of supporters at all levels, while at the same time demonstrating that the candidacy is a credible one, having genuine public appeal throughout the country. It has been said that candidates for the United States presidency had to be "wise and prudent athletes." In recent years that has become more true than ever.

The fifth feature of the process is the action of the national convention itself, either to do the final job of evaluating candidates, or if that has been completed essentially by convention time, of formally certifying and legitimating the decision. In the past that one week at the convention has meant complex bargaining and negotiating among delegates and their leaders—all done in such a way that the public will accept the verdict and not be alienated by it.

The Classic Model versus the New Populism Model

This complex, elaborate, time-consuming, multilevel process is the product of American traditions and political culture. It has always been an elaborate search process, and the party almost tortures itself while making up its mind. In the end it somehow acts as a group and makes the final decision on a candidate. But this process has been undergoing changes in recent years with important consequences for parties, for presidential leadership, and for our system of government. How they got there determines a lot about elites, particularly whether they can be controlled once they get there!

The traditional classic model, the party control model, of presidential nominations which persisted from before the Civil War to the late 1960s had several important elements in it. Its basic purpose was to nominate for the presidency a person who could achieve hopefully both of these goals: contest the presidential election very well, if not win it, and unify the party nationally, if only temporarily, during the period of the campaign.

In the elaboration of this dual purpose there developed a set of operational practices and norms which, given the conditions of American politics, were crucial for party success. One of the basic elements of the classic convention model is the acceptance by all leaders that a *single* nomination would be made by a *majority*, hopefully a strong majority, of the relevant party personnel. Plural nominations spelled disaster for the party (as, for example, 1912 proved for the Republicans with the nomination of two candidates—Roosevelt and Taft). Narrow majority decisions, while acceptable, were not optimal (hence the two-thirds majority rule of the Democrats until 1936, the unit rule, and resolutions to make the nomination unanimous at all conventions despite the division and conflict which actually ensued). Second, the preconvention activities of candidates in appealing to the public and the state and local elites were important aspects of the process, but they were indeed preliminaries. The maneuvers and intrigues of the convention might be influenced by public opinion, but they did not make the decision; the convention remained the final decision maker.

Third, the convention, in arriving at its final decision, did so through power brokerage and political bargaining techniques by which the consensus was built. This was the essential character of the convention. Denis Sullivan and his colleagues, in their study on convention decision making, have specified certain assumptions: Hierarchical party leaders with authority do the bargaining; they are uncommitted and thus can bargain from strong positions, and conflicting elements in the party put aside their differences finally and work together for party victory.[2] M. Ostrogorski early recognized this basic character of the convention about 1900. He said the presidential nomination was "left to the professional politicians" who placed a "high commercial value" on contributing votes to the future president. "In reality, it is all a matter of bargaining: they calculate, they appraise, they buy, they sell, but the bargain is rarely stated in definite terms."[3] In the process of bargaining, however, there is a very canny analysis of, and much debate about, how the party can win while appealing to those interests in the electorate who have to unite behind the candidate. The task of the party convention is to pick "the man most likely to win."[4] And this results in different calculations and different theories, with the majority party, supposedly, having a different nominating task than the minority party.

Finally, the classic model implies that not only is the presidential nomination the consequence of power brokerage, but the total product of the convention, when it is handled properly in all its classical elegance, is a bargain. The convention does other things than nominate someone for the presidency. It also picks a vice-presidential candidate, adopts a platform, selects a national chairman (handpicked by the presidential nominee), and possibly adopts proposals concerning the party organization. The major elements of the party have to be given some recognition of their contribution and role and an incentive for their involvement in the campaign. Thus, in Los Angeles in 1960 when Kennedy barely won the Democratic nomination, the East got the presidency, the South the vice presidency (Lyndon Johnson), the liberals got the platform (chaired by Chester Bowles), and the Western moderates got the national chairmanship (Senator Henry "Scoop" Jackson).

The classic model places much reliance on the party organization's role and function, meeting in convention, to make the crucial decisions for the party. As Theodore White colorfully expressed it, in terms bordering perhaps on caricature at times,

As recently as 1960 one could write of a Democratic convention as it used to be—a universe in itself, a nucleus of 30 or 40 toughminded power brokers, making decisions behind closed doors, while outside the thousands who swelled into convention city made carnival. Tough, surly or corrupt as they might be, the power brokers understood what gave the Democratic party its unique power—its ability to absorb new groups, whether Irish, Italian, Jewish, black, ethnic or labor leaders. The national convention was the anteroom to national executive power.[5]

But it is now argued that the classic model has been replaced today by a new model, perhaps properly called a candidate-centered populist model. At least many scholars are now operating on this basic assumption. Thus White says, " . . . 1972 was to be a rupture of this . . . unwritten process of power."[6] And Jeane Kirkpatrick writes of 1976, "Both the Reagan and Carter feats dramatized what may be the single most important fact about contemporary party politics: The inability of either major American party to control the nominating process for the nation's most important political office."[7] In 1980 certainly this observation would be repeated, since both Reagan and Carter had the required number of delegates to be nominated by the first week of June, long before the conventions.

Sullivan and his colleagues, as well as others, argue very cogently that the assumptions of the classic model are now very doubtful, suggesting that the process has taken on new characteristics. In their opinion, the preconvention activities of the candidates are of greater importance than before. Candidate organizations are more important than party organizations, because of the financial regulations of the federal government and the significance of the large number of preconvention primaries (modified as they have been to provide more candidate control over elected delegates).

The power of party leaders at the convention has been decreased due to the new delegate selection rules, as well as changes in the convention's procedures (elimination of the unit rule, for example). Leaders do not have the hierarchical authority they had before, the convention may not be as open an arena as before (due to delegate commitments), and the coalition-building process of the candidates takes on a different character. The candidate's relationship, and that of his organizational team, to the individual delegate is the heart of the final support mobilization process.[8] The 1980 conventions certainly illustrate this development. There is an expectation that party activists and party identifiers will play an important part in the nomination decision. This may mean somewhat less insistence on the selection of a winner—the primary goal of the professional politician—and somewhat more concern for the policy orientations of candidates. Aspects of the classic model which then are de-emphasized are: consensus building, careful evaluation at the convention of aspirants in terms of party success and party unity, and arriving at a "bargain" which satisfies the major conflicting interests and elements of the party.

There are, then, two models—an old one which is no longer operative, superseded presumably by a new one which more accurately reflects the nature of the presidential nominating process today. How does this new model, the candidate-centered populist model, operate, and with what consequences?

Preprimary Period: The Early Blooming of Potential Candidates

Of the millions of Americans who are interested in politics and perhaps the one hundred thousand who have moved up to some party or governmental elite position, and the one thousand or less who hold (or have recently held) office as governor, United States senator or representative—perhaps fifteen or so give some thought to being a candidate for the presidency. And they do this within a year after the November national election. At least within the "out party" which does not control the presidency, there are several aspirants who become visible very early, either because they tantalize the press with this possibility or because supporters are publicly encouraging them to consider the race. There follows then a two-year period, stage one of the process, leading up to the presidential primaries (which begin in February of the election year), during which the country goes through a special series of actions, events, and developments presumably helpful to decision-making by the public and to a realistic evaluation of the "presidential quality" of would-be candidates by the politicos. Open to question is whether this two-year period is necessary and useful for evaluating these candidates, persuading some of them to drop out, demonstrating the particular appeals and capabilities of others, and gradually leading the American public to a rational decision, first in stage two in the primaries and after that in stage three at the convention (if the decision has not been made by that time).

The timing of the candidate's announcement is a critical decision, of course. One strategy is to seek to establish early credibility and announce early, hoping to head off rivals through good organization and indications of strong support (John Connally in 1978 is an example). Alternatively, the strategy may be to indicate availability without announcing in order to appraise the success of others, and not peak too early, while using public office as a launching pad for the candidacy (as an example, Senator Howard Baker in 1979). And then there is the wait-and-see strategy (Gerald Ford in 1979), which may result in decisions not to compete in the primaries or only in the later ones (Frank Church and Jerry Brown in the 1976 primaries for Democrats), hoping for success in a pluralized convention. Under the populist model this strategy today, it is alleged, is unlikely to lead to the nomination.

In this preprimary period the aspiring candidates have to make some crucial decisions, staking out the political territory they feel is theirs and the political approaches which will win them the nomination. They have to decide, first, what groups or interests within the party, or even outside the party, they wish to appeal to (or they may wish to generalize their appeal) while, second, deciding on what style that appeal shall take. They must decide what image they wish their candidacy to communicate publicly. In addition, of course, they have to decide on the timing of their declaration of candidacy, delaying or expediting it on the basis of certain calculations of advantage. Recently it appears that early declarations are encouraged by the intensity of the competition and the necessity of collecting enough funds to establish the credibility of the candidacy to qualify with the Federal Election Commission for public funds. Early campaign personnel decisions also have to be made, as well as decisions on organizational strategy and publicity.

The key decision, however, for the aspirants in the pluralized "out party" remains that of image—how to picture oneself before the party and the public. This, of course, depends basically on (1) what has been the image of the candidate up to this point; (2) how the other candidates are likely to picture themselves; and (3) what is needed to win. Recent research suggests that four basic styles develop depending on whether one runs as a "partisan" (appealing to the party faithful) or "nonpartisan," and whether one is an "ideologue" (espousing a particular philosophy) or a "coalitional" candidate (seeking to mobilize a wide variety of supporters).[9] Among the Democrats in 1976 Hubert H. Humphrey was a partisan coalitional candidate and Morris Udall was a partisan ideologue; Jimmy Carter was a nonpartisan coalitional candidate and George Wallace was a nonpartisan ideologue. For the Republicans in 1980 John Anderson might be labeled the nonpartisan ideologue, Ronald Reagan the partisan ideologue, and George Bush and Howard Baker as the coalitional types who were appealing more broadly to moderate support, with Bush perhaps less partisan than Baker.

While candidates are attempting to establish themselves in the public eye during the preconvention period and to demonstrate their attractiveness to party leaders at all levels, the public presumably is trying to sift through the available candidates and begin eliminating those who have no appeal. The credentials on which these decisions are made are not altogether clear. Thus Stephen Hess in his discussion of the "routes to the presidency" suggests that the process has become more open than previously. It used to be accepted that the presidential candidate should come from a large state with a large electoral college vote; from those who have had executive experience as governor in such states; and not from among the minority groups of American society—particularly Jews, blacks, perhaps Catholics. But these assumptions have proven invalid in recent years. Small states like Arizona, South Dakota, and Georgia have supplied presidential candidates. Between 1956 and 1976 governors have taken second place to United States senatorial and congressional leaders. And minority groups are considered in many circles very eligible for the presidency, particularly after 1960. Thus the process has become more wide open and the pool of eligibles has been enlarged. Hess argues that the qualities of intelligence, political expertise, a "transcending honesty," a "feel of the nation," a "sense of history," a capacity to communicate and persuade, and tremendous physical stamina are some of the qualities which the public and political leaders use to evaluate the many contenders during the preprimary period.[10]

During this early period, before the presidential primaries begin, very few would-be candidates are persuaded to withdraw. Most candidates wait until the primaries begin or even excuse themselves from the primaries and remain candidates, hoping that the convention will deadlock and still nominate them. An exceptional case was that of Lowell Weicker, United States senator from Connecticut, who on May 17, 1979, withdrew from the race after the reports of public opinion polls revealed that he was trailing behind Gerald Ford and Ronald Reagan. He concluded that he was in third place "and third place in this business is not good enough." Usually early withdrawals of this type do not occur. The would-be candidates develop an organization, solicit funds, attract party activists to their campaign staffs and field forces, talk to party leaders at all levels, and hope that they can establish a credible candidacy. Very little winnowing really takes place until the primaries begin in the presidential election year. Then, sometimes suddenly, dramatic developments occur.

The preprimary period may indeed be very deceiving as to the relative strength of candidates. It may also reveal real weaknesses in their qualifications for the presidency. In the period leading up to the 1968 Republican nomination, Governor George Romney of Michigan looked like a very credible candidate. In the Harris poll of November 1966, he was more popular than President Johnson, 54 percent to 46 percent. But in August 1967, after his trip to Vietnam, he made the fatal mistake of stating that he was "brainwashed" by the military and diplomats in Vietnam, and from that time on his popularity declined, so that in the December 1967 poll in New Hampshire he was the preference of only 12 percent of the electorate, compared to 64 percent for

Richard Nixon. This illustrates the sharp decline that can occur in the status of a contender and the value of the public opinion polls as a device for measuring public sentiment.

Contenders can maintain considerable status during the preprimary period, only to suddenly decline as these candidates face the realities of the presidential selection process in the year preceding the convention. As of January 1972, Senator Edmund Muskie led the field of candidates in the preferences of Democrats in the Gallup poll as follows: Muskie, 32 percent; Kennedy, 27 percent; Humphrey, 17 percent; and McGovern, 3 percent. Yet it was Muskie who soon lost support as the favored candidate, and it was McGovern who was finally nominated.

What really occurs in this early period of two years before the final presidential year is the appearance of a multiplicity of candidates, all of whom attempt to demonstrate their appeal, develop coalitions, communicate an "image" of themselves, solicit funds, and prepare themselves for the presidential primary battles. Few candidates are realistic enough to drop out, as Senator Lowell Weicker did in May 1979. The role of the press in building up and validating these potential candidates is considerable. The public opinion polls chart the progress in their ability to mobilize public support. But few are discouraged. And in February of an election year, most of these candidates remain, ready to compete in the primaries or wait for the conventions. Up to this point the party organizations have had a limited role, the public has had a spectator role, and the press has played a dominant part in the buildup and evaluation of candidates. The candidates as individual political entrepreneurs have pursued their strategies. And everyone who is involved in politics is really waiting for the final stages in the selection process—the series of primary obstacle races which the candidates must run, gathering delegate votes in primaries and in state and district conventions for the final decision at the national convention. The quality and competence and electability of candidates is not definitely judged until the presidential year begins. Then the search process and the sifting process moves into higher gear.

The Presidential Primaries

Stage two of the nominating process begins when New Hampshire holds the first primary in February or March of the election year. In a little over a three-month period, thirty-five states, plus Puerto Rico and the District of Columbia, held such primaries in 1980, in which over 70 percent of the delegates to the national convention were picked. At the same time 25 to 30 percent of the delegates were picked by party conventions or caucuses. With 1980 as a good example, it can be seen that by mid-June the delegate selection processes for the national convention in all the states are complete. This, then, is a very critical period, because the final job of screening the would-be candidates takes place in this time. The results of the early primaries in the East and South, as interpreted by the media, may suggest that certain would-be candidates are front-runners and that the strength of others is minimal. Thus, on March 20, 1980, Hedrick Smith in the *New York Times* argued that Reagan appeared "virtually impossible to beat" after the Illinois primary.[11]

It is argued that there is now a tendency for the results of the primaries to virtually decide the nominee in advance of the convention, and that this tendency stands in sharp contrast to the situation which prevailed earlier. In 1952, for example, Dwight Eisenhower scored impressively with write-in votes in primaries, establishing his appeal over Senator Robert Taft, but the final decision was left up to the bargaining processes of the Republican convention. Estes Kefauver won in the Democratic primaries, but the convention selected Adlai Stevenson. Similarly, John Kennedy in 1960 established his vote-getting ability, despite his Catholicism, in certain primaries (particularly Wisconsin and West Virginia), but his majority was not assured until the convention met in Los Angeles. And even in 1964 the primaries were not decisive. Republican Barry Goldwater did not do well in the primaries, losing to Henry Cabot Lodge in New Hampshire, New Jersey, and Massachusetts, losing to William Scranton in Pennsylvania and to Nelson Rockefeller in Oregon. His victory with 51.5 percent of the vote in California was important, but his victories in the selection of delegates in the conventions of nonprimary states were more decisive. In 1972 the convention's role in the final decision for George McGovern was a large one, since it had to rule on key challenges to delegations—the California and Illinois delegations in particular. Even though his primary victories had made him the favorite, McGovern had to be certified by the Democratic convention. Up to 1976 and 1980, then, the convention's final authoritative role as evaluator and designator of the nominee has remained intact. The question is whether the recent increase in the number of primaries and the alteration of their nature, plus the new rules emphasizing the binding nature of primary decisions, now threaten the basic role of the convention in the nominating process. Has the populist model actually begun to replace the classic model for presidential nominations? And, if so, is this a development of concern?

To answer these questions it is necessary to analyze the origins, increasing use, and different types of presidential primaries which the states have adopted. The presidential primary came into existence first in Wisconsin in 1905 (there are also those who say Florida in 1904). It provided initially only for the direct election of delegates. After Pennsylvania and South Dakota adopted the same system (in 1906 and 1909, respectively), Oregon in 1910 adopted the preferential idea, permitting voters to express their preference for the presidential contenders directly, while also electing national convention delegates.[12] From that point on the special type of presidential primary was experimented with at the state level, by fifteen states in 1912, and after a hiatus until the late 1960s, by over 30 states more recently. In 1980 there were thirty-seven primaries. This represents an even larger proportion of the electorate and delegates than was the case in 1976. Table 12.1 compares the proportion of electorate and delegates for 1968 and 1976.

TABLE 12.1
Comparison of Size of Electorate and
Number of Delegates

		1968	1976
Number of states with presidential primaries selecting delegates	Democrats	17	29
	Republicans	16	28
Percentage of voting age population in these states		56	78
Percentage of convention delegates selected in in these primaries	Democrats	37.5	72.6
	Republicans	34.3	67.9

SOURCE: Austin Ranney, *Participation in American Presidential Nominations, 1976* (Washington, D.C.: American Enterprise Institute for Public Policy Research, 1977), p. 6.

A dramatic change in the relevance of the presidential primary apparently has taken place since 1968. By the 1972 conventions 60 percent of the Democratic delegates and 53 percent of the Republican delegates were chosen by primaries. And by 1976 this had grown close to, or over, 70 percent. By 1980 the proportion was even greater.

Each state has its own special system for selecting delegates to the national convention. The direct primary is only one type of selection procedure. But primaries differ greatly. Some states have primaries in which there is only a preference poll, or popularity contest, for presidential candidate contenders, and delegates are selected by conventions (Michigan is an example of this type). Other states have primaries in which there is only a delegate selection procedure, but no presidential preference poll, and delegates are not committed on the ballot to a candidate (New York is an example). Wisconsin and Florida are examples of states which have both preference polls and separate delegate selection procedures. And then some states combine the idea of presidential preference with delegate selection by having voters select delegates who are bound to a presidential choice. Thus, in one voting action the voter picks delegates and registers his or her preference for a presidential candidate (the California system). Although these are the basic types, there are a variety of other ways in which presidential primary systems differ (see table 12.2). The differentia are (1) whether a strict PR (proportional representation) system is used, or a "winner-take-all" system, or a combination of the two; (2) whether delegates are bound to support candidates at the convention; (3) whether the primary is closed (limited to partisan supporters) or open to everyone; (4) whether the presidential aspirants have to give their consent to being placed on the ballot (volunteer ballot system) or are placed on the ballot irrespective of their consent (blanket ballot system); and (5) whether delegates are selected on a district system or at-large or a combination of the two.

In recent years there have been more PR primaries. In 1976 the Democrats used PR in sixteen states, and in 1980, theoretically at least, in all but two. The Republicans used PR in twelve states in 1976, in twenty-nine in 1980.[13] There were eighteen states, plus the District of Columbia, which required delegates to be bound in 1976. In 1980, although the Democrats technically required this of all delegates, a few states were not able to follow the rule. Hence from twenty-six to twenty-eight states had a binding primary in both parties. The balance between closed and open primaries is close (see table 12.2). Both the blanket ballot and volunteer ballot systems continue to be used. In

TABLE 12.2
Presidential Primaries, 1980

Characteristics	Democrats	Republicans
Number of states and territories	33	36
Percentage of delegates selected through primaries	71	76
Percentage of delegates selected through proportional representation	91	30.5
Number of delegates selected in open primaries	1,054	781
in closed primaries	1,324	735
Number of primaries where primary preference vote is binding	28	26
Number of states with "loophole" primaries (or combinations of winner-take-all systems)	2	21

SOURCE: *Congressional Quarterly Weekly Reports,* February 2, 1980, pp. 283–84, 288; March 8, 1980, p. 648.

primaries at the district level there is considerable variation in states—in 1980 two Democratic primaries used loophole (or winner-take-all) primaries at the district level, and twenty-one Republican primaries used this type.

These specific variations can be confusing. But there are ways of classifying these systems on certain dimensions. Thus, there was party *organization* control over the selection of delegates in twenty-one states, and virtually complete loss of party control to an open primary process in thirteen states; a third set of sixteen states seemed to give the *rank-and-file partisans* major control. But the variations within these three gross categories are considerable.

Another way of classifying these systems is, of course, to rank them on the basis of how well they are designed to *directly* and *accurately* reflect the public's presidential candidate preferences. Certainly then to do this only those systems which pick delegates on a statewide basis strictly proportionate to the results of the presidential preference poll can be considered as most reliable in this sense (for example, the Michigan and Kentucky open systems). Other "open" primaries which are binding are Wisconsin's, for both parties, and Montana's, for the Democrats. However, it is a different matter to consider only those primaries which faithfully reflect the preferences of the *loyal partisans*. Of course, closed primaries are not very closed in many of these states, and individuals can easily register as Democrats or Republicans before primary election day.

For their 1980 national conventions, the Democratic and Republican National Committees (DNC and RNC) specified precisely what rules shall be followed in delegation selection.[14] The Compliance Review Commission of the DNC examined all procedures which the state parties planned to use in selection of delegates to see if they conformed with these rules. (Table 12.3 lists some of the 1980 rules.) The specificity of these rules is immediately apparent. More than ever before the DNC has taken over control of the procedures for the selection of delegates, in the process guaranteeing as well as it can the application of the principles of *proportionality* and faithful reflection of public preferences, the restriction of the process to *loyal partisans*, and the binding nature of the delegate's commitment to a candidate. It was on this latter question that Kennedy sought unsuccessfully to have the Democratic convention in 1980 change the rule, freeing the delegates to vote for him. The RNC has left much of the process up to the states.

Each state's primary, therefore, has to be seen as embodying certain characteristics designed to achieve specific purposes. Some states prefer to select delegates at conventions and have only a "beauty contest" primary; others want to popularly elect and bind delegates to a presidential preference. Some states want a wide-open participatory system,

TABLE 12.3

Examples of Delegate Selection Rules for the National Conventions, 1980

Democrats

2A. Participation in the delegate selection process in primaries or caucuses shall be restricted to Democratic voters only who publicly declare their party preference and have that preference publicly recorded.

2C. A state Party, which is precluded by state statute from complying with this rule, shall adopt and implement an alternative Party-run delegate selection system which complies with this rule.

11A. All candidates for delegate in caucuses, conventions, committees and on primary ballots shall be identified as to presidential preference or uncommitted status at all levels of a process which determines presidential preference.

11H. All delegates . . . shall be bound to vote for the presidential candidate whom they were elected to support for at least the first convention ballot, unless released in writing by the presidential candidate.

12B. At all stages of the delegate selection process, delegates shall be allocated in a fashion that fairly reflects the expressed presidential preference or uncommitted status of the primary voters or, if there is no binding primary, the convention and caucus participants. . . .

Republicans

31n. Except where state law otherwise mandates, only legal and qualified voters who are deemed to be Republicans pursuant to state law or by state party rule shall participate in a Republican primary, caucus, mass meeting or mass convention held for the purpose of selecting delegates. . . .

32a. Participation in a Republican primary, caucus, or any meeting or convention held for the purpose of selecting delegates and alternates . . . shall in no way be abridged for reasons of sex, race, religion, color, age or national origin. The Republican National Committee and the Republican state committee . . . shall take positive action "to achieve" the broadest possible participation by everyone in party affairs, including such participation by women, young people, minority and heritage groups and senior citizens in the delegate selection process.

32b. Unless otherwise provided by the laws of the state . . . the precinct, ward, township, or county meetings shall be open meetings and all citizens who are qualified shall be urged to participate.

32c. Each state shall endeavor to have equal representation of men and women in its delegation to the Republican National Convention.

32d. The provisions of Rule 32 are not intended to be the basis of any kind of quota system.

SOURCE: The Democratic and Republican National Committees.

---

while other states wish to keep the decision in the hands of bona fide party supporters. Some states insist that every person with presidential ambitions be subjected to public scrutiny in their primaries; other states don't insist on that and permit candidates to opt out. Some states, like New Hampshire, want their primaries early, while others want theirs later, or even at the very end of the process, in June. There is thus a bewildering variety of state presidential primary systems spaced from February to June.

In order to bring some order out of all this and to evaluate the role of presidential primaries in the nominating process, only certain issues and features of these primaries will be considered. The basic question of course is whether, as the primary's supporters argued eighty years ago and still do today, the presidential primary improves the leadership search process used every four years in the United States—improves in the sense of providing for a more thorough, more open, more democratic, more equitable opportunity for aspirants to the presidency to demonstrate their competence, for the parties to evaluate their competence, and for the interested public to participate in the selection process in such a way that public support for the process is mobilized and the decisions are legitimized. In a sense the key question is, Do presidential primaries improve the quality of the presidential search process, adding something to that process of sifting leadership beyond what the national convention provides? An answer to this query can be attempted by concentrating on certain specific aspects of the presidential primary systems.

How Much Participation in Presidential Primaries Is There?

An initial concern of primary advocates was the limited number of people involved in conventions and the desire, therefore, of opening up the process so more citizens could participate and participate directly. In terms of sheer numbers there can be no question but that primaries involve more people than those participating in precinct level caucuses in states where the conventions finally pick the delegates (see table 12.4).

In 1980, national surveys done by the University of Michigan Center for Political Studies revealed that in those states holding primaries 37 percent reported that they voted: 63 percent of the strong Republi-

TABLE 12.4
Comparison of Voter Participation in
Primary and Nonprimary States, 1976

Category	Nonprimary States	Primary States (closed primaries)
Average percentage of voting age population participating in Democratic delegate selection	1.9	18.6
Highest percentage of registered Democratic voters participating	19 (Connecticut)	74.0 (California)

SOURCE: Austin Ranney, *Participation in American Presidential Nominations, 1976* (Washington, D.C.: American Enterprise Institute for Public Policy Research, 1977).

cans, 50 percent of the strong Democrats, 34 percent of weak identifiers and Independent leaners, and 18 percent of the "pure" Independents.[15] There are great variations in turnout by states—in 1976 ranging from 11.5 percent of the *voting age population* in Rhode Island to 44.2 percent in Oregon (or from 14.5 percent of the *registered voters* in Rhode Island to 74.1 percent in California).[16]

Despite such variations the message is clear. In many states the primaries can involve many more voters than in nonprimary states—almost six million voters in California in 1976 and 1980, and near or over two million in states, such as, Florida, Illinois, Pennsylvania, Ohio, and Texas.[17]

Over the years there has been an increase in public participation in primaries, although this is dependent on the extent to which the primary contests are genuinely linked to the presidential succession issue and can indeed have an effect on the outcome. There is some argument on this point, however. Thus, in 1976, Ranney argues, there was a "sharp drop-off in turnout" compared to earlier years. His analysis reveals that in competitive primaries during the 1948–68 period the average turnout was 39 percent while in 1976 it was 28 percent.[18] Other scholars are not in total agreement, however, with this conclusion. Rubin has presented data for those states (California, Massachusetts, Oregon, Pennsylvania, and West Virginia) which have had primaries consistently without interruption since 1948. It seems that voters have been "socialized" to participate in them (see table 12.5).[19] There is strong evidence here, then, that not only are there more primaries than ever before but where voters have become used to them they are bringing out the citizenry more than previously.

Who Participates in Primaries—Partisans or Nonpartisan Citizens?

Although the number of persons participating under certain conditions in primaries seems high, sheer numbers should not be the only factor influencing an evaluation of the usefulness of primaries. Who participates may be of greater importance. Over the years there has

TABLE 12.5
Primary Turnout in Five Key States
(as a percentage)

	Registered Voters Participating			
Primary	1948	1960	1972	1976
Democratic	25	37	62	62
Republican	29	42	42	58

SOURCE: Richard L. Rubin, "Presidential Primaries: Continuities, Dimensions of Change, and Political Implications," a paper presented at the Annual Meeting of the American Political Science Association in Washington, D.C. (September 1977).

been a continuous controversy over this matter. Ranney has summarized it well. He identifies three schools of thought on the question.[20] There are those who feel that only the *party regulars* should participate, that is, "people should earn the right to help select their party presidential nominees." The proponents of this position support the convention as the nominating mechanism or, at worst, the mix of primaries and conventions in the pre-1972 period, before the reforms were adopted.

A second group has argued that party regularity should not be the key test but rather that activists in support of candidates and issues *in the year of the convention* should be recognized as having a major right to participation. Ranney contends that the new rules adopted for the 1976 convention requiring "all steps in the delegate selection process" to "take place within the calender year of the Democratic National Convention," and that old party office holders shall not have an automatic right to a delegate position—that such rules are designed to basically alter the concept of who has the right to participate.

A third theory, and one which appears to be more popular all the time, is that any ordinary voter, independent or partisan, loyal or uncommitted, shall have the right to participate in the process of helping the parties decide who their presidential candidates shall be. Thus, in 1976 thirty states held primaries of which at least fifteen were open, so that on primary election day any voter could arrive at the polling place and ask for the ballot of any party. In 1980 the Democrats forbade the selection of delegates in open primaries, although Wisconsin still used such a primary. The Republicans left it up to the states. Some of the states using such open primaries selected large blocs of delegates—Illinois, Michigan, New Jersey, Ohio, Wisconsin, and Texas—representing approximately one-third of all delegates in 1976 and one-third of Republican delegates in 1980. It is interesting that in 1976 these open primaries recorded a significantly lower turnout than for the closed primaries (which required participants to register as a party supporter from nine to thirty-eight days before the primary election date, and which only permitted such registered partisans to vote on that day). Ranney's analysis reveals that in 1976 the percentage of registered voters participating was: 34.9 percent in open primaries and 50.9 percent in closed primaries.[21]

The extent to which there is in fact crossover voting is difficult to substantiate. Presidential contenders openly encourage crossover voting: Lindsay (Wisconsin, 1972), Reagan (generally, but especially in Texas, Indiana, Michigan, and Georgia in 1976), Jackson (Wisconsin, 1972 and 1976). Wallace (Michigan and Wisconsin in 1972), Carter (Wisconsin in 1976).[22] There are also hints of crossovers in the raw data about turnout in certain states when comparing the estimated number of eligible voters.[23]

Two studies based on survey data do suggest that open primaries result in the participation of opposition partisans and Independents. Ranney's study of the New Hampshire and Wisconsin primaries in 1968 revealed that Independents did indeed participate in both of them (54 percent of the hard-core Independents in Wisconsin, 59 percent of the Independent Democrats and 70 percent of the Independent Republicans).[24] In table 12.6 Ronald Hedlund analyzes the 1976 Wisconsin primary. A high proportion of the vote came from other than partisan sources. Further, table 12.7 shows an equally interesting division of the vote by candidates in 1976. Clearly, there was an interesting conflict in both primaries in candidate support. The Democrats in the Republican primary were surprisingly interested in Reagan (as were the Independents)! The Republicans in the Democratic primary were heavily backing Wallace! The distance between the two groups of partisans was considerable (41 percent compared to 7 percent for Wallace—a 34-point difference, and 48 percent compared to 34 percent for Reagan—a 14-point difference). Hedlund argues that there was no "widespread mischief vote" (crossovers to nominate the weakest candidate of the opposition or to embarrass the opposition), or at least not one which had "a critical effect on the primary's outcome." But it is clear that other than partisans were participating, and the Independents and opposition interlopers had distinctly different candidate preferences.

TABLE 12.6
Source of Votes in Wisconsin Primary, 1976

Percentage of vote from	Republican Primary	Democratic Primary
Independents	48	41
Opposition party supporters	10	5
Bona fide partisans	42	54
	100	100

SOURCE: Ronald D. Hedlund, "Crossover Voting in a 1976 Open Presidential Primary," *Public Opinion Quarterly* 41, no. 4 (Winter 1977–78): 498–514.

TABLE 12.7
Voting Behavior in the 1976 Primaries
(as a percentage)

Group	Republican Primary		Democratic Primary		
	Ford	Reagan	Carter	Wallace	Udall
Republican Identifiers	66	34	32	41	15
Democratic Identifiers	52	48	41	7	39
Independents	46	54	29	16	40

The open primary was by Democratic party bylaw forbidden for 1980, although how the states will in fact adjust to this is as yet not clear. And open primaries are still used by the Republicans widely. Hence, the "crossover primary" remains a real possibility, meaning that the party nomination in certain states is not exclusively in the hands of the party regulars.

How "Representative" of the Rank and File Are Primary Voters?

This is a central question in the analysis of primaries, because it was the concern over the representativeness of the early caucus and conventions which was a basic argument in favor of the primaries. And it remains an argument today. *Representativeness* of course means a variety of things and can be interpreted from a variety of vantage points. Thus, representativeness of the delegate selection for the national conventions can be thought of in different senses: It can be the demographic and social characteristics of the delegates and how closely they mirror the rank-and-file partisans whom they are supposed to represent; the ideological orientations of the delegates, and the extent to which they are in this sense a good mirror of their rank-and-file constituents; the characteristics of those who vote in primaries, and their representativeness in relation to the loyal partisans or regular supporters and activists. Or it can mean the presidential candidate preferences which the delegates have, and in most cases which they were committed to when selected, and how faithfully these preferences, as they are recorded in the votes at the convention, represent the desires of their constituents.

One of the problems, of course, with any analysis of representation is deciding what the primary constituency is, or should be, in terms of judging the characteristics and actions of the representers. Some will insist it should be the party leaders or the most activist partisans at the grass roots, others will insist it should be all loyal party supporters, and others will insist it should be anybody in the citizen public. In judging primaries, therefore, these different conceptions of the constituency must be kept in mind. The characteristics of the delegates at the convention and their representativeness will be discussed in the ensuing section analyzing the convention itself. Here we are concerned with the representativeness of *those who vote in the primaries* and of delegate preferences and votes for presidential nominees, compared to constituent preferences.

From the limited studies which have been made of the social characteristics we can deduce that those who do participate in primaries tend to differ by age and socioeconomic status from regular voters (see table 12.8). The older and upper-income groups have the best participation rates in both primaries and general elections. Both types of elections produce a higher turnout for higher status groups. Young voters seem

TABLE 12.8

Voting Behavior of Social Groups in
Primaries and Elections 1976
(as a percentage)

Age Categories	Primaries	General Election
18–21	20	30
22–29	29	43
30–44	45	49
45–59	52	68
60 and over	55	64
Family income		
Under $8,000	34	45
$8,000–12,000	36	46
$12,001–20,000	46	59
Over $20,000	48	66

SOURCE: Richard L. Rubin, "Presidential Primaries: Continuities, Dimensions of Change, and Political Implications" a paper presented at the Annual Meeting of the American Political
Science Association, Washington, D.C. (1977), p. 29, table 4.

to participate less in primaries. This finding is corroborated by Ranney's study of primary voters in Wisconsin and New Hampshire in
1968. Young people were underrepresented among primary voters,
women were overrepresented, and the most conservative persons on
Vietnam and civil rights issues tended to vote in the primaries.[25]

A key question, of course, is, Do delegates faithfully reflect the presidential candidate preferences of their "constituents" (however these
may be defined)? To some persons who feel delegates should be free
to exercise their own judgment at the convention this is unimportant.
To others this is the major issue for evaluating primaries, because delegates are elected to perform one distinctive representative act—vote
for a presidential candidate. Now the primaries create problems which
complicate this matter of representation by delegates of rank-and-file
preferences. One problem is that there may not be an opportunity for
these preferences to be unambiguously stated or communicated. Thus
certain candidates may not be on the primary ballot, or the delegates
running may not be committed to them. The second problem is that
the preferences of the constituents may not be properly or accurately
utilized in the selection of delegates. The third problem is that delegates picked presumably because they favor a particular presidential
candidate may not be bound to support that candidate in the convention and finally do indeed decide to support another candidate. (In
1980, for example, Kennedy lost 112 delegate votes from those pledged
to him before the convention.) A fourth problem is that in the winner-
take-all systems (at the district level particularly, the loophole primaries) there can be a distortion in the representation of constituent pref-

erences, and constituents may be forced to acquiesce in the behavior of a delegate supporting a presidential candidate who has only a plurality of support in their district.

Analysis of the 1976 presidential primaries reveals that to some extent in certain states the results were a distortion of popular preferences.[26] The analysis revealed that the imperfections in the operation of the PR system in fourteen states resulted in an overrepresentation of the Carter vote by an average of 5.1 percent (or 46 delegates). As a result of the loophole primaries in eleven states Carter was overrepresented by 10.5 percent (95 additional delegates). Ford also gained 31 additional delegates because of these two types of situations. Examples in a state-by-state analysis are provided which sometimes reveal gross inequities in the representation of preferences, both over and under what Carter and Ford should have received. In Ohio, Texas, and New Hampshire, with loophole primaries, Carter secured 31 percent, 47 percent, and 53 percent more in delegate votes than he was entitled to if there was pure proportionality (or 108 more delegates in these three states alone). Gerald Ford in Rhode Island, New Hampshire, New Jersey, Ohio, Maryland, and Wisconsin secured from 34 percent to 45 percent *more* than he would have under pure proportionality, and in California, Texas, Alabama, Indiana from 32 percent to 34 percent *less* than he would have under pure proportionality. Loophole primaries, plus winner-take-all systems, plus PR systems which are not "pure" systems, therefore, can seriously distort the preferences of the constituents.

How Competitive Are the Primaries?

The competitiveness of primaries varies greatly by presidential year. In many primaries few contenders appear before the voters, and turnout is low. From 1972 on, however, a majority of primaries have been contested. But few primaries were truly competitive before then. Table 12.9 shows the number of competitive primaries in the postwar period.[27]

Often one major contender will contest in the primaries and the other will not. Thus in 1952 Eisenhower stayed out (although there were often write-in votes for him), as did Adlai Stevenson, yet both of them won the nomination. In 1968 Hubert Humphrey, who won the nomination, was really never involved in any direct contests with Eugene McCarthy or Robert Kennedy. In 1960 John Kennedy could not be on the California ballot, nor could Lyndon Johnson or Adlai Stevenson because of the favorite son candidacy of Governor Edmund G. Brown. And in 1964 Barry Goldwater did not win the nomination because of his successful primary contests (his one major win was against Nelson Rockefeller in California). In 1972 Oregon was the only primary which included the name of Senator Edward Kennedy,

TABLE 12.9

The Number of "Competitive" Primaries

	Winner received less than 65 percent of the vote and turnout of eligible voters was 10 percent or more	
Year	Democrats	Republicans
1948	0	3
1952	4	5
1956	2	0
1960	2	0
1964	2	6
1968	6	0
1972	12	0
1976	23	19
1980	26	15

SOURCE: Reprinted by permission from Richard L. Rubin, *Party Dynamics: The Democratic Coalition and the Politics of Change* (New York: Oxford University Press, 1976), p. 150.

considered by many a potential candidate although an avowed noncandidate.[28]

In 1976 the presidential primaries were rather well contested. Carter, Wallace, Udall, and Jackson entered twenty-two or more of them. Indeed they were so well contested that Carter received only 39 percent of the total Democratic primary vote.[29] In 1980 he received 53 percent; Reagan received 61 percent of the total Republican primary vote.[30]

Under the new presidential candidate funding system it is possible, and in a real sense necessary, for aspirants to compete in more primaries and do well in them. In fact the entire financial support system encourages a multiplicity of candidates and entrance into the early primaries. In 1980 each candidate could spend over $17,500,000 divided as follows: $7,360,000 raised privately from contributions of $250 or less; $7,360,000 in matching funds from the federal government; and $2,944,000 in funds (20 percent of the above) for fund raising costs. By February 14, 1980, ten candidates had raised the necessary private funds to qualify for federal matching funds.

Public Opinion Polls as a Measure of Popular Preferences

During the same period that the presidential primaries are being held there are also a variety of polls measuring public preferences among all the candidates. As William R. Keech says, "The primaries and the polls are the two most important sources of evidence about the relative popularity of the candidates." In his opinion, "the primaries are far more likely to give a confused picture than the polls. . . ."[31] A look at the public opinion polls since 1936, when scientific polling was first really undertaken, shows that the preferred candidate in the polls usually won. In fact, in forty-four years there is only one clear-cut case where the winner in the last poll before the national convention was not also the winner in the convention. Only in 1952, when Estes Kefauver won most of the primaries and the polls, was the rank-and-file preference reversed in the convention, primarily because Kefauver had angered the Democratic party leaders through his charges of the connections between big city Democratic machines and organized crime. In 1964 Goldwater was not the clear choice of the public in the Gallup polls, and it was his build-up of strength among delegates not elected in primaries which eventually won the nomination for him at San Francisco. Aside from these two cases, in eleven presidential years for both parties the conventions' decisions have reflected the rank-and-file partisan preferences. These preferences often emerged over time as the result of the press coverage of the direct primaries. But other factors were also important. The main point is, as Keech maintains, that the conventions have generally mirrored public preferences.

What is interesting also is that the convention has mirrored the preferences of the majority of local party leaders. Since 1952 Gallup has polled the three thousand county party chairmen in the United States as to their preferences in the presidential candidate race. A look at the convention decision in relationship to the preferences of these chairmen indicates a high level of congruence. There was a discrepancy among Democrats only in 1972—the chairman wanted Humphrey, but the convention nominated McGovern. Among Republicans the only discrepancy was in 1952—the chairman wanted Taft, but the convention nominated Eisenhower. Thus the congruence between the preferences of rank-and-file partisans in the polls and the convention decision may be high, while the results of the primaries and the convention decision occasionally may be at odds, or the primary results may be ambiguous or irrelevant.

An Evaluation of Presidential Primaries

There can be no doubt that the increasing use of presidential preference primaries has complicated and changed the presidential nominating process. And the popularity of the primaries, including the public attention attracted to states which have them, indicates it is difficult to envisage a reversal of the recent pattern. Some states have considered changes, and there may be revisions by 1984. Further, in 1981 both national chairmen agreed that changes are necessary—fewer primaries and a shorter primary season, for one reason because of campaigning costs.[32] And there is a major reconsideration of the binding nature of the primaries and the veto power of candidates over the choice of their delegates. Hence, a controversy has developed between those who support the present Democratic rule that all delegates should be bound and those who see that rule as a real threat to the party nomination process.

Major reform of the present primary system will be difficult, however. Considerable support for them remains; and to some people the values and virtues of the primaries are considerable. They do force presidential candidates to demonstrate their vote mobilization talents in trial heats early in the presidential election year, sometimes in intensely competitive multicandidate contests. They do bring out large numbers of citizens in such contests, so that if gross numerical participation is important, the primaries certainly provide it. Further, the primary, in appearance at least, is a more open process, permitting candidates who might otherwise not be considered to enter and attempt to establish themselves as credible contenders.

The arguments against the presidential primary are also strongly presented: The integration of popular preference with delegate selection is not properly done yet, despite efforts to select delegates who have been committed to presidential nominees *and* to bind the delegates to support these preferences. Often only a few of the real contenders for the presidency enter the primary in a particular state, and thus the results of the primary cannot be considered representative and conclusive. The early elimination of candidates because they fail in one or two states (the "sudden death" primary) means that later primaries are less relevant for the total candidate evaluation process. The role of the media is much too influential in interpreting primary results and building up candidates who do better than expected in the early primaries. Further, important credentials for the presidency may be de-emphasized in this drive for mass media support. The crossover primary means that the decision may not be confined to bona fide partisans, that in effect it is not a party decision any longer, and not one the party can be held responsible for. Primaries actually either exaggerate the victory of a winner or understate the extent of his success. The tremendous amount of resources in time, energy, and money required today to enter all of the primaries (thirty-six state primaries in 1980) means that candidates cannot campaign effectively in all of them and the public is then not properly informed in order to make a meaningful, deliberative decision on all the candidates. They, therefore, may misjudge the candidate's capabilities, as well as his position on policy questions. With a limited amount of money available for thirty-six states, to finance campaign personnel salaries, organization headquarters, travel, campaign literature, and mass media advertising, candidates are forced to shortcut the job of communicating with the public and rank-and-file partisans in each state. The primaries subvert the party organizational process, weaken and divide parties, and thus contribute in the last analysis to the deterioration of the party as it functions in leadership recruitment and control. Nominations are not then the authoritative and binding decisions of the party structure. Primaries are not functional to organizational consensus. Public funds are used to pay the costs of all presidential contenders, many of whom may not be credible candidates.

In short, the key question which continues to face the American public is whether to maximize mass participation and do this at the expense of the party structures or maximize party organizational coherence and responsibility. No way to do both has yet been worked out—by having the party organization develop internal procedures for elaborate consultation between its leadership and the rank and file, but with the leadership selection remaining an organizational decision. The move toward the "populist model" of nominations has been in a way harmful to the party organization. This need not be. In the process, the national convention's nature and function seems to have been altered.

The National Convention—Final Phase of the Presidential Nomination Process

Traditional discussions of the convention have laid great stress on its importance as an apparatus in the party structure and its pre-eminent role in presidential nominations. While this may be changing considerably in the move to certain types of primaries, the convention has not yet been definitely made anachronistic. The primaries may either build up a front runner whom the convention merely ratifies, or they may produce blocs of delegates bound to various candidates, none of whom have a majority. If this happens the bargaining process in the convention will again be very important, but certainly differing from the bargaining process of the classic model. In any event, what happened in 1976 and 1980 may not necessarily be the wave of the future. The national convention may still play an important role in nominating presidential candidates. It is, therefore, useful to review carefully what has been the convention's role in the nominating process and to compare what *was* with what seems to be the evolving process today.

It was James Bryce who said long ago that the task of the party convention is to pick a candidate who can win. This was its chief task, in reality, and one which determined the basic orientation of that body. All other actions, in a sense, were linked to that task, whether it is defined as including the final screening and evaluation of candidates, the negotiation among interest subgroups for support of alternative candidates, or merely the final certification of the winner. There is an age-old argument whether conventions actually selected the most electable among the contenders (a Stevenson instead of a Kefauver, a Goldwater instead of a Scranton or Rockefeller, a McGovern instead of a Muskie or Humphrey), and the extent to which ability was sacrificed for electability. But at least the generalization can be made that the party hoped to pick a candidate who could win (or at least run a hard and respectable race), however the assumptions underlying that decision may be questioned from time to time. Implicitly also, the party presumably picked candidates who, if elected, would work effectively with other political leaders and particularly with Congress in order to provide effective leadership.

Linked to this task of selecting an electable candidate was the task of preparing and adopting the party's platform, in which the party presents its analysis of the problems facing our society and its proposals for action. The platform in theory was supposed to maximize the possibilities of winning the election. This was part of the bargaining process of the convention, in the narrow sense of the "aggregation" of the demands of the interest groups who have specific policy positions, and also in a larger sense as part of the total "bargain" arrived at by party leaders at the convention. Thus in 1960, at Los Angeles, John Kennedy accepted a "liberal" platform as part of a bargain which included Lyndon Johnson as the vice-presidential candidate, to placate liberals who objected to that selection. The analysis of most conventions would probably lead to the revelation of similar bargains (except the unsuccessful Goldwater convention of 1964 and the unsuccessful McGovern convention of 1972, where no "bargain" was arrived at among the various elements in the party). Certainly in 1976 and 1980 the Carter conventions can be interpreted in these terms. For the Republicans the same was true in 1976, but in 1980 the platform represented less of a compromise (although the selection of Bush as vice-presidential candidate was a bargaining move).

The platform is, thus, important as (1) part of the effort to win the election; (2) an opportunity for interest groups to be heard; and (3) part of the bargaining process of the convention. It may also be important as a statement of the long-range goals and principles of the party. Pomper argues all these positions strongly:

In order to win elections, the party must also promote, in part, the cause of voter-rationality. The attention to the presumed interests of voting groups in the platforms provides a policy significance to elections. These documents are reasonably meaningful indications of the party's intentions. By their strictures about the past and pledges for the future, a party becomes committed to particular policies . . . platforms provide assistance to voters and indirect policy influences on the parties. Platforms are indeed to run on, not to stand on—but they also can reflect and affect the pace, direction, winner, and meaning of the race.[33]

Other tasks are performed at the convention which may also be important, either for the campaign or for the long-range development of the party. There are the previously noted plenary powers of the convention to make basic changes in the party organization, if it wants to: the decision to change the composition of the national committees, to determine the rules for the apportionment of delegates to the convention, the decision by the Democrats to hold miniconventions two years after each presidential year convention, to regulate the conditions under which the credentials of delegations may be contested. These organizational policy decisions could be very significant. If the national convention decided to set up a national party Council of Fifty with specific power (as recommended long ago by the Committee of Political Scientists in 1950) it could do so by majority vote!

The convention is to be seen as an arena of party bargaining, as an interactive forum of the party faithful from all parts of the United States, and as a mass media spectacle which is a launching pad for the campaign. As a conclave of the faithful it performs a variety of interesting functions. In a chapter in his classic book, *The Politics of Democracy* (1940), Pendleton Herring wrote of "the uses for National Conventions," in which he says, "The value of the convention lies in its permitting the rank and file of the party to participate physically and emotionally in a common enterprise. Here are the men who must carry the brunt of the campaign. Here they have their chance to meet, to shout together, to act together, to feel together."[34] The convention gives new leadership an opportunity to be seen, to be heard, and to mobilize support from the rank and file (as Kennedy did in 1956 and McGovern in 1968, four years before they won the presidential nomination). The convention gives delegates an opportunity to exchange information, insights, and experience about party work, to acquire additional ideas and skills for political work. As Herring put it, the convention "is admirably suited to testing the talents of our politicians. It demands organizational skill and manipulative genius—both of which qualities are exceedingly useful in democratic government."[35]

In the past the convention had many values. As a proving ground for leaders, as an arena which could help promote party solidarity, as a policy deliberating forum, it was important. While its main task was to maximize competition (by picking a candidate who would run well) it also had a basic integrative role to play in the system. Now, with the movement toward more presidential primaries, the question is whether these values and functions will be fulfilled. The question for many is whether the contributions of the primary are of such preeminent consequence that they justify the degeneration of the convention.

The characteristics of the delegates to the convention have been studied extensively of late. Such research reveals the high turnover of delegates—two-thirds or more are new each time.[36] While this provides an opportunity for rewarding local workers and officials, an opportunity greatly sought, it also means less continuity in experience. Yet, those who do come are experienced in party affairs in their localities and states: Up to 70 percent had been active in party work for ten or more years before they came to the convention.[37] They are also a more socially diverse group than ever before—more women, blacks, and young people. They rank high in educational level, and this has not changed much over the years: At the 1948 conventions among the Democrats 78 percent of the delegates had attended college, at the 1972 convention 79 percent had attended college. For the Republicans 82 percent at the 1948 convention, and 85 percent of those at the 1972 convention had attended college. Occupational data reveal also that the delegates are high in socioeconomic status. Despite these similarities the delegates for the two parties can differ strikingly in their ideological position (or their views on policy questions). Several studies since 1956 have demonstrated that the parties are not Tweedledum and Tweedledee in issue positions (see table 12.10). Clearly these delegate groups are rival cadres of activists who despite similar social backgrounds are competitors in policy views. Table 12.11 illustrates how delegates classified themselves ideologically in 1972: The delegates at national conventions in the past were certainly individuals committed to the performance of certain critical tasks for the party. Kirkpatrick's

TABLE 12.10

Comparison of Issue Positions of Republican and Democratic Delegates in 1972 (as a percentage)

Favoring or Having Favorable Attitudes Toward	Democrats	Republicans
Busing children to school in order to integrate	66	8
Government action against inflation	87	63
Political demonstrators	59	14
Welfare recipients	58	25
Having a welfare policy which abolishes poverty	57	10
Action to protect the legal rights of the accused	78	21
Average "distance"	43.3	

SOURCE: Jeane Kirkpatrick, *The New Presidential Elite* (New York: Russell Sage, 1976), pp. 301–7.

study in 1972 presented the delegates with five possible roles and asked them to rank order them (see table 12.12).

While there is general recognition of the need to pick an electable presidential–vice-presidential candidate team, other role orientations are also important. The delegates must be seen as a group of highly motivated activists who are aware of the multifunctional character of the convention—to maximize the party's competitive status, to develop a program or a set of policy positions, to reward able leadership, and to develop party consensus.

What conclusions do the findings of these studies suggest? The delegates have always been and still are a high social status group (although coming from very diverse social backgrounds) with considerable party experience, even though two-thirds of them at any national convention are new to convention politics. They seem to be very purposefully motivated to the achievement of personal satisfactions, as

TABLE 12.11
Ideological Self-Classification of Delegates, 1972
(as a percentage)

	Delegates	
Classifications	Democratic	Republican
Radical	8	0
Very Liberal	41	1
Somewhat Liberal	30	9
Moderate	13	35
Somewhat Conservative	6	44
Very Conservative	2	13

SOURCE: Jeane Kirkpatrick, *The New Presidential Elite* (New York: Russell Sage, 1976), p. 169.

TABLE 12.12
Rank Order of Convention Roles as Perceived by
Delegates, 1972 (as a percentage)

	Those Who Ranked the Role First or Second	
Role	Democrats	Republicans
Pick a winning team	69	85
Adopt correct issue positions	49	52
Nominate deserving candidates	37	28
Unify the party	30	32
Reform the party	18	6

SOURCE: Jeane Kirkpatrick, *The New Presidential Elite* (New York: Russell Sage, 1976), p. 126.

well as fulfilling party functions. They are alert to the tasks the convention must perform. They are also a relatively strongly committed set of ideologues, the Republicans much more conservative and the Democrats much more liberal. And there has not been much change in these characteristics over time, although at particular conventions the delegates may appear much less (or less) representative than at others. Kirkpatrick, for example, argues that the 1972 Democratic convention on the one hand "demonstrates the persistence of class characteristics of political elites" and also "illustrates the errors of concluding that 'open' processes . . . will produce a convention in which 'the people' are represented. . . ." She concludes,

> Conventions based on "open" participatory politics may turn out (as in 1972) to be less representative of party rank and file (and other voters) than conventions peopled by labor leaders, political "bosses," and public officials. . . . A characteristic of the "new breed" may be its remoteness from the party rank and file, and a major consequence of the new rules may have been to open the way for selection of delegates unrepresentative of and unaccountable to either the party rank and file or any ongoing organization whose welfare depends on responsiveness to that rank and file.[38]

This is the observation and the complaint of one scholar. Others will, and do, disagree. Actually there is little solid empirical evidence yet to permit confidential generalizations. The impact of the primaries on the representativeness of the convention has not been clearly demonstrated. The mandatory quotas preceding the Democratic convention in 1972 did produce more blacks, youth, and women. But this was not necessarily and only a consequence of the use of more primaries. The delegates appear in 1972 and 1976 to have come as much from middle-class and upper middle-class backgrounds as previously, to be as liberal or conservative in attitudes as in other conventions, and to be as diversely motivated. There is as yet no evidence to prove that primaries produce more representative sets of delegates or delegates who are fundamentally different in perspective. In sum, there is no evidence either that primaries produce a more, or less, representative convention.

Evaluation of the Presidential Nominating Process

This chapter began by posing the question, Have the reforms produced a new presidential nominating process? The experiences of 1976 and 1980 strongly indicate that a change has been taking place. A populist-oriented process is replacing the classic convention-brokered process. While future developments must be observed before it can be concluded that a fundamental alteration has occurred, if events proceed as they did in 1980 the outcome is obvious. Both the form and the reality of the process seems to be radically transformed of late. Presidential primaries can lead to an overwhelming victory long before the convention. Alternatively they could lead to such pluralization of support that no decision is reached by convention time, a stalemate ensues, and the convention is immobilized.

A further question is whether more reform action will occur. There is considerable criticism these days of the presidential primaries and their consequences for the system. In April 1981, both Charles Manatt, the Democratic national chairman, and Richard Richards, the Republican national chairman, said they intended to establish committees to study the changes which have occurred. In early July Manatt set up a committee under Governor James Hunt of North Carolina to do exactly that. A great number of reforms have been suggested, such as:

1. Reduction in the numbers of primaries, from the present thirty-six to no more than half that number. The action of the Democratic National Committee limiting delegate selection to bona fide partisans may lead to that result in a few states (as it did essentially in Michigan for the Democrats, in 1980, where the caucuses replaced the Democratic presidential primary). But a significant reduction is unlikely.
2. Tightening up the primaries. Make them "closed," insist on proportionality, require all presidential aspirants to be on the ballot, and plug up the loopholes which can distort the results in relation to public preferences. It is clear that some states are inclined to move in these directions, but there is considerable ambivalence.
3. Spacing and grouping primaries by some such arrangement as Representative Morris Udall has suggested: allowing primaries only on four dates, as the first Tuesdays of March, April, May, and June in the election year. The national party committees could implement such an arrangement. It would dilute the influence of the results of one small primary (such as that of New Hampshire), permit more states to be simultaneously involved in the decisions, focus public attention and candidate campaigning on four dates (instead of seventeen dates in 1980), and lead to less of a rush to judgment. A lottery could even be used each year to decide which state would hold primaries on the first date and which later. It might make the primary campaign process less gimmicky, and more rational. It might also persuade a few states not to hold primaries.
4. Regional primaries. A variant of the above is a proposal to have four to six primaries by geographical regions, on different dates over a three- or four-month period. While accomplishing the reduction of primary dates, this proposal would not meet the objection of giving a certain part of the country an advantage over other regions.
5. A national "one shot" presidential primary. This has been proposed for a

long time. The basic idea would be a nationwide primary election at which all Democrats and Republicans, presumably separately, would cast their votes for their preferred presidential candidate from a long list of all aspirants. The decision of such a primary would replace the convention decision. The problems are obvious: Who would be permitted to vote in each primary? Would crossovers be allowed? What would be the party loyalty criteria employed? Who would make up the list of bona fide aspirants? Would a plurality nomination be acceptable, and at what plurality level. Or would there be a run-off primary? These and other difficulties raise serious questions. Yet there are strong advocates of such a mechanism, and there are those who think we are moving inexorably to such a solution.

6. Elimination of "the candidates' veto power over the choice of their own delegates and ... freeing all the delegates from binding commitments of support for particular candidates." This is the proposal of the Duke University Forum on Presidential Nominations, headed by Terry Sanford, issued in October 1981.

Clearly reform is in the air. Many people are disenchanted with the recent transformation of the nominating process. Proposed reforms center on revisions of the presidential primary system. Supporters of that system can indeed point to its virtues: public participation, and opportunities for newcomers to be tested as leaders, opening up the political process. But many feel that the type of process now used verges on an incongruous, even irrational and haphazard race which is not a deliberative "search process," and in which the factors determining success are not necessarily presidential ability or even superior vote-getting talents. Rather the determinants may be money, early media support, plenty of leisure time, and the good fortune to do well in early primaries. For those who feel that way, reform is essential. The primaries have to be made more meaningful tests of leadership potential, in which partisanship can have a significant place, or there should be an attempt to return to the convention. For in the convention are combined party responsibility, programmatic concern for the needs of the society, and the selection of the most important political leadership of the nation.

In its report of October 1981, the Duke University Forum on Presidential Nominations (a bipartisan group of party leaders and presidential aspirants) evaluated the present system in the following terms:

It saps interest, distorts choice, eliminates judgment, narrows the popular base, spans too long a period, and squeezes out of the deliberative process those peers whose evaluations and cooperation the choice of a president vitally requires.... Most significantly, the present system radically erodes the foundation of the one institution most necessary to its effective operation: the political party.

Major recommendations for changes were made, above all, to end binding commitments of delegates to candidates who handpicked them. If such a change is now made the convention can recapture its function of nomination. Many, such as David Broder, feel this may be necessary "to rescue the presidential nominating system from the wounds it has suffered in the last ten years. . . ."[39]

The convention, of course, has its weaknesses also. It is a mass assemblage of party activists and leaders with heterogeneous backgrounds, diverse motivations, different levels of party experience and organizational skill, but all more or less committed to playing a critical role in the life of the party. They meet once in four years in a hectic atmosphere in the heat of summer in a large city, somehow in five or six days to do their work. They go through five days of leadership oratory, patriotic rituals, appearances before television, continuous social affairs, fights over the seating of contested delegates, battles over platform planks, and then they may have to decide on their candidate for the presidency.

In this frantic and confusing context it is a wonder how action is accomplished, how decisions are made. This raises the basic question of how effective the convention has been in the performance of its key tasks. Critics and supporters answer that differently. Of course, the convention's role in the critical matter of presidential candidate selection changes every four years. Sometimes the convention is merely ratifying the selection of an incumbent president—this has been the case in nineteen of the seventy-four national major party conventions. Usually this means there is no contest—the 1976 confrontation between Ford and Reagan was a rare exception. In other cases, there is what is known as "Inner Group Selection" (such as Alfred Landon in 1936) where the convention's screening and evaluating role also may not be important. But certainly where there is a stalemate situation and when there is an inner-party factional battle, the role of the convention has usually been very important.[40] Until recently these two latter patterns were more frequent, and often conventions had to face the necessity of deciding among two or more contenders for the presidency. In the post-World War II period, up to 1980, in sixteen conventions the only occasions when the convention did not play a final decisive role (and when an incumbent president was not running) were the Goldwater nomination in 1964 and Carter's nomination in 1976. In both cases the decision was over before the convention since the candidates had mustered the necessary majority of delegate votes through the primaries and state conventions before the national convention met. Goldwater received 883 out of 1,300 votes on the first ballot; Carter 2,238½ out of 3,008 votes on the first ballot. Last minute efforts to head off these nominations were futile. Aside from these two conventions, however, the decision had not been final until the convention met, deliberated, bargained, and acted. Again in 1980 the nominations were virtually over by convention time.

One of the major problems of the convention historically has been to legitimate the convention decision. Several scholars have pointed to this problem and suggested that if the presidential primaries preempt the nominating decision, legitimation may become even more difficult.[41] By legitimating the decision is meant the rallying of support behind the candidate and his faction in the party, persuading the opposition within the party to accept the nomination and to work for it. If that cannot be done, if the decision is not authoritative and binding, it may result in a division of the party and a loss of the election (as happened to the Republicans in 1912 and almost to the Democrats in 1948). Previously conventions have achieved a legitimacy for the decision by a variety of devices: cooptation of the leadership of the opposition (Kennedy's selection of Lyndon Johnson for the vice-presidency, and Carter's selection of Mondale) is one such approach. Votes of unanimity at the convention often are used to demonstrate that consensus exists. Striking a bargain on the platform and on the selection of the national chair may also be useful for this purpose. But even with such efforts legitimation may be difficult to achieve. It took Eisenhower some time after the 1952 convention, and a personal meeting with Senator Robert Taft, to persuade the Taft forces to support him. Similarly, many of the Republican liberals "sat on their hands" after the Goldwater nomination. And Reagan was too busy to provide much support for Ford in 1976. It is interesting to note that Eisenhower did not get a unanimous vote in 1952 (only 70 percent finally supported him on the bandwagon ballot), and in 1976 not all Democratic delegates voted to make Carter's nomination unanimous—90 percent of the Humphrey and Jackson party regulars did, but only 60 percent of the Brown, Udall, Harris "purists" did! Even in the expectation of victory, therefore, and with attempts to appease the factional opposition, complete legitimation is difficult. How much more so would it be in a pluralized nomination situation where the primaries decided the result?

The great virtue of the convention has been its capacity to achieve organizational consensus (admittedly minimal and temporary) in the face of fierce internal party conflict, to make the presidential nominating decision in such a way that all the major representative elements and forces in the party participate in it, at least participate in it so that they accept it, and do not bolt the convention to nominate someone else! Thus the convention makes a decision which is clearly the *party's decision*, one which the party can be held responsible for. If this consensus role is weakened, if organizational solidarity disappears, then organizational responsibility and legitimacy will also disappear. The candidate may become, then, much less a party candidate.

Finally convention behavior and decisions may be very consequential for the system not only in the type of candidates selected and the party's success in the ensuing election but in how the public perceives the quality of the political process as it is openly displayed to it on television from convention city. Particularly when the party is riven by conflicts, the airing of its differences and the style employed to achieve harmony may be very important. The role of the press in covering the conventions in this respect is crucial, how it portrays the behavior of politicans in this power arena. For party success and for the public's support for the party system, the convention decision-making process may play a seminal role. For many citizens the exposure to parties and politics occurs only in campaigns, and the convention may be the central event in that exposure. "There is something about a national convention," said H. L. Mencken, "that makes it as fascinating as a revival or a hanging."[42] This scene may be "exhilarating" and "gorgeous," or, he added, "preposterous" and "obscene." However it is viewed, its impact can be enormous, because its function in the system is fundamental. The important point is that it does perform a significant function and has done this despite great conflict and diversity in our politics. Can that task and that function be satisfactorily performed by the primary without serious dysfunctional side effects and consequences for the American party system?

Part IV

---

*PARTIES AND
THE CAMPAIGN,
ELECTORAL, AND
POLICY PROCESSES*

Chapter 13

Campaign Process

and Strategy

THE FOCUS of politics for many people and many groups in the United States is the political campaign. The citizen's attention is drawn by the mass media to the events of the campaign. The politician devotes all his energies. The political activist is involved more than ever whether he is working for the precinct or ward organization of the party or as part of a candidate campaign team. The incumbent candidate often leaves everything to go back to the hustings, to the home folks who alone can re-elect him. His opponent, if he is a serious contender, places politics above family and other interests. And the political party presumably takes center stage (presumably, because there are those who say today the party has become less relevant). Parties are theoretically interested in taking control of government and developing policies to meet the needs of society. In a democratic society victory in elections is essential to accomplish this purpose, and therefore the party as an organization allocates its resources to electing its leadership to office. True, as others have said, "*all* the activities of American parties—making nominations, writing platforms, campaigning, organizing government, and the rest—are electioneering."[1] Parties have to constantly be concerned with the impact of their actions on votes in succeeding elections. In this chapter, however, the emphasis will be on the campaigning and electioneering activities of parties in that period directly before the election, even though campaigning is a multifaceted process during which the parties and their candidates are linked to the total society.

Campaigns must be important to the political system, considering all the attention given to them by politicians and the public. Hubert Humphrey said in 1968, as many other losers have said, the election was so close that if the campaign had been a little longer, "surely not more than a week ... my own subjective judgment is that we would have gone on to win."[2] In terms of the money spent, it appears that campaigns are valued highly, no doubt because of what happens as a result of them. The amount of money spent is estimated to have increased from $140 million in 1952 to $250 million in 1968, $300 million in 1972, and over $500 million in 1976. In 1980 the amounts were probably as high, despite public funding, because of the amounts spent by political action committees. Why are people willing to contribute such sums and politicians to spend them?

Not only is it assumed that political campaigns are important to parties, it is also argued that campaigns are critical for the fulfillment of democracy. It is for many citizens the one time that they relate to the political process, the one time that they become attentive to what goes on in the political world. For some of them it is the time that they really become involved with parties, either as activists and workers or as persons exposed to the activities of political parties. Their image of the political process, therefore, may very well be formed during this period and can lead to alienation from politics or enthusiastic support. The campaign process can, thus, be evaluated from two perspectives: (1) How well does the campaign maximize the party's chances of winning; and (2) how well does the campaign involve the public and contribute to meaningful citizen deliberation and decisions about political candidates, parties, and programs? These two perspectives may be in collision with each other. What is good for the party and its success may not be good for the citizen and his effective participation in politics. That is, a candidate and party may engage in campaign tactics which may contribute to party success but they may lead to manipulation of citizens rather than rational deliberation by them over the alternative programs of candidates and parties. This possible disjunction should be clearly kept in mind in evaluating political campaigns.

Scholars have attempted to describe the nature and purpose of campaign strategy and process in various ways. David Leuthold simply conceives of it as "the process of acquiring and using the political resources that can secure votes."[3] In a broader sense Dan Nimmo argues that "political campaigns are, in fact, but one form of persuasive communications designed to influence the actions of people.... Any campaign resembles the basic communication act.... That act involves a source communicating in a specific setting to an audience and receiving responses [feedback]."[4] The political campaign resembles other campaigns in many respects, particularly in its persuasive techniques and in its desire to influence human behavior. It differs, however, in one basic respect: Its aim is power to govern. The goal of a political campaign is control (partial or total) over the governmental apparatus, and the strategic principles employed to that end, therefore, take on added significance. The conduct of campaigns and their results affect the lives of all citizens.

The discussion of campaign strategy presented here will start with the basic theoretical models of campaigning in order to provide a context for understanding the types of techniques and activities which parties and candidates engage in while soliciting support during campaigns. Second, the particular strategic decisions which have to be made during campaigns, and the differential approaches of candidates and parties to these decisions will be considered. Third, the campaign management, in particular the trends in recent years in the utilization of media specialists and technical experts in the running of campaigns, and the consequences of this for the parties will be discussed. Fourth, the extent of our knowledge about the effects of campaign techniques will be reviewed. Fifth, there will be an assessment of the consequences of campaigns for the democratic process.

A profound change has taken place in American political campaigns in the past two decades. Television has radically changed the way in which parties can communicate with voters, affecting the types of candidates who run for office, the substance of their appeals, and the basis for individual voter decision making. Further, it is argued, the professional managers and public relation specialists have taken power from the party organization, assumed control of campaign decision making, and thus subverted the campaign process, weakening the party structures while doing so. There are those, of course, who are not too worried about these trends and feel that the parties utilize these experts for *their* purposes while also maintaining control over the campaign operations. The alarmist thesis must be kept in mind, however, in our analysis of the nature and operations of the campaign process today.

Theoretical Models of the Political Campaign

Every campaign has a basic thrust to it, however subdued and inarticulate it may be. True, for some campaign managers the idea of a fixed strategy is abhorrent, the argument being that the campaign operation must be flexible and adaptive (sometimes called incremental) so that the candidate and his team can respond easily to new issues and developments.[5] Despite different degrees of rigor in specification of a strategy and its implementation, a basic concept for the campaign does usually exist.

Political campaigns vary in specifics, but one notes that they have four common characteristics. They utilize the principles of a communication model and operate with certain basic ideas of how best to communicate with the voters. They employ a coalition-building model wherein victory is conceived in terms of appealing to certain interest sectors of the public who can be mobilized to produce a majority. They are based on a model (or theory) of attitude influence which assumes that individual citizens' political perceptions and attitudes can be appealed to, or changed, in such a way as to influence their voting behavior. They implement a model of ideological competition, appealing to the public with certain ideological orientations, however general and obscure, in such a way as most efficiently to attract votes on the basis of issue positions while also counteracting the ideological appeal of the political opposition.

An elaboration of each of these elements of the campaign process can possibly help develop a theory of the political campaign into which can fit most of the activities of parties and candidates during the typical campaign. First it is necessary to see the campaign as a communication process (see fig. 13.1). Each party with its candidate and strategy team is confronted with the basic question of deciding how to communicate most effectively in order to maximize chances for victory. The public has to be visualized as not just an aggregate of voters, but subgroups of voters with differing interest orientations (defined in terms of partisan predispositions, ideological perspectives, social class status, and demographic characteristics, such as age, religion, sex. The party thus must make certain communication decisions, such as what interest sectors should be appealed to, with what types of messages (differentiated for these interest sectors), using what types of media, in order to achieve the effect of penetration and to minimize the possible effects of boomerang and bypass, and how to do this to counteract most effectively the appeals of the opposition.

According to this model the essence of campaigning is the rational planning of the entire operation to adapt the messages and appeals to selected groups in the population using the most effective media for each target group, thereby achieving a breakthrough, meaning the mobilization of the maximum possible votes from the group. Clearly in this ideal model one must have considerable intelligence about the behavior of the voters in each target interest sector, as well as great expertise in the use of media. The problem with such a rational model, of course, is that it makes assumptions that are not tenable and which, therefore, require constant revisions of strategy. Thus, as L. Froman has pointed out, this type of rational choice model has to face up to

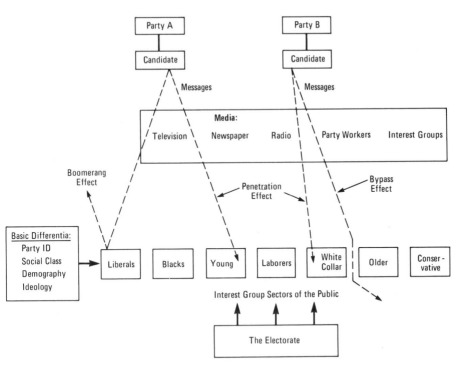

FIGURE 13.1
A Communication Model of Political Campaigning

groups who are not politically neutral at the outset of a campaign, but have a history of support for a particular party; voters with partisan predispositions which limit their availability to persuasion, including their selective exposure to campaign appeals; candidates with biases which also limit the credibility of their appeals to certain types of voters.[6] These and other nonrational considerations have to be continuously reviewed in the implementation of campaign decisions. Yet each campaign has its own communication assumptions and goals.

A major element in campaign strategy is the need to put together a coalition of interest groups which, if appealed to properly, will constitute the winning margin. Parties are, on the one hand, alliances of group interests appealing for group support in an election campaign, both by activating and re-enforcing the support among their own interest subgroups and by expanding the appeal to other interests in the community needed for victory. The particular interest groups which are targeted will, of course, vary greatly by community. As part of the strategic problem, there is always the possibility that an appeal to one group will offend another group of supporters. It is then necessary to estimate the probability of this occurring, the extent of such damage, and ways of minimizing losses or offsetting such losses with other appeals.

The difficulty in devising a campaign strategy which is a design for victory in interest-coalitional terms is that individual voters are complex human beings. To identify their dominant interest orientation and appeal to that interest is necessary, but such calculations are not always easy. Further, the absence of political solidarity in interest-group sectors of the American public, as well as the lack of homogeneous party loyalty, makes it difficult to mobilize a strong majority in such groups. Elmer Schattschneider called this the "law of imperfect political mobilization of interests."[7]

Another concept in any model of campaigning is that of ideological competition. In most campaigns, after all, two or more candidates face each other, each with his or her own issue positions on current problems facing the community. What they say (or do not say) about each of these issues in the context of political combat presumably plays a role in providing greater vote support for one candidate and less for the other. In a sense this is an application of Anthony Downs theory (discussed in chapter 1) to campaign strategy.[8] Since citizens theoretically will refuse to vote when parties (and candidates) take positions too extreme for them and will support that party whose issue positions are closest to theirs, the party must devise a campaign strategy which will attract the votes necessary for victory.

Since there are many issues, the party and its candidate must devise a strategy which is multidimensional, appealing to groups on differential fronts.[9] A party may take a liberal position on welfare to attract poor voters and a conservative position on government spending and taxation to attract more affluent voters. This suggests a campaign strategy which is flexible enough to tailor appeals to different groups using different issues, which requires determining which issue is most relevant for each group, and collectively developing and adopting a set of issue positions which has the greatest chance of mobilizing support.

Finally, any campaign process model must incorporate a theory of *individual* behavior which is the consequence, in part at least, of attitudes and perceptions of the political environment which are brought into play by these campaign stimuli. As the campaign unfolds the individual's basic orientations to politics are activated, involved, and utilized in a perception of the candidates, the parties, and their appeals. Usually the campaign does not change attitudes, although it may well influence immediate perceptions of political events and actors. It is not attitudinal change which normally occurs but the development of preferences (for candidates, policies, and parties) which are linked to basic attitudes and colored by immediate perceptions. These voting preference decisions arrived at, often early in the campaign, are then reality tested during the course of the campaign by discussion with friends, associates, family members, and by exposure to the media's analysis of politics and lead ultimately to a voting booth decision on election day. The campaign strategy, therefore, must face the necessity of developing messages which (1) influence the voter's perceptions of the candidate-actors; (2) engage basic attitudes in such a way as to lead to particular voting preferences; and (3) throughout the campaign reenforce these initial voting preference decisions. The process can be visualized, then, in the type of model suggested by figure 13.2.

Nimmo argues for this type of model of persuasion for a campaign. He states that "the intent of persuasion is not to change attitudes directly but rather to break through the weak perceptual barriers and convince the individual of alternative ways of acting."[10] He suggests, as an illustration, that campaign propaganda may be aimed at convincing a loyal Republican to alter his perception of a Democratic candidate so that he perceives the Democrat as having the qualities which he expects in an effective leader. This is precisely what many loyal Republicans did in 1964 in choosing Lyndon Johnson over Barry Goldwater[11]—and probably also in 1980 in the persuasion of Democrats to accept Reagan.

These four approaches, or models, of campaign strategy tend to fit together. They suggest that campaigns have to be planned and yet flexible; they must have a basic strategic concept and yet this must be adaptable; they must be aimed at particular groups and yet be aware

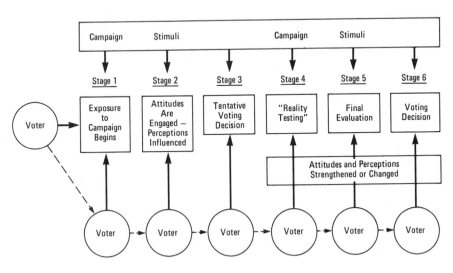

FIGURE 13.2
A Stimulus-Response Model of the Campaign

SOURCE: Bernard Berelson, Paul Lazarfeld, and William McPhee, *Voting* (Chicago: University of Chicago Press, 1954), p. 278. The diagram has been modified and supplemented for use here. Earlier discussions with Daniel Katz were very useful in developing these revisions.

that there are cross-pressures; they must calculate how to develop messages which penetrate but accept the probability that many appeals will bypass. Above all the campaign must have a communication theory, an ideological self-consciousness, a coalition-building theory. Finally there is "the law of the unearned increment of politics"—that parties get votes which surprise them, for which they did not appeal. And such votes increase as the campaign gathers momentum.[12]

System Constraints on Campaigning

Attempting to develop and implement a careful campaign plan under the conditions of the American political system is difficult. This is due to a variety of special constraints, expectations, and requirements which complicate the task. First, there are the electoral system constraints. The special features of the election system make party campaign calculations difficult. For example, the electoral college system for electing the president means that it is a majority of 538 electoral votes, not of the popular vote, which is necessary for victory. Further, persons are elected to many different positions (president, Congress, United States Senate, state governors, legislatures, judges, county officials) and often all at the same time. Therefore the merits of a variety of candidates have to be argued before the public simultaneously, and the funds and manpower mobilized to support all these candidates for office at the same time. This makes the job of coordination difficult.

In Britain the election campaign is focused exclusively on one type of office—the House of Commons *or* the local municipal council. The simplicity of that party competitive context stands in sharp contrast to the chaotic jungle of American electoral contests. In addition, our system of registering voters requires each citizen to take the initiative to register with the local clerk. Ours is a voluntaristic registration system, while in Britain, again, the government assumes the responsibility of seeing that all eligible persons are registered. There are other aspects of our elections which complicate campaign management—the large size of our election districts, the failure to hold elections on a special holiday, and the financial regulation of parties and candidates which requires detailed and frequent reporting of contributions and expenditures.

A second constraint is political/cultural in nature. In a two-party system, such as the United States has, the expectations concerning the nature of campaigning assume that parties will need to spend a great deal of time and effort to communicate with the electorate about candidates (many of whom are self-starters with little visibility), particularly in large and heterogeneous constituencies. Further, it is assumed that to bring voters to the polls in our low turnout culture poses particular problems. As a consequence our culture tolerates (indeed some would say demands) long campaigns, in which much canvassing at the home or by telephone is undertaken, and during which there is a great expenditure of funds for mass media propaganda. Indiscriminate use of television if funds are available to pay for it is permitted. In a parliamentary system such as one finds on the Continent campaigns are shorter, house-to-house convassing is discouraged, the parties in a multiparty system appeal to their own clienteles for the most part and engage in much less expensive vote mobilization efforts. The use of television is usually carefully restricted. In Britain the campaign is twenty-one days long and, therefore, very intensive. There is no need to mobilize unregistered voters nor to acquaint the public with many obscure new leaders who are seeking office without previous visibility. In our system campaigns are more protracted, diffuse, and expensive. They may also be more tiring and alienating.

Campaign Organization and Management

To create a campaign battle plan in such a complex set of environmental constraints and to carry it out efficiently is extremely difficult. The conditions in the arena of combat are almost too diffuse and demanding for rational planning to emerge. Indeed, often it appears as if there is no plan. In 1963, at the time of Hubert Humphrey's nomination, his campaign consultant Joseph Napolitan was astounded to discover the absence of a basic strategy and was quoted as saying to Humphrey's managers, "Do you know there isn't any campaign plan?" He then took the first ten days of the campaign to develop one.[13] Often campaigns are poorly coordinated; indeed there are those who will argue that incremental campaign decision making under certain conditions may be preferable to a comprehensive ideal campaign model.[14]

Despite the desirability of maintaining flexibility in campaign operations, it is nevertheless necessary to establish a managerial group of some type to organize the planning for the campaign at the outset. The tasks of campaign management are explicit and have to be undertaken early, however open and ambiguous the particular strategy shall be. This leads to the initial decisions concerning the authority locus for the campaign: Who is going to be in charge, what will be the relationship between the manager and the candidate, and to whom will the various divisions of the campaign organization be responsible? Further, the question of centralization of control over the various layers or echelons of the campaign operation has to be answered. As one study remarks, Who will be "the collective brain for the living campaign?"[15] Ideally a campaign team is put together which includes representatives, on the one hand, of the key interest groups which will be targeted (as soon as *that* decision is made), as well as those responsible for particular aspects of the campaign operation (publicity, itinerary, finance, and local organization). And ideally this should be a cohesive team of utterly loyal and hopefully congenial persons who will meet regularly to coordinate all top-level strategic decisions and operations while wisely allowing considerable decentralization in the tactical implementation of these decisions by lower level personnel, who are consulted, advised, cajoled, encouraged, but not dominated. A proper balance, therefore, between central coordination and supervision at the top and responsible utilization of initiatives and imaginations at the base of the whole campaign structure is highly desirable. In practice it is difficult to achieve.

Presidential campaigns illustrate the difficulties in setting up the management for a campaign. Decisions have to be made as to who will be campaign manager and whether that will be the national party chairman; if not, what will be the role of the chairman. Then there is the establishment of state organizations and the identification of the key personnel in each state with whom the national campaign team will deal, a matter of great sensitivity at the state level and critical for activation of the state and local organization. In addition, of course, the leaders of the big city or county organizations have to be pulled into the campaign communication network. Previously, the financial organization used to be critical, but with the complete public funding of the presidential races after the national conventions the problem now is not how to raise the money but how to allocate economically the limited funds (less than $30 million in 1980) that exist. The decisions are needed on mass media contracts and on polling research, who will be responsible for managing these two operations. Countless other activities have to be planned and supervised: scheduling of itinerary and events, preparation of speeches and publicity releases, laying the groundwork for candidate appearances at each stop, special contacts with interest-group representatives, et cetera. Coordination and management of all these activities require the recruitment of skilled personnel and their efficient guidance and control.

Presidential campaign management takes many different forms. In 1932 Roosevelt turned to Jim Farley, his national chairman, as Eisenhower did to his national chairman in 1956. But John Kennedy relegated his national chairman, Senator "Scoop" Jackson, to a secondary role in 1960 while Robert Kennedy ran the campaign. Stevenson ran his separate campaign from his personal headquarters in Springfield, Illinois, in 1952, which is what Jimmy Carter did with his Georgia group who were headquartered in Plains, Georgia, in 1976. In 1968 Humphrey's campaign was improvised and created at the last minute with the candidate virtually pleading with Lawrence O'Brien to become national chairman and run the campaign. In contrast the Nixon campaign was set up efficiently, run out of three sets of offices on Park Avenue in New York City with John Mitchell, Herbert Klein, Maurice Stans, and company at headquarters and John Ehrlichman, H. R. Haldeman, Ron Ziegler and company with the candidate.[16] Thus, in a variety of ways campaign managerial teams come into existence and vary in the efficiency and quality of their operation. The care with which the managerial concept is developed, the extent to which it provides for the integration of all relevant activities, and above all, the systematic control over the policy direction of the operation, in which the candidate plays a significant role—whatever the managerial style—are the components of campaign management which are probably key requisites for party success.

Strategic Decisions

Aside from the basic initial decision concerning the type of campaign management, any political campaign has a series of other very important decisions to make. Some of these are made early in laying out the campaign strategy and others later as the campaign unfolds, and are contingent on the strategy of the opposition, as well as on considerations such as the amount of money available. A discussion of these decisions will highlight the difficulty of the American campaign process.

How broad should the coalition be? Very early it is necessary to decide what the target groups in the population should be if the party and candidate are to win. This requires a careful review of all research on the electorate ("profiling the electorate," Dan Nimmo calls it in *The Political Persuaders*), particularly concerning the partisan history and turnout behavior of the relevant groups in the population. Once this knowledge is in hand the managerial team becomes aware of what is needed for victory. Yet, mistakes are often made in making the decision on strategy in these terms. Nelson Polsby and Aaron Wildavsky argue, for example, that the "underdog strategy" of the Republicans often has been disastrous because of incorrect decisions on how to put together a majority. The strategy of blurring the differences between the parties and not appealing directly to the known Republican vote (the "me-too-ism" of Thomas E. Dewey, for example) has never won, they argue, nor has the strategy of mobilizing the "hidden Republican vote" by a highly ideological appeal (Goldwater in 1964). But the Republican strategy of appealing directly to all Republicans plus the Independents (Eisenhower in 1952) has been successful.[17]

What should the interest group strategy be? How can you appeal effectively to all the critical interest groups in the coalition and at the same time minimize the losses to any one of these groups due to the necessarily conflicting character of some of these messages? A good illustration of this dilemma for the Democrats was in 1960, when Kennedy and his advisors were faced with the decision whether to emphasize the Catholicism of the candidate and discuss it openly or to play it down hoping thereby to antagonize fewer Protestants, particularly in the South. The Catholics had normally identified at the 63 percent level with the Democrats, but in 1956 they had split in their voting behavior with 50 percent supporting Eisenhower. The decision was made to speak openly on the issue (Kennedy stating that he hoped that he was not ineligible for the presidency on the day he was baptized!). A postelection analysis revealed that Kennedy did in fact win 80 percent of the Catholic vote in 1960 but in the process lost a large number of Protestant Democrats, particularly in the South (see table 13.1) The countervailing effect on Protestants of Kennedy's Catholic support made the 1960 election very close. In virtually every campaign such calculations of interest-group gains and losses are necessary. Goldwater's appeal to the South and to the conservatives was based on incorrect assumptions of where potential Republican votes were and on a misperception of how damaging this appeal would be to his chances in the North and East, in the big cities and with the moderates. The coalitional realities of party politics become strikingly clear at election time.

What should be the basic theme(s) or substantive thrust of the campaign? At least two questions must be faced: How can the campaign be pictured as having a positive and affirmative stance, rather than a defensive

TABLE 13.1
Catholic and Protestant Vote in Kennedy Election
(as a percentage)

Vote Change	South	Outside South	Nationally
Kennedy Catholic gains from Republicans	+ 0.7	+5.2	+4.3
Kennedy losses from Protestant Democrats (defected to Nixon)	−17.2	−3.6	−6.5
Net Kennedy gain or loss	−16.5	+1.6	−2.2

SOURCE: University of Michigan SRC/NES, 1960, reported in P. Converse et al., "Stability and Change in 1960: A Reinstating Election," *American Political Science Review* 55 (June 1961): 269–80.

posture? What central theme should be adopted which will communicate this positive stance and the particular concept on which the campaign will hinge? In some campaigns it seems difficult to escape being on the defensive, which puts the candidate at a great disadvantage. Goldwater's campaign manager Denison Kitchel complained in 1964 that it seemed impossible for the candidate to engage the Democrats in that philosophical discussion of conservatism versus liberalism for which he so ardently yearned, because he spent all his time defending himself against attacks that he would drop the bomb, that he would cut people off social welfare, and so forth. In contrast, Nixon's campaign plan in 1968 was "Attack, attack, attack!"

American campaigners are ingenious sometimes in the themes they give campaigns. One of the most effective was John Kennedy's "Get America Moving Again," which he used often, particularly in his television debates with Nixon. Eisenhower stressed "Crime, Communism, and Korea" and on election eve said that if he won "I will go to Korea," implying that peace would arrive if he were elected president. Goldwater used "In Your Heart You Know He's Right" (which had more than one connotation and, research showed, was not regarded highly by the public).[18] Humphrey in 1968 could only conceive of the concept of "Trust," which proved inadequate. In 1980 Reagan's campaign used the theme "Together, a New Beginning."

What should the issues strategy be? What issues should be emphasized and how precisely and explicitly should they be presented? There are those who will argue that "election campaigns are fought not 'on the issues' but on the themes."[19] And this is still probably the prevailing folklore of politics in the United States: appeal to everybody, be general, try everything, don't be specific. And yet issues can become fairly important and even specific in certain campaigns. Recent research has argued that there is a closer linkage now between issues positions and the vote than ever before. Samuel Huntington claimed that in 1948 Truman's campaign was relatively specific. In his "Give 'em Hell" speeches as he crossed the country by train he attacked the "Do-nothing" Congress.[20] On the other hand, certain candidates who have taken precise positions recently, which have also been rather extreme, are Goldwater and McGovern, both losers. Goldwater promised the liberation of Eastern Europe, argued that only victory could end communism, suggested that commanders in the NATO forces should have the power to use tactical nuclear weapons on their own initiative in an emergency, and ruminated about a possible end to social security.[21] McGovern's proposals concerning a guaranteed annual income, amnesty, immediate withdrawal from Vietnam, and other issue positions were much more extreme and specific than usual.

One can classify campaigns in terms of issues by using the following four-cell concept:

Issue Positions

	Extreme	Moderate
precise	Goldwater McGovern	Truman
vague		Most U.S. campaigns

The type of issue strategy actually used depends a great deal on the groups to be appealed to, the nature of the opposition, and the characteristics of the electorate. One can argue much more strongly today for fairly precise (if moderate) issue strategies, but the folklore of American politics is for moderation *and* ambiguity.

What image of the candidate should be consistently communicated? There is a heavy emphasis on candidate imagery in these days of television and the media specialist. Since attractive candidates are more important than ever the packaging of the candidate requires much planning. Nimmo reports that Richard Nixon was discovered in 1946 by a professional campaign which advertised for an attractive candidate to face Democrat Gerald Voorhies in the race for Congress in the Los Angeles area. A few professionals do pretest potential candidates, but most of them give expert advice as to how the candidate can be most effectively presented to the public.[22]

Merchandising the candidate incorporates many things, including his wife and other members of family. It communicates an image about the candidate's record in private and public life, his or her rectitude and honesty, competence and experience, extent of group support, and possibilities of winning. Perhaps one of the best image-saving jobs done on television was Nixon's "Checkers" speech in 1952, when he was accused of having used a private slush fund for political purposes while in Congress. Another notable example was that of Edward Kennedy in his first race for the United States Senate in 1962. The problem was to convince the voters that he had the requisite ability (his public service consisted of having been a member of the Board of Trustees of Boston University and chairman of the Massachusetts Cancer Crusade). By using extensive coaching on issues by a brain trust and the candidate's contacts with the White House, as a substitute for expensive and massive use of television and other propaganda, the inexperience of the candidate was overcome and his credibility as a candidate successfully communicated.[23]

In 1976 the image Jimmy Carter wanted to create was that of a new political personality. In 1980 Reagan communicated an image of a conservative who was a pleasant and competent alternative to Carter.

What channels of communication or media should receive top priority?

Since knowledge of the effects of what is done in campaigns is very thin, the attempt is to "try everything," the buckshot approach. We put out brochures, use billboards, posters, campaign buttons, bumper stickers, as well as, of course, newspaper ads, radio, and television. In presidential campaigns now there is more care and selectivity, since the amounts that can be spent by the candidate's organizations are limited ($22 million in 1976, but closer to $30 million in 1980). Nevertheless, choices still have to be made in presidential campaigns, and these choices now may be harder than ever.

The media available are extremely diverse, including telephone campaigns with recorded messages, house-to-house canvassing, radio (which for certain voters traveling in cars and for certain candidates who are not telegenic may be of great value), newspaper advertising, as well as free newspaper publicity and editorials, and campaign biographies. Then there is a great variety of campaign literature, display media, to say nothing of personal appearances, Hollywood shows, rallies, and so forth. Whatever one uses has to be planned for carefully. An example of poor planning was the Humphrey television appearance in West Virginia in 1960 in his primary race against Kennedy. He used $750 for a telethon but had no money to arrange for production, so he faced the television camera alone, answering telephone calls himself directly. The first call was from an elderly lady who shouted, "You git out! You git out of West Virginia, Mr. Humphrey!" The call staggered Humphrey, and then an operator came on to demand that Humphrey hang up because of an emergency! The program was, as a result, a complete catastrophe.[24]

Great emphasis has been placed in the past on the use of television. Close to 50 percent of the money spent goes to television normally. The television "blitz" at the end of the campaign, which Nixon's team used so effectively and which Humphrey in 1968 had no money for, is a major development in campaign operations. Since television receives so much money, other channels are starved. There are those who argue that the role of newspapers can be extremely important in informing the public about candidates, and therefore they should not be neglected. Furthermore, in the past a certain amount of money was available to precinct workers, particularly to round up the voters in the last days of the campaign and to bring them to the polls on election day. Such funds now, it is argued, are not available to the extent they were in the past.

From a strategic standpoint it is necessary to determine carefully what media will be useful in communicating with what groups, as well as most useful in terms of the candidate's personality. Television probably helps an unknown figure in politics, like Carter in 1976, a great deal. It can also create a favorable image or replace a negative one—Nixon in 1968 compared to 1960 may be a case in point. And it permits the candidate to appeal directly to the public with messages which might otherwise never be communicated. There are many examples of this utility for television. One of the most dramatic was in 1964. The Johnson media advisors (Doyle, Dane, Bernbach) devised some very telling television spots. One was the famous "Daisy Girl" spot, a close-up of a little blond girl plucking petals from a daisy, counting the petals as she went, until the film faded to a countdown of an atomic testing site with the scenes of a mushroom cloud. The Republican objections were so loud that it was shown only once. Another spot showed the fingers of two hands tearing up a Social Security card—a spot played throughout the campaign and probably having great "penetration."[25]

What should the strategy be in the precincts? Nimmo states that campaign organization requires the coordination of "the pros" (professional managers), "the pols" (politicians and political party workers), and "the vols" (volunteer workers at all levels).[26] This is certainly an apt way to put the problem of integrating the elements of a campaign. One critical part of this is the proper utilization of the precinct workers. It is the systematic deployment of these workers which is important; indiscriminate and unplanned activation of them may be useless. There are many instances of effective use of precinct workers. For example, Senator Eugene McCarthy won 42 percent of the primary vote in New Hampshire in 1968 with campaign help of 3,000 college students who contacted 60,000 households, leading to the launching of the McCarthy for President campaign.[27] In September 1964 a Gallup poll reported that Republican party workers had contacted 7,100,000 households for Goldwater, Democrats 3,800,000 for Johnson.[28] The potential for grass-roots activism is considerable.

What should be the psychological direction or character of the campaign? Every campaign has an image, or psychological character. That image can be of a candidate who is aggressive or quiet and inoffensive— either "Give 'Em Hell, Harry" (Truman) of "Keep Cool with Coolidge." It can be a low-keyed operation or one which is on the attack. It can be intellectual in character (as Adlai Stevenson's was) or appeal more to visual imagery and candidate charisma (Eisenhower). The psychological strategy of any campaign must be worked out carefully, including the timing and pacing of the campaign. If the campaign peaks too early, the last few weeks may see the erosion of support. In 1976 although Gerald Ford started out with the polls 60 percent to 40 percent against him, he utilized a gradual build-up of support so that by election day the polls were calling it even, and Carter barely won. In 1980 Reagan peaked in the last week of the campaign after the second television debate.

Underlying all these campaign strategy decisions, of course, is the question of money. The development of a campaign budget so that there is careful determination of how much money will be available, and what expenditures are necessary to produce the desired results is absolutely critical for the whole operation. Being able to plan the campaign on the basis of adequate funds ensures maximum campaign effort. The Goldwater campaign of 1964 is cited by Theodore White as an example of the lack of coordination. The early difficulty in mobilizing funds led to the cancellation of television presentations for the latter part of the campaign. By late October, however, money was flowing in great quantities into the campaign coffers, but it was too late to repurchase prime television time. Similarly in 1968 Humphrey was hurt badly by the early lack of funds so that when $5 to $6 million became available it was too late. Lawrence O'Brien argued that the Democrats would have won in 1968 with more funds, particularly if television time could have been purchased early in California, a key state. He said, "We could have licked Nixon."[29]

Campaign Management: The Take-Over of Political Campaigns by the Specialists?

Much has been made of late concerning the development of a new industry of media specialists, public relations firms, polling experts, and other consultants who have assumed command of our campaigns presumably and in the process infiltrated the political process, making decisions as to how our politics shall be conducted.[30] The rise of the public relations profession in the 1920s led eventually to the application of these techniques to politics in the 1930s. Clem Whitaker and Leone Baxter in 1933 set up their famous business for this purpose in California and became so successful that many other firms followed their lead. After World War II these trends in expert application of public relations principles to campaigns spread throughout the country. By the 1960s both national parties, most candidates for state office in the large states, and many senatorial and congressional candidates hired campaign management firms. Different firms specialize in particular aspects: fund raising, newspaper advertising, polling, television shows, and consulting on strategy. Some of these firms are full-service agencies, large firms with several clients and a considerable staff, handling all details of the operation. As for public opinion polling, although Roosevelt, as early as the 1930s, contracted for surveys, 1946 was the year when such polls really came into prominence. By the 1970s over two hundred firms did polling.[31]

The conditions under which these management firms operate and the possible consequences of them for our politics are important to note. The firms have a close working relationship with the candidate and usually have considerable authority over certain key aspects of the campaign. How far this extends and to what extent they remain subordinate to the candidate and his campaign team depends on the situation, but their influence can obviously be considerable. These firms apply the basic principles of merchandising to political campaigns. They are selling a product (a candidate) and they therefore will use whatever mass persuasion techniques of a manipulative nature to do this job. Further, they operate for profit, and their success in the long run is linked to how many people buy their product—vote for their candidate, on whatever basis they decide to merchandise the candidate. They may come close to deciding who, or what type of person, shall be the candidate. Even though normally they accept the candidate as a given, they have been known to actually be part of leadership recruitment screening activities, arguing that only certain types of candidates are saleable and electable.[32]

These campaign specialists provide a wide range of services, including what used to be the work of the party organization, such as house-to-house canvassing in a precinct, circulating petitions to get enough signatures to get a name or a proposal on the ballot, and taking over the organization of the campaign itself. Campaigns have become much more "scientific," in appearance at least, since these specialists have entered the picture. Precampaign polls are used to determine the probable chances of election against the major contenders. In 1967–68 President Johnson's private polls indicated he would lose, while Robert Kennedy's polls showed he would defeat Johnson in the California primary.[33] In addition, the information from polls on the image of the candidate helps make image decisions, helps identity where the public stands on issues, what groups hold what views, and how to adjust campaign strategy during the course of the campaign.[34]

What Do We Know About the Effects of Campaign Techniques?

The extent to which we have precise knowledge of the utility of particular campaign media is still an open question. To some we are still in the dark, working with myths and folklore because we have only "pre-scientific" knowledge. Others would argue that we are better informed today than previously. What does our research reveal?

First, we know there is limited conversion of partisans, but for most people exposed to a campaign there is some effect. Long ago Paul Lazarsfeld and his associates concluded from their study of Erie County,

Pennsylvania, reported in *The Peoples' Choice,* the following types of campaign effects: [35]

	Percent
Reinforcement	53
Activation	14
Conversion (from one party to another)	8
Partial conversion (from one party to independent status)	6
Reconversion (from one party to another and back to the original party)	3
No effect	16
	100

The authors of *The American Voter* stated that "only about one person in twenty said the campaign had failed to reach him through any of the principal media of communication." [36] No one has been inclined to challenge this overall assessment in recent years. It is true that in particular elections there is the defection of a large proportion of partisans, in our volatile system; 1980 was probably an example. But in an attempt to pin down what the campaign itself does normally, "conversion" is not the major effect. Campaigns *are* effectual, but their reinforcement and activation roles seem to be of predominant importance. Added to this might be what is called the "depressing" effects of campaigns, that is the alienation of voters from participation. The decline in voting participation since 1960 in the United States to 54 percent turnout in 1980 suggests that campaigns may have such an effect.

A second observation concerns the use of television. Americans, while continuing to be exposed to campaigns via the newspapers, have in the past quarter century found television as the major new medium of information. Table 13.2 presents the basic trends since 1952. The striking jump in exposure to television in 1956 and its continual increase in use since then, combined with the drop in exposure to radio for campaign purposes, is most impressive. Television has become the most frequently used source for information about the national campaign. [37] But for many citizens the other three media are still of value. In 1976 the Center for Political Studies found that in the Ford-Carter television debates 83 percent of the voting population said they watched at least one debate (compared to 73 percent using newspapers, 48 percent magazines, and 45 percent listening to radio programs). Further, the Center reports that the television exposure was high for all groups in the population, although those with higher education were more inclined to watch more debates, which was the case also for whites and for older citizens. [38]

TABLE 13.2

Public Uses of Mass Media in Presidential Campaigns

(as a percentage)

Followed Campaign Through	1952	1956	1960	1964	1968	1972	1976	1980
Television	51	74	87	89	89	88	89	86
Radio	70	45	42	48	41	43	45	47
Newspaper	79	69	80	79	75	57	73	71
Magazines	40	31	41	39	36	33	48	35

SOURCE: University of Michigan SRC/CPS/NES, 1952, 1956, 1960, 1964, 1968, 1972, 1976, 1980.

The third question concerns the relevance of exposure to the mass media for voters' knowledge, attitudes, and behavior. Arthur Miller reports on the basis of the 1976 data that "respondents' information about the candidates increased systematically as the debates were broadcast. In addition, their perceptions of differences between Carter and Ford became clearer as they watched more debates."[39] In a much earlier study based on the 1952 national survey, exposure to television, as well as to other mass media, was linked to voting participation (see table 13.3). This suggests a causal relationship between media exposure and voting turnout. Of course, the relationship could be reversed, and a variety of other factors may also be relevant to explain the participation of voters. Nevertheless, the evidence is highly suggestive, and undoubtedly today television is still relevant for voting turnout.

The 1960 debates between Kennedy and Nixon are also cited as an

TABLE 13.3

The Extent of Nonvoting by

Exposure to Mass Media

(as a percentage)

Exposure to Media	Nonvoters, 1952
High	
Television	12
Newspaper	12
Radio	24
Moderate	
Television	30
Newspaper	30
Radio	46
Nonusers	69

SOURCE: Morris Janowitz and Dwaine Marvick, *Competitive Pressure and Democratic Consent* (Chicago: Quadrangle Books, 1964), p. 67. Reprinted by kind permission of the Institute of Public Policy Studies, the University of Michigan.

example of television impact. The survey by Elmo Roper at the time concluded as follows: A high proportion of the viewers (44 percent) said they were influenced by the debates, 6 percent (4 million viewers) said they voted on the basis of the debates (3 to 1 for Kennedy); this meant a shift to Kennedy of 2 percent.[40] In 1980 it is claimed that the television debates helped Reagan convert "a 4 percent deficit into a 5 percent lead" over Carter.[41]

The evidence that television is effective is very limited. Yet there is a strong feeling that the way in which network news teams handle the campaign and particularly how they build up candidates during the primaries, as well as how they interpret the news of the campaign, can have a profound effect on voters' perceptions of candidates. In this connection an experiment in 1976 by a psychology professor at the University of Notre Dame indicates the possibilities of such influence. Using 254 students, randomly selected and asked to listen to the second debate between Ford and Carter, he exposed one-third of the group to the CBS postdebate coverage and interpretation, one-third to the ABC coverage of the debate, and one-third were not exposed to any network team's evaluation of the debate. He determined by interview what their candidate preferences were: 47 percent Ford, 27 percent Carter, and 26 percent Don't know. The shift to Carter was 27 percent for the CBS group and 22 percent for the ABC group. The conclusion of the investigator was, "This shows that the media have a powerful impact, perhaps more so than the debate itself. Newscasters were able to change viewers' opinions of something they themselves had just witnessed and formed an opinion on."[42]

A fourth question concerns the effectiveness of the party work which is done in the precincts, the registering of voters, door-to-door canvassing, telephoning, and the work on election day to "round them up" and bring them to the polls. It is important to note that over the years the two major parties have been expending more energy, rather than less, in contacting potential voters. Parties or candidates personally contacted 12 percent in 1952, 30 percent in 1976, and 24 percent in 1980. Michael Wolfe's analysis of the data since 1952 indicates that during the period when big city machines have presumably been declining and local party organization is atrophying, there has been a continual increase in the proportion of the electorate contacted by local party workers.[43] This appears anomalous and suggests either that the theories of party decline are unsubstantiated or that this type of organizational work is superficial, directed at those who vote anyway, and is not very relevant for party success. Yet, 85 percent of those who were contacted did vote in the elections, and this was the same in 1980 as in 1952. Above all, these data reveal that local party work continues, and the local organization is not moribund.

The potential effectiveness of the local party organizational activity has been discussed previously. Studies in Detroit and Gary, Indiana, in the 1956–57 period demonstrated that a good precinct organization for one party, if confronted with a poor precinct organization by the other party, could make a difference of 10 percentage points in the vote for a presidential candidate.[44] William Crotty has suggested that the effect of the local organization's activities may even be greater in connection with campaigns for local office (such as the sheriff and state legislators).[45] In a propaganda experiment designed to test the effectiveness on voter turnout of personal contact of voters by the parties (or other groups) versus mail propaganda, it was clearly demonstrated that either house-to-house canvassing or telephoning was much more effective in getting citizens to vote. Thus, among those who had never voted in local elections before, over 25 percent were mobilized by personal canvassing (telephone or at the home) while 10 percent or less were mobilized by mail.[46] Thus, from previous studies it is apparent that party contact efforts are reported by more eligible voters than previously and that under certain conditions local organization effort can pay off.

One of the most fascinating aspects of campaigns is the extent to which cross-pressures influence citizen voting behavior. Early studies noted that as a campaign proceeds, it produces voters whose decisions have been made (the crystallizers), as well as those who become undecided (the waverers), and, of course, the changers (the 8 percent who shift from one party to another). The early Lazarsfeld study suggested that cross-pressures occurred for many citizens; that is, they were subjected to certain social and political influences in favor of Candidate A, as well as social and political influences in favor of Candidate B, and that these conflicting pressures led to (1) delayed vote decisions; (2) decreased interest in the election; and (3) more variable voting intentions. This early study demonstrated that those under such cross-pressures, if their interest in politics was low, were indeed more likely to change parties and to delay a voting decision.[47] Similarly, Morris Janowitz and Dwaine Marvick pointed out that a high proportion of people were in a conflicted primary group situation so far as politics was concerned (68 percent in 1952) and that those persons were less inclined to vote (32 percent were nonvoters compared to 7 percent and 20 percent, respectively, of Republicans and Democrats with no cross-pressures).[48] A more recent study by Peter Sperlich suggests that under certain conditions cross-pressures and tensions for a voter in the course of a campaign can activate him or her to participate rather than to withdraw from politics.[49] Obviously new studies are needed to explore this question in depth, particularly these days when voting participation is low, to ascertain whether the bombardment of the voter by particular campaign stimuli constitutes a type of overkill and lessens the voters' willingness to be involved.

A final empirical question is whether candidate behavior in a campaign really has an effect. Again, the research that has been done on this question is very limited. One study of congressional candidates in 1964, at the time of the Goldwater campaign, analyzed what happened to those Republican congressmen who endorsed Barry Goldwater—49 of the 159 congressmen who were up for reelection. Goldwater received 38.7 percent of the two-party vote and 39 Republican congressmen were defeated. The correlations of presidential and congressional votes: +.49 for Republicans endorsing Goldwater, −.01 for Republicans not endorsing him. Other factors were also important, including the margin of victory in preceding elections and the type of ballot (whether "party column" or "office block"). But the impact of declaring an association with Goldwater was apparent.[50] What the candidate does in the public eye may be of considerable importance!

To evaluate what is known about campaign effects is not easy. It can be argued that campaigns may trigger short-term changes in perceptions and voting behavior but they do not by themselves change basic attitudes. But these short-term influences can be important and can cumulate to a resounding defeat or victory. The candidate and party which wins is the one which develops a coalition of interests to whom he or she appeals through a communication technique which achieves penetration—appeals that are *meaningful* stimuli in the lives of the respondents appealed to, are *direct and attention demanding,* and are *credible* (that is, the voter feels it is in his interest to act in terms of the appeals). To achieve such a breakthrough with a large number of different types of voters, particularly in terms of their established attitudes, selective self-exposure to campaigns, and the countervailing influences of other appeals is extremely difficult. The more personalized the appeal the more it will be efficacious. Nimmo speaks of the "law of minimal consequences," by which he means that the "conversion potential" of campaigns is reduced by "a host of intervening conditions" and "prior inclinations."[51] To swing voters to another candidate and party requires effective persuasion. It is also becoming more difficult to activate the disinterested voters because of prior inclinations and intervening conditions. This is equally the function of campaigns.

Final Evaluation of the Campaign Process

The study of American campaigns, their management, and their effects raises a good many questions, as many as it begins to answer. Campaigns are supposed to serve particular functions, for the parties and the system, and it is well to attempt to reflect on how well campaigns perform these functions. Campaigns seem to arouse the interest of citizens, to make them more aware of the characteristics of the candidates, perhaps to know more about the saliency of the issues, to have better images of the parties. The question is, however, does all of this help the voter make an intelligent decision, to produce a deliberative election result, rather than a manipulative election result?

V. O. Key posed this question long ago. He said that "the picture of the voter that emerges" from much of the "folklore of practical" politics as well as from "the new electoral studies is not a pretty one." The voter is seen as "an erratic and irrational fellow susceptible to manipulation by skilled humbugs. . . ." But he argues then that

voters are not fools. . . . in the large the electorate behaves about as rationally and responsibly as we should expect, given the clarity of the alternatives presented to it and the character of the information available to it. In American presidential campaigns of recent decades the portrait of the American electorate that develops from the data is not one of an electorate straitjacketed by social determinism or moved by subconscious urges triggered by devilshly skillful propagandists. It is rather one of an electorate moved by concern about central and relevant questions of public policy, of governmental performance, and of executive personality.[52]

The issue posed by V. O. Key is a basic one. Does the campaign process as we know it contribute to responsible electoral behavior or not? There can be no question that American campaigns are much more protracted affairs than is normal in democratic systems. They revolve around a multiplicity of offices of various types (rather than just the election of members of a parliament), they bombard the public with a variety of messages through different types of mass media, and they are extremely expensive. The job of the parties is complicated, and coordination of the diverse campaigns is difficult. The job of the American voter is, hence, also very complicated, more so than that of voters in other democratic systems. The way campaigns are conducted does not simplify this task for the voter. The candidates for president, senator, governor, House and county office do not usually campaign as a unified team. Each has his campaign operation, financial organization, issues, and coalition-building strategy, and the voter must sort out the diverse appeals from those running at all levels. The parties as structures do not simplify this job, and their communication as a party with the voter leaves much to be desired. Party and candidate appeals are often tedious and confusing, and one can understand why voters withdraw from involvement in a politics which is so complex.

On the other hand, it is important to emphasize that American political campaigns are often hotly contested, represent major efforts by the parties and candidates to inform the public through a variety of media, ranging from expensive television programs to canvassing in the precincts. And all the evidence indicates that what happens in the campaigns does make a difference, does affect the great majority of voters—whether by activating lazy citizens or reenforcing the waverers or informing the ignorant or, unfortunately, encouraging some voters to stay home! All the evidence is as yet not in, but clearly only a minority of the voters is unaffected by what goes on in a campaign. And what evidence there is suggests, as V. O. Key says, that many voters are engaged in a careful, deliberative, decision-making experience. There are indeed manipulative components of the campaign process, but those who say that the parties have lost control of the process or that the public is the dupe of the media specialists go much too far. American elections, probably more so than those in most democratic societies, are massive efforts to communicate with all potential voters, on as personalized a basis as possible, and over a longer time period than is usual, by two highly competitive political parties, both of which are constantly seeking to expand their clienteles, utilizing highly sophisticated communication techniques, and expending vast amounts of money in the process. If one wants competitive, deliberative, exhaustive, comprehensive, and expensive political communication, one certainly finds it in the American campaign. And thus voter knowledge and responsible behavior should theoretically be enhanced. The American problem may be campaign overkill for certain American voters—too much noise at a time when their voting task is too complex. The problem is certainly not that campaigns are irrelevant.

Chapter 14

Money in Political Campaigns:

Its Use, Abuse, and Regulation

FOR over a century America has struggled with the problem of party finance, with the question of how and by whom money should be collected or solicited and spent in the election process. Periodically since the Civil War the public has become very concerned about the amounts of money spent, the sources of the money, and the types of expenditures. When this concern becomes intense enough, as reflected in public opinion, as reported in the press, and as crystallized by Senate and House investigations, new legislation is adopted in an attempt to deal with the problems. But we always seem to fall short of satisfying ourselves that the problem has been solved. And so the cycle goes on: reports of abuses or irregularities, press criticism of the use of money in elections, legislative investigation, a new party finance law, and then a subsidence of concern until new abuses or irregularities come to light. At the present time we are in a "downward slope" of concern, because we have enacted a post-Watergate campaign finance law, the Federal Election Campaign Act (FECA), and this law with Supreme Court interpretations and modifications has seemed to satisfy for the time being major concerns about how parties and candidates get and spend money. But new rumblings of discontent, new revelations, new shortcomings in the legislation have been pointed out by scholars of party finance. And so we may shortly again be, and indeed to some extent already are, heading into a period where changes in party finance legislation may be demanded.

It is necessary to think about the use of money in elections from several different theoretical perspectives. First, of course, it must be realized that elections in a democracy such as ours require the expenditure of much money if the job of communicating with the public about the parties, issues, and candidates is done properly. There are perhaps an estimated eight hundred thousand elected positions filled in the United States at all levels in any one year. For the public to vote intelligently the candidates (and political parties) need to spend large sums to inform citizens of their positions and records. If the democratic process is to work effectively money equal to the need for parties and candidates *to compete* strongly for public office is needed *to inform* voters. Any law regulating the use of money in elections must contribute to these two requisites of democracy.

Another perspective to keep in mind is the need and the right of citizens and interest groups to organize politically and to mobilize resources in order to influence governmental action. If an individual citizen wishes to use private finances in order to influence governmental elites and public policy and does it legitimately, it is assumed that he or she has this right. And the same is true for any group of citizens with a particular interest in policy they wish to promote. They cannot be forbidden to use individual or group funds for political objectives. The problem is to what extent can the use of such funds be limited and how to get adequate disclosure of who is financially supporting whom. The law certainly can provide for an open accounting, for publicity, of such individual and group expenditures. But the question is how far to go in permitting the use of such funds by wealthy individuals and groups in *direct* support of parties and candidates. Again, any attempt at regulation of party finance must take a reasonable approach and one which restrains "improper influence" in the linkages of financial contributors to those in public office. So we want *free speech* but also *restraints on improper political influence* by the affluent sectors of our society.

A third concern is the role of government in the regulatory process. As David S. Broder has written,

The direct role of the federal government should be kept as small as possible. We ignore at our peril the fact that, historically, the worse threat to freedom has come from the power of the state, not the influence of private interests. If, in trying to reduce the influence of private interest money, we give government officials the power to decide who can compete effectively for public office, we risk something far worse than Watergate . . . in distributing funds the government should be as neutral as possible.[1]

The campaign process is critical for society, and what must be carefully maintained is a finance system which permits adequate *information*, protects party *competition*, preserves *freedom* of political action, insists on *openness* in our knowledge of who is paying the political bills—in short, as rational and democratic a set of standards as can be achieved. And in all of this the goal is *restraint* in the financial relationships between donors and candidates. It is important to have as deliberative (versus manipulative) a process as possible, to approximate as closely as possible a situation where voters have access to all relevant information about candidates and parties—what they stand for, who is behind them—so that the public can weigh the pros and cons of the contestants and select the individuals most qualified to serve in terms of their ability and beliefs. Similarly, we wish to elect persons to public office in such a way that when in office they feel free to consider proposed legislation in such a way that they are not coerced by "improper influence relations" which developed during the campaign and which might interfere with their better judgment. These are "rationality" and "restraint" expectations which admittedly may be ideal, but we certainly should work toward their achievement if we are to have an informed electorate, competitive parties, and deliberative public officials. Money in politics creates moral stress on the policy process. Its improper role should be reduced and its proper place maximized in the system, thus freeing the citizen from ignorance and freeing the legislator or executive from undue pressure.

The Costs of Campaigns

The first major concern is the increasing amounts of money spent by all political candidates in the United States. It is a long way from the Civil War period when the presidential campaign of Abraham Lincoln cost $100,000 (in 1860) and $125,000 (in 1864).[2] Theodore Roosevelt spent $2 million in 1904, Hoover over $6 million in 1928 and Nixon $62 million in 1972.[3] In the same election years the Democratic costs rose as follows: Stephen Douglas (1860) $50,000, Alton Parker (1904) $700,000, Al Smith (1928) $5 million, and George McGovern (1972) $50 million. In 1976, the analysis of Herbert E. Alexander, the best informed student of party finance in this country, reveals that $159,700,000 was spent in the presidential campaigns alone, while total political spending in the United States, so far as can be determined, was $540 million.[4] This contrasts with the amount spent in the May 1979 parliamentary election in Britain, which was about $3 million.[5]

In 1980, under public funding, the national party committees and candidates for the presidency spent close to $200 million—$118 million in the primaries and $78 million in the conventions and the postconvention campaigns. These are estimates; the final figures may be larger.

Campaign costs are divided into presidential, congressional, state, and local disbursements, by candidates, committees, and the political action committees. To secure precise data on all campaigns is virtually impossible. However, basic trend data resulting from the most extensive and reliable research done to date by scholars working in this area can be presented. Table 14.1 presents the trend in postconvention presidential campaign costs since World War II. They reveal a phenomenal rise between 1968 and 1972—from $37 million to $112 million. And the total cost per vote which for the first time rose to almost 60 cents in 1968 jumped in 1972 to almost $1.50.

However, the actual total spent including all expenditures in presidential campaigns, from before the first primary to election day, was actually even greater than these figures indicate (see table 14.2).

TABLE 14.1

General Presidential Post-Convention Campaign Costs Since World War II (in thousands)

Year	Total	Republican	Democratic	Total Cost
1948	$ 4,864	$ 2,127	$ 2,736*	$ .106
1952	11,642	6,609*	5,033	.190
1956	12,885	7,779*	5,107	.209
1960	19,925	10,128	9,797*	.292
1964	24,783	16,026	8,757*	.353
1968	36,996	25,402*	11,594	.587
1972	112,000	62,000*	50,000	1.492

SOURCES: Up to 1972: Reprinted by permission from Herbert E. Alexander, *Political Financing* (Minneapolis: Burgess, 1972) p. 6; the 1972 figures are estimates taken from *Dollar Politics* 2 (Washington, D.C.: Congressional Quarterly, 1974) p. 72; Frank B. Feigert and M. Margaret Conway, *Parties and Politics in America* (Boston: Allyn and Bacon, 1976), p. 266.
NOTE: * denotes winner.

TABLE 14.2

Total Costs for Presidential Elections, 1968–80 (in millions)

Party	1968	1972	1976	1980
Democrats	$37	$ 67.3	$ 83.2	$ 73.8
Republicans	45	69.3	74.5	107.7
Other	9	1.2	2.0	14.3
Totals	$91	$137.8	$159.7	$195.8

SOURCES: Herbert E. Alexander, *Financing the 1976 Election* (Washington, D.C.: Congressional Quarterly, 1979), pp. 166–67; for 1980, see Federal Election Commission Record reports for September 1980, April 1981.

According to Alexander these totals for presidential campaigns are only a part, perhaps a third or less, of *all "political spending"* in a presidential election year. His research indicates that this latter figure was $300 million in 1968, $425 million in 1972, and $540 million in 1976. These figures suggest a 75 percent increase in presidential campaign costs from 1968 to 1976 and an 80 percent increase in total political spending. A breakdown by governmental level of such spending reveals the following: presidential, 33 percent; House and Senate, 23 percent; and state and county, 44 percent.[6]

Of course, a major factor in recent costs in presidential campaigns has been the increase in the number of presidential primaries and the provision for federal matching funds for presidential candidates in the preconvention period. The number of such primaries was thirty-seven by 1980. Each candidate could receive $7,360,000 in *public funds* in the preconvention period. He could thus spend twice this amount, plus 20 percent for fund-raising costs. Actually not all candidates continued in the race and, hence, the total amount spent was much less (see table 14.3). Table 14.4 lists candidates receiving the largest amount from the government in 1976 and 1980. These amounts contrast strikingly with the amounts which investigators report were spent in previous preconvention campaigns. In 1952 Eisenhower and Taft are estimated to have spent $2.5 million each. Kennedy is reported to have spent a

TABLE 14.3

Presidential Primary Expenditures (in millions), 1980

Funds	Democrats	Republicans	Anderson	Totals
Public	$10.6	$18.0	$ 2.7	$ 31.3
Private	26.2	52.7	7.4	86.3
Totals	$36.8	$70.7	$10.1	$117.6

TABLE 14.4

Candidates Receiving Most Government Funds, 1976, 1980 (in millions)

1976	Amount	1980	Amount
Gerald Ford	$4.5	Ronald Reagan	$7.3
Ronald Reagan	4.5	George Bush	5.7
Jimmy Carter	3.6	Jimmy Carter	5.1
George Wallace	3.2	Ted Kennedy	4.1
Henry Jackson	2.0	John Anderson	2.7
Morris Udall	1.9	Howard Baker	2.6

SOURCE: Federal Election Commission press release, August 1979.

little over $900,000 in 1960. But in 1968 the expenditures went up sharply:[7]

Richard Nixon	$10,000,000
Eugene McCarthy	11,000,000
Robert Kennedy	9,000,000
Nelson Rockefeller	8,000,000
Hubert Humphrey	4,000,000

And this trend seemed to continue in 1972 when all candidates are estimated to have spent $33 million. In 1976 this amount was almost doubled; in 1980 it was $118 million.

The Costs in United States Congressional Races

Running for the United States Congress has become more expensive also. As table 14.5 reveals, there has been a tremendous leap in such costs in recent years—an increase of over 200 percent in six years from 1972 to 1978. The *Congressional Quarterly* reports that these increases were 34 percent above the increase in the Consumer Price Index for that period.[8] The two major parties appear fairly evenly balanced in their efforts to win congressional seats, from a financial standpoint at least (see table 14.6). In 1980 for Senate and House seats the Democrats spent a reported $125 million, the Republicans $117 million.

A further statistic on the House and Senate expenditures relates to the increased demands made on those seeking office in the United

TABLE 14.5
Campaign Cost Breakdown by Party, 1978

Party	House	Senate	Totals
Democrats	$46,221,817	$27,026,792	$ 73,248,609
Republicans	41,092,235	37,996,430	79,088,665
Others	667,685	504,013	1,171,698
	$87,981,737	$65,527,235	$153,508,972

SOURCE: *Congressional Quarterly Weekly Report*, September 29, 1979.

NOTE: Larger amounts are reported in an earlier (June 29, 1979) Federal Election Commission release, which calculated expenditures of the congressional candidates for the entire 1977–78 period, as follows

TABLE 14.6

Congressional Campaign Costs for House and Senate

Costs	1972	1974	1976	1978	*Percentage of Increase 1972–78*
Total Expenditures (in millions of dollars)	$66.4	$74.0	$99.0	$153.5	231
Overall average per candidate (in thousands of dollars)	44.8	54.6	73.4	100.9	225

SOURCES: *Congressional Quarterly Weekly Report*, September 29, 1979; Herbert E. Alexander, *Financing Politics* (Washington, D.C.: Congressional Quarterly, 1980), p. 225. Average expenditures based on research reported in Edie Goldenberg and Michael Traugott, "Resource Allocations and Broadcast Expenditures in Congressional Campaigns" (a paper presented at the Annual Meeting of the American Political Science Association, Washington, D.C., September 1979).

States House of Representatives the first time. The *Congressional Quarterly's* analysis documents an increase of over 100 percent for the 1974–78 period. Whereas in 1974 the average amount spent by House first-time winners was $106,000, by 1976 that became $141,000, and by 1978 it was $229,000. And the costs for reelection decline the longer one is in the House. The average amounts spent for reelection in 1978 were: $143,000 for the class of 1976; $127,000 for the class of 1974; and $87,000 for the classes of the period before 1974.[9] It is the initial try for high legislative office which is most expensive. Once one becomes an incumbent, it appears that a candidate's financial status may change considerably.

The status of the candidate—whether an incumbent, a challenger to an incumbent, or a candidate in an open race (no incumbent running)—is critical for the mobilization of money. First, challengers spend the least and candidates in open races spend the most (see table 14.8) House incumbents will spend, on the average, almost twice as much as challengers, while in the United States Senate races the discrepancy will be even greater. In open races the expenditures are the greatest since no incumbent monopolizes the financial resources available and more than one candidate sees a realistic chance of winning. The winners do tend to outspend their rivals in House races (see table 14.7).

Second, not only do House incumbents, as well as open-seat candidates, spend more in aggregate terms, the amount they receive from party committees appears to be closely linked to the proportion of the vote the candidates received in the preceding election (see table 14.9). When the incumbent is not threatened, the flow of funds is restricted and diverted to areas where the chances of an upset are greater. The same is true in party support for challengers. For both the incumbent

TABLE 14.7
House Race Average Expenditures
(in thousands)

Candidates	1972	1976	1978
Winners	$55.4	$87.2	$126.5
Losers	34.3	53.9	76.1

SOURCE: Edie N. Goldenberg and Michael W. Traugott, "Resource Allocations and Broadcast Expenditures in Congressional Campaigns" (a paper presented at the Annual Meeting of the American Political Science Association, Washington, D.C., September 1979).

TABLE 14.8
Average Expenditures by Status of Congressional
Candidates (in thousands)

	House			Senate	
Candidates	1974	1976	1978	1974	1978
Incumbents	$63.5	$ 79.8	$111.0	$842.6	$1,341
Challengers	39.9	48.9	54.5	331.8	351
Open races	94.2	114.9	160.0	800.0	507

SOURCES: Herbert E. Alexander, *Financing Politics* (Washington, D.C.: Congressional Quarterly, 1980), pp. 220–23; *Congressional Quarterly Weekly Report*, September 29, 1979, p. 2151.

TABLE 14.9
Party Campaign Contributions in 1976 to House Candidates
Linked to Incumbency and Political Strength in Their Districts, 1976
Types of District[a]
(Averages per candidate)

Party	"Sure" Districts (60.1 percent or more)	Moderately "Sure" Districts (55.1 percent to 60 percent)	Marginal Districts (55 percent or less)	Difference Between "Sure" and "Marginal" Districts
Democrat				
Incumbents	$1,781	$ 7,054	$ 9,114	+411.7%
Challengers	1,660	3,090	4,617	+178.1%
Republican				
Incumbents	6,112	8,005	12,627	+106.6%
Challengers	4,396	13,581	18,633	+323.9%

SOURCE: Roland D. McDevitt, "Interest Groups and Political Parties: Their New Roles in Congressional Campaign Finance" (paper delivered at annual meeting of American Political Science Association, Washington, D.C., 1979); data taken from Gary Jackson, *Money in Congressional Elections* (New Haven: Yale University Press, forthcoming).

[a] Percentages indicate winner's share of adjusted two-party vote.

and the challenger, the differences are in some respects tremendous; they are particularly striking among Democratic candidates. Thus, in 1976 an incumbent Democratic candidate in a "sure" district (where he got over 60 percent of the vote previously) received only 20 percent of the party contributions given to a Democratic incumbent in a "marginal" district. Similarly, a Democratic challenger in a "sure" district received only 33 percent of what a challenger in a marginal district received. Republican party contributions were more generous in all districts, but they too were more inclined to support challengers and incumbents more heavily in marginal districts—twice as much for incumbents and four times as much for challengers.

Third, incumbents are the most likely beneficiaries of contributions from the special interest groups which have their own political action budgets (the PAC's). The Federal Election Commission's data reveals that the 1978 contributions of such groups to House and Senate candidates favored incumbents by a wide margin (see table 14.10).

TABLE 14.10

House and Senate Candidates' PAC Contributions, 1978
(in millions)

	Incumbents	Challengers	Open Races
Numbers of candidates	414	971	524
PAC contributions	$19.23	$7.55	$7.34

SOURCE: Federal Election Commission press release, June 29, 1979.

Clearly those already in office attract much more financial help than those trying to get in.

A major worry in congressional spending is the virtually unlimited amounts which candidates can spend. The United States Senate campaigns are notorious—the number of million-dollar Senate campaigns has increased from four in 1972 to seven in 1974 to ten in 1976 to fourteen in 1978. Examples of "big spenders" in 1978 were:[10]

Jesse Helms–Republican–North Carolina	$5,969,317
John Tower–Republican–Texas	3,157,981
Robert Kreuger–Democrat–Texas	1,700,948
Howard Baker–Republican–Tennessee	1,326,567
William Bradley–Democrat–New Jersey	1,216,485

Recent Supreme Court interpretations have permitted the unlimited expenditure of funds for and by Senate candidates, including no limits on the use of their own fortunes. One major question, of course, is whether this is good policy.

The Sources of Campaign Funds—Who Contributes?

The extent to which the American citizen public is involved in the financial support of parties and candidates has been a major source of concern for some time. Although the parties have sought to broaden the base of their support by soliciting funds from the public generally, their efforts have not always been successful, and such efforts have by no means displaced the large wealthy contributor and his family. Although many citizens do contribute to party campaigns (9 percent of the adult population in 1956 and 10 percent in 1972),[11] there appears to be a decline in the proportion who are giving in response to solicitations. According to the best data available 19 percent of the adult population in the United States was solicited for contributions in 1956 and 9 percent made contributions; 30 percent was solicited and 10 percent contributed in 1972. Nevertheless, the *number* of contributors has increased—from three million in 1952, to eight million in 1956, to almost twelve million in 1972.[12] The major question, of course, is how important these public contributions are to the total amounts contributed to candidates and spent by them. It is very difficult to answer this question since complete data on all small contributions are not available—records need be kept only for contributions of $50 or more. However, research suggests that the large contributions increased considerably in recent years and have accounted for the greatest share of all money contributed and spent (see table 14.11). In the House and Senate races of 1978 the *Congressional Quarterly* reports reveal that only

TABLE 14.11
Comparison of Campaign Contributions, 1952, 1972

Contributions	1952	1972
Number giving $500 or more to federal campaigns	9,500	51,230
Number giving $10,000 or more	100	1,254
Amounts given by those contributing $10,000 or more	$1,937,000	$51,320,000

SOURCE: Herbert E. Alexander, *Financing Politics* (Washington, D.C.: Congressional Quarterly, 1980), p. 86.

10 percent of the contributions came from individuals giving between $100 and $499. Other sources made up the other 90 percent.[13]

It is the role of the big contributors which has alarmed many scholars of party finance. In 1972 the following persons contributed big sums:

W. Clement and Jessie V. Stone	$2,141,666
Richard Mellon Scaife	1,068,000
Stewart Mott	830,339
Anne and Frank Forsyth	703,000
Leon Hess	481,000

The Rockefeller family gave over $2 million in 1968, and over a half million in 1972. There were twelve prominent families (among them, the DuPonts, Fords, Mellons, Rockefellers, Pews) who together gave $1,154,000 in 1956 and by 1972 this was close to $4 million.[14] It is not merely that such large amounts have been contributed which is disturbing or that they are increasingly relied on. Rather, the relationship of these contributions to influence attempts heightens the alarm, particularly when ambassadorships are linked to such contributions, or government contractors make contributions to members of House or Senate committees up for reelection who are most responsible for financial decisions relevant to the business of such contractors.[15] And finally a particularly upsetting discovery was that some of these contributions were illegal, specifically those of twenty-two corporations in 1972 (which gave a total of almost $1 million, mostly to Nixon's campaign). Such firms as American Airlines, Gulf Oil, Goodyear Tire and Rubber Company, Phillips Petroleum, all of whom were found guilty of violating the law.[16] These revelations shocked the public into a new awareness of the role of money in politics. As the California politician Jesse Unruh said, "Most people who put money into political campaigns aren't contributors—they're investors."[17]

It isn't that the public is unwilling to contribute to parties and political campaigns, for a large number do indeed contribute, and 30 percent say they would contribute if asked.[18] Further, when given a chance of a tax checkoff for political purposes on their income tax forms, over 25 percent in 1975, did agree to such a checkoff.[19] Rather, the big spender has been traditionally the source of funds, at least up until recently. The new limits imposed by the Federal Election Campaign Act ($1,000 in direct individual contributions to a candidate in the primary and again in the general election campaign, and $25,000 total direct contributions to all campaigns in a particular calendar year) may limit the role of the large spenders. Yet, "indirect" contributions and expenditures as well as money spent via the PAC's while not permitting contributions of the magnitude seen previously, may yet maintain the influence status of the big giver, or result in the substitution of the "interest group" for the "financier-patron saint" of earlier days.

Interest Groups and Campaign Finance

The direct (and indirect) financial involvement of interest groups in American electoral politics has been a concern for a long time. The early contributions of corporations led to the 1907 act outlawing contributions by "any national bank, or any corporation organized by authority of any law of Congress" to the election of presidential, vice-presidential candidates or those running for the United States Senate and House. In the 1930s labor unions began to be active in Democratic campaigns, and this led to the prohibitions under the Smith Connally Act of 1943, for the war period, and under the 1947 Taft-Hartley Act, which forbade "any corporation whatever or any labor organization to make a contribution or expenditure" related to any aspect of the election process for national elections (including primaries, conventions, and caucuses). The matter rested there until the 1970s so far as *direct* involvement was concerned. Labor unions did set up political action and political education committees, however, which spent their own funds (established with voluntary contributions). This paralleled the contributions given by individual officers and directors of corporations and interest groups to parties and candidates. Thus, both labor and business interests circumvented the law by substituting personal and voluntary contributions for group and corporate giving. Alexander Heard has documented well the involvement of these groups through personal contributions. In the 1950s, as table 14.12 demonstrates, their financial roles were considerable. Over 90 percent of the corporation money went to the Republicans and the opposite was true

TABLE 14.12
*Financial Involvement of Labor and Business Groups in
1952 and 1956 Elections*

Group	1952	1956
Labor PAC disbursements	$1,817,622	$1,690,297
Officers and directors of 100 largest U.S. corporations' personal contributions	1,014,909	1,920,322

SOURCE: From the *Costs of Democracy* by Alexander Heard. Copyright 1960 The University of North Carolina Press. Reprinted by permission.

for the labor political action money. Further, Heard's investigation of the role of other groups revealed the percentages of the officers and/ or directors of these groups who gave money in the 1952 national elections to the parties and candidates; for example:[20]

	Percent
American Petroleum Institute	37
U.S. Chamber of Commerce	36
National Association of Manufacturers	24
National Housing Conference	11
American Iron and Steel Institute	14
American Bar Association	4
American Legion	3

Corporate executives continued to give as did labor, primarily through its action committees after the 1950s. By 1964 the ten largest labor committees were spending almost $3 million, and by 1968 this had increased to $5 million.[21]

The linkage of such economic interests to national electoral politics was radically altered by the new Federal Election Campaign acts since 1971. This legislation ultimately restricted *direct* individual contributions to $1,000 for any particular candidate ($1,000 in both the primary and general election, separately) and $5,000 in *direct group* contributions. As a result the act triggered the creation of new political action committees which were set up by business firms, corporations, and other groups. These groups were permitted to solicit funds and spend them as they pleased to further their objectives in the election of candidates for public office. The mushrooming of such PACs in the 1970s can be seen from the data in table 14.13. Between 1974 and 1976 there was a 63 percent increase in the number of PACs and another 95 percent from 1976 to the end of 1978. By 1981 there were 2,551 political action committees, double the number in 1977.[22] The total increase (1974–78) was primarily the result of nonlabor activity: 5 percent of the increase was from the creation of new labor PACs, 55 percent by corporations, and the rest from the establishment of PACs by trade organizations, cooperatives, and health or other groups. Some of the leading corporate PACs now are: General Electric, Union Oil Company of California, Texaco, Chrysler, Coca Cola, Southern Railway Company. In 1976 corporate and business-related PACs gave more than $6.9 million to congressional candidates in general elections, while labor PACs, including teacher associations, gave nearly $8.1 million.[23] Almost 60 percent of the corporate PAC money went to Republicans, while over 95 percent of the labor PAC money went to Democrats.[24] But incumbents are favored by all PACs—68 percent of corporate PAC money in 1976 went to incumbents and 63 percent of labor PAC money. As Fred Radewagen of the United States Chamber of Commerce said, "The prevailing attitude is that PAC money should be used to facilitate access to incumbents."[25] What is particularly important to note, therefore, is that corporate PAC money often goes to *Democratic* incumbents *in preference to Republicans* challenging these incumbents. Thus, in 1976, where there was a Democratic incumbent–Republican challenger situation corporate and business PAC money was distributed as follows: 70 percent to the Democratic incumbent, 30 percent to the Republican challenger.[26] Clearly the aim is to secure influence with those already *in* power rather than elect new representatives *to* power.

One other type of group with explicit conservative ideological objectives has also appeared on the national election scene with more money and more clout in recent years. New Right groups, such as the National Conservative Political Action Committee, Citizens for the Republic, Gun Owners of America, Fund for a Conservative Majority spent a reported $1 million in 1976 in support of House and Senate candidates, but in the 1977–78 period they spent over $6.4 million,

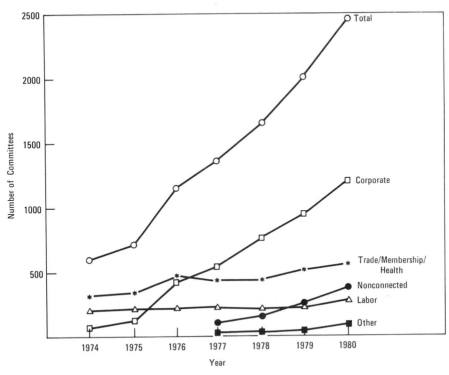

FIGURE 14.1

SOURCE: Federal Election Commission *Record*, vol. 7, no. 3 (March 1981).
[a] This graph includes all political committees that are not authorized by a federal candidate and are not established by a political party.

TABLE 14.13

Increase in Number of Political Action Committees

Group	Reported by Federal Election Commission as of						
	Dec. 31 1974	Nov. 24 1975	May 11 1976	Dec. 31 1976	Dec. 31 1977	Dec. 31 1978	Total Increas.
Corporate	89	139	294	433	538	821	732
Labor	201	226	246	224	216	281	80
Trade, Membership, and others	318	357	452	489	544	836	518
Total	608	722	992	1,146	1,298	1,938	1,330

SOURCES: *Electing Congress*, Congressional Quarterly, Inc. April 1978, p. 30; Federal Election Commission press release, May 10, 1979.

according to reports filed with the Federal Election Commission.[27] Of course, these groups were also active in the presidential contest in 1976, the Citizens for the Republic supporting Ronald Reagan and leaving a million-dollar surplus for his use after that campaign.[28]

The essence of the matter is that candidates for Congress these days, as well as candidates for many other offices, are becoming much more aware than previously of the existence of PACs. They are also beginning to rely on them for a sizeable proportion of their costs. Roland McDevitt has brought together the data necessary to see this trend (see table 14.14). Close to 25 percent of all campaign receipts of House candidates in 1978 came from the PACs directly, and 13.5 percent of the receipts of United States Senate candidates. In the face of the limitations on direct group contributions under the new federal law, and keeping in mind the other solicitation efforts of these candidates, this proportion is not insignificant. For incumbents it is much higher—perhaps closer to 50 percent. Further, the support of PACs is not limited to *direct* contributions. As long as there is no collaboration with the

TABLE 14.14

Trends in PAC Contributions to House and Senate Candidates, 1972–78 (in millions)

Receipts	1972	1974	1976	1978
House candidate receipts	$38.5	$45.7	$65.7	$92.2
Percentage from PACs	15.9	18.4	22.4	24.8
Senate candidate receipts	$23.8	$28.2	$39.1	$66.0
Percentage from PACs	11.6	11.3	14.8	13.5

SOURCES: Roland D. McDevitt, "Interest Groups and Political Parties: Their New Roles in Congressional Campaign Finance" (paper presented at the 1979 Annual Meeting of the American Political Science Association, Washington, D.C., August 1979). The data came from Robert A. Diamond, ed., *Dollar Politics: The Issue of Campaign Spending* (Washington, D.C.: Congressional Quarterly Press, 1973); Common Cause, *1974 Congressional Campaign Finances* (Washington, D.C., 1976), and the Federal Election Commission reports.

TABLE 14.15
PAC Contributions to Congressional Races in 1980 Election

Political Action Committee	Amount Contributed	Percentage to		Percentage to			Success Rate	
		Republicans	Democrats	Incumbents	Open Races	Challenges	Won	Lost
AFL-CIO COPE	$ 748,920	3.4	96.6	57	19	24	49	51
UAW Voluntary Community Action Program	1,359,676	1.4	98.6	67	15	18	62	38
American Medical PAC	1,219,410	72	28	60	15	25	79	21
Realtors PAC (Nat'l Association of Realtors)	1,226,115	67	33	68	13	18	80	20

SOURCE: *Congressional Quarterly Weekly Report*, Nov. 22, 1980, p. 3406.
NOTE: These figures are for contributions from Jan. 1, 1979 to Oct. 15, 1980.

candidate directly, PACs can spend as much money as they want in supporting the candidates of their choice.

Obviously, interest groups of many types are more involved in the financing of electoral politics than ever before. Obviously, also, they want to influence those *in power*, directly if possible, indirectly if that is the only way left to them. In 1979 the Federal Election Committee reported that 1,459 active PACs during the 1977–78 election cycle had spent $77.8 million. Of this, $35.1 million went to federal candidates— almost $20 million to incumbents.[29] This attests to the "new" level of *organized* interest-group participation in parties and elections.

The latest reports on PAC activity in the 1980 election reveal even greater evidence of their importance. By January 1981 there were 2,551 PACs, compared to 1,146 in 1976.[30] Table 14.16 shows the expenditures by a sample of key PACs in 1980. Approximately $75 million were collected by PACs for use in the 1980 campaigns according to the *Washington Post*. And certain right-wing or conservative PACs are taking credit for the Republican victories of 1980. The National Conserva-

TABLE 14.16

Expenditures by Political Action Committees, 1980 (in millions)

Conservative and Right-Wing	Amount Spent
Citizens for the Republic	$2.3
Committee for the Survival of a Free Congress	1.6
Gun Owners of America	1.3
National Rifle Association	1.0
Life Amendment (anti-abortion)	.6
Unions	
United Automobile Workers	1.5
International Ladies' Garment Workers	1.2
United Steelworkers	1.0
United Transportation	1.1
National Education Association	1.0
Corporate	
International Paper	.3
General Motors	.2
General Electric	.2
Trade	
National Realtors	1.6
American Medical Association	1.3
National Automobile Dealers	1.0

SOURCE: The *Washington Post*, January 27, 1981. Data was compiled by Morton Mintz, Valarie Thomas, Cindy Detrow, David Worthy, Marv Liekweg, and Lydia Delris.

tive Political Action Committee (NCPAC) reportedly spent over $4 million. The Moral Majority also was deeply involved, as was other groups such as the Religious Roundtable and the Christian Voice. The claims that these groups did indeed influence, or decide, certain elections are strongly disputed. The arguments used emphasize that those people defeated in 1980, such as Senators George McGovern and Birch Bayh, were already vulnerable and nearly defeated in 1974. Further there are those who argue that the charges of the NCPAC and similar groups in 1980 were unfair, erroneous, and resented by many people, and actually worked against the influence of such groups. Finally, Republican leaders believe that it was their party's organizational renovative leadership at the head of the ticket and campaign efforts which were responsible for their 1980 successes, not the efforts of these conservative PACs.[31] In any event, apparently we have entered a new era of a large number of well-financed committees committed to spending large funds related to their political objectives. It is interesting that the liberals are opposing them by creating their own new PACs. George McGovern has set up a group called Americans for Common Sense, and Senator Edward Kennedy and former Vice-President Walter Mondale have set up their own action committees. Several other senators who are reportedly targets for these conservative committees for 1982 are also active in this way. "We were outgunned last year [1980], said Senator Alan Cranston of California, "but we don't intend to let it happen again."[32]

Purposes for Which Money Is Spent in Campaigns

American political campaigns are expensive because there are no governmental limits on the use of radio and television (contrary to the practice in other countries), *and* because these publicity media are expensive. In the earlier study of the national campaigns of 1952 and 1956 radio and television already consumed a major portion (up to 40 percent) of the money spent.[33] Both parties competed fairly evenly in their allocations for broadcasts. And this pattern remained basically the same through the 1972 presidential election. If only national committee expenditures are used for presidential campaigns the proportions committed for television and radio remained markedly similar (see table 14.17). It appears that the decline in such expenditures in 1960 was a phenomenon for both parties, as was the rise in 1964 and 1968. In 1972 the two parties had different strategies. Nixon's campaign was based on the concept of the "stay at home president," with limited television exposure and more use of direct mail to particular

TABLE 14.17
Percentage of Campaign
Funds for Television
and Radio

Year	Democrats	Republicans
1952	30	31
1956	35	37
1960	12	18
1964	53	40
1968	53	50
1972	27	7

SOURCE: Herbert E. Alexander, *Financing Politics* (Washington, D.C.: Congressional Quarterly, 1980), pp. 20, 28.

groups of voters, while McGovern needed much more national visibility and used television for this purpose.

The great variety of purposes for which funds are spent in political campaigns is almost impossible to specify in detail. Some idea of the use of presidential campaign funds can be obtained with a look at the Nixon and McGovern allocations in 1972 before the new law restricted the presidential candidates to less than $22 million each in 1976. The massive Nixon campaign in 1972 (over $61 million) which outspent McGovern's group 2 to 1 reveals the magnitude of certain types of expenditures. One-fourth of the funds were funneled to state organizations (less than 20 percent for McGovern). Nixon spent $10 million for research and surveys, fund raising and legal fees (McGovern spent much less). The broadcast and publicity operations, including direct mailings, took $14 million (about $10 million for McGovern). Headquarters and travel costs were over $8 million (but only $2.5 million for McGovern). These sums are large, and they attest to the heavy use of mass media (and their price), of professional services, of headquarters overhead expenses, and the mix of the national effort, the effort through state organizations, and the effort through ancillary groups and structures. If the purposes, as well as the total expenditure level, are kept in mind, a better perspective can be had in evaluating the complaints that in 1976 and today there is not enough money for what has to be done. If the ceiling is set at $21.8 million, as it was in 1976 (closer to $30 million in 1980), and $7 million of this is for television, radio, and broadcast advertising, the balance may restrict campaign operations considerably. Further, there has been an increase in broadcast rates—from 1972 to 1976 it is reported that rates for television ads increased 64 percent.[34]

A recent analysis of expenditures in congressional races in 1978 reveals that they are heavily media/broadcast oriented.[35] The average expenditure for all 1978 House races was $79,800 ($130,200 in open races where there was no incumbent running), spent for the following purposes:

	Percent
Staff	18.0
Research	4.3
Events	6.3
Direct mail	14.7
Broadcasting	23.9
Other media	17.1
Travel	4.3
Door-to-door	8.5
Other	2.9
	100.0

The authors of this analysis test a variety of theories to explain differential levels of expenditures. For example, campaigns varied greatly in the amounts spent on radio and television—from nothing to $168,000. The question posed was, Why the variation? The preliminary results of this research suggest that reactive spending (responding to what one's opponent does) is a major factor in decisions to allocate funds to broadcasting, particularly in open races. A further finding in this study was that congressional races have become increasingly professionalized. Whereas 27 percent had salaried campaign managers in 1976, in 1978 40 percent did (plus 9 percent with managers on a paid consultant basis). In addition 53 percent had paid ad specialists, 24 percent had paid accountants, and 10 percent had paid legal aids.[36] These congressional contests thus cost more and are more professional than previously.

Regulating the Use of Money in Campaigns

For most of this century the United States Congress has been struggling to design a legislative approach to the problems of the use of money in campaigns for federal office. As mentioned at the outset of this chapter, there are periodic revelations about alleged abuses of the use of money, followed by legislative investigations, as well as mass media exposés and public concern, which lead to the adoption of new legislation, then a quiet period until new revelations begin the cycle all over again. Our most recent cycle began about 1970, which led to new federal regulations, and there now appears to be a period of relative quiet.

Probably our earliest concern was the exploitation by parties of federal employees for money-raising purposes, and this led to the provision in the Civil Service Reform Act of 1883 that federal government employees could not be solicited on governmental premises for funds to support parties or candidates. The first approach to regulation was, thus, to dry up one of the sources of campaign funds—federal appointees. But this act was only a beginning and did not really impose any stringent limitations. In the elections of the period from 1888 on, the Republicans, particularly, under the financial leadership of Mark Hanna, their national chairman, were able to secure huge sums from wealthy businessmen, as well as from corporations.[37] Standard Oil gave sums ranging from $100,000 to $250,000 in the elections of 1896 to 1904. This situation raised a hue and cry which resulted in a 1907 act prohibiting the direct contribution of corporations to federal campaigns, an act which essentially has been retained since that date. Again, the aim was to close a source, linked to a desire to limit the direct influence of a particular interest group with ample funds which they desired to use to control the presidency. In 1912 Woodrow Wilson, very aware of this danger, directed his finance chairman that "no contributions whatever be even indirectly accepted from any corporation" and that none of the money used in the campaign should come from "three rich men in the Democratic party whose political affiliations are . . . unworthy."[38]

Aside from these legislative attempts to dry up the sources, a second approach was that of publicity and disclosure—forcing candidates to reveal the sources of their funds. In 1910 Congress passed a law requiring periodic financial reports by candidates in general elections; in 1911 this law was extended to include primaries and conventions. But there was considerable debate at the time over the propriety and constitutionality of such legislation and its interference with First Amendment rights. The Supreme Court did indeed rule in 1921 that Congress had no authority to regulate primary elections.[39] It was not until twenty years later that the Court reversed this position.[40] In the meantime because of the great public concern, again, about the state of party and campaign finance, Congress passed a new basic law, the Federal Corrupt Practices Act of 1925. This act spelled out the publicity and reporting requirements rather comprehensively for congressional candidates, but not for presidential candidates. All political committees seeking to influence the election of federal candidates and functioning in two or more states were required to report to the Clerk of the House several times a year all contributions and expenditures, including the name and address of every person contributing $100 or more in a calendar year and the name and address of every person to whom an expenditure of $10 was made. Further, all individuals spending $50 or more to influence such federal elections had to file, as did all candidates for both houses of Congress—House candidates with the Clerk of the House, and Senate candidates with the Secretary of the Senate—such reports ten to fifteen days before the election and within thirty days after the election. This law remained on the books until superseded by the 1971 and subsequent legislation.

The same 1925 Corrupt Practices Act included provisions to deal with the use of political money in a third way—by placing *ceilings on the amounts* that might be spent. It limited House candidates to $5,000 and Senate candidates to $25,000 (the exact amount linked to the votes cast in the last election). Certain major expenditures were, however, exempted: personal travelling and living costs; stationery, printing, postage; distribution of letters, circulars, or posters; and telephone and telegraph service. Although considered largely ineffective, because of decentralization in campaign operations and the loopholes in the law, as well as nonenforcement of its provisions, this approach remained. And in 1940 in the Hatch Act a ceiling was placed on the amounts which national committees could spend—a maximum of $3 million being specified as a permissible aggregate amount. This approach, too, was debated at length, those opposed contending that it led to more auxiliary or separate committees (each of which could spend $3 million!).

The Hatch Acts also approached campaign finance in a fourth way— by imposing a limit of $5,000 on the amount that any person could contribute in any calendar year to the nomination or election of a candidate to federal office or to an organization working for a candidate or to the national political party. This prohibition was intended (by some congressmen) to limit the sources of party funds, or at least to limit the probability that big donors could "buy" candidates. However, contributors who wanted to give more than $5,000 were facilitated by the creation of more committees (to each of which $5,000 could be given). Yet, the act did tend to change the big donor's role, while not, however, controlling the total amount he could give.[41]

The final major act adopted prior to the 1970s was the Taft-Hartley Act of 1947, which prohibited labor unions and corporations from expending or contributing organizational general funds on behalf of the nomination or election of federal candidates. In a sense the purpose was to *break the direct financial linkage of interest groups* to political parties. The way was left open, however, for the creation of voluntary political action committees, to which labor union members could contribute money if they so desired and which could spend money on their own initiative in support of candidates for federal office. This opportunity, plus the propriety of spending certain funds from union treasuries for the publication of political information and for "political education," was upheld by the Supreme Court. This, in a sense, was the precursor of the development recently of the political action committees.

After the Taft-Hartley Act nothing was done although there was considerable concern about various aspects of party finance. In 1956 Senator Francis Case of South Dakota revealed that he had been offered a $2,500 campaign gift by natural gas lobbyists for his vote on the Harris-Fulbright Natural Gas Bill. (President Eisenhower later vetoed the bill.) President Kennedy set up a Commission on Campaign Costs, which made an excellent set of recommendations on all the major aspects of party finance reform and also suggested the use of public funds on a matching basis to finance candidates for federal office. But nothing happened during the 1960s despite more revelations about the improper use of money by Bobby Baker, aide to Lyndon Johnson, and by Senator Thomas Dodd of Connecticut, who used political funds for private purposes. Abortive legislation was proposed in Congress; indeed one act (the Long Act of Senator Russell Long) was adopted and then repealed. This set the stage for the Federal Election Campaign Act of 1971 (FECA), which replaced the 1925 Corrupt Practices Act. New provisions were included also in the Revenue Act of 1971. FECA 1971 was in turn changed by the FECA 1974, and this was supplemented by amendments in practically every year, including 1979. In addition, Supreme Court interpretations of these acts have modified the law substantially. A summary of the basic elements of the federal legislation to 1980 may be helpful.

Current Federal Regulations of Party Finance

The present regulations reflect to a certain extent the experience of the past, particularly the ineffectualness of some of these earlier attempts. But they also embody the good elements of that legislation and introduce some new concepts. Of course, the Watergate crisis precipitated much discussion of the uses of money, particularly the large cash contributions which were unreported, the "laundering" of contributions, the direct (illegal) contributions of corporations, and so forth. These revelations on top of the previous findings against congressmen and senators led to the feeling that a new law was necessary. To a certain extent the FECA represents new approaches to an old problem, approaches designed to tighten up and specify more precisely the limitations on the use of money in federal campaigns.

Publicity Requirements

Careful and detailed bookkeeping by political committees and candidates, or their financial representatives, is now required. This continues and extends the requirements first initiated in 1910 and supplemented in 1925. *Candidates* must have one official committee whose treasurer is responsible under the law for reporting. The candidate must keep records of all contributions of $50 or more (by name and date) and must provide detailed reports on all contributions of $200 or more, including the occupation and principal place of business of the contributor; all cash on hand, all money raised by special events (dinners, rallies), all loans and obligations. In short, almost all financial transactions must be carefully recorded. Quarterly reports must be filed every year, as well as ten days before an election and thirty days after an election. Also all contributions of $1,000 or more received in the last two weeks must be reported, up to two days before the election. Every political *committee* spending or receiving money in excess of $1,000 must file with the Federal Election Commission. It must report the names and addresses of all its members, as well as a variety of information about its relationships to other groups, its accounts, the candidates it supports, and of course its contributions to candidates or committees supporting candidates, as well as its expenditures on its own initiative. *Individuals* are treated like committees if money is spent in order to influence the election of a candidate. Thus, those who must report are: the treasurer for the candidates' committees, all other political committees, including party committees, and individuals—all who contribute to or spend money in connection with federal elections.

Limits on Contributions and Spending

Individuals may directly contribute $1,000 maximum to a candidate in a primary campaign and $1,000 in a general election—for a total of $2,000 maximum to any particular candidate. The limit an individual may contribute directly is $25,000 to all candidates and committees in any one calendar year. Individuals may contribute up to $5,000 to a political action committee and $20,000 to a national party committee. Individuals may make "independent" expenditures supporting a candidate but these must not be coordinated with the candidate's operations.

Candidates for the Senate and House may spend as much of their own funds or family fortunes as they wish to (the 1971 act limiting Senate candidates to $35,000 and House candidates to $25,000 was invalidated by the Supreme Court). Presidential and vice-presidential candidates, however, who accept public funding may only spend $50,000 from their own private (personal or family) funds.

Party committees are limited in the amounts they can spend on behalf of candidates. For the national committees in 1980 it was $4,638,000 (based on a formula using the voting age population, which was 157.5 million, and the Consumer Price Index). Similarly the Federal Election Commission published limits for each state that party committees may spend in United States senatorial races (ranging from $29,440 to $485,000, in California). For all candidates for the House the *party* expenditure limit was $14,720 in 1980.[42]

Groups have a basic limit of $5,000 in direct contributions to a specific candidate in a particular election but no aggregate limit on the amounts which may be contributed to all candidates and committees. The Federal Election Commission ruled that unions, corporations, and other groups may set up PACs from voluntary contributions, and such PACs could spend unlimited funds in support of candidates, as long as they did this "independently" (without collusion with the candidate's representatives). Further, all PACs of a particular company or union would be treated as a single committee and the $5,000 limit for direct contributions to a candidate would be applied in this sense.

Party committees have special limits on the amounts they may contribute to particular candidates or their committees, as well as expenditure limits which vary by state depending on the size of the voting age population. The 1979 amendments provided liberal exemptions to party committees in determining their contributions. For example, payments for campaign materials, legal services, and voter registration drives are exempted.

Miscellaneous regulations require that loans be treated as contributions; no cash contributions of over $100 are permitted.

Public Funding

A "tax checkoff" was allowed (by the Revenue Act of 1971) for all those paying a federal income tax, amounting to a $1 deduction ($2 for those filing joint returns) from their tax as a contribution to a general fund for all eligible presidential candidates. This fund is used to support candidates running in the preconvention and post convention periods, as well as to support the costs of national party conventions. The tax checkoff takes place every year, but money is paid out only in presidential election years. Over 25 percent of those paying taxes have been using the checkoff recently. The total amount available to be spent in 1976 was $94.1 million. In the 1980 survey done by the Center for Political Studies, National Election Survey at Michigan, 32 percent said they used the checkoff.

Funding for candidates was provided in the preconvention period on a matching basis. A candidate had to establish credibility by first raising $100,000 consisting of private contributions of $250 or less which would add up to at least $5,000 in each of twenty states. Contributions of this size would then be matched by the federal government up to a total of about $5.5 million. The total amount (in 1976, at least) that a candidate could spend was thus almost $11 million, plus 20 percent (raised privately) for fund-raising costs, or a total of $13.2 million. In 1980 it was raised to $17.7 million. In 1976 fifteen candidates qualified for federal funds in this way; in 1980 ten did.

Candidates are subjected to two other requirements, however: (1) they must receive 10 percent or more of the vote in two consecutive presidential primaries in order to remain eligible for federal funds; and (2) if they fail to remain eligible or withdraw from candidacy they must return the balance of funds received from the government after previously incurred debts are repaid.

Both national conventions could receive help to defray costs, the amounts being $2.2 million each in 1976 and $3 million in 1980. A broad interpretation by the Federal Election Commission permitted certain financial assistance by the host state and city, as well as corporations, but corporations were forbidden to make direct contributions for this purpose alone.

The law provides now for direct allocations through a Presidential Election Campaign Fund, to presidential candidates who are nominated by their parties, to be spent in the postconvention period. The major party candidates (those who receive 25 percent of the votes cast in the preceding presidential election) would secure full funding. This amounted to $21.8 million each in 1976, almost $30 million in 1980. This would be adjusted each election year to the Cost of Living Index. No public funding would be provided unless the presidential candidates agree to use only such public funds in the campaign—thus eliminating direct private contributions to presidential campaigns. Minor parties who received 5 percent or more of the vote in preceding presidential elections would be entitled to receive funds after the election. The proportion of the maximum amount such a presidential candidate could receive is based on a formula which relates the vote of the minor party to the average popular vote in the presidential elections of the Republican and Democratic parties.[43] After the election minor party candidates who did not previously qualify for funds could apply and get the public funds they were entitled to under this formula. The public funds received by major and minor parties also constitute spending limits for the campaign, except that there is also an allowance for the national committees to spend a limited amount from *party funds* for the presidential campaigns ($3.2 million for the Republican and Democratic National committees each in 1976; in 1980 it was $4.6 million). The total maximum expenditure permissible for postconvention costs in 1976, therefore, was $25 million for each major party. In 1980 it was over $30 million.

Administration of National Party Finance Regulations

The basic new agency for administration is the Federal Election Commission which, after a controversial history, now consists of a bipartisan body of six members appointed by the president and confirmed by the Senate. The members must terminate outside business interests one year after coming on the commission. A major effort has been made, thus, to make it an independent agency. The 1976 amendments gave the commission powers to prosecute violations of the campaign finance law and generally increased its monitoring and supervisory roles. The commission aims at voluntary compliance with the disclosure requirements of the law although it has the responsibility to take action to secure compliance, but on the basis of sworn, written, complaints. The processing and analysis of the disclosure reports is a major task, since it is estimated that some 100,000 such statements were filed in 1976 by 2,500 federal candidates and 7,500 political committees.[44] While the commission initially ran into opposition from Congress, and its earlier regulations (concerning congressional "slush funds" and filing requirements) were turned back by Congress, it has acquired considerable legitimacy now. It works with the Department of Justice in handling criminal violations.

The criminal penalties under the law are considerable. They provide that knowingly violating the campaign law (involving sums over $1,000) is punishable by a one-year jail sentence and a fine of $25,000 or three times the amount of the contribution or expenditure violation. Civil penalties are fines of $5,000 ($10,000 if knowingly committed), or twice the amount involved in the violation of the contribution or expenditure limits. The 1974 act provides also that a candidate who failed to file reports could be excluded from candidacy for the term of that office plus one year; this is no longer true under the present law. In addition there is still on the books the prohibition on the use of promises of public appointments, contracts, or other benefits for the purpose of securing a person's support for a candidacy—fines of $1,000 and/or one year prison terms are the minimal penalties provided.

The State of Party Finance and Its Regulation Today

The history of America's efforts to adopt satisfactory regulations for the use of money in elections has been a tempestuous one, a long period of trial and error, which has forced some very difficult decisions. There are serious dilemmas over questions concerning major moral issues, such as the permissible extent of direct financial influence over political leadership, the need to rectify inequalities in wealth of aspirants to high office, the proper role of interest groups in the party process, and the need of the public to know the money sources of those in political power or seeking political power. On occasion the debates over these issues have been so acrimonious as to lead to their resolution in the United States Supreme Court. The most recent instance of this kind was the case of *Buckley* v. *Valeo*[45] which was decided in January 1976. The plaintiffs in this case were a strange assortment ideologically: the conservative Republican Senator James L. Buckley, the liberal former Democratic Senator Eugene L. McCarthy, the Conservative Party of the State of New York, the New York Civil Liberties Union, the Mississippi Republican party, the Libertarian party, and others. Defendants included the Attorney General, FEC, Common Cause, the Secretary of the United States Senate and Clerk of the House, the League of Women Voters and so on. The key issue was the free speech question, that is, the relationship between expenditures of funds in political campaigns and the adequate opportunity of individuals, candidates, and groups to communicate effectively to the electorate. "Free speech is money and money is free speech" was the Court's position, and it decided for a broad protection of the right to speak. This meant that individual expenditure limitations could not be imposed on persons or on candidates in the use of their personal resources, but those candidates accepting public funding (the presidential candidates) could be held to expenditure limits. Further the Court held that direct contributions to candidates and parties could be limited because these were not necessarily restrictions on free speech and that there might be a coercive influence, and at least an appearance of corruption, if large contributors were permitted to make *direct* contributions. Finally, the Court upheld all the other basic elements in the law, for disclosure of amounts received and spent and the administration of the law under the Federal Election Commission.

In effect, there is now a major new party finance law at the national level. The controversies are not over by any means, but the issue has subsided for the time being. The most important recent development has been the proposal again to provide public funding for House and Senate candidates, but this has failed in Congress. In the meantime, the state governments have adopted new legislation, often patterned after the national law. All but one state requires the filing of reports by state and local candidates and forty-three states require disclosure *before* the election as well as *after*.[46] About half the states have bipartisan election commissions like the FEC and have limits on individual contributions. A fourth of the states provide subsidies for certain candidates. There is considerable progress, therefore, in altering the legal context in which parties and candidates receive and spend money throughout the political system.

How should the new legislation on party finance, particularly as it has operated in recent elections, be assessed? What are its strong points? First, the prominent role of the wealthy contributor who gave huge sums directly to the presidential campaign has presumably disappeared. As Anthony Lewis wrote in his November 7, 1975, column, "When Jimmy Carter takes the oath next January, his situation will differ from that of other recent newly elected Presidents in one interesting respect: He will not be obligated to a single large campaign contributor." There may still exist "fat cats" who spend money, but they now must spend it independently on their own, without being able to give a lot of money in direct support to the candidate. No one can contribute more than $1,000 directly to a presidential candidate in the campaign. A new variety of "fat cat" support has appeared, however. In 1975 it was especially noticeable in the form of "personal services," particularly by those in the entertainment industry. Thus, Carter hosted a reception for members of the Recording Industry Association of America, and the proceeds of this and concerts by Southern rock stars (the Allman Brothers, Marshall Tucker, the Outlaws, and others) raised close to $300,000 as start up money for Carter. Jerry Brown raised $170,000 from a single concert by Linda Ronstadt and the Eagles. Such funds (at $15 or so a head) are the "up-front" money needed to get a campaign underway.[47]

A second major advantage of the new legislation is its publicity concept. The insistence that each candidate must have a committee with a treasurer who is responsible for all contributions and expenditures by all committees working with the candidate, a concept developed long ago in the British theory of finance regulation, is fundamentally sound. It introduces the idea of responsibility into the American system. And the periodic detailed reports during the entire calendar year at least provide the opportunity for the public and the press to know who is supporting whom.

Third, some of the most blatant evils of the Watergate era and before have been outlawed. That is, the large secret slush funds, the use of cash contributions and of funds laundered through several bank accounts, as well as the huge direct contributions by individuals or groups—these abuses are presumably no longer possible.

Fourth, the change in the approach to ceilings on the amounts that House and Senate candidates can spend is considered by some a real advantage. The old limits were entirely unrealistic and were not obeyed. Now the amount that can be spent is flexible, contingent on the type of campaign, the nature of the district or state, the amounts that can be collected from individual $1,000 contributions, and the wealth of the candidate. The latter amounts can be considerable, as witness the 14 million-dollar Senate campaigns of 1978, and the huge sums particular individual candidates can give or lend to their own campaigns (John Heinz, III, of Pennsylvania, for example, loaned $2.6 million to his 1976 campaign, none of which was repaid). Still, the earlier legislation of 1974 which placed limits on these campaigns was so low and so inflexible that the advantage was clearly in favor of the incumbents. Now House and Senate candidates operate in a free enterprise environment for incumbents and challengers but with strict limits on *direct* contributions and with disclosure requirements. True, incumbents will always have the advantage because of their large staffs, expense accounts, mailing privileges, and multiple offices in their districts. This has been estimated as a half-million dollar advantage which is taxpayer financed. Despite this, the present law does provide more opportunity for a challenger than under the old 1925 act or the 1974 act, when the ceiling was $70,000 for all House races—a figure which was less than the average expenditures in the past.

Fifth, the present legislation is more realistic in its handling of the interest-group involvement in party campaigns. The limit of $5,000 in direct contributions is severe. But the right of groups to collect voluntary funds and to spend them on their own in pursuit of electoral goals is protected by the courts. Not only labor unions and corporations but other interest groups as well can now openly solicit such funds (within certain reasonable rules laid down by the FEC) and spend them independently. There were over 2,500 such PACs actively involved by 1981. While this court decision is not an unmitigated blessing and does draw the fire of certain critics, it does consistently apply First Amendment rights and it does bring such spending into the open.

Finally, in support of the present legislation there is a much improved Federal Election Commission which is in charge of administering the law, implementing the basic policy laid down, and receiving reports and making these available to the press and the public. It is a bipartisan committee. And it has not, thus far, been reluctant to investigate delinquencies and report them to the Justice Department for prosecution. The first person convicted of violation of the new finance law was Representative Richard A. Tonry of Louisiana, who was sentenced to one year in prison in August 1977 on four misdemeanor charges of accepting contributions in excess of the $1,000 limit on personal donations. Perhaps the new law does indeed have some teeth in it!

There are still many criticisms of the law and proposals for more revisions. One of the most frequently heard is that the amounts now allowed for presidential campaigns ($25 million each in 1976, over $30 million in 1980) are inadequate in order to inform the American electorate. In 1976 almost half of these sums were allocated by Carter and Ford to media advertising. After personal travel expenses took another large cut from the budget, there was not much left, so it was claimed, for state and local organizations and for all the little extras needed for a campaign. In 1976 there were fewer buttons, banners, and bumper stickers, and not even enough money for campaign literature used in personal canvassing. This depresses citizen participation. As one organizer in the Carter camp said, "There just aren't as many people able to get involved. Fund raising used to generate a lot of activity: bazaars, concerts, cookouts, the little old ladies making Swedish meatballs—a lot of nickel and dime events that got people excited. The new regulations make it almost impossible to do this now, and I miss it."[48] Further it is argued that the low ceilings puts the presidential challenger at a disadvantage compared to the incumbent with all the privileges and free publicity of the White House. Herbert Alexander has advocated recently that we increase the presidential campaign ceilings to $40 million.

Ironically there are also those who will argue that too much money is being spent on election campaigns. Is the estimated grand total of $540 million in 1976 for all campaigns really necessary? If the use of the mass media, particularly television, were strictly limited, couldn't those enormous expenditures be cut down? The problem, of course, is a composite of the number of elections, the cost of the media, the problem of communication, and the availability of resources. Cutting down on the totals spent would require a drastic overhaul of the entire system.

Some people will also argue that the problem of special influence under the new laws has not really been solved. By opening up the opportunity for interest groups to spend unlimited amounts in connection with campaigns (even though direct contributions are severely limited), wealthy people have been let back into the game after having had the door on them closed earlier. As one Federal Election Commissioner said, "If I were a member of the fat-cat society, I'd find a splendid way of operating under the new ruling."[49] And *Common Cause* argues that "special interest group money pouring into political campaigns is contributing to legislative paralysis and interest group domination of Congress."[50] There is a difference now, however, in that *direct* influence is limited. How important a difference this is remains to be seen.

There is a variety of other charges against the present law. Smaller parties, it is claimed, are put at a disadvantage under the public funding provisions for presidential campaigns. "Too much red tape" is the cry of those who have to hire personnel to keep the records and file the reports. In 1980 the FEC cut some of the red tape, reducing the number of reports by a committee each "election cycle" from twenty-four to nine. "Invasion of privacy" is the charge of certain groups who have to report their sources of funds.[51]

A major concern, particularly of those hoping to strengthen party organizations and to make them more responsible structures, is that the new legislation operates to weaken parties. This is because the presidential campaign funds are given to the candidate, not to the national committee or some other party body. This places in the candidate's hands, it is argued, vital control over the campaign which he can run through his own campaign organization while ignoring regular party organs. This can mean that a presidential candidate can select the party personnel he desires to work with at the state level as well as at the national level. Those most alarmed by this development see this as just another step in weakening parties by taking a vital power—the financial power—out of the hands of regular party leaders.

Certainly the present legislation is still controversial. On balance, however, it seems quite clear that there has been great progress. Present campaign finance law operates with a new set of theoretical approaches. The older approach was to put ceilings on the amounts to be spent, to try to limit individual contributions *and* expenditures, to discourage groups from participating with their funds in the electoral process. The new approach sanctioned by the Supreme Court is to lift the ceilings (except in presidential races) to permit individuals to spend their money on politics if they wish, to allow groups under voluntaristic rules to be involved in the process, and to provide public funding. It appears that we are closer to realizing at least some of the principles we have been aiming at:

1. Complete disclosure and detailed knowledge of the amounts, sources, and purposes of money used in the electoral process, so voters can have access to the relevant information *before* as well as *after* elections.
2. The discouragement of improper influence relationships, at least of a direct nature, between the affluent interest sectors of society and those seeking public office.
3. A greater equalization of opportunity for all candidates for office on the one hand by providing public funds in presidential races and, on the other hand, by eliminating unrealistic ceilings on candidates in congressional races.
4. Re-enforcing the First Amendment rights of citizens and groups to use money, within reason, to work toward political goals.

There is indeed more evidence today of rationality, openness, equality of competition, and intelligence in our regulation of the use of money in elections. It may be a moral crisis which we are beginning to surmount. Inequities and inadequacies still exist in today's finance laws, but hopefully with more experience there can be a continued improvement on a regulatory system that has many sound operating principles. In the meantime we are functioning with a system in which, as the court has said, "money is speech, and speech is money," and in our society the demands for freedom to speak and to influence politics, while kept in rein, are strongly championed.

Chapter 15

Parties and

the Election Process

ELECTIONS are in a very real sense a major test for political parties in democracies. After all their leadership selection activity, their organizational effort, their intensive campaign work, the election tells parties and their candidates where they stand vis-à-vis the public. Since parties must win elections (or demonstrate that they have the potential for winning) if they are to be taken seriously, elections force a discipline on parties that cannot be matched by any other aspect of democratic life. Although there are many ways to look at elections, certainly a central perspective is their relevance for testing the strength, viability, and power potential of the parties.

Scholars have over the years seen elections as fulfilling different functions in democratic systems. Elections are *expressions of the interest of citizens* in the political system and its leadership selection processes. By voting citizens may be responding to a desire to be involved in politics, to have some say in what decisions are made, and to a "sense of efficacy"—a conviction that ordinary persons can be effective in the system. Nonvoters may not necessarily be negative about voting; they may stay home out of a confident feeling that the system is functioning satisfactorily. And not all voters are optimistic that they can influence political decisions. Yet, the act of voting does represent for many an interest in politics, if only at a minimal level.

Elections are communication opportunities for citizens. In one sense people can merely communicate their preference for one set of leaders over another set.[1] In a more radical sense, elections may represent opportunities for people to protest, even to "revolt" against those in power and the policies they stand for and have adopted. President Lyndon Johnson said "the vote is the most powerful instrument ever devised by man for breaking down injustice...."[2] This is a strong statement and probably exaggerated today in the light of the complexity of issues and the difficulty of mobilizing support for change. But as a vehicle for political action the voting act is vital. It may be an act of reprisal against leadership, communicating at the same time a desire for a leadership of a different type or one which behaves differently. George Bernard Shaw claimed "a general election enables the people to do," if they choose to, what the French did in their revolution— they "overthrew one set of rulers and substituted another."[3]

Elections may be institutionalized *representative mechanisms*. In the process of voting for particular candidates with particular socioeconomic backgrounds, committed to particular objectives linked to perceived interest-group demands, the election may be an instrumentality by which people, in groups or individually, see themselves as placing *their representatives* in public office. There are, of course, other ways that these groups may seek to implement group objectives, through lobbying and direct contact with those in public office, but the election itself may be a major means to channel the demands of groups and to make them legitimate, because by an election one achieves a breakthrough into the formal decisional process itself.

Elections provide the basis for *power acquisition and power rationalization*. Joseph Schumpeter wrote that an election is the "institutional arrangement for arriving at political decisions in which individuals [those who would be leaders] acquire the power to decide by means of a competitive struggle for the people's vote."[4] This refers, of course, to a democracy in which presumably there is freedom for rival leadership cadres to compete for power. Elections are one means by which people can get power, but in a democracy it is a crucial and distinctive means which distinguishes democracy from other forms of power acquisition. Thus, the election process is vital for the acquisition and exercise of power in a democratic system.

There are those who would argue that elections in democratic societies are a sham or a ritual or merely manipulative exercises by the elite in power. Some years ago, the Soviet newspaper *Pravda* ridiculed Western elections thus:

What are elections in capitalist countries? This is a serious question. But we shall take the liberty ... of posing the jesting question: how can one trap all the lions of Africa? The answer is: It is necessary to run all Africa through a sieve. The sand will then fall through, but the lions will remain. Strange though it may be, elections in capitalist countries are a kind of legislative sieve through which, under the name of "general and equal elections," the whole people is passed. All the working people, all the poor ones. lean and scraggy people, are sifted through, but the plump and rich ones remain. Elections in capitalist countries are the falsification of elections. . . . On the electoral sieve is written in large letters: "Democracy." But everyone reads the word "Deceit." Everything is arranged so as to guarantee the unrestricted power of the biggest capitalists, the dictatorship of an individual and financial bourgeoisie, the autocracy of the monopolies. . . . Do the electors realize what happens? Undoubtedly. The majority of the people of the USA well realize the worth of the elections. They look upon them as legalized swindling. It does not matter at all to the inhabitants who gets in at the elections—it will in any case be a local rich person: a big capitalist in a large centre; a publican, the owner of a brothel or gambling house, in a small town. The majority of the electors do not go to the elections, are indifferent to them. This is called absenteeism.[5]

This paints a striking picture, to most of us a caricature. While it does give pause for thought, most scholars see elections as meaningful institutions in our democracy, performing important functions. And, contrary to *Pravda*, all of the functions of elections specified are considered important and they have much to do with parties; in a very real sense parties participate in the selection of candidates and in running campaigns, and their representatives adopt the policies of government. Thus, elections are directly relevant to the status of parties in the system. Through elections the public is expressing an *interest* (or lack of interest) in parties, is *communicating* something about or to parties, is designating which party should *represent* its interests, and is providing support for, or *giving power* to, one set of party leaders (and taking power away from another set of party leaders).

This view, which sees elections as linked to the parties, as evaluations of, and reactions to, parties is a major perspective to keep in mind. But what do elections tell us about the state of the parties in the public's view?

The Election System Imposes Constraints on Parties

The special nature of the American election system should be kept in mind as the factors determining voting and nonvoting in the United States are examined. First, it is important to remember that our voter registration procedures are *voluntaristic,* requiring every person to take the initiative to go to the local clerk of elections to register at age eighteen or thereafter. In Europe the government assumes the responsibility for registering voters. The job of the voter and the party is more burdensome here.

A second feature is the "long ballot" in the United States. Others have called it the "bedsheet ballot," by which is meant that we elect many different types of officials at many different levels of government, and we do this frequently (that is, for short terms in office). This makes the job of the citizen difficult—he has to weigh the merits of many different candidates for many different offices. It is no wonder that after elections, when the votes are analyzed, there appears the phenomenon of "ballot fatigue"—the tendency for fewer people to vote for those at the bottom of the ballot (for register of deeds, for example) than for the candidates at the top of the ballot (for president or United States, Senator or governor). The heavy task this imposes on the parties is obvious. They must mount and finance and coordinate, if possible, a great variety of campaigns simultaneously, and they must communicate effectively with the public the merits and policy positions of all their candidates so that they maximize their chances of electoral success. It is a far cry from the European system where the voter goes to the polls to elect a member of Parliament or (at a different date) a member of a local municipal or county council—but no one else. The ballot in such a system is small, the election issue is focused, and the task of the citizen and the party is much more simplified.

A third critical feature is the "winner-take-all" single member district (SMD) concept of elections in the United States, in contrast to the proportional representation system which obtains in most European countries, except Britain. The candidate who secures the largest number of popular votes in a state or a district wins the election. The task of parties, therefore, is magnified since they must win a plurality or they get nothing.

There are other obstacles to voting in the United States which make the parties' task of getting out the vote onerous. Election day is not a national legal holiday as it is in many European countries where workers have the day free and can vote at any time. Further, the polls are open longer in many countries (until 10:00 P.M. in England, for example). It has been suggested that in the United States voters might be permitted to vote over an entire twenty-four hour period, thus expanding the time-span in which they can participate. Absentee voting is difficult in many states and could be simplified greatly.

Finally, the length and expense of American campaigns certainly places a burden on the parties and also on the citizen who is exposed for months to party propaganda which may alternatively confuse, bore, or anger him. British parliamentary elections take less than one month (technically twenty-one days). Our presidential campaigns last at least nine months (from the February primary in New Hampshire to the first Tuesday after the first Monday in November). Our off-year election campaigns to Congress last at least four months (July to November) and often longer. Add to this the great cost of the campaigns and the need to raise huge sums of money during the campaign when energy should be devoted to mobilizing votes, and one can see how the parties' task is complicated and multifaceted in the United States.

There are those who argue that ours is a "low turnout culture"—that is, one in which voting participation is not emphasized nor valued, the way it is in Europe. This may well be, and the subsequent analysis of data will seek to examine this argument. But it must be admitted that the characteristics of our election system make involvement in elections a demanding activity, both for the individual citizen and the parties.

Voting Participation and Nonvoting

The decline in voting turnout in American elections since 1960, and in a longer range perspective since the 1890s, *may be* a significant indicator of the public's acceptance of parties, the campaign process, the election system itself, and the performance of governmental leadership. There are, however, alternative explanations of low aggregate participation. That there has been a decline, however, cannot be refuted easily. Figure 15.1 reveals the ups and downs, as well as the periods

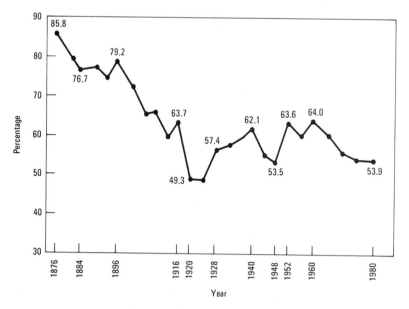

FIGURE 15.1

Fluctuations in Turnout in Presidential Elections, 1876–1980

SOURCES: U.S. Bureau of the Census, *Statistical Abstract of the United States,* 99th ed. (Washington, D.C., 1978), p. 520. For earlier data see also Robert E. Lane, *Political Life* (Glencoe, Ill. Free Press, 1959), pp. 20–21; and W. D. Burnham, "The Changing Shape of the American Political Universe," *American Political Science Review* 59 (March 1965): 11, fig. 1.

of greatest and least turnout, in presidential elections. American citizens who were eligible were attracted to the polls in large numbers before 1900—close to 80 percent or more participated. After the realigning election of 1896 it appears that a decline set in which was only temporarily checked in 1916 when President Woodrow Wilson was re-elected. The decline continued through the World War I years and the arrival of woman suffrage in 1920 and lasted until 1924 (when the all-time low of 49.1 percent was reached). With the new realignment of the late 1920s and early 1930s, turnout picked up, reaching the high points of about 60 percent in 1940 at the time of World War II. The small proportion of absentee soldiers voting contributed to the low of 55 percent in 1944. The Dewey-Truman contest motivated even fewer voters proportionately in 1948 and the turnout dropped to 53.5 percent. After 1960 another period of decline began, culminating in the 1980 turnout of only 54 percent of the eligible voters. Thus, since the 1890s there have been three major periods of decline: from 1896 to 1924, a 30 percent decline; from 1940 to 1948 a 9 percent decline; and from 1960 to 1980 a 10 percent decline. The high level of voter interest of the latter part of the nineteenth century has never been restored.

In comparison to other countries United States voting turnout percentages are low. For recent elections they compare as follows:[6]

Country	Percent
Austria	85
Yugoslavia	82
Britain	77
Netherlands	77
Japan	72
India	59

Even at our recent high point in 1960 the United States is below most of these countries by 9 to 22 percentage points, and by 1980 the differential had become much greater.

In elections below the presidential level, turnout is often much lower. Those participating in elections for the House of Representatives normally represent 3 to 4 percent less of the eligible voting population than those voting in the presidential election, suggesting "ballot fatigue" even for this important national office. Further, the number of those voting in off-year congressional elections is still smaller. A two-year sequence shows the drop-off in participation by those of voting age in nonpresidential years: In the 1960 election, 63.1 percent voted for a presidential candidate, 59.4 percent for members of Congress, and in the succeeding off-year congressional election 48.9 percent voted. In the 1976 election, 54.4 percent voted for a presidential candidate, 49.6 for members of Congress, and in the succeeding off-year

37.9 percent voted.[7] The turnout in gubernatorial, county, and city elections can be still lower, with fewer than 30 percent of the voters participating. In primary elections the national average in recent years has been 27.5 percent of the eligible population.

Some of the major characteristics of this recent decline in turnout should be noted (see table 15.1). First, voter registration has declined considerably over the years—over 7 percent from 1968 to 1976. Second, there is a decline of smaller proportions of voters among those registered. After the 1972 election the decline in interest in elections was significant, with a partial resurgence in 1976. Third, as Thomas Cavanaugh's analysis documents, the decline in voting represents large numbers of dropouts (former voters who have stopped voting)— 10 million dropped out in 1974 alone, and in 1976 over 27 million former voters did not vote. Fourth, the number and proportion of "core nonvoters" (those who are eligible but do not vote in two successive presidential elections) is increasing: 19.5 percent of the total eligibles in 1968, 23 percent in 1972, and 29.6 percent in 1976.[8]

The South used to be the major location of low turnout, but this is no longer as true today. States have differed radically in their records of voting participation, however. Lester Milbrath has presented detailed information on the average turnout for each state in its elections for governor, United States senator and president (see table 15.2). From these data can be seen the great range in participation between the consistently high turnout states (such as Utah in the West and Connecticut in the East) and the states of the Deep South—from a 50 to 60 percent difference in 1960, but a differential of 20 percent or less in 1976.

Since 1960, however, the South has been catching up. Table 15.3 shows the participation tendency in presidential elections. Clearly, while the national percentage has been declining, the Southern percentage has been increasing, suggesting that the source of the aggregate decline is non-Southern. Voter registration has been increasing in the South as a result of the Civil Rights Acts of 1957, 1960, and 1964

TABLE 15.1
Decline in Voting Participation Nationally, 1968–76
(as a percentage)

						Change	
Voters	1968	1970	1972	1974	1976	1968–76	1970–74
Eligibles who were registered	74.3	68.1	72.3	62.2	66.7	−7.6	−9.9
Registered who voted	91.3	80.2	87.1	71.9	88.8	−2.5	−8.3

SOURCES: U.S. Bureau of Census, Current Population Reports, Series P-20, cited in Thomas E. Cavanaugh, "Changes in American Electoral Turnout 1964-1976," a paper presented to the Midwest Political Science Association, Chicago, April 19-21, 1979. See also V. Lance Tarrance, "Suffrage and Voter Turnout in the United States: The Vanishing Voter," in J. Fishel, ed., *Parties and Elections in an Anti-Party Age* (Bloomington, Ind.: Indiana University Press, 1978), p. 80.

TABLE 15.2
Differences in Voter Turnout in Selected States
(as a percentage)

Rank	Average for Governor and U.S. Senator, 1952–60	President			
		1920	1940	1960	1976
1 Idaho	64.6	57.9	75.1	80.7	61.0
2 Utah	64.3	63.8	80.3	80.1	69.4
3 Connecticut	63.4	43.6	67.4	76.8	62.6
15 Illinois	55.3	53.1	78.4	75.7	60.6
15 West Virginia	55.3	67.8	81.4	77.3	58.1
17 New Hampshire	55.0	56.6	72.4	79.4	58.8
23 Ohio	52.3	56.8	72.4	71.3	55.4
24 Wisconsin	51.3	45.9	69.6	73.4	65.8
25 Michigan	51.2	47.3	61.8	72.4	58.7
35 Arizona	43.5	35.4	52.0	54.5	48.6
36 Maryland	42.6	49.7	55.7	57.2	49.6
37 Oklahoma	40.9	47.6	60.3	63.8	55.6
46 South Carolina	11.9	8.6	10.1	30.5	41.7
47 Georgia	10.7	10.4	17.6	30.4	43.1
48 Mississippi	4.2	9.4	14.7	25.5	49.5

SOURCES: Lester Milbrath, "Political Participation in the States," in Herbert Jacob and Kenneth N. Vines, eds. *Politics in the American States* (Boston: Little, Brown, 1965), pp. 38–40; for 1976 data *Congressional Quarterly Weekly Reports*, (October 25, 1980). 3194.

TABLE 15.3
Participation in Presidential Elections: National and Southern State Comparisons

	1960	1964	1968	1972	1976
United States	64.0	61.9	60.8	55.4	54.4
Average for 11 Southern states	38.8	44.7	51.3	44.1	47.5
Difference	25.2	17.2	9.5	11.3	6.9

SOURCES: Based on U.S. Bureau of Census, *Statistical Abstract of United States, 1976*, p. 469, table 752; and Current Population Report Series, pp. 25–626, table 1, p. 6; used in Seymour M. Lipset, ed., *Emerging Coalitions in American Politics* (San Francisco: Institute for Contemporary Studies, 1978), p. 322.

and the Voting Rights Act of 1965. These acts used a variety of procedures to eliminate discrimination and intimidation in registering voters—voiding literary tests, assigning of federal examiners to examine applicants and to register voters in districts which presumably discriminated, and reducing residency requirements to thirty days. As a result, there was a phenomenal leap in the registration of nonwhites in the South (see table 15.4). Thus from a less than 30 percent average in 1960 for nonwhites there was an increase to over 63 percent in 1970, indicating how a change in the rules of the political game can radically change behavior! The average difference in registration between whites and nonwhites in 1960 was 34.1 percentage points; in 1970 that had shrunk to 8.8 percent!

Finally, the national election surveys of the University of Michigan's Center for Political Studies reinforce the same point with data for individual voters. In 1952 in the South 65 percent of the black males were nonvoters and 12 percent of the white males were nonvoters. In 1976 the figures were 23 percent and 14 percent, respectively. Among females, in 1952, 87 percent of the blacks and 33 percent of the whites were nonvoters. In 1976, the numbers were 28 percent for black females and 18 percent for white females who were nonvoters. In 1980 surveys reveal that nonvoting among southern blacks was the same as southern whites—close to 30 percent. There obviously has been a dramatic increase in the South in turnout for blacks, while national turnout has declined. If we are to pinpoint the factors associated with nonvoting, therefore, we must recognize these findings for race, sex, and geographical region.

TABLE 15.4

*Percentage of Voting-Age Population
Registered to Vote in Southern States*

| | Nonwhite | | White | |
State	1960	1970	1960	1970
Mississippi	5.2	71.0	63.9	82.1
South Carolina	13.7	56.1	57.1	62.3
Alabama	13.7	66.0	63.6	85.0
Georgia	29.3	57.2	56.8	71.7
Virginia	23.1	57.0	46.1	64.5
Louisiana	31.1	57.4	76.9	77.0
Arkansas	38.0	82.3	60.9	74.1
North Carolina	39.1	51.3	92.1	68.1
Florida	39.4	55.3	69.3	65.5
Texas	35.5	72.0	42.5	62.0
Tennessee	59.1	71.6	73.0	71.6
Averages	29.7	63.4	63.8	72.2

SOURCES: *Historical Abstract of the U.S., 1971* (Washington, D.C.: Government Printing Office, 1971); original report, *Voter Registration in the South,* prepared by the Southern Regional Council, Voter Education Project; see Frank Feigert and M. Margaret Conway, *Parties and Politics in America* (Boston: Allyn and Bacon, 1976), pp. 84–85.

Factors Linked to Nonvoting

A variety of theories, with supporting evidence, can be advanced to explain the low level of voting in the United States. Any theory has the burden of dealing with the long-range decline in voting since the 1890s, the fluctuation in voting turnout since World War II, the differences in turnout for the various levels of government, and above all the considerable contrast between voting in the United States and in European countries. Why should 54 percent of American eligible voters participate in presidential elections but 90 percent or 85 percent participate in national elections in Germany, Britain, the Netherlands, or even Portugal? Several answers to this query present themselves, none completely satisfactory by itself.

Election Laws

First, of course is the theory of the complexity of the American election system. The American system indeed makes more demands on citizens than that of probably any other country, because of our registration system, lack of national holiday or time off for voting, the long ballot, and other constraints. Early research revealed that suffrage restrictions used to be a barrier to voting, particularly for blacks.[9]

These data established the fact that if election laws impose extreme qualifications for voting (such as literacy tests, poll taxes, residency requirements), they will certainly discourage voting. But since the civil rights legislation from 1965 on these tough requirements have almost disappeared and the federal government closely monitors state regulation and administration of the suffrage. Nevertheless, some states still have requirements, such as registration provisions that do restrict turnout. Other states are making registration easier, some even making it possible to register on election day itself. One study demonstrated that in states which had changed their registration laws to this easier system, there was an increase in participation in congressional elections from 1972 to 1976 of as much as 4 percent (while the national percent was declining by 1 percent).[10] Congress did not adopt President Carter's proposal for a Universal Voter Registration Program, but if it had it seems likely some increase in turnout would have occurred. However, there are arguments against such a program, that a preelection registration system was adopted in the United States to protect against election fraud. Whether that protection is still as necessary as it was presumably in the nineteenth century is an arguable matter.

Another example of how election laws may affect voting is the difference between states providing workers with time off to vote and those which did not. In the 1972 congressional elections the percent of eligible voters who went to the polls in the first group of eighteen states was almost 57 percent while in the latter states it was 49 percent—a sizeable difference![11]

There are scholars who conclude that election law requirements are the major explanation for low participation.[12] But it is significant to note that despite the reform in election laws, the liberalization of registration requirements, and the passage of voting rights legislation, the proportion of *nonvoters* has increased, not decreased.

Political Socialization

The election system certainly makes some difference, but it cannot be the major explanation for nonvoting. A major theory is that Americans are often not influenced in the home while they are growing up to consider political participation important. This argument rests on the proposition that the norm of voting (or nonvoting) is acquired early in life and then persists into adulthood. This theory was advanced in some of the early studies of political socialization. Thus, Herbert Hyman asserted in 1959 that "there is much evidence that individuals learn their patterns of political participation early."[13] Very little research linking early political upbringing to a sense of obligation to vote has been done. In a 1963 study Gabriel Almond and Sidney Verba did find that in homes of lower educational status, persons who remembered participating in family decisions were more likely as adult citizens to have a feeling of political competence and therefore were more likely to be voters.[14]

Important research was done on socialization by Kent Jennings and Richard Niemi, who interviewed both parents and children in a panel study covering the period 1965 to 1973. The study deals with the early development of party identification and shows the importance of family politicization in the child's adoption of partisan orientations. Although voting participation attitudes are not explicitly dealt with, clearly studies of this type are relevant. Identifiers turn out at the polls more frequently than nonidentifiers and apolitical types.[15]

Further, a sense of citizen duty (to vote and to be involved in society), which is probably the result of family and other socialization influences in childhood, is linked to voting turnout. In 1976, 79 percent of those with a weak sense of citizen duty were nonvoters while at the other extreme those with a very strong sense of duty were voters (only 16 percent staying home from the polls).[16]

The influence of the family, or of friends, on voting turnout after a person has achieved adulthood was suggested as relatively important in the early study of the 1952 presidential election:[17] If the spouse did not vote, 59 percent reported they did not vote in 1952. If family members did not vote (for unmarried respondents), 74 percent said they did not vote; if friends were nonvoters, 90 percent said they did not vote. Although the proof of family influence on voting participation is not directly demonstrable, there is an inference in the data that interest in politics, feelings of confidence about participation in politics, and the importance of voting are linked to early family influences. A study in England found that 60 percent of those who reported that neither parent was interested in politics also said that they were not interested, while only about 30 percent of those who remembered their parents as interested were themselves not interested.[18] There is also some evidence from these early studies that those who were under conflicting political pressures from friends and family members were less likely to vote (33 percent nonvoters) compared to those whose friends and family's partisan preferences were all homogeneous (11 percent nonvoters).[19] These data suggest that nonvoting is associated with the individual's social interactions while growing up, as well as after he or she reaches voting age. But the evidence is not yet conclusive.

Age and the Twenty-Sixth Amendment

In 1972 eighteen-year-olds were given the right to vote, and some people have argued that this explains the decline in overall voting participation. Eleven million young people were added to the potential voting population in 1972, and their turnout record in 1972 and since then has been relatively low. In 1980 national survey data revealed the following differentials: 45 percent of the age group 18–29 did not vote; 25 percent of the group 30–49 did not vote; 20 percent did not vote in the 50–64 age group; and for those 65 and over, 22 percent did not vote.[20]

Associated with this is the higher residential mobility of young people. One early study revealed a striking contrast for age groups in mobility. For those under 30 years of age, 73 percent had moved once in a four-year period while in the next age group it was 52 percent, and the mobile proportion decreased steadily until for the oldest age group (over 65 years) only 16 percent had moved. For the young, then, the probabilities of nonregistration, as well as nonvoting either because of inability to meet election system requirements or of limited commitment to a community, are much higher.[21]

However, the *decline* in voting participation is not one which is attributable primarily to the young or new voters. As Cavanaugh points out, the decline has cut across all age groups since 1964 (see table 15.5). The dropouts (former voters), are responsible basically for the depression in voting, and the behavior of the youngest voters, while not very participative, does not constitute the primary reason for the decline. Just as voting turnout declined *before* women were given the right to vote in 1920, so young voters cannot be held accountable solely for the decline recently.

TABLE 15.5
Decline in Voting Turnout by Age Categories

Age Cohort	Percentage decline in voting turnout 1964–76
21–24	5
25–28	8
29–32	9
33–36	10
49–52	9
53–56	7
57–60	6
61–64	6
65–68	5
69–72	7

SOURCE: Thomas E. Cavanaugh, "Changes in American Electoral Turnout, 1964–1976" (a paper presented at the Midwest Political Science Association Meeting, Chicago, April 1979), p. 23.

Social and Economic Status

It has been a common theme of American politics in the past that lower-class, less well-educated citizens are less motivated to vote. The expectation was, then, that as more persons achieved higher education and as the population became better off economically, voting turnout would improve. But that hasn't been the case. However, it continues to be true generally that those with less education and income and lower status occupations tend to stay home on election day (see table 15.6). But what can be seen is that in *all* social status groups there has been a decline in voting turnout, and the gap between the upper and lower status groups has widened. For example, the gap between those with elementary and college education was 26 percent in 1964 (85 percent compared to 59 percent), but in 1976 the gap was 30 percent.

It is these twin phenomena of decline across all groups, and particularly for lower groups, which introduces a greater social bias, as Cavanaugh notes, into the election results than ever before. Lower-class citizens were particularly inclined to stay home in 1972, and from this low point of 1970–72 they never have recovered their interest in voting. (Young southern blacks, 21–24 years of age, are an exception to this: They increased their turnout from 34 percent in 1968 to 36 percent in 1972.) But young voters generally lost interest after 1972 and have not regained interest (see table 15.7). The data on turnout for eighteen- to twenty-year-olds suggests that in a search for explanations for nonvoting the disinterest of those in the lower social classes

TABLE 15.6

Voting Turnout in Presidential Elections by
Social and Economic Status
(as a percentage)

Status	1964	1976	Net Change
Education			
Primary school	59	44	−15
High school	72	56	−16
College	85	74	−11
Family Income			
Low	58	46	−12
Medium	75	53	−22
High	85	68	−17
Occupation			
Blue-collar	66	50	−16
White-collar	82	72	−10

SOURCE: Thomas E. Cavanaugh, "Changes in American Electoral Turnout, 1964–1976" (a paper presented at Midwest Political Science Association meeting in Chicago, April 1979), p. 23; based on U.S. Bureau of Census Reports, Series P-20.

TABLE 15.7

Voter Turnout for 18–20-Year-Olds by
Regions (as a percentage)

	South		Non-South		Nation
	1972	1976	1972	1976	1980
Whites	43	36	54	43	38
Blacks	25	21	36	25	25

SOURCE: Thomas E. Cavanaugh, "Changes in American Electoral Turnout, 1964–1976" (a paper presented at the Midwest Political Science Association meeting, Chicago, April 1979), p. 23, University of Michigan CPS/NES 1980.

and the youth should be a major focus of attention, although the phenomenon of apathy is rather widespread throughout all sectors.[22]

As for other social sectors similar patterns of decline in voting turnout can be found (see table 15.8). The "surge and decline" pattern in turnout differed somewhat for various sectors of the population. But for all sectors 1972 was a low point in participation, and in 1976 most groups (except families of union members) did not recover.

A Fifth Explanation: Citizens' Views About Politics

These trends in nonvoting for major sectors of the population are interesting but they do not really answer the question "Why?" The reasons people give for not voting are many: "no way to get to the

TABLE 15.8

Decline in Voter Turnout by Religion, Union Membership, and Community Size in Presidential Elections, 1952-76 (as a percentage)

								Shift
Category	1952	1956	1960	1964	1968	1972	1976	*1960-76*
Religion								
Protestant	58	56	61	60	60	53	54	− 7
Catholic								
(and non-Protestant)	76	72	74	72	68	65	55	−19
Union Membership								
Union member in family	66	64	60	69	61	58	62	+ 2
Non-union	61	58	65	61	62	55	52	−13
Community size								
Large cities in 12								
metropolitan areas	68	63	74	65	63	60	58	−16
Nonmetropolitan areas	61	60	63	63	62	55	54	− 9

SOURCE: Robert Axelrod, "Where the Votes Come from: An Analysis of Electoral Coalitions 1952-1968," *American Political Science Review* 66 (March 1972); 68 (June 1974); 717-20; 72 (June 1978); 622-624; and 72 (September 1978); 1011.

polls" (4 percent in 1976), "could not take time off work" (72 percent), "out of town, away from home" (14 percent), and "illness" or "emergency" (20 percent). Many of these may be rationalizations. In 1976, 22 percent of nonvoters said they were not interested or "didn't want to get involved."[23] But the key question remains, Why? One major clue to the decline in voting may be the attitudes of citizens toward parties and politics. The basic attitudes which are probably relevant are citizen interest in politics, trust in government, and a "sense of efficacy" about political participation, as well as the more specific orientation to, or identification with, political parties. As for the strength of party identification, it is linked to voting participation. In 1976 and 1980 national survey data reveal consistent differences (see table 15.9). It is clear that party loyalty is associated with voting participation.

On all of these basic attitudes there has been a change since the late sixties. Figure 15.2 reveals the coincidence in the decline in those measures of citizen interest and belief in politics. The greatest movements downward since 1960 have been in citizen efficacy and trust in government, with the net result that today only one-third of the public is confident of their role in the political process and feels government is trustworthy, compared to more than 70 percent in 1960. This is a staggering development, much more so than the decline in political interest, since less than 40 percent of the public has shown a strong interest in campaigns. What is significant, however, as Norman Nie and his colleagues point out, is that recently the uninterested have become more distrustful of government. In the 1960s only 20 percent

TABLE 15.9

Non Voting
By Party Identification

Party Identification	1976	1980
Strong Identifiers		
Republican	8	12
Democratic	19	16
Weak Identifiers		
Republican	27	23
Democratic	33	35
Independent Leaners		
Republican	26	25
Democratic	29	31
Pure Independents	47	45

SOURCE: University of Michigan SRC/CPS/NES.

to 25 percent were distrustful (they were just more likely to be indifferent to politics), but by the 1970s the proportion had risen to 60 percent.[24] So those who have lost interest or never had much interest seem to stay away because of lack of trust in the political order.

There has always been an association between these citizen orientations and their voting participation. The earliest study of this, using the 1956 presidential election survey data, found that nonvoting was more likely to be found among the less interested, less efficacious, less concerned voters.[25] The same finding is corroborated in recent research (see table 15.10).

TABLE 15.10

Nonvoting by Attitudes Toward Political
Efficacy and Sense of Citizen Duty

Attitude	Percentage of Nonvoters		
	1956	1976	1980
Sense of efficacy			
Lowest category	48	40	35
Highest category	9	8	13
Sense of citizen duty			
Weakest group	87	79	76
Strongest group	15	16	18

SOURCE: Bruce Campbell, *The American Electorate* (New York: Holt, Rinehart & Winston, 1979), pp. 237–38; for 1980, University of Michigan CPS/NES.

NOTE: 1980 data basically comparable despite possible differences in efficacy items used.

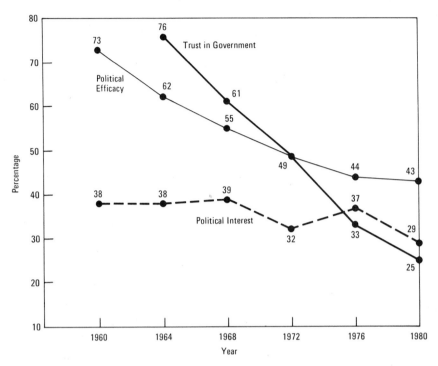

FIGURE 15.2
Trends in Citizen Views of Politics

Trust in government: "How much of the time can you trust the government in Washington to do what is right?" (Those responding "Always" or "Most of the time.")
  Political efficacy: "I don't think public officials care much what people like me think." (Those disagreeing.)
  Political interest: Expressed strong interest in presidential campaign.
  SOURCES: University of Michigan SRC/CPS/NES; see also Norman H. Nie, Sidney Verba, and John R. Petrocik, *The Changing American Voter* (Cambridge: Harvard University Press, 1976); Arthur H. Miller, "Political Issues and Trust in Government: 1964–1970," *American Political Science Review* 68 (September 1974): 951–72.

Care should be taken, however, in assuming that all of these attitudes are equally relevant in explaining nonvoting, although it appears that there could be a causal connection. Since electoral participation has declined since 1960 at the same time that there has been a
decline in trust, efficacy, and interest, the two phenomena seemed
linked causally. While these trends together do indeed provide an attitudinal context in which to try to comprehend what is happening in
American politics, one must be careful about jumping to conclusions
as to what causes nonvoting. Evidence is not strong on what the causal
sequence is, but the recent data suggest strongly that of all these orientations the most important is *sense of political efficacy*. This can be illustrated by use of the data on trust in government and on efficacy for
the 1972 election, based on the Center for Political Studies (CPS) analysis of the national survey results (see table 15.11). While there is a

small increase in nonvoting among those who do not trust government—the cynics—the real attitudinal factor seems to be lack of a
sense of efficacy, even among those who are not cynical. It was, therefore, not lack of trust which was linked to nonvoting but a feeling that
participation was not worthwhile, that the individual citizen was not
heard and could not be effective through political involvement, such
as voting.[26]

TABLE 15.11

Nonvoting Link to Low Sense of Political Efficacy Rather Than to Distrust of Government, Presidential Election, 1972

(as a percentage)

| Respondents | Level of Trust in Government | | | All Respondents |
	High	Nonvoters	Low	
All respondents	26	(N=568)	35	(N=611)	
By extent of sense of political efficacy					
High	11	(N=318)	16	(N=92)	13
Low	41	(N=250)	38	(N=519)	39

SOURCE: Arthur Miller and Warren Miller, "A Majority Party in Disarray: Policy Polarization in the 1972 Election," *American Political Science Review* 70 (September 1976): 753–78.

Exposure to Parties and Media During the Campaign

What goes on during the course of a campaign, the types of stimuli
and contacts to which people are exposed, may be a major explanation
for low turnout and for the decline in participation in the last two
decades (see figure 15.3).

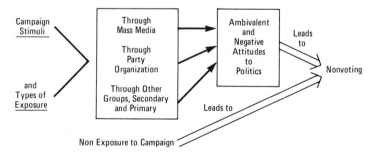

FIGURE 15.3

Pattern of Relationships Between Campaign Stimuli and Voting Pattern

What goes on during a campaign can activate, reinforce, and convert voters. Campaigns can also deactivate and demobilize citizens, and even for those who are committed partisans the campaign may discourage them from participating in the election. This could happen, theoretically, if the campaign has one of the following effects on the individual: (1) the campaign produces confusion due to the *lack of information* as to where the candidates and parties stand on issues; (2) the campaign produces cross-pressures and *conflicting messages* concerning the positions of parties and candidates; and (3) the campaign produces *negative evaluations* of the parties and candidates. American campaigns have been criticized as too long and too tedious, leading to a kind of political informational overkill. This may indeed be so. But probably it is less the *length* of the campaign than what types of *images* are communicated to the voters during the course of the campaign. If these images are not clear, unambiguous, constructive, and positive they may result in disinterest in voting (or in failure to even register to vote).

Close to 90 percent of the American public report that they follow the campaign to some extent on television (an increase from 51 percent in 1952), while 33 percent to 60 percent also follow the campaign in newspapers, radio, and in magazines. Television has clearly replaced radio and newspapers in frequency of use for political information, and close to 70 percent report now that it is their most important source of political campaign information.[27] There is great variation in the use of the mass media, however; 25 percent to 30 percent are mass media (particularly television) "fans," and close to 40 percent are infrequent users or nonusers.

The party organizations also have increased their effort to reach the public. Since 1952 national survey studies have asked respondents whether they have been contacted by party workers in the campaign. The proportion reporting that they have been contacted has increased from 12 percent in 1952 to 30 percent in 1976, and 24 percent in 1980. Both parties have been active, the Democrats more than the Republicans up to 1980, when survey data reveals the Republicans were mentioned more frequently as the party which contacted persons in the campaign (12.5 percent compared to 11.5 percent).[28] Thus, while we have had a decline in voting turnout there has been no decline, indeed an increase, in exposure to the parties and in the reliance on television for political campaign knowledge. Previously the research which related party activity to *getting out the vote* was reviewed and it was noted that a strong party organization could be effective in all types of elections (but particularly in local elections) where one party clearly was more active than its opposition in contacting the public. Further national studies found that 86 percent of those contacted since 1952 do turn out to vote in presidential elections.[29] The other side of this coin, however, is that *many people who are exposed to party effort stay home and do not vote!* The two relevant questions, therefore, are, (1) Is party effort related to a negative reaction to parties for some people? (2) Are those not contacted by the parties also securing negative reactions to parties which lead to nonvoting?

The same query has been posed by students of the role of television in politics. Michael Robinson, among others, has argued that television may contribute to cynicism toward political institutions and to a decline in feelings of political effectiveness.[30] He claims that the message of nightly television broadcasts is "none of our national policies work, none of our institutions respond, none of our political organizations succeed. . . . " Similarly, Gary Wamsley and Richard Pride speculate that "it is a possibility that the characteristics of TV news . . . result in a sum total of effects that is denigrative of political system authority symbols rather than supportive."[31] Television may thus make a "contribution to the demise of the political party."[32]

To produce evidence that exposure to the campaign via parties, media, or other sources leads to negative orientations to politics, and thus to nonvoting, is difficult. From previous research it is known that nonusers of the mass media are also nonvoters, as the following data demonstrate: In the 1948–52 period, of the media fans only 11.5 percent were nonvoters; of those who were moderate media users 32 percent were nonvoters; of the nonusers of the media, 60 percent were nonvoters.[33] Those exposed to party contact in presidential campaigns are very likely to vote, 86 percent compared to only 55 percent or less for those who are not exposed. Indeed, special studies at the local level indicate that those not contacted by the parties are more likely to stay home on election day, a difference of over 30 percent on the average.[34]

Further, from previous research it is known that many of those who acknowledge that they have little interest in politics can apparently be mobilized to vote by exposure to parties and to the mass media (see table 15.12). Despite these findings there are those, even with a high or medium exposure to the campaign, who are nonvoters, such as the 13 percent with a great deal of interest who were contacted by the parties but still did not vote. The suggestion implicit in such data is that party contact for some persons is not functional to participation but may even be dysfunctional and lead to withdrawal from political involvement. This was true in the early studies of elections (1948–56) and is true today.

There are a large number of persons for whom a political campaign is a confusing experience. As many as two-thirds of the citizen public may find the stimuli and pressures conflicting so far as preference for the party candidates are concerned. Thus, of those in a conflicted peer group context, 32 percent were nonvoters, in contrast to 7 percent for those living in homogeneous Republican circumstances and 20 percent

TABLE 15.12

*Mobilization Role of Mass Media and
Party Organizations Among Voters with
Different Levels of Political Interest*

| | Level of Interest | | |
| | High | Medium (not voting) | Low |
Exposure		percentage	
To parties			
High	13	16	29
Low	19	25	41
To mass media			
High	8	17	21
Low	28	31	50

SOURCE: Paul Lazarsfeld, Bernard Berelson, and William McPhee, *Voting* (Chicago: University of Chicago Press, 1954), pp. 176, 249.

living in homogeneous Democratic circumstances. Considerable exposure to the campaign via the media reduced this nonvoting tendency to 22 percent among the conflicted and to 10 percent and 4 percent among those in a homogeneous Democratic and Republican peer group context, respectively.[35] Nevertheless, the media by no means resolve the confusion for many of those confused by the campaign. While exposure to the media may mobilize some citizens to vote, they may indeed confuse others, make them cynical, and incline them to withdraw from electoral involvement.

The campaign may also leave some citizens basically uninformed. A very significant analysis by Philip Converse demonstrated long ago that the link between "information flow" and turnout, as well as partisanism, was important. He found in the 1956–60 elections that 32 percent of those with a "low" level of information about candidates and parties did not vote in either election while only 5 percent of those with a "high" level of information stayed home.[36] While much information is disseminated these days about politics in campaigns, there are still large numbers of people who are not actually informed by the media, and these people are more likely not to vote, although apparently large numbers are also regular voters!

In the final analysis what is the role of parties, and the public's involvement with parties, in relationship to the public's attendance at the polls? Perhaps it can be a double role—both encouraging and discouraging. That is a key concern for American politics today. There have been major trends in the public's attitudes toward parties which coincide with the decline in turnout. As pointed out in chapter 4, there has been a decline in the positive evaluations of parties from a high of 70 percent or more in the 1952–60 period to a low of 49 percent in the 1972–76 period.[37] Since the 1950s people are taking a much more neutral (rather than overtly negative) position in evaluating the parties.[38] The same pattern emerges in the cognitive orientations of citizens toward candidates. They do not use *party* now as much as previously in discussing candidates. After 1968 the decrease was particularly sharp. And as a parallel development citizens are not using their partisan evaluations of the candidates as much in deciding how to vote. According to the analysis by Nie, Verba, and Petrocik the decline in correlation of partisan evaluation of presidential candidates and the vote was as follows:[39]

1952	.50
1960	.49
1964	.39
1968	.36
1972	.14

A striking decline apparently in the relevance of "party" for the vote! Figure 15.4 describes the developments in public attitudes toward politics which may help explain the nonvoter.

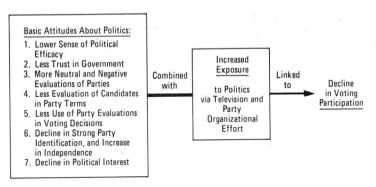

FIGURE 15.4
Development of Public Attitudes Toward Politics

This configuration of trends strongly suggests the linkage of certain attitudes, *despite* or *because of* increased exposure, to nonvoting. Nonvoting characterizes persons who are *not* in touch with the political system. Evidence now also suggests that nonvoting may result from certain types of contacts and exposures *to* the political system. For example, those in the youngest age groups are most likely to exhibit the characteristics noted above (see table 15.13).

TABLE 15.13

Political Orientation of Young and Older Citizens
(as a percentage)

Orientation	18–20	35–44
Nonvoting (1976)	56	21
No party identification (1976)	52	43
Positive evaluation of parties (1972)	36	48

SOURCES: University of Michigan CPS data; Norman Nie et al., *The Changing American Voter* (Cambridge: Harvard University Press, 1976), p. 69; see also William Flanigan, *Political Behavior of the American Electorate* (Boston: Allyn and Bacon, 1972), p. 260.

The youngest citizens are least positive about parties, more independent, and also the highest nonvoting group. These factors appear, then, to be associated.

FIGURE 15.5

Types of Nonvoters

Attitudes Toward Politics and Parties	Exposure to Campaign Through Media and Parties	
	Exposed	Not Exposed
Positive–Accepting, Optimistic About Own Role	Conflicted or Disfranchised	Satisfied– Not Motivated
Negative–Critical, Pessimistic About Own Role	Alienated but Informed Cynics	Hostile Peripherals
Neutral–No Strong Convictions About Politics	Informed Intelligent Apathetics	Uninterested and Uninformed Apathetics

Conclusions

There are clearly several types of nonvoters (see figure 15.5). Those *not* exposed to politics and not inspired to vote divide into three subgroups. From an attitudinal standpoint they may be very satisfied with the system and their nonvoting may be an expression of consent for the status quo. They are not motivated to vote. Or they may be persons who are hostile to politics while also not very well informed about what is going on—"the hostile peripherals." A third group of those not exposed may have no opinions on politics, are not interested at all, completely withdrawn from politics, with no significant attitudinal linkage to the system. Among those *exposed* to politics there are also three types of nonvoters—those who feel positively toward parties, elections, and the system generally but who for a variety of reasons do not vote. They may be in a cross-pressure situation or not able to meet registration requirements or highly mobile persons. At the other extreme are those who know a great deal, are exposed, but have no strong connections leading them to vote—intelligent apathetics. And a third group consists of those who are informed, alienated nonvoters with negative feeling about politics—the informed cynics.

The two key groups which may be on the rise in recent years are the informed cynics and the informed apathetics with a possibility that the hostile peripherals have increased among those not much exposed to politics. There is very little evidence that the satisfied uninvolved nonvoter is on the increase, and it is hard to argue that there is more reason for those with positive evaluations of politics to stay home. There seems to be more hostility, more alienation, and more apathy, despite more exposure and information about politics—linked to negativistic and neutral orientations to politics. When people are motivated and have a sense of efficacy, despite their low economic status, they can be involved in politics.[40] But if they object to the political scene, see themselves as not having a meaningful role, and deprecate the value of parties and elections as instruments for political action, then withdrawal, often hostile withdrawal, can result.

The American party system may well under certain circumstances lead to and play a part in the development of attitudes leading to nonvoting. When crises develop in the society and people do not see political party leaders effectively solving their problems, the system does not have fail-safe mechanisms which will ensure loyalty and turnout—at least not at the levels maintained by European party systems with their 80 percent to 90 percent turnouts. In European systems there are mass-membership parties with their own clientele support groups, paying dues to the party and committed to the party in traditional, class, or religious group terms, as well as in ideological terms. High turnout is assumed under such systems, particularly for the lower socioeconomic classes which have a direct clientele relationship with the parties. In the United States, where turnout of educational and income groups shows wide variations (1976 college-educated, 74 percent, but primary school education only 44 percent), the mobilization of all relevant groups is more difficult because the party system is different and the political culture is different. In a multiparty culture there are more options for the citizen to select. Thus, in Europe, the mass-membership, group-oriented, ideology-based, multiparty system may help to maintain voting support for the system in times of crisis, of cynicism, even distrust. Despite negativism, people will still turn out to vote, particularly when the system facilitates that participation. But the burden on our parties to generate citizen support and involvement is perhaps greater, given the nature of our parties and the system and culture in which they must operate.

The Impact of Voting

Americans have always had considerable faith in the effectiveness of the electoral process, believing that voting is central to the proper functioning of a democratic system. It provides a means by which the voter can express himself in relation to authority. "Voting is the foundation stone for political action," said Dr. Martin Luther King, Jr.[41] It is a way in which the citizen can act against, or in support of, the system. Also, elections and voting are supposed to restrain and influence elected officials (and possibly also appointed officials) in a democracy. Long ago Samuel Adams was quoted as saying, "Where annual elections end, tyranny begins.[42] Or, to put it differently, democracy is a system where elected leaders are always on probation. The assumption underlying these assertions of faith is that voting makes a difference, voting can be effective. By the same token, nonvoting and changes in the pattern of voting can have significant impact. What are the consequences of increased voting or of nonvoting?

The answer to this question is not easy. A great deal of research has been directed at the question of leadership responsiveness to constituency opinion and the extent to which this is due to the actual or anticipated results of elections. Research reveals that members of Congress do feel that they will be judged, if not immediately, at least eventually, by how they vote in the House, even though they also sense that much of the public is apathetic or ignorant about policy matters. At least 80 percent believed that the electoral verdict in their districts "had been strongly influenced by the electorate's response to their records and personal standing."[43] Another study of Congress concluded that many congressmen fear that a "wrong" vote may be used as a weapon against them by the opposition in an election.[44] Still another study of California legislators discovered that the roll-call votes of representatives (California senators in this case) were more clearly correlated with the opinions of constituents as the election approached (a correlation of .41) than after the election (a correlation of .07).[45] There does indeed appear to be an electoral connection! Although it is true that incumbents are more regularly returned to office than ever before (close to the 90 percent level), it is also true that over 50 percent are re-elected at least once with a margin of less than 5 percent. The potential for defeat for a congressman out of touch with his constituency is, therefore, real.

The linkage between local political leadership and the activists in the public (who are attentive to issues and voting as well as involved in other ways) has also been explored. Sidney Verba's study of *Participation in America* has revealed that in communities where there is a high level of participation (including voting) the "concurrence" between leaders' views on issues is closer to that of citizens than in communities where there is a lower level of political activity. This is so particularly when there is a strong consensus among citizens in their positions on issues. This leads Verba to conclude that "where citizens are participant, leaders are responsive."[46] Implicit is the inference that elections and voting make representatives aware of the possibility of defeat, force them to be more aware of the views of the public (particularly as the election approaches), and presumably lead to legislative votes which are more representative of public desires than would be the case if the electoral process was a formality only.

It appears that currently we are going through a period of decline in voter interest and turnout, as well as a decline in strong partisanship. The effects of this on the parties and on the political system cannot be ignored, although no clear evidence has been produced documenting these effects irrefutably. However, there is the possibility that a period of this type can be destabilizing, with less partisan loyalty, more independence, more split-ticket voting, more issue voting, more volatility in voting patterns, and more nonvoting as a result of a low sense of efficacy. With such phenomena occurring at least some short-term effects and possibly some long-run imprints on the system can be expected.[47] Incumbents may be less easily defeated and this realization may be associated with less representative policy-making behavior, or at least legislative behavior less linked to elite perceptions of constituent preferences. Party becomes less important in politics, both for the voter and the leader and, hence, party voting in the House will decline. Party conflict may well be exacerbated during a period of declining party organization influence. Other groups appear to play a much more important functional role in the political arena than previously, achieving more success with legislators and leading to more divided governmental control. The strategies of party politics change in such a period, both in campaigns in arriving at calculations as to how to win (with party appeals being demeaned) and in calculations of mobilizing support for legislation in Congress or in state assemblies. There may be less consistency in policy positions over time, less clear identification of policy with party as politicians are more independent and on their own, struggling with formulae for political victories—in elections and in legislatures.

Above all, the basic public support for parties and party leaders atrophies during a period of low turnout and the dynamism of an active and participative system may be replaced by withdrawal, low interest, and above all a politics less responsive to the public. All this is speculative, but it certainly is a scenario with high probability. It suggests the critical role which voting involvement and partisan commitment play in a democratic political system. The vote has been called a "powerful instrument" and a "foundation stone" for a system like ours. If that be true, when many citizens lose faith or interest in it, the system may well suffer. As Paul Beck has said, " . . . changes in American electoral behavior have widespread effects on patterns of elite [or governmental] politics . . . dealignments . . . have a discernible impact . . . they remove much of the structuring to both mass and elite politics by minimizing the role of political parties. Without this structuring, policy change becomes disjointed. . . ."[48] Electoral behavior may indeed be the mainspring of American politics.

Chapter 16

Parties, the Government, and the Policy Process

THE INFLUENCE of parties on the policy decisions of governmental leaders is one of the most important questions for democratic societies. It is the "governing function" which affects us all. Does it make any difference how well parties organize, how carefully they recruit candidates, how well they are led, how effectively they campaign, how persuasively they mobilize voters and win elections—for policy outcomes? This is not the only process parties are involved in or the only basic function they perform. Parties engage in a variety of other functions—leadership selection, socialization, communication, agenda setting, government monitoring, and consensus building. But certainly their role in determining policy is a central concern. If they have no policy function, they may still meet other needs of the system, but they could then share, or yield, center stage in the governmental arena to other groups which are important in governmental action. As V. O. Key said, "There are two radically different kinds of politics: the politics of getting into office and the politics of governing."[1]

Obstacles to Party Influence in the United States

The traditional view is that American parties are too fragmented, dispersed, and undisciplined to have much influence over policy determination. This view argues that if one wants to explain the basis for the legislative decisions of members of Congress, United States senators, state legislators, or local policy makers one cannot explain them primarily on the basis of party influence. Even when strong mayors, governors, or presidents dominate the policy process, it is not their party roles so much as their personal appeals, personal bases of electoral support, and personal attractiveness and expertise which is important in explaining their success in getting new laws adopted. In this traditional view parties are not considered as policy leadership structures which can mobilize support to determine or significantly influence, legislative, executive, judicial, and bureaucratic decisions.

One of the major reasons for this alleged policy impotence of parties, it is argued, is the structural character of the American governmental system. The principles of our constitutional system theoretically do not facilitate a role for parties; indeed, they were designed originally to make it difficult for parties to have such a role. In *The Federalist* James Madison argued that the proposed constitution would make majority control by a party group virtually impossible. The key principles he had in mind, of course, were separation of powers, federalism, and bicameralism. The dispersion of governmental power under these principles constitutes a major challenge to parties seeking to control government for the purposes of policy initiation and innovation. Obstruction is more likely under such principles than the translation of new ideas into new laws. Structural principles, thus, can be critical for the policy process. Our peculiar principles pose a challenge to party leadership seeking to bridge and coordinate the different arenas of governmental authority.

It is not these constitutional principles alone, however, which are obstacles to party influence in the policy process. It is also the fragmentation of authority within the legislative body itself. The United States House of Representatives, up to 1910, was a body with strong leadership, with a speaker who had considerable power. But in that year there was a revolt against Speaker Joe Cannon, and in the seventy years since there has been no return to anything like the centralization of authority which Cannon had. The committee chairmen, the floor leader, the party policy committees, the whips, the party caucus—all these agencies of House operations have divided up the party's power. In addition special groups such as the Democratic Study Group (DSG), with 200 liberal Democrats, or the Republican special group, the "Chowder and Marching Club," have contributed to the decentralization of power in the House and made leadership and policy coordination difficult. Further, as William J. Keefe points out:

Congress is an institution vulnerable to invasion by others. The three principal external forces that interact with Congress, seeking to move it along lines congenial to their interests, are the chief executive (including the bureaucracy), interest groups, and the constituencies.[2]

Rather than moving in harmony, these actors in the policy process are often in dissonance. There is legislative-executive conflict, a struggle among opposing lobbies, and pressures from different types of constituencies. As Keefe says, on certain issues the party often seems "to fly apart."[3] It *appears* that what we have in the United States—and perhaps want, but certainly tolerate—is "a shared, multiple-leadership form of government."[4]

The traditional model, then, is one which plays down the role of parties in the policy process because constitutional principles disperse power, internal party organization in legislative bodies is not cohesive, and external pressures produce conflicts. The implicit argument is that parties cannot overcome these features of the system—parties as organizations or as leadership groups do not coordinate policy making, parties in fact are secondary to other influences on policy making, and partisan considerations and motivations do not explain policy actions.

This model, further, is usually contrasted to the parliamentary model, such as is found in Britain. It is argued that party plays a much more important role there because there is party discipline in the House of Commons, there is centralized party leadership which determines the party's position on policy questions, there is no dispersion of power as in the American constitutional system (Parliament is supreme), and external pressures play no such negative role (indeed constituency influences facilitate the relevance of party in the policy process). The majority in the party caucus (Labour, Conservative, or Liberal) in the House of Commons selects its leadership, together they decide on policy, defections from these majority decisions are not sanctioned but punished, and thus normally the party as an organization makes policy. There is, thus, *theoretically* a sharp contrast between the United States "fragmentation of party power" model and the parliamentary (British) "party dominance" model.

Evidence of Party Influence on National Policy Decisions

Despite the negative expectations about the role of American parties on policy decisions, research suggests caution in reaching that conclusion. True, parties are organizationally fragmented, power is dispersed, leadership is not centralized and party discipline of the parliamentary system doesn't exist in the United States. Nevertheless, policies do change as the strength of parties ebbs and flows.

The economic policies of the national government are one important substantive area where it may indeed make a great deal of difference which party wins the election. Edward Tufte has studied this matter and concludes that "the real force of political influence on macroeconomic performance comes in the determination of economic priorities." He then argues, "Here the ideology and platform of the political party in power dominate . . . the ideology of political leaders shapes the substance of economic policy."[5] Indeed, his position is that one can generalize for modern democratic societies, including the United States, as follows: Parties of the Right (including the Republicans) favor "low rates of taxation and inflation with modest and balanced government budgets; oppose income equalization; and will trade greater unemployment for less inflation most of the time." Parties of the Left, (including the Democrats) favor "income equalization and lower unemployment, larger government budgets; and will accept increased rates of inflation in order to reduce unemployment." The platforms of the national parties reveal these differences. Thus, in 1976 the Democratic platform pledged "a government which will be committed to a fairer distribution of wealth, income and power." The Republican platform in 1976 pledged "less government, less spending, less inflation." In 1980 the Democratic platform promised to fight inflation but not by increasing interest rates or unemployment. The Republicans said that "our fundamental answer to the economic problem is . . . full employment without inflation through economic growth."

The public's expectations concerning the performance of the two parties are clearly illustrated by their attitudes on the unemployment issue in 1976. When asked to assess the job which President Gerald Ford and the Republicans had done in dealing with unemployment, only 11 percent of the sampling responded that it had been a "good" performance, 57 percent a "fair" job, and 32 percent a "poor" one. Table 16.1 reveals the results of a study asking which presidential candidate and party would do the best job of reducing unemployment. The public clearly expected Carter to do more about unemployment. Similar results emerged when the sample was asked, "Do you think the problems of unemployment would be handled better by the Democrats, by Republicans, or about the same by both?" The results were: 39 percent Democrats, 10 percent by the Republicans, and 52 percent the same for both parties. The 1980 results were different, however: 19 percent Democrats, 23 percent Republicans, and 58 percent about the same for both parties.

Tufte demonstrates that the actual employment statistics over time reveal a linkage between presidential elections and unemployment and inflation rates. These data point to the following "rules":[6]

1. Both Democrats and Republicans will reduce inflation or unemployment if there is an economic crisis and an election is approaching.
2. If there is no real crisis, the Republicans will do much better in reducing inflation than unemployment; the Democrats will do better in reducing unemployment.

TABLE 16.1

Public's Opinion on Which Party Will Best Deal with Unemployment (as a percentage)

Public View	President Ford	Candidate Carter
Candidate will reduce unemployment	31	52
Candidate will not reduce unemployment	46	24
Difference	−15	+28

SOURCE: University of Michigan CPS/NES, 1976.

Whether Carter's actions in 1980 supported these observations is an arguable matter!

Another scholar, Douglas Hibbs, has also explored this problem. He concludes that "inter-party differences in government-induced unemployment levels is 2.36 percent"—a sizeable difference in national employment levels as a result of a Democratic or Republican administration. Thus, "the Kennedy-Johnson administration posture toward recession and unemployment stands in sharp contrast to Eisenhower's, . . . the basic economic priorities associated with the Eisenhower era were re-established during the Nixon and Ford administrations" and were "deliberately induced." Hibbs concludes, "The real winners of elections are perhaps best determined by examining the policy consequences of partisan change rather than simply by tallying the votes."[7]

A study of the policies of our government over the years finds that whichever party is in power for a longer or shorter period of time is crucial for the content of public policy. In an exhaustive study of laws adopted by the United States government from 1800 to 1968 (requiring analysis of 60,000 pieces of legislation) Benjamin Ginsberg was able to determine when the peak points in the adoption of new policies and new laws occurred. He concluded that the peak points were 1805, 1861, 1881, and 1933. These were years after major elections in which a shift in the power of the political parties occurred, called in some instances major "realigning elections." His basic interpretation is that "clusters of policy change" do come as a result of partisan change in electoral choices. He summarized as follows:

Our findings suggest that voter alignments are, in effect, organized around substantive issues of policy and support the continued dominance in government of a party committed to the principal elements of the choice made by voters during critical eras. . . . Partisan alignments form the constituent bases for governments committed to the translation of the choices made by the electorate. . . . The policy-making role of the electorate is, in effect, a continuing one.[8]

In other words, the voters' decision on what party should govern determines the basic direction of public policy!

Party Unity and Disunity on Policy in Congress

The agreements and differences between Republican and Democratic party leaders have been documented in various studies. In a Columbia University study of various types of Democratic and Republican leaders in 1971–72, Allen Barton found issues of *consensus* and issues of *conflict* (see table 16.2). On certain issues, at that time at least, the top leadership of both parties agreed essentially, such as on the use of nuclear weapons or antipollution tax measures. On some other issues they were divided, particularly on certain economic issues, on defense spending, on social welfare programs—these are the types of issues on which the Republicans were less liberal or less supportive of governmental intervention. Substantial conflict between parties is revealed in the leadership positions on these types of issues.

Analyses of roll-call voting in Congress differ concerning the part that party loyalty seems to play. However, as Keefe says, "Even though weakened, party affiliation is still the most important variable in influencing the voting behavior of members of Congress."[9] To substantiate this is not easy, and students of Congress disagree as to the strength of the evidence. "Party unity scores" for members of Congress reveal that on a majority of issues Republicans vote with Republicans, and Democrats vote with Democrats (see table 16.3). In general, since the 1950s, although there has been a decline, from 60 percent to 70 percent of the time there is party voting when a divisive issue confronts the Congress. True, this is not a matter of *all* Republicans versus *all* Democrats as in the British system. That yardstick as applied by several studies finds partisan conflict in roll call voting only a very small percentage of the time—probably below 10 percent of the time.[10] Yet, as Keefe says, "Certain kinds of public policy questions regularly produce conflicts between the parties, or at least between large majorities of each party."[11]

TABLE 16.2

Patterns of Consensus and Conflict Among Top Level Republican and Democratic Politicians and Officials, 1971–72 (as a percentage)

Issues	Republicans	Democrats
Consensus		
1. Wage-price controls are needed	62	82
2. Polluting industries should be taxed	57	70
3. Socialist governments in Latin America should be accepted	76	82
4. Tactical nuclear weapons should not be used in Asia	83	84
Disagreement		
5. Oil depletion allowances should be ended	35	68
6. Poverty could be ended in 10 years	34	66
7. Withdraw or negotiate in Vietnam for a coalition government	31	59
8. Defense spending should be reduced	43	73
9. FBI practices threaten civil liberties	24	57
N=	86	39

SOURCE: Allen H. Barton, "Consensus and Conflict Among American Leaders," *Public Opinion Quarterly* (Winter 1974–75): 507–26. This was part of a study to interview 545 leaders in ten different leadership sectors, 1971–72, by the American Leadership Project at Columbia University.

TABLE 16.3

Party Unity Scores in Congress (as a percentage)

Years	House		Senate	
	Democrats	Republicans	Democrats	Republicans
1954–60	70	70	67	71
1961–63	73	72	68	66
1964–68	65	70	59	63
1967–73	61	65	62	61
1980	69	70	64	65

SOURCES: *Congressional Quarterly Almanacs* in Frank B. Feigert and M. Margaret Conway, *Parties and Politics in America* (Boston: Allyn, Bacon, 1976), p. 215; for 1980, *Congressional Quarterly Weekly Report*, January 10, 1981, p. 800.

NOTE: Percentage of time average Democrat and Republican voted with his party majority in disagreement with the other party's majority.

One problem in such analyses, of course, is the split within the Democratic party between the southerners and the northerners. The southern wing of the party is much more conservative on certain types of policies than the rest of the Democratic congressmen or senators (see table 16.4). In a sense there are four ideological-partisan groups in Congress because the Republicans also seem to be consistently split between its eastern and noneastern wings. Keefe has demonstrated how distinctive these wings are on certain types of issues. In recent sessions of the United States Senate, for example, up to 40 percent of the eastern Republican wing was prolabor in its votes while zero percent of the southern Republican wing was.[12] As a consequence there often is a "conservative coalition" in the Senate and House which can be very effective, an alliance of southern Democrats and Republicans which may work together from 20 percent to 30 percent of the time to pass or to block legislation. And when it does work together, it has in recent congressional sessions been successful 60 percent to 80 percent of the time.[13] The Reagan administration in 1981 quickly moved to establish a "conservative coalition" in order to push through its legislation. When this happens, party unity suffers.

Despite such occasions of party disunity among our representatives there still is more party "cohesion" than one might expect under our system. In a recent analysis David Brady and his colleagues traced this cohesion for the House of Representatives back to before 1900 and found that average cohesion has not declined very much (see table 16.5).[14] "Cohesion" has not fluctuated greatly over the years, but "inter-party conflict" has declined, apparently partly because of the rise of "the conservative coalition."

Variations in Party Role by Type of Issue

Although in aggregate terms there may be higher cohesion than might be expected, the role of party apparently varies considerably by the type of issue before the Congress. The research findings of Aage Clausen demonstrate this clearly. He examined the relevance of several factors in explaining the variation in policy positions of congressmen on five different issues and found that "party" was most influential as an explanatory factor on issues concerning governmental management of the economy—the same types of issues which Tufte and Hibbs argued were genuinely "partisan" issues (see table 16.6). The evidence here suggests that parties in Congress divide much more on domestic issues than on international issues. But on certain domestic issues, such as civil rights, it is a regional split and a constituency

TABLE 16.4

Contrasts in "Liberalism" Within Democratic Party in the Senate, Second Session, 1972 (as a percentage)

Scoring High on Liberalism	All Democratic Senators	Southern Democrats	Northern Democrats	Republican Senators
Americans for Democratic Action ratings	45	6	63	7
AFL-CIO Committee on Political Education	65	0	95	20

SOURCES: *Congressional Quarterly Weekly Reports;* see also Frank B. Feigert and M. Margaret Conway, *Parties and Politics in America* (Boston: Allyn, Bacon, 1976), p. 216.

NOTE: "High on Liberalism" means a score of 60 percent or more on the rating.

TABLE 16.5

Party Cohesion in House of Representatives (as a percentage)

Years	Average Cohesion	
	Democrats	Republicans
1890–1900	68.9	74.6
1920–30	63.5	71.1
1958–66	69.5	66.5

SOURCE: David Brady et al., "The Decline of Party in the U.S. House of Representatives 1887–1968," *Legislative Studies Quarterly* 4, no. 3 (August 1979): 384. Reprinted by permission of the Comparative Legislative Research Center of the University of Iowa, copyright holder.

TABLE 16.6

Factors Explaining Variations in Congressmen's Votes (percentage of variation explained by factor)

Type of Issue	Party	Region	Urban and Blue-Collar Constituency	Other Factors
Government management of the economy	92	2	0	6
Agricultural assistance	62	7	10	21
Social welfare	29	23	11	37
Civil liberties	8	45	26	21
International involvement	0	22	19	59

SOURCE: Aage Clausen, *How Congressmen Decide: A Policy Focus* (New York: St. Martin's, 1973) p. 168.

NOTE: Data based on voting in 85th Congress (1956–58).

split, more than a party split. Party plays its most dominant role in the economic welfare and social welfare policy areas. Care must be taken, therefore, in generalizing either way about party cohesion or inter-party conflicts in Congress. Neither blanket statement that party controls most voting decisions in Congress or it influences none of them can be made. It depends on the issue, but the "party" of a congressman *can* be very influential.

How Party Influences Congressmen Even Though They Deemphasize "Party"

Congressmen's attitudes often indicate that they are less overtly concerned with straight party voting than other considerations. Thus, in one study when they were confronted with the question of whether a congressman should support the party (on a bill which was important to the party's record) "even if it costs him some support in his district," the congressmen's replies were as follows: support the party, 35 percent; undecided, 7 percent; not support the party, 52 percent; and no answer, 6 percent.[15] Of course, what "support the party" means and whether such a direct conflict occurs often is an unresolved question.

In a 1969 study of congressional decisions John Kingdon found that few members of the House spontaneously mentioned party leadership as the "actor" or consideration of importance to them in making up their minds on a given piece of legislation (see table 16.7). Despite this finding that party leadership in the House appears to be unimportant because congressmen do not emphasize party, Kingdon recognizes the differences which exist in the voting patterns of Republicans and Democrats and attempts to explain these contrasting voting patterns in Congress:

The fact that party regularity in voting remains, despite the apparent unimportance of the leadership, leads one to search for alternative explanations. Party voting seems to begin with constitutency differences; the parties have very different demographic bases and supporting coalitions. Building on constituency differences are the patterns of interaction within the House. Congressmen rely heavily on informants within their own party grouping. Common campaign experiences cement the party regularity, since Democrats and Republicans are electoral opponents both nationally and locally.[16]

On this matter of friendships and interactions in the House, Kingdon presents some very interesting evidence of the partisan nature of such contact patterns. In 75 percent of the decisions, congressmen reported that other members of the House were important informants

TABLE 16.7

*Factor Spontaneously Mentioned by Congressmen's
as Influencing Their Decision Making*

"Actors"	Percentage
Party leadership	10
Constituency	37
Fellow congressmen	40
Interest groups	31
"Administration"	25
Staff	5
Reading (of materials about the legislation)	9

SOURCE: John Kingdon, *Congressmen's Voting Decisions* (New York: Harper & Row, 1973), p. 18.

helping the respondent arrive at a decision on a particular issue. The distribution of these informants by party is very revealing (see table 16.8). The congruence in partisan associations found in these data is significant. They suggest that the House consists of definite partisan clusters—although southern Democrats are less predictable on this than northern Democrats and Republicans. Yet, in 70 percent of the cases congressmen are turning to their own partisan colleagues for information and advice.

TABLE 16.8

*Source of Guidance and Advice for Congressmen
(as a percentage)*

	Respondent's Party		
Informant's Party	Northern Democrat	Southern Democrat	Republican
Northern Democrat	85	14	3
Southern Democrat	4	51	1
Republican	0	6	71
Mixed	11	29	25
N=	54	35	75

SOURCE: John Kingdon, *Congressmen's Voting Decisions* (New York: Harper & Row, 1973), p. 78.

The Role of the Party Leadership in Congress

What is the role of the party organization in the House and Senate in influencing roll call voting? Earlier, in chapter 6 on the national party organization, the types of party organs which exist in the House and

Senate were described in detail—the floor leaders, the whips, the policy or steering committees, the campaign committees and the caucuses or conferences. The point was made there that this organization is fragmented and as a consequence there is no strong, focused leadership of the parties in the Congress, certainly not a leadership which can regularly impose sanctions on members and thus force them to vote a "party line." It is not, of course, completely true that there are no sanctions because the leadership does have certain favors to dispense, such as committee assignments. Kingdon quotes one congressman as follows:

... the party leadership will punish you if you vote wrong too much. It especially happens on committee assignments ... if you want a real plum—like Ways and Means or Appropriations, the guys that vote against the leadership too much don't get them.[17]

Other "favors" relate to expediting (or delaying) legislation of congressmen, or withholding support for public works in a congressman's district. Randall Ripley found, for example, that only one-third of the congressmen said that nothing could be done to them, that there were no sanctions at all if they bucked against the party leadership.[18] And he reported that most congressmen felt there were strong appeals made to them, often on a personal basis. Yet, Kingdon concludes that "sanctions are not very effective," because they may not be critical to the careers of congressmen.[19] This depends of course on the particular situation in which congressmen find themselves. If they are electorally insecure and fearful of losing in the next election, they may feel that they should not defer to the wishes of the party leadership in Congress, particularly if that leadership suggests voting positions at odds with what they perceive to be constituency orientations. Kingdon indeed finds this to be true.[20] Further, length of time in Congress seems to be related to willingness to go along with the party leadership. Junior representatives in the Northern wing of the Democratic party reject the party leadership 74 percent of the time.[21] Thus, the status of congressmen and their perceptions of the "ideological stance" of the party leadership, plus their calculations of how they are to be re-elected, are crucial factors in the extent to which they support the party leadership line in their voting decisions. In 1981 it was clear that those forty to fifty congressmen, mostly from the South, who left their party to support Reagan on the budget cuts did so to protect themselves from Republican opposition in 1982 when they would be running for re-election.

The Role of the Party in the Constituency

Parties can influence congressmen through their role in the constituency or legislative district. They may do this in a variety of ways. The party organization may be very active in seeking candidates to run initially and hence also in recruiting persons to run against a congressman who is seen as behaving contrary to the local party organization's wishes. Another way is by giving or withholding a variety of organizational resources—manpower, money, records and files on voters, forums for presentation of the congressman's viewpoints. Further, the organization may influence key decision-makers in the area who are important to the success of any candidate—those who control the newspapers, radio stations, television stations, as well as interest-group leaders and prominent financial supporters. Thus, the organization may be very important to the candidate for Congress or the incumbent congressman. If, in addition, he or she has come up through the ranks of the local party organization, where the friends and earlier associates still remain, the relevance of the party organization may be enhanced. In one careful study of this relationship between congressmen and their district organizations (for thirty-six congressmen in seven states in 1964) it was discovered that this linkage could be very strong (see table 16.9). Where the district organization was coherent and well developed the local organization did indeed have a very influential role. In one-third of the cases the party organization was relied on for the nomination, while in an additional 19 percent of the

TABLE 16.9
Congressmen's Reliance on District Parties
(as a percentage)

Electoral Relationship of District Organization to Congressmen	All District Organizations	In Districts with Well-Organized Party
Relied on for nomination and election	22	60
Relied on for nomination or election	33	30
No help—congressman developed own organization or worked with special faction of party	44	10
	99	100

SOURCE: David M. Olson, "The Electoral Relationship Between Congressmen and Their District Parties," (a paper presented at Annual Meeting of American Political Science Association, Washington, D.C., 1977).

cases the party was relied on for the election campaign. These findings tend to support those of the study by Barbara Greenberg of New York congressmen (see table 16.10). Such data suggest that the apparent independence of congressmen from party while in Congress may be offset by a real dependence on party in their home districts.

TABLE 16.10

The Relation of Congressmen to Local Parties (New York)
(as a percentage)

Role	New York State Congressmen
Asked by the party to run	23
Strongly supported by the local party organization	57
Active in party work or held a party organization position before running for Congress	74
Supplied by local organization to campaign:	
Money	57
Workers	74

SOURCE: Barbara Greenberg, "New York Congressmen and Local Party Organization," Ph.D. dissertation, University of Michigan, 1972.

The district is indeed very important to the member of Congress. He or she agrees most of the time with the public's perceptions of what the relationship between the congressman and the district should be (see table 16.11). Certainly the congressman accepts the necessity of "servicing" and communicating with constituents on a regular basis. And the partisans among such constituents must be particularly important.

TABLE 16.11

Mutual Expectations of How a Congressman Should Perform—Views of
Congressmen and Constituents Compared
(as a percentage)

Expectations	Public Views	Congressmen's Views
Get back to the district to stay in touch with the constituents	68	74
Help people in the district who have personal problems with government	62	57
Take time to explain to citizens what government is doing to solve important problems and why	67	54

SOURCE: Adapted from survey data of House Commission on Administrative Review (1977), used by William J. Keefe, *Congress and the American People* (Englewood Cliffs, N.J.: Prentice Hall, 1980), pp. 27–28.

The increase in the personal staffs of congressmen has been phenomenal in recent years, increasing from a total of 2,344 in 1960 to 5,109 in 1974. And whereas only 14 percent of these staff personnel were functioning in their districts in 1960, 34 percent were operating in the districts in 1974.[22] Further, the amount of contact with constituents has mushroomed. It was calculated that the pieces of mail received by congressmen from constituents in 1969 was 14 million; by 1975 it was three times that—42 million pieces of mail![23] The emphasis seems, therefore, more than ever to be on the district, and in a sense on the support needed in the district for re-election and, thus, on the evaluation by constituents of the congressman's service and voting record. As part of that relationship the linkage of the congressman with his party—its leadership, its activist cadre, and its potential body of supporters—is not inconsequential.

One of the major questions in all of this is how important is a congressman's policy stand for the voting behavior of his constituents. Will a voter defect from his own party if he sees his candidate for Congress as representing policy positions which the voter cannot support? The answer seems to be, yes; often this is true, *if* he or she sees the opposition candidate's policy position as preferable, and also *if* the incumbent is a member of the opposite party. A special analysis of this problem by Gerald Wright for the 1966 election, based on interviews with a cross section of voters and candidates, provides interesting evidence to support this position (see table 16.12). The probability of defection is twice as great when the voter sees himself closer to the opposition party's candidate's policy position than that of his own party's candidate. And this 47 percent defection increases to 65 percent if the opposition party's candidate is also the incumbent. When his own candidate is the incumbent *and* the voter agrees with his candidate's poli-

TABLE 16.12

Responsiveness of Voters to Policy Positions of Candidates for Congress (Percentage of Voters Supporting or Defecting from Own Party When Own Issue Position Is Closer to:)

	Voter's Own Party's Candidate	Neither Candidate	Opposition Party's Candidate
Percentage *not supporting* own party's candidate	23	42	47
Percentage *supporting* own party's candidate	77	58	53
N =	240	202	127

SOURCE: Gerald C. Wright, "Candidates' Policy Positions and Voting in U.S. Congressional Elections," *Legislative Studies Quarterly,* vol. 3, no. 3 (August 1978): 453. Reprinted by permission of the Comparative Legislative Research Center of the University of Iowa, copyright holder.

cy position, defection in voting is cut to 9 percent. This is strong evidence that policy stands, as well as party affiliation, do count.

The work of Warren Miller and Donald Stokes on this question of the relationship of the voter (his knowledge and perception of the congressman) to the behavior of Congressmen is valuable. They demonstrated that the extent of the voter's knowledge of the candidates for the House (the "saliency" of the candidate) was related to the vote. Thus, if party identifiers had knowledge only of *the other party's* candidate, 40 percent would vote for that candidate (of the opposition) compared to only 2 percent defection in behavior by those who were familiar with *their own* candidate only.[24] Further, Miller and Stokes demonstrated that "congressmen feel that their legislative actions may have considerable impact on the electorate" even though *in fact* a large proportion of constituents [about 50 percent in 1958] knew practically nothing about their representatives. They concluded, "Our evidence shows that the Representative's roll call behavior is strongly influenced by his own policy preferences and by his perception of preferences held by the constituency."[25]

These combined pieces of evidence show that (1) constituency influences on the congressman are important; (2) the policy position and roll call voting behavior as perceived by voters are important; and (3) the "party" of the candidate and voter, by itself, is important. All the complexities of the association of the congressman and his or her constituents have by no means been unraveled. To the extent that there is "party voting," there is a strong possibility that a congressman is self-consciously aware that his or her re-election may depend on what the party organization in the district will do in the next primary or election campaign, and particularly what his partisan-support group in the district will do. Party therefore seems to play a variety of subtle roles in a variety of direct and indirect ways in the congressional policy process.

Concluding Observations on Party in Congress

It is fashionable to argue these days that party doesn't account for much in American politics, particularly in the behavior of United States congressmen. Studies of the nature of public attitudes about the role of parties in Congress, such as the work of Jack Dennis, in 1964, are quoted to suggest extreme negation (see table 16.13). Yet, these early data note that the public was not overwhelmingly opposed to parties in legislation—rather, the public was split. Average antipartisanship was over 40 percent, while another 15 percent was ambiva-

TABLE 16.13

Public Attitudes Toward Partisanship in Congress (as a percentage)

Attitude	Agree	Uncertain	Disagree	"Anti-Party"
"A senator or representative should follow his party leaders even if he doesn't want to."	23	9	63	63
"The party leaders make no real effort to keep their promises once they get into office."	36	28	33	36
"We would be better off if all the Democrats in government stood together and all the Republicans did the same."	30	12	54	54
"Our senators and representatives ought to follow their party leaders more than they do."	41	20	33	33
Average anti-partisanism				46.5

SOURCE: Jack Dennis, "Support for the Party System by the Mass Public," *The American Political Science Review*, vol. 60, no. 3 (September 1966): 605.

NOTE: Based on Wisconsin sample in 1964.

lent. Even though there are indications that since the 1960s antipartisan attitudes have increased, the public is still unclear as to how parties should function in the policy process. Unfortunately, there is almost no trend data on attitudes toward the role of parties in campaigns.[26] Congressmen are also ambivalent about the role of parties—less than half feel they should stick with party "through thick and thin," particularly if the party's stand collides with their own views of constituency opinions.

Despite such findings, analysis presented in this chapter shows there is strong evidence that party policy positions of the leadership differ, that party platforms differ, and that the actual policy outcomes of Republican and Democratic administrations differ. Therefore, party is often important to the individual legislator at the national level, and a change in party power in government can indeed have policy consequences.

This does not mean that parties are all-powerful in Congress. Party leadership is often not important. Nor does it mean that the "doctrine of party responsibility" has taken hold of the national policy process. This doctrine, which will be examined in more detail in the concluding chapter, argues that parties should (1) develop distinctive programs of action; (2) recruit candidates for office (president, United States Senate, House, and state and local) on the basis of this program;

(3) hold their legislative (and executive) representatives "responsible" for implementing this distinctive program when they are in office, and thus the public should vote on the basis of this "responsible" behavior of the party's elected representatives. This "responsible party doctrine," which is similar to the concept of parliamentary discipline, is by no means operative on the American scene. Both the "party man" and the "maverick" are found frequently in American politics and particularly in Congress. That makes the puzzle of the importance of party a complicated one to solve. For, clearly, party is important to most legislators, in the associations with colleagues in Congress, in their relationship to the president and his administration, in their contacts with the party organization leaders back home, and in their relationships to their constituents. Yet, American parties operate in our Congress quite differently from British or Continental parties in their parliaments. Since the environment is more pluralistic, fragmented, undisciplined, and decentralized here, parties function quite differently also. In Congress American parties can be important while often appearing irrelevant. Despite this, parties may indeed often "govern" even though it appears as if they don't.

Partisan Bases of Presidential Leadership

The American presidency is a unique institution of governmental power, one of the most powerful offices in the world. Although the exercise of this potential power ebbs and flows with the philosophy and personality of the individual who holds the office, the central place of the office in the American political system is unquestioned. The president is head of a vast army of civil servants numbering over two million. He directs a large White House staff who are his political appointees. He is commander-in-chief of the armed forces. He appoints the judiciary with the advice and consent of the Senate. He is a legislative leader with constitutional responsibility for proposing legislation and with great opportunities for influencing the agenda and decisions of the Congress. He is the leader of the mass public in more than a symbolic sense. And in all of this he is the chieftain of his political party, presumably designated by his national party convention (or through primaries today) as its "leader" elected on a program of that party, in a campaign in which that party's organizational resources (among others) were mobilized and deployed in his election. Thus when he takes office he is the leader of his party in the government. True, he can be characterized as much more than that and indeed is much more than that—he is the nation's leader.

Many people say they would prefer to have a president "above party politics." But this is never realistically possible. The president is a "partisan," although the degrees of intensity and consistency with which he exhibits his partisanship vary from president to president. And in all aspects of his leadership his party origins, his party relationships, his party ideology, and the demands of his party on him influence greatly how he performs the variety of functions which are his when he assumes the presidency. Richard Neustadt once said, "The Presidency is a place for men of politics."[27] In its broadest sense, this means, among other things, that he is the product of a competitive party system and more or less conscious of his role in that party system.

An important aspect of the American presidency to keep in mind is that it is an institution of shared power. Because of the nature of the institutions of government in the United States, the dominance of the policy-making process by any office or body or person or collectivity of persons is difficult. That in a sense was the intent of the Founding Fathers and to a certain extent that has become reality. As Neustadt remarked, we have "a government of separate institutions *sharing* powers."[28] The president shares powers with others while also participating in the exercise of others' powers. And in order to achieve results in policy making this means "bargaining," the willingness and capability to work with others, particularly members of the House and Senate, in order to make decisions. The most capable presidents are, therefore, experts in bargaining or, as Harry Truman insisted, in the power to persuade. There are limits to command in the American system, due to the separated institutions, the limits on the control which the leaders of one institution have over another, the lack of discipline, the divided partisan control between House, Senate, and the presidency, and the absence of a parliamentary system with a cabinet collectively accountable to a legislative body. In the absence of a parliamentary system with such accountability, close linkage between executive and legislative responsibility, and party discipline, our presidential system relies on the politics of bargaining and persuasion.

Earlier, a discussion of "The American Party System" (chapter 3) showed that although our system was "majority oriented," in the sense that there were only two major parties, one of which could theoretically secure a majority, in actuality ours was often a system of "divided government." Since the Civil War, 53 percent of the time we have had either divided control or marginal party control. In the most recent period, for example, 1960–80, in only 30 percent of the time was there "strong party control," where one party (the Democratic party, actually) controlled the presidency and Congress, with a 60 percent or more majority in both houses of Congress. This divided government characteristic is reflected in, as well as is a result of, split voting in elections. This tendency has been increasing since 1920.[29]

In addition, there is sectionalism in the voting behavior patterns for the president and Congress, particularly in the Democratic party. In the 1977 session, for example, only 9 percent of the Southern congressmen were scored as "liberals" (on the COPE Liberalism Measures) while 66 percent of the Northerners were "liberal." One further piece of information about the Congress with which the president has to deal, namely the entrenched power of incumbents in Congress and the difficulty of defeating them once they get there, reflects the context within which policy bargaining has to take place. Table 16.14 illustrates the increasingly entrenched nature of congressional leadership. Clearly, the Congress is a body which may not easily be bent to presidential wishes. It often is not of the same party or only marginally so. It is a body with sectional cleavages, where members achieve status and power and command of political resources in their own right, and electoral reprisal against them is extremely difficult.

There are, then, two foci of political power and decision making, the president and Congress, in a divided government with separated institutions. As Everett Ladd says,

... the President and Congress are two major centers of power, and the avenues to control of each very different. . . . Voting for President is heavily shaped by the pull of national issues and images, while the fabric of political argument in Congressional races is more parochial.[30]

These two institutions formally at least are not mutually dependent, are often in conflict and rarely in harmony, look to different bases and sources of political support from different constituencies, jealously guard their prerogatives against encroachment and can, because of their independent power statuses, resist attempts at control and dominance. This does not mean the two are always in conflict. Indeed often at the beginning of a new presidency there is the so-called honey-

TABLE 16.14
Entrenchment of Representatives in Office

Year	Percentage of Members of the House Elected More than Once	Percentage of U.S. Senators Elected More than Once
1871	53	32
1915	74	47
1935	77	54
1961	87	66
1977	85	58

SOURCE: William Keefe, *Congress and the American People* (Englewood Cliffs, N.J.: Prentice Hall, 1980), p. 9.

moon period, in which the president has the support of a majority of the Congress, at least until the crucial partisan issues emerge or the crucial divisions between the liberal and conservative wings in the parties become visible. It is then that the character of the presidential role and the personality and philosophy of the incumbent becomes apparent and is tested.

The way in which presidents conceive of the office in party leadership terms and, hence, their style and strategy in dealing with the public and with Congress, determines how they will deal with conflicts in the system and consequently what the president's impact on policy will be. The contrasts in presidential role conceptions can be illustrated by looking at the party leadership philosophies of Kennedy and Eisenhower. Kennedy summarized his conception as follows:

But no President, it seems to me, can escape politics. He has not only been chosen by the nation—he has been chosen by his party—if he blurs the issues and differences between the parties—if he neglects the party machinery and avoids his party's leadership—then he has not only weakened the political party as an instrument of the democratic process—he has dealt a blow to the democratic process itself.[31]

In contrast here is Eisenhower's view:

. . . in the general derogatory sense you can say that, of course, I do not like politics. Now on the other hand . . . it is a fascinating business. . . . But the word "politics" as you use it, I think the answer to that one would be, no. I have no great liking for that.[32]

Obviously these two presidents saw their "party political" and "politics" role differently. Kennedy saw himself as the party leader; Eisenhower shrank from that image.

David Barber has developed a four-fold typology of presidential role conceptions using two basic dimensions: policy activism or passivity, and positivism or negativism in the way they view their presidential responsibilities. These dimensions yield the types suggested by figure 16.1. Barber's analysis suggests that presidents differ in the ways they look at their functions and this in turn is linked to their role in the policy process.[33]

FIGURE 16.1
Presidential Role Conceptions

Affect Toward His Activity	Level of Activity	
	Active	Passive
Positive	Truman	Taft
Negative	Nixon	Eisenhower

Presidents can have a significant imprint on policy. But this depends on what kind of leaders they are. Great presidents have "led" the society, their parties, and the Congress—as Jefferson, Jackson, Lincoln, Wilson, and Franklin Roosevelt did. And they were policy leaders while also being partisans.

In his relations with Congress, the president has "formidable advantages," as Keefe explains.[34] These are (1) expectations of presidential leadership; (2) information and expertise; (3) visibility; (4) dominant trader in a trading system; (5) party leader; and (6) fragmentation of congressional power. Together these advantages make it possible for the president to be successful with Congress in its policy decisions 50 percent, perhaps 60 percent, of the time. But this depends on whether he wishes to assert his leadership potential. Many members of Congress look to the president, whose prestige can be great, for support for their proposals. If he doesn't "lead" they may be upset or, alternatively, take advantage of his indifference. What the public looks for in a president is an expert, and the great danger is that we will get a politician who is not knowledgeable or wise in political leadership. The public attention focused on the president enhances his potential for influence, and television is the media which is particularly useful in his role as pressurer of Congress. Some presidents are very capable horsetraders—they know what congressmen want and can thus parlay favors, logrolling, promises of future support, and patronage into votes needed to get a particular piece of legislation. Presidents like Lyndon Johnson are great traders. Presidents like Jimmy Carter are not. "I am not much of a trader," Carter confessed, "that is one of my political defects for which I have been criticized a great deal."[35]

Is the party the bridge which helps in part to close the gap and reduce the tension between Congress and the president? This is a critical concern for American politics; and one on which scholars differ. There are those who argue that party used to be the bridge but that today its role in bringing together the presidential and congressional wings of the party has declined. Kingdon reports, for example, in his study during the Nixon administration that "the administration" ranks poorly as an actor influencing the voting decisions of congressmen. Yet the administration's impact was not completely inconsequential, as his own data reveal. For both Republicans and Southern Democrats in Congress the Nixon administration's influence was considerable. And this, despite the fact, as Kingdon reports it, that in 55 percent of the decisions he studied, the Nixon administration engaged in no direct communication with members of Congress.[36]

Sometimes dramatic "turnarounds" can be seen in leadership attitudes and behavior as a result of presidential leadership. Allen Barton reports one such reversal in 1971, when (on August 15) President Nixon announced that he favored and planned to institute wage and price controls. In a study of Republican and Democratic leaders Barton discovered that while Democrats and Independents had been in favor of such controls before Nixon came out in favor of them, the Republican leadership had been in opposition. But the Nixon decision *for* controls changed the attitudes of the Republican leaders. Before Nixon's announcement 22 percent favored controls; after his announcement 70 percent favored the idea.[37] In this case the impact of presidential leadership was impressive!

The president, of course, can employ a variety of tactics to influence the policy decisions of congressmen. Under the Constitution he has three: to recommend legislation, to veto, and to convene Congress in special session (to hear his proposals). In addition, he has a variety of powers in his other capacities, which can be brought to bear to secure support for his positions: patronage appointments, support during a congressman's campaign for re-election, invitations to the White House, and support for projects in the home constituency. The story is told of Senator Frank Church of Idaho, who opposed the Vietnam War, showing President Johnson an article on war by Walter Lippmann and Johnson replying, "All right, the next time you need a dam for Idaho, you go ask Walter Lippman."[38]

The president's use of appointments for his party's advantage is, of course, well documented. It is indeed strikingly apparent that the

TABLE 16.15
*President's Appointments to Judiciary
From Own Political Party*

President	Percentage
T. Roosevelt	95.8
W. Wilson	98.6
C. Coolidge	94.1
F. D. Roosevelt	96.4
D. D. Eisenhower	94.1
J. F. Kennedy	90.1
L. B. Johnson	94.6
R. Nixon	93.2
J. Carter	86.0

SOURCES: Adapted by permission from Table 3, page 382 in Frank Sorauf, *Party Politics in America*, 3rd ed. Copyright © 1976 by Little, Brown and Company, Inc.; Robert H. Blank, *Political Parties, An Introduction* (Englewood Cliffs, N.J.: Prentice Hall, 1980), p. 192; earlier sources are Charles L. Sheldon, *The American Judicial Process* (New York: Harper & Row, 1974) p. 121; Harold W. Chase, *Federal Judges: The Appointing Process* (Minneapolis: University of Minnesota Press, 1972); Evan A. Evans, "Political Influence in the Selection of Federal Judges," *Wisconsin Law Review* (May 1948), pp. 300–51; for Carter see *Congressional Quarterly Weekly Reports*, 1981, p. 300.

president acts *as a party leader* in making these appointments. Table 16.15 shows presidential court appointments.

If this is true of the judiciary the political appointees to administrative positions outside the civil service would certainly be no less partisan. It is in consultation over these appointments that the president can attempt to exert some influence over the Congressional members of his party. But this is a reciprocal relationship: He must "clear" appointments with congressmen and senators, while also communicating to them that these appointments are part of his "bargain" with them for their support.

In the last analysis, how successful does the president seem to be in Congress? This depends on the Congress (whether of the president's party or not) and on the president (whether he vigorously works to secure passage of his preferred legislation), and on the policy issue before Congress. Table 16.16 presents the data from recent congressional sessions on the support for the president by his party on these bills in the president's program. It can be seen that the majority of the party supports a president on major aspects of his legislative program. When Kennedy and Johnson were in the White House, from 57 percent to 72 percent of the Democrats in the two chambers supported presidential programs on the average. When Nixon was the president, from 57 percent to 66 percent of the Republicans in Congress supported his programs. These are not overwhelming majorities, as might be found in a parliamentary system such as the British have. Nevertheless, they are majorities, and usually majorities in a divided Congress, with a majority of the opposition voting against the president. This suggests genuine partisan conflict; it also suggests congruence between the president and the majority of his party on legislative objectives.

To bring this even more up to date and to make the point even more direct, the behavior of Congress during the first year of President Carter's administration can be used as an illustration. Carter was criticized

TABLE 16.16
Party Support for President's Legislative Program
(average percentage of members voting in favor)

Selected Years	Party of President	Senate		House	
		Democrats	Republicans	Democrats	Republicans
1962	Democrats	63	39	72	42
1966	Democrats	57	43	63	37
1969	Republicans	47	66	48	57
1973	Republicans	37	61	35	62

SOURCE: *Congressional Quarterly Weekly Reports;* also exerpted by permission from Table 3, page 357 in Frank Sorauf, *Party Politics in America,* 3rd ed. Copyright © 1976 by Little, Brown and Company, Inc.

as a president who did not get along with his own party in Congress, and did not have the political know-how to get support among House and Senate Democrats for his program. Yet in 1977, using the "key votes" on which the administration took a position, often a very strong position, despite Carter's alleged lack of skill in dealing with Congress, he won out more often than he lost, being particularly successful in the House on seven of eight "key votes" on which he took a position (see table 16.17). In the Senate on the average he secured almost 65 percent of the Democratic vote and in the House almost 75 percent. It is interesting to note how much of the defection in Democratic ranks came from the Southern legislative party wing. In 1977, in the House 30 percent of all Democratic legislators came from the South and 42 percent of them voted against Carter on key issues; 31 percent of all Democratic senators were from the South and 55 percent of them voted against Carter on key issues. The Southern Democrats in the Senate thus constituted a major roadblock to Carter's success in getting his legislation adopted in 1977. Despite this he did quite well. However these data throw much light on how and why Reagan was successful in 1981 with a House in which the Democrats had a majority of 243 to 192. Reagan won over many Southern Democrats and won a crucial vote 217 to 211.

Presidents have been remarkably successful in getting support on issues on which they have taken clear cut positions. Table 16.18 shows the percentage of victories of presidents in the past twenty years on key issues.

The American presidency is a powerful institution. And it is an institution of party power. The incohesiveness of the Congress and the separateness of the institutions of policy making in our system demand political bargaining, persuasion, and integrative political tactics.

TABLE 16.17
*Support and Opposition for President Carter's
Legislative Program in Congress, 1977*

Votes	Senate		House	
	Democrats	Republicans	Democrats	Republicans
Number of "key votes" on which the Carter administration took a position	9		8	
Number won by Carter	5		7	
Average percentage of support for the administration on the "key votes"	74.1	27.6	64.6	28.8
Percentage range in support	48–100	8–58	39–86	1–86

SOURCE: Based on data in *Congressional Quarterly, Electing Congress*, 1978.

TABLE 16.18
Success Rate of Presidents
on Key Issues

President	Average percentage	Number of years
Kennedy	85	3
Johnson	83	5
Nixon	67	6
Ford	58	3
Carter	76	4

SOURCE: *Congressional Quarterly Weekly Reports,* January 3, 1981, p 37.

Support for policy has to be mobilized. The president in his capacity as party leader, despite the incoherencies of our system, can be very effectual in mobilizing a majority policy coalition. Indeed there are those who would say that without such party leadership, power will not be coordinated or will fall into the hands of special interests.

Parties and Public Policy in the States

For a long time political scientists have been aware that the states differ considerably in their policies—whether in their expenditures for education or for social welfare or for transportation or for a variety of other purposes. Similarly, certain states adopt legislation which is much more promotive of civil rights objectives or supportive of labor unions or more progressive in tax policies than other states. Many scholars have puzzled over the general question of what factors explain these variations in state policies. One major factor is the nature of the party system in individual states. In 1949, V. O. Key, in a classic analysis of this matter, argued that if a state had a competitive party system with parties strongly organized, there was much more probability that the policies in that state would be "redistributive" (that is, policies assisting the poorer strata of the society) than in states without a well-organized two party system. "The factional system of the one-party state simply provides no institutional mechanism for the expression of lower-bracket viewpoints," argued Key.[39] We need, he said, "continuing competitive groups" to "carry on the battle." Key's argument for well-organized, competitive parties actually can be broken down into several specific propositions: (1) parties provide for responsibility in the system since organizations retain an identity over time (while a faction has a shorter life); (2) parties provide continuous leadership and thus help voters make their decisions in the highly complex multicandidate American electoral system; (3) they are rallying points for the opposition, particularly for those who are discontented with governmental policy; (4) parties adopt programs or platforms for the long-run and thus as organizations they are less erratic in policy changes than factions; and (5) parties help the disadvantaged in society (if they are truly competitive) because they will compete for votes wherever it is necessary in order to win elections.[40] Thus competition, organization, program, continuity, and responsibility are the characteristics of a party system most functional to the adoption of policies incorporating the demands of the community, particularly the underprivileged segments of the community.

Whether the competitive party system is more responsive to the demands and problems of the total society than a system which is not competitive has intrigued scholars, and since 1949 has led to a voluminous body of research.[41] Duane Lockhard did a study of New England politics in 1959, which tested Key's thesis, and found considerable support for it in the contrasted politics of the states of Vermont and New Hampshire (which were one-party bifactional systems), Maine (which was a one-party multifactional system then), and Massachusetts and Connecticut (two-party systems). He did indeed find that there was a tendency for two-party systems to have less regressive tax systems and to expend more funds per capita for such social welfare programs as aid to the blind, old age assistance, and Aid for Dependent Children (ADC).[42]

Since these early studies, however, there has been much research, not all of it confirming these findings, about the relevance of the competitive party system for policies favoring the have-nots in society. In some of these studies the differential level of economic resources and development for the states has been argued as more important then the type of party system. Other aspects of the party system beside its competitiveness have been also assessed, such as the organizational cohesion of parties, the level of turnout in elections, the extent of unity in primary elections, and the conditions of conflict and other behavior in the state legislature and in the relations between the legislature and the governor. It will not be possible here to review all the different types of research which have been done. An attempt will be made to summarize some of the key findings concerning the relevance of parties for state policy outcomes.

States vary considerably in the policies they adopt to deal with the key problems of their populations. The range in the level of their support is illustrated by the data in table 16.19. The students in New York get 2½ times the support for education per capita that the state of Alabama spends on them. And in welfare expenditures, states such as Alaska, Hawaii, Illinois, Massachusetts, and Connecticut spend four

TABLE 16.19

Variations in State Support for Education and Welfare

States	State Expenditures for Public Elementary and Secondary Schools (per pupil in attendance), 1973–74		State Welfare Expenditures (Percentage of Total Expenditures from State Funds), 1970–71	
Five Highest	New York	$1,809	Alaska	66
	Alaska	1,597	Hawaii	57
	New Jersey	1,432	Illinois	54
	Delaware	1,388	Massachusetts	54
	Maryland	1,322	Connecticut	53
Five Lowest	Tennessee	804	Minnesota	22
	Mississippi	787	Mississippi	21
	Arkansas	773	Montana	18
	Kentucky	727	North Carolina	14
	Alabama	716	Arkansas	14

SOURCE: Frederick M. Wirt, "Education Politics and Policies," and Robert Albritton, "Welfare Policy," in Herbert Jacob and Kenneth N. Vines, eds., *Politics in the American States* (Boston: Little, Brown, 1976), pp. 327, 365, respectively.

times the proportion of the welfare budget that states like Arkansas and North Carolina spend. In specific welfare areas, studies revealed, for example, that while New Jersey in 1968 was contributing $322 a month in support of needy families with dependent children, the monthly assistance dropped to as low as $55 in Mississippi.[43] Virginia Gray has made a study of the innovativeness of states in adopting policies in the areas of civil rights, education, and welfare and ranks states on an overall index of innovation. States are ranked from California (most innovative) to South Dakota (least innovative). But their ranking varies a great deal by the particular policy area. Thus on welfare expenditures South Dakota is in the middle of the ranking of states while lower on civil rights and educational policies. California ranked high overall but was not very high in its civil rights legislation.[44]

Tremendous variations for the states occur in their policy actions dealing with critical problems facing their publics—in education, welfare, civil rights, as well as other areas. The key question intriguing many scholars is, To what extent are such variations, in the past and today, explained by the type of party system in the state? And the further quetion is, To what extent are other factors, such as the economic resources of the state, more useful in explaining the variations in state policy than the conditions of the party system in the state? Some scholars have argued that the level of economic resources of a state, its relative affluence, is the determining factor. Others see the party variables as relevant "if one holds economic conditions constant"—that is, among wealthy states *and* among poor states, looked at separately, the conditions of party organization and competition influence the policy outcomes. Thus Thomas Dye found that if one controlled for economic development, there was a significant relationship between Democratic party control of state legislatures and governorships, on the one hand, and certain aspects of state education policy on the other.[45]

A review of all the studies done since V. O. Key presented his hypotheses leads to the conclusion that there is still much controversy, but that also certain generalizations emerge:

1. The income of a state, its industrialization, and its urbanization levels are important considerations for explaining those state policy outcomes involving financial commitments.
2. Certain characteristics of state party systems may indeed be relevant for explaining variations in state policy—notably that it may well be true that interparty competition is beneficial to the have-nots in a state's population.
3. One of the difficulties in demonstrating the independent effect of party system competition is that competitive states tend also to be more affluent. Thus, the correlation between competition and economic status (percent of the state population falling below the poverty line) is $-.85$. Such a high correlation means that it is difficult to demonstrate that party competition *by itself* is *the* critical factor.
4. Despite such problems, recent research has provided more support for the theory that the type of party system in a state is important as a determinant of state policy outcomes. The key aspects of the state party systems which have been examined besides competition are: voting turnout in state elections, legislative party conflict, and the extent of party organization unity in state parties.

David Nice's recent work, examining the relevance of these variables in great detail, pushes beyond the research of other scholars. He uses a variety of measures of state party systems to determine which, if any, seem to be related to state policies.[46] He finds considerable support for the theory that party system characteristics are important as explanatory factors. For example, in the area of civil rights legislation, using a scale developed initially by Richard Hofferbert[47] (related to whether a state has civil rights laws dealing with public accommodation, employment, education, and public and private housing), and controlling for the size of the minority population in the state, Nice found significant relationships. As table 16.20 reveals there was a significant correlation in 1960 between the adoption of civil rights laws and the type of party system in a state. Similarly, although the correlations are not as impressive for the policies requiring financial outlays for education and welfare, the correlations are with one exception in the right (expected) direction. The evidence here is not overwhelming, but it strongly confirms the view

TABLE 16.20

Relation of Type of State Party System to State Legislative Policy Outcomes (partial correlations, 1960 data)

	Interparty Competition	Election Turnout	Party Organizational Unity	Legislative Party Conflict
Civil rights scale	.39	.30	.51	.44
Welfare expenditures per capita	.16	.20	.14	.28
Educational expenditures per capita	−.06	.10	.35	.41

SOURCE: David Nice, "The Impact of Barriers to Party Government in the American States," Ph.D. dissertation, University of Michigan, 1979.

NOTE: Socioeconomic traits are controlled for in this table. The "Interparty Competition" measure used here is the Ranney Index (in Herbert Jacob and Kenneth N. Vines, eds., *Politics in the American States* [Boston: Little, Brown], 1965 and 1971); "Election Turnout" is derived from Lester Milbrath, Ibid., 1971; "Party Organizational Unity" is percent of vote for winner in gubernatorial primaries 1956–62; see David Nice, "Barriers," p. 229; "Legislative Party Conflict" is from the research of Wayne Francis, *Legislative Issues in the Fifty States* (Chicago: Rand McNally, 1967).

that, as Nice says, "Party system variables all have at least some policy impact but . . . the levels of predictive power vary substantially . . . most of the relationships of any size are consistent with Key's hypothesis that strong, well-organized parties tend to benefit the disadvantaged . . . ,"[48] that is, if they genuinely compete against each other for public support. Since 1960, research suggests that in those policy areas where the federal government has assumed a major responsibility for funding the states and where these funds begin to pre-empt the states' own funding roles, the "party factor" declines in importance. Thus, federal social welfare grants to the states rose from $912 million in 1963 to over $5.6 billion in 1973. By 1972 the federal government financed approximately half of all public welfare costs.[49] With such huge allocations to the states the influence of the state parties on the level of state funding for welfare declines. In policy areas where such federal intervention has not occurred, state parties still can play a very important role. As the Reagan administration cuts back federal funds to the states, the role of state parties can again be increased in the decisions made at the state level. Whether national parties are adopting legislation funding programs for the disadvantaged, or state parties adopt such policies, there is strong evidence that the original argument of Key was largely correct—the conditions of party competition, organization, and mobilization activities can influence considerably the content of public policy. Walter Burnham argued at one time that parties provide "countervailing collective power on behalf of the many individually powerless . . . against the relatively few who are individually or organizationally powerful."[50] This conception of party was at the heart of democratic theory. Parties may not always be effective, but as cohesive, combative structures they *can* be.

Part V

PARTY SYSTEM
CHANGE
IN AMERICA

Chapter 17

Party Realignment
in America:
Fact or Fantasy?

IS THE American party system undergoing a radical crisis today, leading to a major transformation of the system and the eventual appearance of a new party system? Or after surviving many threats since the Civil War, is the party system finally in the process of collapsing? Certain scholars in recent years have argued that this is indeed occurring. Walter Burnham wrote in 1970,

The political parties are progressively losing their hold upon the electorate. A new breed of independent seems to be emerging. . . . This may point toward the progressive dissolution of the parties as action intermediaries in electoral choice and other politically relevant acts. It may also be indicative of the production of a mass base for independent political movements of ideological tone and considerable long-term staying power. . . . There is considerable evidence that this country is now in a realigning sequence and that we are enroute to a sixth party system.[1]

And right after the 1980 election David S. Broder suggested that we might well be heading into a realigning era. He said,

Sifting through the returns of [the] election [of 1980] makes it clear that for the first time in a generation it is sensible to ask whether we might be entering a new political era—an era of Republican dominance. . . . To find an earlier example of the kind of basic realignment of party strength some observers think may have begun this month, you have to go all the way back to the Roosevelt-Democratic victories of 1932 and 1936 . . . something like the reverse of that occurred this month.[2]

Other scholars are less alarmist. After examining the evidence in their study of *The Changing American Voter*, Nie and his associates conclude that although there is some evidence of changes which "clearly point to a realignment . . . all in all, we see little prospect for the emergence of a new party system from the disarray of the present system."[3]

Similarly, James Sundquist, after a careful analysis of realignment, concluded in 1973 that a radical transformation of our system was not clearly in evidence:

In the long run, the prospect may well be for a further gradual decomposition of the two-party system. But there is at least as much reason to believe that in the shorter run the headlong march toward decomposition . . . will be checked and even reversed. The New Deal party system will be reinvigorated, and most of those who ceased identifying with one or the other major party . . . will reidentify.[4]

The Theory of Realignment

Realignment means different things to different people, although all who discuss the phenomenon see it as a change in the basic pattern of public support underlying the party system. For some, realignment is a *sudden* happening occurring at the time of a "critical election" (such as 1860, 1896, or 1932) which saw a minority party become the majority party and remain dominant for a considerable period of time. For others, realignment is a *gradual* change in party support—called secular realignment. Again, for some writers realignment means electoral replacement (older voters of Party A replaced by new voters supporting Party B). Realignment also means to some primarily a change in the party loyalties and the voting behavior of the public, while for still others realignment means much more—a change in the organic structure of the party process, in the citizen's relationship to that process with significant consequences for the political system.

In the views of the most prominent writers on the subject, the nature of realignment can be described as a series of changes which take place in a society.[5] These views can be summarized as follows.

During any era of party control (such as the period after World War I when the Republicans were the dominant party and the Democrats were in the minority), social and economic changes occur which may be the result of specific crises (such as war, economic recession, racial conflict), or gradual changes in the nature of the population (economic well-being, technological improvements, changes in population movements, and changes in the public's attitudes toward issues). New groups may appear along with these social and economic changes, making new demands on society.

New political issues appear as a result of these crises or "social maladjustments," or because of the gradual changes occurring in society. These issues will replace the older controversies and will relate to the role of government in the society or economy (such as, whether the government should provide more social welfare, do more to end discrimination against blacks in education, withdraw from Vietnam, or pardon all deserters). Certain of these issues may trigger confrontation between or within the parties and result in ideological polarization. Issues become more important to politics than ever before at these times, both for political leaders and for citizens. Further, interest in politics presumably is intensified during this period of issue conflict, often resulting in the involvement of citizens previously disinterested.

The response of the political parties to these new issues, or to the single triggering issue, determines the extent and nature of party realignment. Since these new issues usually cut across both the Democratic and Republican parties, the leaders and activists (and finally the voter support groups) have to take positions on the issues and somehow resolve the conflict. The response of the parties may take the following forms:

1. No significant response, or at least a very slow reaction to the crisis, and the opponents of change, or those who want to straddle the new issues, win out in both parties. (Some writers would argue that this was the scenario of the Democrats and Whigs before the Civil War in their failure to deal with the slavery issue.) A major realignment occurs through the replacement of both old parties, if the crisis continues.
2. One major party, either the Republican or Democratic, responds affirmatively, with the "new issue adherents" who seek more progressive policies winning out in the control of the party. The other major party does not respond affirmatively, continuing to straddle the issues. (Perhaps the party crisis of 1928–32 during the Depression fits this scenario.) A major realignment occurs—one party attracts the progressives, the other the conservatives.
3. Both major parties respond to the new issue politics by developing new issue positions which are "progressive"—that is, the internal struggle within the parties is won in both cases by the "progressive" new issue adherents. (After Hoover's defeat, the Republican party was changed considerably, so that by the 1950s both parties were more "liberal" and

"internationalist.") The old party system survives, although changes occur in both parties.

4. A new third party appears on the scene, organized on the basis of the new issue controversy. But, this new party is eventually absorbed, because one, or both, of the older major parties responds affirmatively to the crisis, thus making it difficult for the newly formed third party to maintain itself. (The Populist party threat in 1892 may be a prime example of this.)

5. The new third party may withstand efforts for its absorption into one of the major parties, and thus a new type of party system is born, which includes a viable third party as a meaningful, continuous threat to the older major parties (as in Canada), or which in fact replaces one of the major parties (as the Liberal Party in Britain was replaced as a major party by the Labour Party after World War I).

Depending on which scenario takes place at these times of national crisis, the party system may be modified considerably, transformed into something different, or maintained as it was. But in each case, even if it is maintained in basic form as it previously was, political realignment of some type occurs in the society. The following *types of changes*, according to realignment theory, are likely to occur:

1. There will be a shift, suddenly or gradually, by groups or "blocs" or categories of voters away from support for the party to which they have been loyal. Not by all the individuals in a particular group or "bloc" but by a significant proportion, large enough to indicate that the coalitional character of the parties is changing.

2. There will be a loosening of individual citizen ties of loyalty for and identification with parties, depending of course on the citizen's perception of how satisfactory is his/her party's response to the new issue politics.

3. Issues will play an important role in the citizen's support for the parties during this realignment period. "Issue polarization" develops within and between the parties. The citizen's own position on the issues is sharpened and then is related to that of the parties and their candidates. The vote is then more closely linked to issue positions.

4. During realignment, citizen interest in politics and voting participation will increase. This is not necessarily so for all sections of the country or for all groups, however. Participation increases for those groups most concerned about the new issues.

These phenomena should be looked for in seeking to discover whether a "realignment" has occurred or is occurring. Theoretically, this is what happens to a society like ours when there is a basic change in the party system. As V. O. Key said, a "critical election," one in which a "sharp and durable realignment between parties" occurs, is one "in which more or less profound readjustments occur in the relations of power within the community."[6]

American Party Realignment in the Last Decade

It is generally admitted that in the United States there have been four major party realignments, linked to the elections of 1828, 1860, 1896, and 1932. These are spaced at fairly regular thirty-two- to thirty-six-year intervals, a fact which to some scholars is very important. This leads to major questions: Did the U.S. enter into a new realigning era with the election of 1968, and if not, when will the next realignment occur? Has 1980 begun a new realignment process?

On the surface, a look at elections and voting behavior, as well as party identifications of citizens from the 1950s to 1980, does not indicate any great change in the strength of the Republican and Democratic parties *from 1968 on* compared to the preceding period. The parties have alternated in control of the presidency, and there has been some fluctuation in the extent of party control of the House and Senate, but election results do not indicate any sustained swing in the support for the two major parties. George Wallace's third party movement in 1968 secured 13 percent of the vote, and John Anderson's almost 7 percent in 1980. But there has been no durable vote for third parties. Similarly, in national surveys when the public was asked, "Generally speaking, do you usually think of yourself as a Republican, a Democrat, an Independent, or what?" the proportion who identified with the two major parties did not decline greatly after 1968. Table 17.1 shows the results of these surveys.

This aggregate change over a quarter century is not great. The Republican proportion is only 4 percent less; the Democrats 6 percent. Almost two-thirds of the public still recognizes a loyalty to one or the other of the two major parties. The change since 1968 does not appear

TABLE 17.1
Party Identification, 1952–80
(as a percentage)

Date	Democrat	Republican	Total Support for Two Major Parties
1952	47	27	74
1960	46	27	73
1964	51	24	75
1968	45	24	69
1972	40	23	63
1976	39	24	63
1980	41	23	64

SOURCE: University of Michigan CPS.

strikingly different. In terms of these data, the parties are almost as strong as ever in public support. This is only on the surface, however! A more careful study must be made of the kinds of changes which are hidden by these summary percentages.

The Erosion of Party Loyalty ("Dealignment")

To begin, there has been some change in the *strength* of party identification in recent years. In table 17.2 the data strongly suggest a change after 1964. This represents a decrease of over 30 percent in strong partisans in the population.

At the same time that this was happening, an increase in independent voting took place. The number of the bona fide Independents has tripled, while the number of "partisan" Independents (those leaning to the Republicans or Democrats) has increased slightly (see table 17.3). The change that occurred was noticeable particularly in November 1966.[7] During the period from early 1965 to 1968 the nation experienced continuous conflict and strife over Vietnam and racial questions. In 1965 the war effort was escalated, B-52 bombers were used for the first time, Hanoi was bombed, and the draft was expanded. The Voting Rights Act of 1965 and subsequent enforcement efforts produced opposition and confrontations (not the least of which was that between President Lyndon Johnson and Governor George Wallace). Other episodes in racial conflict occurred at this time also, such as the violence in Selma, Alabama (in March 1965), and the urban riots and torching of ghettos of Watts, California, and Detroit, Michigan. Opposition to American involvement in Vietnam continued from 1965, leading to Johnson's decision in 1968 not to seek re-election. This issue provoked both the liberals and conservatives, as did the continuing controversy over race. All of these developments appeared to be linked to the public's attitude to the parties. As Nie, Verba, and Petrocik wrote,

The issues which loosened party ties were racial conflict and Vietnam, capped off in recent years by Watergate. These issues caused substantial discontent. They led the public to turn against the political process more generally.[8]

In chapter 4, "The Public and the Parties," it was pointed out that this "dealignment" was particularly noticeable for the younger voters. The change after 1964 is particularly significant (see table 17.4). While some change occurred in all age groups, it was the youngest group which really demonstrated a decline in party attachment. The significance of this for the future is considerable, since one-half of the new voters are beginning their involvement with electoral politics under conditions of weak party loyalty or complete independence.

TABLE 17.2
Strong Party Identifiers
(as a percentage)

Year	Democrat	Republican	Total
1952	22	13	35
1964	26	11	37
1968	20	10	30
1972	15	10	25
1976	15	9	24
1980	18	8	26

SOURCE: University of Michigan SRC/CPS/NES.

The 1980 election revealed a continuation of independence for the youngest age cohort but not for the 26–30 age group. Indeed, the 1980 results are mixed and no basic change in the pattern since 1968 toward more partisanship can be inferred.

TABLE 17.3
Voters Calling Themselves Independents
(as a percentage)

Year	Bona Fide Independents	Partisan Independents	Total Independents
1952	5	17	22
1960	8	15	23
1964	8	15	23
1968	11	19	30
1972	13	22	35
1976	15	21	36
1980	13	22	35

SOURCE: University of Michigan SRC/CPS.

TABLE 17.4
Voters Calling Themselves Independents by Age
(as a percentage)

Age Group	1952	1960	1964	1968	1972	1976	1980
21–25 (18–25 from 1972 on)	25	39	33	53	51	49	48
26–30	32	26	29	41	50	50	41
51–65	19	21	18	24	26	25	29
66 and over	20	13	14	15	19	22	23

SOURCE: University of Michigan SRC/CPS.

Shifts in Group Support for the Parties

A political party is a coalition of socioeconomic groups the majority of whose leaders and members support the party because of the conviction that the party can do more (and will do more) to promote the interests and needs of the group than any other party. A good example is the Democratic New Deal coalition in 1932 which consisted of the South plus certain groups in the big cities of the North, particularly ethnic groups, union members, and blacks. The Republicans were left with a coalition of white-collar and nonunion whites found mainly in the rural and suburban North, Midwest, and West. When a "realignment" occurs, theoretically it means a basic shift in the support which such groups give to the political parties. Thus, there must be evidence of such shifts, of a durable nature, to demonstrate that a realignment is occurring.

In assessing the evidence on this question, it must be recognized at the outset that the major groups making up the party coalitions can shift dramatically in their vote for candidates (see table 17.5). Labor union members, a significant element in the Democratic coalition, shifted away from the Democrats and supported Nixon strongly in 1972. The same was true of the Catholics who had backed Kennedy with an 83 percent vote in 1960, but supported Nixon in 1972. Both groups, however, came back in the Democratic fold by 1976. But major shifts occurred again from 1976 to 1980 (see table 17.6).

The fact that such shifts in voting behavior can occur due to the vagaries of particular election campaigns and the personalities and credentials of presidential candidates should not be taken as convincing evidence, however. The key question is, Is there a *sustained* shift in the loyalties of these groups to the parties over time, a shift which is durable enough and profound enough to reveal that the group-coalitional basis of the parties is changing? This question has been an-

TABLE 17.5

Shifts in Group Support of the Parties

Shift	Percentage
Catholics	
To Democrats, 1956–60	36
From Democrats, 1964–72	39
Union Members	
To Democrats, 1956–64	30
To Republicans, 1964–72	40
To Democrats, 1972–76	21
Blacks	
To Democrats, 1956–64	36

SOURCE: University of Michigan SRC/CPS.

TABLE 17.6

*Changes in Support of Major Groups for Parties in
Presidential Elections 1964–80 (as a percentage)*

Voting for Democratic Presidential Candidates	1964	1968	1972	1976	1980
Catholics	79	60	40	56	41
Jews	89	92	69	66	50
Blacks	100	96	87	94	93
Union members	83	53	43	63	51
Grade school education	80	60	40	69	62
College education	52	38	38	43	32

SOURCE: University of Michigan CPS/NES, 1964, 1968, 1972, 1976, 1980.

swered in the affirmative by Nie, Verba, and Petrocik in their book, *The Changing American Voter*. They argue that the changes which took place from the 1950s to the 1970s in "the social correlates of party identification . . . clearly point to a realignment of the parties."[9]

In a detailed and complex analysis they present evidence in support of this position. The essence of their argument is as follows:

1. In the South since the 1950s there has been a decline in Protestant white support for the Democrats, particularly native white southern support. As a result the proportion of Democratic loyalty among these southerners declined from 78 percent in 1952 to 57 percent in 1960 to 47 percent in 1972. Many southerners called themselves Independents—over 40 percent by the late seventies. In 1980, 61 percent of the southern whites voted for Reagan.
2. The blacks in the South, who had already embraced the Democrats, during this period were gradually moving more completely to a Democratic identification (over 80 percent by 1964). Recently, blacks are also inclined to see themselves as Independents (27 percent by 1972). In 1980, 93 percent of the southern blacks voted Democratic.
3. In the North the Democrats were in a sense making up for their southern white losses by cutting into Republican strength in their traditional sectors—among northern white Protestants, even among upper status white Protestants. The Goldwater candidacy in 1964 was critical for this development. Again, what happened was not an increase in Democratic identification but rather a *decrease* in Republican support, coupled with an increase in independence (see table 17.7).
4. The black support for the Democrats in the North also increased considerably (from 55 percent in 1952 to 71 percent by 1972, and 92 percent voted Democratic in 1980).
5. The Catholic identification with the Democrats declined somewhat (from 55 percent in 1952 to 47 percent in 1972 to 43 percent in 1980). This was not seen as a major change. There was also some attrition in the Jewish vote. The development of independence in party affiliation among both the Catholics and Jews in recent years is particularly notable.

TABLE 17.7
Party Identification of Northern White Protestants (as a percentage)

Party	1952	1964	1972	1980
Republican	43	37	33	34
Democratic	31	38	27	30
Independent	26	25	39	37

SOURCE: University of Michigan SRC/CPS/NES.

After an evaluation of the relative contribution of these groups to the Democratic and Republican coalitions of the fifties and the seventies, the conclusion reached by Nie and his colleagues was that a gradual alteration in the coalitional character of the parties has been taking place. The white South has declined as the central component of the Democratic coalition. It used to constitute 30 percent or more of the Democratic party strength; now it is 20 percent or less. Blacks have become more prominent in the Democratic coalition, and this, plus a small increase in the relative Democratic strength of the upper-status northern WASPs (or a decline in their Republican support), has shifted the group orientation of both the two major parties' coalitions.

However, in 1976 and 1980, had the elections again altered the nature of the parties' coalitions? Did Carter in 1976 win back the white South? It is true that Carter did much better in the South than McGovern had done, winning 118 electoral college votes (compared to none for McGovern) and 54.1 percent of the votes in the South. But at least one scholar, Everett C. Ladd, has concluded that Carter "failed to win a majority of the vote among Southern whites," because he received only 45 percent of their vote.[10] In 1980 Carter received only 35 percent of the southern white vote, Reagan received 61 percent; this continues then the trend for the Democrats to lose the white Protestant South.

Increasing Importance for Politics of Citizen Attitudes on Issues

In the theory of "realignment" there is a great emphasis on the rise of new political issues, the emergence of party conflict in the dialogue over these issues, the role of these issues in mobilizing and influencing citizen involvement in politics, and the linkage of issue positions to the vote. To what extent since 1964 have political issues become a more decisive, salient, and relevant aspect of American politics, particularly for mass political behavior?

It is not difficult in most elections to find issues on which the Republican and Democratic voters differ. Table 17.8 depicts the differences for party identifiers on some of the major issues discussed in the 1980 campaign by Carter and Reagan.

TABLE 17.8

Differences on Selected Major Issues Discussed in 1980 Campaign
(as a percentage)

Issue	Democrats	Republicans	Across Party Difference
Government aid to minorities			
Favor	31	11	20
In between	28	28	
Oppose	41	61	
Within party difference	10	50	
Increased government services			
Favor	60	27	33
Stay the same	19	20	
Decrease	22	53	
Within party difference	38	26	

SOURCE: University of Michigan SRC/CPS.

The Democrats and Republicans were in conflict on such issues in 1980, and there was considerable internal disagreement among each party's identifiers. The Democrats were really more split on the minorities issue, and the Republicans more split on the government services issue. There was then both cross-party conflict and internal party disagreement. This was not as serious in 1980 as it was for the Democrats in, for example, 1972,[11] but the contrasts were significant.

Important in the theory of party realignment, however, is not whether differences exist in the attitudes of the supporters of the different parties but whether new issues have emerged which influence the voting behavior of the public *and* result in changes in individual and group support for the parties. It is difficult to demonstrate that this has been happening since the mid-sixties in the United States. Probably, this is what happened in 1932. New issues commanded the political arena, issues focused on the role of government in dealing with the economic crisis (particularly about the responsibility of the government in providing welfare assistance, social security, and aid to the farmers). The parties responded differently to these issues in 1932, the public's party loyalties and voting behavior was linked to its positions on these issues, and this presumably led to the major realignment in the basis of party support in 1932. Is this pattern being repeated since 1968, although more gradually than was the case in 1932?

The issues which have confronted the American public in the sixties and seventies are quite different from those of the Eisenhower years 1952–60. In the Eisenhower presidency the country was relatively prosperous. The Cold War was on people's minds, but after the Korean

War was settled American military involvement was not an issue nor was race an issue yet as the Supreme Court had outlawed school segregation. McCarthyism preoccupied and divided the nation, but by 1956 that too was on the wane. There were issues for partisan dialogues in the fifties—aid to foreign countries, national medicaid programs, full employment, and aid to education. But they were low-keyed, nonpolarizing dialogues, and studies reveal that the votes of citizens in 1952 and 1956 depended much more on party identification and candidate personality perceptions than on issue positions.[12]

After 1960, new issues, or new versions of old issues, demanded the attention of the American public—how to implement racial justice, military involvement and success in Vietnam, the social and economic crises of urban areas, the economic recession which developed in the seventies, pollution of the environment, as well as a whole series characterized as "new politics" issues. Warren Miller and Teresa Levitin have identified four such "new politics" issues of the sixties: dealing with political protest (marches, the occupation of buildings), law and order (individual rights versus community rights), counterculture (new lifestyles, defiance of conventional values and morality), and social control (attitudes toward the police and military and their approach to maintaining social order). They argue that these new issues dominated politics and elections in 1970 and 1972, polarized the public, and remained relevant for 1976.[13] The new politics analysis remains controversial. Its value is in identifying the new issue climate within which Americans voted from the mid-sixties on.

In the elections of 1976 and 1980 there was a return to the economic issues of inflation and unemployment. It is clear from recent research that these were the salient issues for the public. In 1976, 32 percent of the public saw unemployment as the most important problem, while 27 percent saw it as inflation. In 1980 the proportions were 11 percent for unemployment and 33 percent for inflation.

The following questions emerge from this research on the role of issues in elections: How important were issues to Americans in the 1960s and 1970s? How consistent were their issue positions? How important were issues to their votes? Can shifts in party loyalty be associated with "issue-voting"?

As to the saliency of issues for voters, there seems to have developed a striking change since 1964. In the national studies from 1952 on people were asked to evaluate presidential candidates by stating what they liked and disliked about them. Their comments could then be analyzed to determine to what extent the references were to "issues," to "personal attributes," or to "party." Table 17.9 shows the increase in "issues references" found in one study. While the personal record and qualities of the candidates continue to maintain the interest of voters, it is interesting to note the rise in the reference to issues

TABLE 17.9

Percentage of Respondents
Mentioning Issues, Party Ties,
Personal Attributes

Year	Issues	Party Ties	Personal Attributes
1960	54	42	82
1964	77	34	84
1968	68	40	82
1972	67	24	72
1980	78	24	80

SOURCE: Norman H. Nie, Sidney Verba, and John R. Petrocik, *The Changing American Voter* (Cambridge: Harvard University Press, 1976), p. 142. University of Michigan SRC/CPS/NES.

in 1964 and the continuance of this at only slightly lower levels thereafter. In 1980, however, it returned to the 1964 level of 78 percent.

On the question of issue "consistency" the data also seem to indicate that the public's attitudes to politics have become more structured. The Nie-Verba-Petrocik measure of attitude consistency indicates that whereas only 26 percent of the American public in 1956 and 1960 could be classified as consistent, this figure rose to 40 percent in 1964 and, according to their data, stood at 44 percent in 1973.[14] It is interesting to note from their analysis also that more attitudinal or ideological polarization existed in the 1970s compared to the 1950s: 26 percent were on the extreme "liberal" end (of a 10-point liberal-conservative continuum) in the seventies compared to 15 percent in the fifties; further, 24 percent were at the extreme conservative end of the continuum in the seventies compared to 16 percent in the fifties.[15]

Furthermore, their data reveal that within the parties the division of opinion on issues has become slightly more "extreme" recently. Thus, in the Democratic party, the supporters were considered 15 percent liberal on the issue scale in 1956 compared to 26 percent in 1972; 11 percent of the Democrats were considered conservative in 1956, but 17 percent in 1972. The corresponding percentages for Republicans are: liberals 9 percent and 11 percent; conservatives 18 percent and 23 percent.[16]

The relation of issues to the vote seems to have increased considerably in recent years. Some scholars have argued that after 1964, contrary to the elections of the 1950s, issues became more relevant to the vote. But there is much controversy over this matter. The analysis by Nie, Verba, and Petrocik is seen in table 17.10. Clearly, if these data are valid, issues since 1964 have become much more important in explaining the vote. But other scholars question the methodology on which these data are based. Nevertheless, even among the skeptics there is support for the importance of issues in explaining the vote in presidential elections since 1964.[17]

The final question is the relationship, if any, of issue positions to the shifts in party loyalty. Since the 1950s there has been a gradual shift in the nature of group support for the parties. The white Protestant southerners have been leaving the Democrats while the blacks have been moving toward the Democrats; on the other hand the upper-status northern Protestants have been leaving the Republicans. In addition there have been slight shifts among lower status northern WASPs and Jews, while the Catholics have in the long run not changed much. Are these shifts linked to attitude changes since the 1950s? The evidence suggests very strongly that they are (see table 17.11).

The most prominent attitude changes concern the native southerners of lower and upper status (more conservative) and the blacks (more liberal). This confirms the expectation of the loss to the Democratic

TABLE 17.10

Correlations Between the Vote and the Issues, 1956–72

Issue	1956	1964	1968	1972
Welfare, including redistribution policies (job guarantees, minimum wage, collective bargaining)	.29	.61	.51	.54
Foreign policy	−.03	.66	.36	.64
Race	.08	.44	.41	.47

SOURCE: Norman H. Nie, Sidney Verba, and John R. Petrocik, *The Changing American Voter* (Cambridge: Harvard University Press, 1976), p. 188.

TABLE 17.11

Shift in Liberal-Conservative Position on Issues (as a percentage)

Group and Basic Position	1950s	1970s
Conservative position on issues		
Middle- and upper-status native white southerners	37	50
Lower-status native white southerners	16	35
Catholics	12	18
Liberal position on issues		
Blacks	48	76
Jews	32	48
Higher-status northern white Protestants	11	20

SOURCE: Norman H. Nie, Sidney Verba, and John R. Petrocik, *The Changing American Voter* (Cambridge: Harvard University Press, 1976), pp. 243–69.

party of the "white South"; on the other hand, the blacks became a central element in a liberal Democratic coalition, which contains a high proportion of Jews (only 10 percent of whom are very conservative), a slight loss of Catholics, and possibly on the periphery some attrition of northern high-status Protestant support for the Republicans. There is evidence then that the gradual change in the character of the group support for the parties since the 1950s is not superficial. It is an attitude change grounded in reality, at a time when attitudes are more salient, consistent, and linked to voting behavior.

Decline in Political Interest and Participation ("Demobilization")

There are two theories on party realignment. It has been assumed that an intensification of public interest in politics and an increased turnout at the polls would accompany a realignment. More recently there has been some argument that "demobilization" or the withdrawal of people from participation in politics may just as well be linked to realignment. A party system can be modified, or even break down, if a large proportion of citizens turn away from it and are alienated enough to eschew all participation in the system. This is as possible as the earlier theoretical scenario which pictured the involvement of a larger number of persons who were captivated by the new issues and made demands on the parties leading to party system change.[18] Which theory about public participation seems most appropriate for the last ten to fifteen years?

To begin with, it is quite clear that there has been a consistent decline in voting turnout in presidential elections during the sixties and seventies (see table 17.12). The 1976 and 1980 figures are the lowest since the 1948 figure of 51.1 percent. Other data seem to confirm that fewer people may be involved with party and election politics than

TABLE 17.12
*Voting Age Population
Casting Votes in
Presidential Elections*

Year	Percentage
1960	63.1
1964	61.8
1968	60.7
1972	55.4
1976	54.4
1980	53.9

SOURCE: U.S. Bureau of the Census, *Statistical Abstract of United States*, 1976, p. 469; for 1976, Current Population Report Series, pp. 25–626, table 1, p. 6.

previously. Thus the Nie-Verba-Petrocik study reports that the number of persons stating that they are "very interested" in the presidential campaign has declined slightly from 38 percent in 1960 to 32 percent in 1972. Also, the proportion who are "involved" (both interested and follow the campaign in newspapers and magazines) declined from 23 percent in 1960 to 13 percent in 1972. What is interesting in these data more than the absolute percentages is the fact of a decline, not an increase during a period when new issues were appearing in American politics. Further, it is significant that this decline took place in all age and education groups, significantly among those with a college education (where the decline in the percentage "involved" was from 44 percent in 1960 to 25 percent in 1972, at the time of the McGovern candidacy)![19]

The decline in the trust and confidence which Americans have in their government and political institutions seems clearly associated with this decline in voting and political involvement. The details from recent studies about such decline were presented earlier. The findings are truly startling. Less than one-fourth of the American public was rated as high in trust for our government in 1976. In 1980 it dropped even lower. In 1960 the proportion was 60 percent.

A final point must be made about this growing body of cynics and distrustful and alienated citizens. Many of them apparently are staying home on election day rather than taking part in political action to change the system. The study of the 1972 election revealed that many of those who were cynical of government and who felt a lack of a sense of efficacy about their role in the system did not vote in that election. In fact, their voting turnout was 27 percent lower than that of the opposite group—those who were supportive of government and had a high sense of political efficacy.[20] This is important evidence indicating that "demobilization" is indeed occurring among those who might be expected to be aroused.

There is strong evidence here, then, that if a party realignment has been occurring since the mid-sixties, contrary to theoretical expectations, it is taking place during a period of decline in participation rather than an increase. This decline seems to occur when there is a loss of confidence in government and in political action.

The 1980 Election: Its Significance for Realignment

After each election there is a temptation to allocate blame and to predict the future, to assess the trends in political behavior, the patterns in public attitudes and ideology, and the state of the parties. The aim is to arrive at an understanding of the meaning of the election for our society. The problem is that there are often conflicting developments and, hence, contradictory interpretations.

In terms of the general results in the 1980 election the Republicans and Reagan won a stunning victory. Reagan won the electoral college vote overwhelmingly (489 to 49), the Republicans were victorious in the United States Senate races, winning 12 more seats (thus holding a balance of 53 to 47), and they picked up 33 seats in the House, although the Democrats retained control (243 to 192). Carter's vote dropped from 51 percent in 1976 to 41 percent in 1980. However, Reagan's majority was only 51 percent. In twelve of the states in which Reagan won he did so with a plurality of less than 50 percent of the vote. In fact Reagan won 224 electoral college votes in nineteen states that he won with less than 54 percent of the vote. Ten of the Republican Senate seats were won by a margin of 4 percent or less. Of course, the vote for John Anderson was responsible in many states for making the election close. His vote (overall 6.7 percent) was over 10 percent of the total in ten states.

In one sense, then, this was another one of the many close elections this country has had (1960, 1968, 1976, 1980). It was also a low turnout election. Only 53.9 percent of the eligible voters participated in the presidential election, or, to put it another way, an estimated 75 million voters stayed home. Further, many voters were not very enthusiastic; one study showed that only 38 percent of the voters said they strongly favored the candidate they voted for.[21]

An important concern in a study of 1980 is, how much defection was there by party identifiers? There was a great deal, and that disloyalty behavior was more complicated than is the case usually because of Anderson's attractiveness. The national data are presented in table 17.13. From such findings it can be seen that the greatest defections

TABLE 17.13

Loyalty and Defections of Party Identifiers and Independents, 1980
(as a percentage)

Party Identification	Presidential Vote			House of Representatives
	Reagan	Carter	Anderson	Democratic Vote
Strong Democrat	10.8	86.2	3.1	85.2
Weak Democrat	32.1	59.7	7.5	69.3
Independent Democrat	31.1	47.6	21.4	69.9
Pure Independent	65.1	22.9	12.0	56.3
Independent Republican	78.0	11.9	10.1	32.0
Weak Republican	86.8	4.6	8.6	26.4
Strong Republican	92.0	4.5	3.6	22.5

SOURCE: University of Michigan CPS/NES, 1980.

were by the weak and Independent Democrats. Almost a third of these left the party, more than in 1976, but they did not all go to Reagan. In fact 21 percent of the Independent Democrats supported Anderson. The Independent Republican switch to Anderson was also considerable: 10 percent. And the strong Republican support for Democratic candidates for Congress was high (22.5 percent), greater than in 1976. Thus there is a set of mixed results, and certainly it must be concluded from this that the power of party allegiance continues to be on a "declining slope" in both parties.

A second question concerns the important groups in the parties' coalitions and their voting behavior in 1980. The behavior of these groups has been referred to previously, but here it must be noted that the desertion of large numbers of individuals in these key Democratic groups was critical in the Carter loss (see table 17.14). The suggestion implicit in these findings is that the traditional (post-New Deal) Democratic coalition was deeply invaded by Reagan, although the Anderson appeal was partly responsible. Even those of the Jewish faith supported Carter with only 50 percent of their vote, although a sizeable proportion of the remainder went to Anderson and not to Reagan. The blacks backed Carter overwhelmingly (92.5 percent) as did those with a grade-school education (62 percent). But Carter's support was low in other socioeconomic groups.

Another measure of the decline is found in the big city vote and its movement in some cities (but not in all of them) to the Republicans (see table 17.15). These metropolitan areas have been the heart of the Democratic coalition, but in 1980 the Democratic decline was severe in many of them. Only a few of them could buck the tide: Baltimore, New Orleans, and perhaps Detroit, Chicago, and Pittsburgh.

Several observations emerge from the 1980 election studies regarding the question of the role of issues and ideology in the election. As usual a great many issues were raised during the campaign, including women's rights, abortion, and national morality, in addition to the basic economic issues of inflation, unemployment, and interest rates; and

TABLE 17.14

Decline in Democratic Vote, 1976–80

Voter Group	Percentage Supporting			
	Carter	Reagan	Anderson	Change
Union members	51	41	8	−12
Catholics	41	50	9	−15
Jews	50	37	13	−16
Young (age 18–29)	35	51	14	−17
Southern whites	35	61	4	−11

SOURCE: University of Michigan SRC/CPS/NES.

TABLE 17.15
Change in Big City Vote, 1980 (as a percentage)

City	Reagan	Carter	Anderson	Change in Democratic Percentage 1976–80
Los Angeles	50	40	7	−10
Seattle (King County)	45	39	13	− 6
Denver (County)	42	41	14	− 9
Miami (Dade County)	51	40	8	−18
Pittsburgh (Allegheny County)	44	48	6	− 3
New York City	38	55	6	−11
Chicago (Cook County)	40	52	7	− 1
Detroit (Wayne County)	35	59	5	− 1
Baltimore	22	72	5	+ 4
New Orleans (Orleans Parish)	40	57	2	+ 2

SOURCE: *Congressional Quarterly Weekly Reports*, April 25, 1981, p. 714.

a variety of foreign issues, particularly Iran and defense policy aimed at the USSR. Furthermore, the candidates themselves and their records were clearly at issue—up to 40 percent of the participants voted *against* either Carter or Reagan. Of all the substantive issues, economic questions and foreign policy matters seemed to be critical as explanations of the Carter defeat. At the time of the election inflation was 12 percent, interest rates at 15½ percent, and 8 million people were unemployed. And the hostages were still in Iran. During most of 1980 Carter's popularity had declined, basically because of the evaluations by the public of his performance in these issue areas (see table 17.16). There was an almost consistent decline in support on the critical issue areas right up to the fall of 1980. The voting behavior in the election of those who disapproved (and approved) of Carter's record on these types of issues reflects the impact of issues (see table 17.17). In 1980 these issues were uppermost in peoples' minds. For example, on de-

TABLE 17.16
Public Approval of Carter Position on Issues
January–August, 1980
(as a percentage)

Issue	January	March	June	August
Foreign policy	45	34	20	18
Economy	27	23	18	19
Iran	55	49	29	31

SOURCE: Cited in Gerald Pomper et al., *The Election of 1980* (Chatham, N.J.: Chatham, 1981), p. 100; based on CBS/*New York Times* polls.

TABLE 17.17

Voting Patterns in Presidential Election as Reflected in
Attitudes Toward Issues, 1980 (as a percentage)

	Voted for		
Issue	*Reagan*	*Carter*	*Anderson*
Carter performance on Iran			
Approved	24	72	5
Disapproved	68	21	10
Carter performance on inflation			
Approved	16	80	5
Disapproved	65	25	10
Defense spending			
Closer to Reagan	77	16	7
Equidistant	52	40	8
Closer to Carter	18	69	12

SOURCE: University of Michigan CPS/NES, 1980.

fense spending, in 1976 two-thirds of the public approved a *decrease* in such spending, but by 1980 70 percent wanted an *increase.* Economic issues also were important, both in 1976 *and* 1980. The public felt that Reagan and the Republicans were more likely to deal with these problems, although a large proportion (one-third or more) had misgivings about both candidates.[22]

Finally, so far as ideology is concerned, there were two developments: an increase in conservatives to about 44 percent of the national sample in 1980 (compared to about 37 percent in 1978), and the defection of a large number of both liberals and moderates from Carter. Only 61 percent of the liberals supported Carter (18.5 percent went to Anderson), and only 35 percent of the moderates voted for Carter (54 percent went to Reagan). Reagan held on to 72 percent of the support of the conservatives and then added to this the support of moderates, plus 21 percent of the liberals. This meant an erosion in the ideological backing of Carter.

A variety of other factors occurred during the campaign which were of importance, but their role was linked to the public's evaluation of the candidates' ability to deal with the critical issues most salient to them. The debates just before the election were apparently of some significance, although more research needs to be done to measure their impact. One study claims that Reagan won the debate and convinced the public he was a satisfactory alternative, converting a "4% deficit into a 5% lead over Carter."[23] Whether true or untrue, the polls in November gave Reagan 51%, and Carter had indeed lost his lead in October of a few percentage points over Reagan.[24] The election results confirmed this division of public opinion.

Since the election a variety of interpretations have been presented. The two most prominent are that the country has "gone conservative," and that a new realignment has begun. As for the first of these, there is much dispute. Pomper argues that there is really not much change in the ideological patterns of voting. Rather he finds much continuity between 1976 and 1980 and no basic change in the ideological composition of the party coalitions in the two years—the conservatives constituted 43 percent of Ford's support group in 1976 and 42 percent of Reagan's in 1980.[25] It is true, however, that 7 percent more of the population called themselves conservatives in 1980 than in 1978. And conservative positions on issues such as defense spending and economic controls are more popular than before.

As for realignment, it is certainly not clear from the 1980 election results nor from the national surveys of 1980 that a realignment has occurred. Party identification is at the 64 percent level (as in 1976), divided very much as in 1976 between the parties. There were party defections in both partisan directions in 1980, not just away from the Democrats. Public interest was not high; turnout was the lowest it has been since 1960. Post-election commentators are claiming that 1981 surveys reveal a major additional shift to the Republicans, among those voting groups which can be used to build a new Republican majority coalition. To Broder this suggests "the possibility that we are witnessing a major realignment that will make the Republican party the new majority party." But other observers are more cautious.[26] Above all much depends on whether President Reagan can deliver on his promises, and if the Republicans can hold the loyalties of those Independents and Democrats within those key social groups who supported them in 1980. Perhaps 1982 will provide additional insight, but certainly no major trend will be visible until 1984.

Conclusions

In reflecting on the meaning of what has been presented here one should not be too dogmatic. Clearly, party loyalties have been loosened. Clearly, "the American public has been entering the electoral arena since 1964 with quite a different mental set than was the case in the late 1950s and early 1960s."[27] Clearly, the evaluations of parties are less positive. Most important, a new cohort of young citizens has entered the electorate, almost half of whom are Independents. Their voting behavior (when they vote) may be more issue oriented than previously. Nevertheless, one should not jump to extreme conclusions. As scholars like Philip Converse and Gregory Markus report, there is great stability in party loyalty and in its relevance to the vote.[28] The party system has been undergoing significant changes in the loyalty of its supporters and in the character of its coalitional base, but the two major parties *are* functioning, with the support of over 60 percent who are identifiers. This support is not as intense, but the parties' performance must be evaluated over the next years as they continue to attempt to respond to the demands of the 1980s before the American party system can be written off. That system has been remarkably resilient and adaptive in the past. Perhaps it can also cope with the "new politics," liberal and conservative.

Chapter 18

Party Decline and
Party Reform

POLITICAL parties are complex institutions and processes, and as such they are difficult to understand and evaluate. There are several different yardsticks by which parties could be evaluated: whether they are democratic structures in which rank-and-file supporters can participate effectively; whether they produce competent leaders who deserve public support; whether they propose (and adopt) policies which meet the needs of our society; whether they are coherent and responsible organizations; and whether they communicate in such a way with the public that citizens feel confident about parties and their performance in our political system. These concerns about parties as "linkage structures" have been a major focus of this study of parties. Controversies abound today over these questions, and the complex issues they pose. An attempt shall be made here to present some concluding observations about the state of our parties today.

Certain basic positions have been maintained in this book fairly consistently:

1. Parties are structures which developed early in societies in order to perform certain key processes and functions, which are central to the performance of the system. In democracies, such as the United States, they were necessary in order to develop the linkage and mediating functions between political leadership and the mass public.
2. The types of functions parties perform can be understood by visualizing them in three basic senses, or by using three "images," of their relationship to the society: as groups competing for formal governmental power, as co-

alitions representing the major socioeconomic interest sectors, and as ideological competitors defining issues and setting the agenda for society. Parties must not be conceived in a narrow "electoral power" sense, but as structures penetrating the social fabric, and involved with the major social forces of the system.

3. Parties and party systems differ by society and culture. The United States party system differs in significant respects from the party systems in other countries, and the dimensions on which our system differs have been described in detail. The major point is that long-term forces such as tradition and historical experience with parties and party politics conduce to the emergence of a special party culture in terms of which party leaders, organizations, and the public behave. While this nation is not irrevocably locked in to the system for all time, nevertheless the constraints of the party culture make change difficult.

4. The durability of a party system over time, as functionally central to a system, is a consequence of its "relevance," by which is meant its tie to social reality, interests, demands, conflicts, and needs. Whatever its deficiencies, and despite many threats, the United States party system model has, since the Civil War, developed in its own way, and it has survived because of this "relevance" in its functional performance in our society.

There have always been serious criticisms of, and attacks on, the American party system. At the level of government the role of parties has been seen as anarchic, fragmented, leaderless, and undisciplined. In leadership selection it has often been criticized as too decentralized in control, or undemocratic, or both. In the way parties conduct campaigns they have regularly been characterized as nonrational, uncoordinated, improvisational, unsystematic. As organizations they are viewed, aside from the big city machines (which are denounced as too efficient oligarchies), as loose aggregations of factional subgroups, ideologically at odds and minimally active. All these criticisms have been heard for years, and yet the United States party system has been far from dysfunctional. To many citizens this party system has remained through all these trying years, years of serious threats, as a meaningful set of social and political groups to which they can relate and be loyal. They have remained important linkage and mobilizational structures, performing critical functions. In the last analysis, the great policy decisions are those that parties, and the leaders produced by parties, have had a major role in—whether it was the Emancipation Proclamation, the anti-trust legislation, the New Deal legislation, the civil rights acts, energy legislation, or any other piece of significant legislation. The *parties*—not the Chamber of Commerce, not the UAW, not the American Legion, not the American Medical Association—usually are the *prime movers* in the adoption of such landmark laws *and* are usually held responsible for such actions.

Nevertheless, despite the recognition of their contributions of the past, parties and party systems change. The United States party system has been changing also, so much, as a matter of fact, that serious question is now raised as to the suitability, centrality, indeed the viability of the system. Students of parties see two major developments in recent years: demobilization (decline in involvement) and dealignment (decline in party identification). And they argue from this that the parties have been losing their "relevance," their critical capacity in responding to social needs and problems. Thus their support by the American public and their ability to maintain the loyalty of citizens in this party system is in decline. Today, many scholars do not see parties as great actors on the American scene. Rather, they see the decomposition, dismantling, and atrophying of parties. It may be, however, that what is occurring is a metamorphosis in the forms of party organization, not a decline. Our parties may be as active and relevant, but in new ways. This question of the changes in parties is the subject of this final evaluation.

The Meaning of Party "Decline"

Parties in all systems undergo "change"—in organizational nature, in types of leadership, in policy direction, in electoral strength, in social group support, and in competitive relationships to other parties. But in the United States the basic concern is over the decline in the *role* and *significance* of parties in the system. Two major foci of concern relate to our conceptions of the "parties in the electorate" and "parties as organizational systems." Thus, one kind of change which observers of the American parties are primarily preoccupied with is the alleged decline in *the public's support relationship* to the party system. This can be variously specified as: (1) a decline in the strength and extent of partisan loyalty and commitment; (2) a decline in interest in elections and voting; and (3) a decline in a feeling that parties are important for policy decisions, and for governing generally.

Linked to these meanings of the decline of parties are the views of scholars that parties have declined as *organizational systems*. Again, there are several ways of operationalizing this concern, and the emphasis can be on the decline in (1) the existence and amount of organization; (2) the power of leaders and agencies in the organization; (3) the capacity and competence (particularly in the professional skills) of the party organizational leadership; (4) the activity of the organization; and (5) the importance of the organization in performing its key functions (such as nominations, campaigns, policy deliberation, decision making)—in comparison to the role of interest groups, mass media, candidate-centered committees or specialists in propaganda.

In essence, the decline conceived of often is in the institutional nature of parties—that the parties as organizational apparatuses have atrophied. The writings of many scholars referred to earlier can be cited to document these observations—among them, Burnham, Wilson, and Kirkpatrick. Thus, Wilson in 1973 argued that parties, as organizations, "have become if anything weaker rather than stronger—parties are more important as labels than as organizations."[1] And to Jeane Kirkpatrick, 1976 provided "fresh evidence of the parties' decreasing capacity to represent voters, mount campaigns, elicit resources, and recruit leaders who were devoted to the institution," and one of her central theses is that the decisions to reform the parties have been responsible for "hastening party deinstitutionalization."[2]

Here is the convergence of two streams of concern or alarm—the alleged decline in the public's support for and interest in parties, and the decline of the party organizations as active and effective entities. Both of these streams emphasize the declining "relevance" of parties for the system, for the society, for the solution to our problems as important instrumentalities for political action, and, in the final analysis, for the lives of Americans as they are affected by government.

It is important to distinguish here between *what is alleged, what is perceived,* and *what is reality.* Scholars may assert that there is no organization, *but* that may be an inference not supported by reality. Or scholars may assert that the public is disillusioned with parties because parties have no important policy role, *but* to support such an argument two types of evidence are important: Is that in fact the public's perception? Is it factually correct that parties have no policy role? In analyzing party decline, then, both *perceptions* and *performance* must be examined. It may very well be argued that what is perceived is more important than what is reality, since attitudes of disillusionment by the public (and by scholars) reflect perceptions. But if there is a divergence between perception and reality, we have only begun to understand the problem and we then need a careful analysis of why. The analytical context for the discussion is suggested by figure 18.1.

Many scholars assume that the situation of Box D in the diagram obtains, and if it does, parties may well be responsible for negative attitudes. But this must yet be demonstrated. If, on the other hand, the conditions of Box C exist, then there is a conflict between perceptions and actual performance. This too needs to be demonstrated and the factors responsible for the disjunction identified. Box A suggests the conditions which many assume to have existed in the past when we had higher turnout, less independence, and so forth. But actually we may have had Box B conditions all along—to secure evidence on this historically is very difficult.[3] In any event, when the "decline" in our parties is discussed it is necessary (1) to document the change in the level of party organizational performance; (2) to document the change

FIGURE 18.1
Evaluations of Parties: Four Basic Types

Perceptions of Party Performance and Relevance	Party Organizational Preference	
	High	*Low*
Positive	A Healthy Condition if It Ever Existed	B Very Possibly What May Have Been True in the Past
Negative	C Basic Conflict	D Party Role in System Negative or Neutral

in the content of public perceptions of parties; (3) to document the extent to which the decline in one is related to the decline in the other; and (4) if the two do not co-vary, to explore explanations for the decline in public affect for parties which may not be linked to party organizational effort. This is a major research task, and the evidence now available and relevant to that task will be presented here. But by no means is all the information needed to enlighten definitively and correctly all aspects of this phenomenon of party decline yet at hand. It is a puzzle which can only partially be pieced together at this point.

A First Major Question: Has Party Organization Activism Declined at the Local Level?

The familiar refrain in commentaries on American parties these days is that the rise of the direct primary and of new campaign technology has meant the loss of control by the party organization, as presumably it existed in the past, over nominations, campaign strategies, candidates, issues, resources, elected leadership, *and* that this has meant "the decline of local party activism" as Robert Agranoff explains.[4] But what is the evidence of the decline in local party activism? None of the scholars making these general assertions have demonstrated that this is the case. In fact, there is evidence to suggest that the opposite may be true. Wolfe's careful analysis of the Center for Political Studies' data from 1952 on indicates that the proportion of the American public who have been contacted by party campaign workers in recent years is much greater than previously (see table 18.1). Whereas in 1952 only 12 percent of the public report contacts, by 1976 it was close to 30 percent; in 1980 it was 24 percent.

TABLE 18.1

Percentage of United States Public Reporting Contacts by Local Party Activists

Party	1952	1956	1972	1976
Democrat	6	11	19	17
Republican	7	11	13	13
	13	22	32	30
	13	22	32	30

SOURCE: Michael Wolfe, "Personal Contact Campaigning in Presidential Elections" (a paper presented at the Annual Meeting of the Midwest Political Science Association, Chicago, April 1979), p. 11a.

What is interesting to note is the extension of such local party contact efforts in all parts of the country, to blacks, as well as whites, and to lower educational groups, as well as to the college educated (see table 18.2). True, those with low socioeconomic status are not as frequently the targets of campaign activists as are those of higher status, but there is some evidence of expansionism in contacts, particularly for blacks and those with a middle (high school) educational status.

TABLE 18.2

Extension of Party Activism Efforts Geographically, Racially, and by Educational Level (as a percentage)

Category	Contacted by Party Canvassers Each Year				Increase
	1952	1956	1972	1976	1952–76
Regions					
South	9	15	18	21	+12
Border	9	16	25	20	+11
Mountain and Far West	20	18	40	36	+16
Northeast	15	17.5	19	30	+15
Mid-Atlantic	12	15	26	28	+16
Midwest	12	20	40.5	32.5	+20.5
Race					
Whites	12	16	28	27	+15
Blacks	6	12	18	18	+12
Educational Level					
Completed college	15	22	33	35	+20
High school	13	22	29	27	+14
Less than high school	10	13	19	16	+6

SOURCE: Michael Wolfe, "Personal Contact Campaigning in Presidential Elections" (A paper presented at the Annual Meeting of the Midwest Political Science Association, Chicago, April 1979), pp. 8a, 6a, 16a. Based on University of Michigan SRC/CPS data.

In this connection it is instructive to look at the results of the 1980 national surveys which also asked all those in the sample if they had been contacted in the campaign. Although there was a slight decline in the overall percentage (to 24.4 percent), the characteristics of those who were contacted are revealing (see table 18.3). The Republican effort was slightly greater in 1980, particularly among conservatives (41 percent), young persons (44 percent) as well as the oldest citizens (41 percent) and, of course, among Republican identifiers. The Democrats seemed to spend more canvassing effort among liberals (46 percent), those with a lower educational status (50 percent) and, of course, among Democratic identifiers (55 percent). What is significant also, however, is that both parties appealed to all groups, including each other's partisans. One-fifth to one-fourth of strong partisans were called on by the opposite party. The same phenomenon holds true for other categories of voters. In the light of the election results perhaps the overall net advantage to the Republicans lies in their greater effort with Independents. They seemed to have contacted about 10 percent more of them than the Democrats did. And since 85 percent of those

TABLE 18.3

Characteristics of Persons Contacted by the Parties and Candidates, 1980

(as a percentage)

Respondents	Total for Group	Contacted by			
		Republicans	Democrats	Both Parties	Other
Contacted in Campaign	24.4	36.4	33.5	21.6	8.4
Ideology					
Liberal	31	23	46	23	
Moderate	25	39	31	22	
Conservative	26	41	22	28	
Party Identification					
Strong Democrat	30	20	55	18	
Weak Democrat	21	36	34	18	
Independent Democrat	21	35	27	27	
Independent	23	42	20	29	
Independent Republican	21	42	36	23	
Weak Republican	27	44	24	24	
Strong Republican	30	53	24	18	
Age					
Young (18–29)	17	44	30	11	
Older	25	33	33	28	
Old	30	33	39	24	
Oldest (65 and over)	29	41	32	17	
Educational Level					
Grade school	17	21	50	14	
High school	22	37	37	16	
College	29	39	26	28	

SOURCE: University of Michigan CPS/NES, 1980.

contacted said they voted (an exaggerated report, but nonetheless the proportion was still high), this extra Republican effort may have been relevant to Republican success.

A great many questions can be asked of these data, including who the canvasser was (whether a party organization person or not), what the content of the contact was, and whether these recalls of contacts are at all reliable. Obviously, many more adult citizens are being contacted now by party and campaign personnel than ever before. Although there is a continuous socioeconomic bias in these efforts, such contacts are reaching out to a larger proportion of blacks and less well-educated people than ever before, and this seems to be going on throughout the country. There has always been much organizational slack in the performance of the key tasks by the local party organization, except in certain big city machines, but there is really no convincing evidence that recently the local party is less active or less efficient than formerly. In fact, the data on Detroit and Los Angeles, comparing local party activity of 1980 with 1956, suggests no decline, as does the Wolfe analysis above.

A Subsidiary Question: Are the Local Party Activists Less Likely to Be Competent Workers than Previously?

Although it may be true that local parties are as active as previously, it is contended that the party activist today is different in two respects—he, or she, is more ideological and less pragmatic, and also less professional (and more amateur). This type of argument uses data particularly about the delegates to the national conventions, relying heavily on the 1972 delegate studies, a year which certainly on the Democratic side was perhaps somewhat abnormal. The Democratic National Convention in 1972 certainly did see what Jeane Kirkpatrick has called a "new breed" of activists—more youth, more black, more women, and presumably more amateur and ideological. But, as Kirkpatrick herself has stated, the 1976 Democratic convention had more delegates with "prior party experience, more who had held party and public office, fewer who were indifferent to winning. . . ."[5] Yet she is still concerned about the presence of activists in both parties who are not loyal to the party, who are candidate-oriented, who have limited professional competence, and who are unrepresentative in social and economic status in relationship to the parties' rank and file. David Broder is similarly concerned, citing figures that governors and congressmen are represented much less at recent Democratic conventions.[6] But in 1980 this trend presumably was altered with the adoption of the new rule that 10 percent of the delegate seats in a state are set aside for elected party leaders.

The American parties have always been wide open structures. They have always had ideologues (a minority) and pragmatists, amateurs and professionals, those intermittently involved and those making a career out of party organizational work. To argue that our parties have changed radically, have declined, because there are today many more nonprofessional, nonpragmatic ideologues than formerly is not substantiated by any trend data available.

Another Subsidiary Question: Is Party Organization at the Local Level Less Important Today?

The point has been made by several writers that the local party organization is less critical today for our parties and for political campaigns, that state and national parties operate independently, that candidates depend less on the local organization, and that the mass media have replaced the local doorbell ringer as the major source of information about politics and the major stimulus to voting. As has been seen in the previous analysis of the research on the media, there can be no question but that since 1952 television particularly is relied on heavily by voters. But this has not meant a decline in the proportion of Americans exposed to the efforts of the local party organization. As for the extent to which candidates rely on the party organization in their districts, the evidence reviewed earlier by no means suggests that the new specialists in campaign technology have over time replaced the local organizations—for registration drives, for money, for mobilization of campaign pesonnel, for "getting out the vote." Scholars of Congress are inclined to emphasize the congressman's relationship to his constituency, and this includes his district party organization, through which he often rose to the top, whose views about politics he shares, and which could run an opposition candidate against him if that organization feels ignored. Again, the evidence on this point is not by any means overwhelming, and the importance of the local organization apparently varies greatly from state to state and from community to community. But to dismiss the local organization as superseded by the mass media or scorned by the candidate-centered campaign or ignored by the incumbent congressman (or state legislator), *particularly as something which has happened recently,* is not supported by the available data.

A Second Major Question: Has Party Organization at the State and National Levels Become Weaker?

Have state and national party organizations declined in power and influence in the role they play in campaigns, leadership recruitment, and policy decisions? Contradictory arguments are advanced. One argument is that there is a nationalization trend and that state parties are losing out. But it is also maintained that the parties have lost control over nominations and campaigns to public relations agencies, professional consultants, and candidate organizations.

The evidence that state and national party organizations have lost power is not conclusive. Thus, the Democratic National Committee has expanded its control over the selection of delegates to the national convention both through the Compliance Review Commission, to which state organizations must submit descriptions of the process they use in selecting delegates, and in 1980, by informing the states that delegates selected in open primaries, not confined to declared Democrats, will not be acceptable at the national convention. The assertion of these two powers alone has meant a modest centralization tendency in American parties. True, those who would have "europeanized" our parties at the Kansas City mini-convention of 1974 by giving the national committee much more authority (over party policy, for example) were defeated. But the national committees have never been centers of party power, and thus recent developments represent, if anything, a slight increment in national committee power, rather than a decline.

As to the question of the decline in the role of the state and national organizations over nominations and campaigns, there is probably no question that some attrition has occurred. In 1980, and for the Democrats in 1976, the national convention did not make the final decision on the presidential nomination. The primaries selected over 70 percent of the delegates, and Reagan and Carter won the majority of the delegates needed for nomination long before the conventions met. This does depreciate the role of state organizations at the national convention—then and now. But, the national convention may still be important in nominations in the future. In the meantime it remains a major plenary body of party decision making—on the platform and on the rules and permanent organization of the party—as well as being a major forum for consensus building and party unity.

As for the role of the national parties in the campaigns for president and vice-president, the national organization was often only peripherally involved and rarely central in the planning and executing of campaign strategy. This role depended on the pleasure of the presidential candidate. Certainly Carter, Nixon, Johnson, Kennedy, to name only a few, did not place the national committee in the center of the campaign operation. It is true that the Federal Election Campaign acts since 1971, by providing public funds for presidential campaigns, most of which are given to the candidate, not to the committee, may appear to have weakened the role of the national committee. Yet, the Republican national organization under Chairman William Brock is credited with a major role in the 1980 presidential victory. Brock worked to renovate state and local organizations, organized training sessions on campaign techniques, the use of the media, and the use of surveys of public opinion, and actually ran a "campaign management college." Above all, large sums of money were collected and funneled through the national organization to United States senatorial, congressional, and state legislature candidates.[7]

A major study of state party organizations recently has concluded that since 1960 the budgets of state organizations have more than tripled and their staffs have increased greatly. The authors conclude, "If state parties were in the undeveloped state ascribed to them by political scientists in the 1950s and early 1960s, they have since developed into relatively strong and durable organizations."[8]

In short, to argue that party organization at the state and national levels has been decisively weakened in recent years is difficult to substantiate, and such claims assume strong parties in the past. In reality this country has always had a decentralized and stratarchical party organizational system, and some would argue that that is the strength of our parties. It has forced parties to be responsible to local interests, to adapt to local differences, to force upper-level party structures to be truly consultative of lower-level structures and to maintain, thus, a minimum of rapport in a very heterogeneous system. If anything, the national committee has more power today, and the party caucus in Congress is asserting its authority more than it has for many years. The decline in our parties, therefore, is difficult to demonstrate, empirically or in terms of a historical perspective.

Third Basic Question: Has There Been a Decline in the Public's Affect for, and Confidence in, the Parties?

This may turn out to be the critical question in the party decline controversy. For, in the last analysis, it is *the* test of the viability of any particular party and of any particular party system. If there is a continuous decline in the public's positive evaluation of parties, rooted in disaffection over party capability and performance, then a withdrawal of public support will occur which is meaningful and difficult to reverse, a concern about which empirical evidence is available.

There are several components of this concern which are separable. First, to what extent is there a change in the extent to which the public *thinks* in "party content" terms at all? If "party" is less salient to people, something they spontaneously talk and think about less frequently, that in itself is a significant development. The little data available on this matter indicates that, indeed, such seems to be the case today (see table 18.4).[9] Surveys show a decline in the 1970s in the public's

TABLE 18.4

Measures of the Public's Interest and Confidence in Parties (as a percentage)

Interest	1952	1956	1960	1964	1968	1972	1976	1980
Use of "party" in evaluating candidates (all citizens)	46	41	41	34	40	24		
Use of "party" in evaluating candidates (identifiers)	52	46	47	37	44	27		
Positive evaluation of own or both parties	74	72	74	64	59	49	49	50
Feel parties "help a good deal in making the government pay attention" to the public				41	36	26	17	28
Do not mention one or the other of the parties as doing the best job on a problem the respondent considers most important (that is, the percentage who are neutral or indifferent)			38	34	48	51	54	50

SOURCES: Norman H. Nie, Sidney Verba and John R. Petrocik, *The Changing American Voter* (Cambridge: Harvard University Press, 1976), pp. 56, 58, 171; Jack Dennis, "Trends in Public Support for the American Party System," in Jeff Fishel, ed., *Parties and Elections in Anti-Party Age* (Bloomington: Indiana University Press, 1978), p. 10; Martin Wattenberg, "The Decline of Political Partisanship in America: Negativity or Neutrality?" *American Political Science Review* (December 1981); all data based on University of Michigan CPS/SRC/NES.

inclination to evaluate candidates in "party" terms, a finding that holds true for party identifiers also. Second, when people do think of parties, they are less positive in their general evaluations of them than previously—a steady decline since the 1960 election, when 71 percent were positive, to 49 percent by 1976. Third, this does not necessarily mean an increase in negative evaluations but seems to be associated with more neutrality in the way people view parties. When people are asked, "Which party can do the best job in dealing with the most important problem(s), as you perceive those problems?" more citizens are inclined to say, "the parties are about the same," or "no party" or "neither party." And this is perhaps the most significant development of all—that close to 50 percent of the public today has great difficulty in identifying one or the other of the parties as best capable of solving our problems. In 1960 the proportion was 38 percent. These are the people who seem more inclined to stay home on election day.

The decline in the relevance of parties for the solution of problems may well be the nub of the matter. The general decline in affect for parties may be the result of a change in the image of the role of parties—from positive to neutral—in the policy process. It is not so troublesome that large proportions of the public over the years do not perceive clear-cut differences between the parties. That has been going on for years—the United States studies in the 1950s revealed that less than 20 percent of strong identifiers saw important differences between the parties on issues.[10] Rather, what is new and significant is the declining relevance in public cognitions of parties combined with an increased neutralism and indifference to parties. This in turn may be linked (although scholars differ on this) to a decline in the correlation of partisanism to the vote—a drop after 1952 from .50 to .14 in 1976. To understand why that has occurred would lead to a closer understanding of the meaning of the decline of parties.

The "puzzle" as it has emerged thus far is: Compared to most other countries, the United States is unsurpassed in level of political activity and in amount of party identification, but far down in rank in voting turnout (54 percent in the presidential election of 1980, compared to 75 percent or more in most European countries and also Japan). Further, political activity is not declining in the United States, nor is party effort declining on the basis of the reports from the respondents in surveys since 1952. The parties are contacting a larger proportion of the citizens. At the same time our politics seem more competitive than before (closer elections in many parts of the country, including the South). There is more issue awareness and ideological involvement with politics recently which, at least in the interpretations of some scholars analyzing these data, indicates citizens are linking their issue positions to the vote more than they did before. In all of this, however, the image of parties has been declining, is less positive; parties are seen as less relevant to problem solving. Thus, the "puzzle" (see figure 18.2).

This poses the "why" question in a particular theoretical context. It suggests that the way *the image* of political parties is communicated recently, as having relevance for today's issues and problems, is changing, and this in turn may be partly responsible for nonvoting. Further, it suggests that all this is going on *because of, or despite,* the activities of political party organizational personnel and activists. It also suggests that the type of politics which interests people these days and with which parties and their activists must be engaged is different—special issue and special interest politics. Above all, it suggests that there should be a careful examination of *what is being communicated to the public about parties* and *by whom.* What is being communicated by party workers, by party organization leaders, by candidates for office, by incumbents in office, by television, by newspapers and other mass media, by opinion leaders, by interest group leaders? If the image of parties is declining despite a relatively consistent level of organizational contact work and political activity, then it is not the inactivity which is at fault, but *the message.*

Much more research needs to be done on the question of why, before there can be any definitive answers. A configuration of forces seems to be at work, which can be summarized in the following terms.

Party canvassing and contact efforts may today emphasize the party less frequently and less effectively than in the past. There is little reliable research on this question, but it is strongly suggested by Wolfe's analysis. He reports that those who were contacted in the fifties by party workers reported more frequently that the appeal was a "pure party" appeal than in the sixties—26 percent in 1956 compared to 7 percent in 1964 (the only times when such data were reported for national cross sections).[11] Wolfe argues that parties may be adapting to the changing conditions of our political environment, responding "to the electorate's growing willingness to split votes between parties," thus requiring canvassing efforts which more and more solicit votes for candidates rather than parties. This fits in with the argument that the ad hoc candidate-centered campaign is replacing the party-orient-

FIGURE 18.2
Relationship of Party Decline to Party Involvement

A. A Decline in Positive Evaluations of Parties, Particularly as Problem Solvers *Plus* B. Decreasing Voting Turnout	*At the Same Time There Is*	1. Much Party Activity 2. Still Relatively High Party Identification 3. No Decline in *Personal* Political Activity 4. More Issue Politics

ed campaign. The evidence, however, to prove that campaigns in the past were not as candidate-centered as today is not really available.

Party canvassing efforts can always have, and in the past have had, negative, as well as positive, effects. This has been suggested by previous research, including the reference to possible boomerang effects in stirring up the opposition. One study of the 1952 presidential election suggested that "the workers of each party helped the cause of the rival party."[12] This occurred because the parties' efforts sometimes activated the "wrong" voters or could not persuade some of those they activated to support the party or antagonized some of those they had activated. The evidence on this point—that is, the possible incitement of negative reactions by those canvassed by the parties—is documented to some extent by the author's study in Detroit in 1956.[13] Although the positive aspects of local party organizational work are also clearly indicated in that study, certain negative consequences suggested by the data must not overlooked.

These negative effects should not be exaggerated, because there are many indications that local party contact work does pay off—in stronger partisanship, more knowledge about politics, higher interest in political affairs, and a greater source of political efficacy, for example.[14] But it is possible that recently, despite a high level of local party activism, the image of the party communicated by such efforts has also produced indifference, neutrality, and independence in the public's view of parties.

A second point to keep in mind is that the way party leaders and candidates think about parties and talk about parties in their appeals to the public may be a major factor in the public's image of parties. If the leadership plays down parties, if candidates de-emphasize their party affiliation or seek to maintain aloofness from the party organization, then indeed the public's rejection of parties will be encouraged. Earlier studies of local party organizations have revealed that they were a diverse, multiple-motivated group of leaders, with no more than 50 percent consciously talking about party loyalty as a major factor in their involvement in party work. From 10 percent to 20 percent felt ideological or issue-oriented concerns were very important; another 20 percent were initially interested in trying for a personal career in politics or in improving business contacts; and many were involved because of social friendships and contacts.[15] When these precinct leaders were asked whether they ever felt that they would be justified in voting for candidates of the other party, up to 50 percent of the Democrats and over 70 percent of the Republicans said yes.[16] Thus, the data from this research suggest that local party leaders have always been less than 100 percent loyal to the party and less than 100 percent reliable as communicators of positive affect toward party in their contacts with the public.

The point at issue now, however, is whether there is evidence of an accentuation of party criticism and disloyalty among party leaders today. No systematic study has been done on this question, but some recent findings are suggestive. In a study by Kirkpatrick of the delegates to the Republican and Democratic National conventions in 1972 questions were asked concerning the delegates' incentives for party work, as well as their trust in government. The results indicate the variability in positive support for their party and for the government. Table 18.5 reveals a decline in party loyalty incentives as one moves from the older to younger political generations—that is, those delegates who entered politics long ago were more likely to be party oriented in their responses. The delegates who entered politics from 1968 on appear to be less concerned about supporting the party, less committed to unifying the party, and more involved with issues and party reform. Further, what the study reveals, which is disturbing, is the high level of cynicism about government among delegates (see table 18.6). Even among Republicans, who were in power at the time, there was considerable cynicism. These data are from 1972 and may not be representative of 1976 and 1980. The key point, however, suggested by such data is that if these party leaders are low in trust and communicate such attitudes to the public, then the decline in the public's attraction to, and affect for, parties begins to be understandable.

The third approach to explaining the decline in the public's positive images about parties is to lay the blame on the mass media, including not only television but also radio, newspapers, and other printed media. There has been some research on the role of the media in campaigns. The extent of the research directly related to the question of the impact of media content on the voter's images of political parties is much less, however. Some recent studies are more pertinent and do indeed suggest that the mass media role may be significant.

TABLE 18.5

Attitudes Toward "Party" by Delegates at National Conventions, 1972
(as a percentage)

	By Era of Original Party Involvement				By Presidential Preference (Democrats)	
	Pre–1945	1946–59	1960–67	1968–72	McGovern	Humphrey
Incentives for Involvement						
Support for the party	84	81	69	42	44	89
Civic responsibility	87	84	80	66	68	87
N=	(300)	(752)	(766)	(521)	(881)	(195)

SOURCE: Jeane Kirkpatrick, *The New Presidential Elite* (New York: Russell Sage, 1976), pp. 100, 126.

TABLE 18.6

Comparisons on Statements by Convention Delegates Regarding Trust in Government, 1972 (as a percentage)

	Agreeing to Statements		
Statements	McGovern Delegates	Humphrey Delegates	All Republican Delegates
Government wastes a lot of money	68	60	71
Government is a run for the benefit of a few big interests	91	63	21
Quite a few people in government don't know what they are doing	57	36	39

SOURCE: Jeane Kirkpatrick, *The New Presidential Elite* (New York: Russell Sage, 1976), pp. 176–77.

Much of the public is highly exposed to television and newspapers during campaigns as the only real source of political information, ideas, and images. Television has, since the 1960s, gradually become the major source, replacing newspapers, for certain types of voters, particularly those in the lower economic brackets. Both television and newspapers are extensively utilized and thus must be primary sources of political awareness. Certain scholars, such as Michael Robinson, have argued that persons relying on television have a lower sense of political efficacy than those relying on newspapers, radio, or magazines for their political information.[17] In a special study of the television coverage of the New Hampshire presidential primary of 1976, he argues that his data reveal that television produced misperceptions about the meaning of the primary, particularly by exaggerating its importance. And he infers from this that this type of reporting contributes to the "continuous decay of the American party system."[18] Robinson argues that we have a "videomalaise," contending that research has demonstrated "a relationship between exposure to television . . . and feelings of political malaise," partly because of the "anti-institutional theme in network news programs." He concludes that "television news . . . often injects a negativistic, contentious, or anti-institutional bias . . . [which] evokes images of American politics and social life which are inordinately sinister and despairing."[19]

Securing hard data on the impact of the media to support or refute such charges is difficult. In Thomas Patterson's book on the role of the mass media in the 1976 election he presents new findings on trends in media coverage since 1940, when Lazarsfeld, Berelson, and Gaudet did their pioneer study. He documents the following significant developments.[20]

1. The press (television and major newspapers) in 1976, compared to 1940, emphasized much more the competitive struggle between candidates. In 1940, issue positions, leadership qualities, and group commitments were more emphasized. The balance has shifted, in fact has been reversed, from 35 percent of the media attention in 1940 going to the fight between candidates and over 50 percent to issues and leadership, to just the reverse of this in 1976.

2. The journalistic model which tends "*not* to view the election primarily as a contest over the directions of national policy and leadership," but rather "as a power struggle between the candidates" pervades all aspects of the presidential campaign coverage. This was clearly apparent in the coverage of the presidential primaries—with the winner in one state such as New Hampshire (Carter, with 28 percent of the vote) projected as a national winner. His press coverage was much more extensive than anyone else (2,600 lines in *Time* and *Newsweek*, for example, for Carter, but only 96 lines for Udall, who got 23 percent of the vote).

3. The voters' response to such coverage (based on a panel survey of 1,200 respondents nationally) is significant particularly in two respects. One, the voters in 1976 were less concerned about the candidates' policy position and qualifications than in 1940. In their conversations in 1940 about the election, 67 percent of the voters talked about policy, but in 1976 only 34 percent were "concerned with substance, while 50 percent focused on the contest, mostly in direct response to news stories about the race." Second, the knowledge level of voters was less in 1976 than in elections in the 1940s—fewer people (25 percent compared to 37 percent earlier) knew the issue positions of the candidates in August of election year. Patterson concludes, "Although the press and the political party both serve to link candidates with voters, these two intermediaries are very different in kind." The press is in "the news business" and thus "simply is not an adequate guide to political choice."[21]

A final piece of evidence directly linking the press content to public disaffection with the system is the product of a complicated analysis by Miller, Goldenberg, and Erbring of the 1974 national election. The survey of the public in that election was combined with a content analysis of the front pages of the daily newspapers read by these respondents—ninety-four newspapers throughout the country during a sample ten days in October and November preceding the election. The results permitted analysis of the linkage between the type of newspaper content (extent of media criticism of institutions), the actuality and intensity of voter exposure to such media content, and the public's disaffection with the system. This was then a more rigorous test of the relevance of media coverage.

This research revealed that a few newspapers (6 percent), in their front-page stories praised our system, a larger proportion (31 percent) were critical, and the remainder (63 percent) were neither of the above. What was significant for our discussion here was finding that political parties were particular targets of criticism. Thus, the authors found:

TABLE 18.7
Critical Newspaper Coverage
(as a percentage)

Stories About	Percentage Which Were Critical
Political parties	70
Congress	42
Administration	40
State and local government	34
Supreme Court	25

SOURCE: Arthur H. Miller, Edie N. Goldenberg, and Lutz Erbring, "Type-set Politics: Impact of Newspapers on Public Confidence," *American Political Science Review* 73 (March 1979), pp. 67–84.

This was 1974, of course, and the Democrats were in conflict with President Ford in the Watergate aftermath. Nevertheless, the *relative negativism* concerning parties stands out. What is, finally, extremely significant in this study is the finding that political disaffection (of the public) was significantly related to newspaper criticism in 1974, even after controlling for education and media exposure. Further, a test was made to determine to what extent the policy dissatisfaction of citizens or their negative attitude toward particular incumbents ("incumbency effect") influenced results. They found that media content had an independent role in influencing public attitudes. The authors conclude, "Readers of papers containing a higher degree of negative criticism directed at politicians and political institutions were more distrustful of government ... [and] higher levels of exposure ... [yielded] higher levels of cynicism and feelings of inefficacy...."[22]

Implicit in such research is the clear implication that public feelings toward institutions are influenced by what the media communicate. Parties as key institutions are often treated poorly by the media. The criticism of our politics by the media appears clearly linked to cynicism, and this in turn may well exact its toll on the public's view of parties. Because of negative stories about parties and the cumulative impact of negative reporting a frame of reference emerges in terms of which the citizen judges what the party organizations and party leaders do, and this affects the nature of his identification with and belief in the party system.

Party Reform

Since the beginnings of parties in the United States, scholars and politicians have talked about party reform, with many proposals being advanced over the years. Today there seems to be a preoccupation with the subject of reform, because of concern about party decline. Any discussion of reform cannot ignore the conditions of our parties and the strong evidence that the public has become less positive in its evaluations of parties. There are three approaches to the charges of party decline: the sanguine approach (nothing much of a substantial nature has happened, and the public will return to party support soon at the same levels as in the past); the alarmist approach (the party system is already disintegrating and will be replaced by a new type of party politics); and the incremental change approach (modest changes have and will occur in the party system and the parties must and will adapt to the new conditions of American society, gradually modifying our parties but not radically changing the system). It is highly likely that the latter scenario is taking place. The questions really posed are: What changes should be encouraged? What should the aim of "incremental" reform be? What is feasible given the restraints of our political culture?

A great deal of party reform has occurred in the American system. The nation has not been irrevocably locked into one type of system with no movement toward change. A survey of the history of American party politics notes that the system has been modified considerably. Austin Ranney has described these changes, in historical sequence, in detail.[23] Beginning with the changes in the party structure at the national level, particularly the demise of the congressional caucus in the 1820s as *the* authority in the nominating process, and then the adoption of the national delegate convention in the 1830s, we have proceeded at subsequent periods in our national history to change the organizational character and control relationships in our parties significantly. The progressive movement from 1890 to 1920 was a period of legal regulation of parties, the adoption of nonpartisan elections, and the advent of the direct primary. After World War II we moved in the direction of making party conventions more representative and attempted to strengthen the party organs at the national level. Ranney suggests that we have had three types of reformers: the regulators (the most influential group of reformers who feel parties are not private associations and their internal organizations and processes must be carefully controlled by law); the representative party structure people (who focus primarily on making parties reflect rank-and-file desires and characteristics), and the responsible party people (who wish to make parties programmatic entities).

All three types of reformers have been active in the last thirty years. The reform proposals and actual changes adopted concerning the party organizations in Congress, the national committees, the national conventions, the presidential nominating process, the state direct primary systems, the election system, and party finance have been discussed in detail. What is important to remember now is that considerable reforms have indeed been accomplished. The Democratic party now has a new party charter, adopted in 1974, which provides for a new National Committee of 350 members, a Judicial Council to review and approve plans for the selection of delegates to the national convention, a Finance Council to fund party activities, a National Education and Training Council to implement plans to "reach every young citizen as they enter the electorate," recommended "mini-conventions" every two years, banned discriminatory practices and endorsed affirmative action programs, and among other things, has urged the national party to develop policy positions acceptable to both leaders and supporters.[24] The new National Democratic Committee has asserted itself as to the procedures to be used by states in the selection of delegates to the national convention, and the courts are generally inclined to support the national party. So, change in the Democratic party *has* occurred at the national level—in Congress (the new role for the caucus since 1973), in the composition and work of the national committee, and in the convention.

Similarly, the Republican party has been making changes. The 1972 national convention adopted a series of reforms opening up the delegate selection process and the meetings dealing with delegation selection, as well as a broadening of representation of the party's executive committee. In addition, affirmative action procedures were incorporated into the rules of some state Republican organizations. And after 1972 the Rule 29 Committee dealt with the question of how to make the Republican party more open to minorities, as well as how to prevent the recurrence of Watergate-type abuses in the use of money in elections.[25] The Republicans had much internal conflict over representational and affirmative action reform, and by 1980 these conflicts had not yet been resolved. For example, there apparently were fewer blacks at the 1980 convention than previously, but the representation and role of women was to be increased significantly (for example, in 1980 they said that 50 percent of the delegates should be female).

Despite these reforms, the parties have not re-established themselves before the American public as strong, relevant, policy-oriented, effective structures, according to the data on the decline in public affect and support for parties. There are those who will argue that the parties are more nationalized than ever before, with the allocation of more authority to the national organs.[26] There are those who see parties as more competitive than ever before in the fifty states, and view this as "the most encouraging development for the cause of responsible party government."[27] There are those who remark that national conventions (and committees) are more representative than ever before. But despite such progress, the decline of parties is still with us, and for some *this decline is the result of reforms*. Thus, Jeane Kirkpatrick argues that the "trend toward party decomposition is still in process" *and* that "the most important sources of party decomposition are the *decisions* taken by persons attempting to reform the parties."[28]

It is difficult to demonstrate the validity or falsity of this position. There is no question that primaries have contributed to the weakening of the party organization's role in recruitment and that recent campaign finance reform is more candidate-oriented than organization-oriented. But whether these and other reforms are responsible for the decline in public affect for parties is arguable. First, note that the weakening of party organizations has been going on for some time via the primary (if that is the cause) but the decline in the public's attitudes is relatively recent. Also, there are areas in the United States where the parties retain the support of the public and party organization has not atrophied, despite these reforms. And, finally, the recent countertrends in reform, to strengthen party organization at the national level, seem to have had no significant effect in reversing negative public attitudes. Thus, the direct causal linkage between reforms and the decline in public support is not easily demonstrable. What has been happening is the result of a more complex set of forces, which probably has to do with the way in which the party organizations, leaders, and mass media communicate with the public.

The need for more effective party structures is as important today in the United States as in the past—party structures which are perceived as relevant intermediary structures between citizens and government. The controversy has been over what type of party system *should* we, and *can* we, move toward in order to make parties more effective linkage structures. One such model which has evoked a tremendous amount of advocacy, as well as opposition, over the years is what has become known as the "responsible party model." This model was specified in detail by a committee of the American Political Science Association in 1950.[29] This committee's report took the basic position that our party system was inadequate "in sustaining well-considered programs and providing broad public support for them," that "with growing public cynicism . . . the nation may eventually witness the disintegration of the two major parties" and the possible emergence of "extremist parties." Further, the authors argued that we needed a party system which is "democratic, responsible and effective." This meant (1) "parties which bring forth programs to which they commit themselves"; (2) parties with "sufficient internal cohesion to carry out these programs"; and (3) the basic concept of the "responsibility of both parties to the general public, as enforced in election," as well as, "responsibility of party leaders to the party membership." Thus, *program, cohesion, and accountability* were primary objectives of the responsible party reformers in 1950.

Some specific reforms were recommended by the Committee:[30]

A. *Organizational Changes*
   1. A national party council of fifty members with power to adopt platforms, recommend candidates for Congress, discipline state and local parties deserting the national platform;
   2. Professional staffs for the national committee;
   3. National committees more representative of party strength;
   4. Smaller national conventions, but more frequently held (every two years).
B. *Platform Writing and Implementing Process*
   1. Members of Congress active in writing the platform;
   2. The party council to adopt and interpret it;
   3. State party platform to be adopted *after* national platform is adopted;
   4. Platform binding on all party office-holders;
   5. Members of Congress deprived of committee chairmanships if they opposed the party program.
C. *Congressional Parties*
   1. All Senate and House leadership positions to be consolidated in one leadership committee;
   2. The caucus of party members to be more important, to meet more frequently, and the decisions of caucus to be binding.
D. *Nominations*
   1. Closed primaries;
   2. More pre-primary conventions;
   3. A national presidential primary.

These were the 1950 proposals. Many people were worried then about the directions of our parties. But few of these reforms have been adopted. The most important ones perhaps to be accepted are the moves in the Democratic party to closed primaries, to more representative conventions and committees, and the mini-convention every two years, by the Democrats. But this is a far cry from moving toward the responsible party doctrine. The idea of cohesive, program-oriented, disciplined, centralized parties with (1) candidates selected because of their commitment to programs; (2) party workers recruited on the basis of programs; (3) voters identifying with parties and supporting them primarily on the basis of programs is a conception of the American party system which clearly, in its major outlines, has not been embraced and is probably not attainable.

Rather, we have continued to work with what is often called the pragmatic model of the party system. Such a system consists of parties which are moderate, eclectic, and somewhat opportunist in ideology.

Organizationally such parties are decentralized and internally pluralized, containing factions and subgroups often in considerable conflict over programs (conflicts which are papered over often, but not resolved). These are open structures (some would say wide open) with great diversity in the characteristics and orientations of the working cadre of activists. Protest is tolerated, and the insurgents seldom expelled. There is much local autonomy, stratarchy, and respect for adjustment to local conditions. Such parties are presumably heterodox and adaptive structures—not consensual, not monolithic, not closed, nonhierarchical, and not rigid in control relationships. And this may well mean also that they will often not be very efficient! These are the elements in the so-called pragmatic model which approximates what we have in the United States. Many believed in 1950 that our system was different from Britain's or the Continent's, where presumably the responsible party model prevailed. But most observers today do not accept this, and British scholars are the first to argue that such a position cannot be substantiated and is, in large measure, a misconception of the British party system.

In any efforts at major party reform one must remember, first, that our pragmatic model has emerged after a long history of political development, after much experimentation with a variety of parties and party organizational systems. It is part of our political culture and constrained by many elements of that culture: our populism, our disinterest in strict discipline, our acceptance of duopolistic competition, our dispersion of power, our structural openness and tolerance of protest, our eclecticism in ideology, and our capacity for volatile electoral change. As our party system has evolved, particularly since the Civil War, we have come to appreciate certain virtues of that system. By and large it has been a stable system, maintaining an equilibrium of power between two major parties, strongly competitive, but nonpolarized and not extremist—a dynamic and open system, yet stable. Ours is a system which has demonstrated considerable consensus, but not a stagnant consensus for the most part. While competitive in orientation, it has been also integrative in function. And it has permitted us to get things done—to produce great leaders, great laws, an affluent economy, a society as free and just as any.

What then do we say about reform? Clearly some reform actions are necessary, and any system however successful must adapt to changing conditions in its society. If there is evidence, as there is, of a decline in public support for the parties—in the vitality of the organizations, and in their functional relevance—then we should seriously consider change and reform. But we should not delude ourselves into thinking that we can move very close to the responsible party model, although we can work toward certain of its proposals. There are empirical difficulties in implementing the responsible party model, as well as cultural constraints. Evron Kirkpatrick has questioned the two key assumptions in the 1950 American Political Science Association report that our parties can formulate unified programs and enforce them, and that our voters can and will act primarily on the basis of their knowledge of the policy stands of the parties.[31] These are difficult empirical problems. And combined with the cultural constraints, the probabilities of reform seem well-night impossible. And yet, the reality of "decline," of dealignment, nonvoting, and disaffection must be faced. The organizational strength and functional performance of our parties must be supported and encouraged.

The following proposals are made as reform "directions" or goals toward which to work. They are advanced in the spirit and belief that change is necessary, that our parties must adapt to changed conditions, and that change is possible.

1. More *coherent policy leadership* is necessary at all levels of our parties. Not that we have no such leadership, for, as Broder notes, most of the key issues in our politics in recent years have been decided in Congress on partisan votes. "Party lines and party loyalties play more of a role in decision making of Congress than we sometimes imagine."[32] Yet, the image people have is one of decline in the party's role in the policy process. Anthony King noted in his discussion of Western systems ten years ago a "general decline" of parties as bearers of ideology and a concomitant decline everywhere in their role in policy formation."[33] And our empirical analysis of the public's attitudes toward parties in the United States reveals that the public is less inclined to see parties as having solutions to the "most important problem" people see confronting the society. There must be visible evidence of a more coherent party leadership working together on policy questions and clarifying policy alternatives. This can and should occur at the national committee level, in Congress, in national conventions, and in the state and local organizations also.

2. We need party organizations which are more *deliberative* (and deliberating) on questions of policy and leadership. Anyone associated with American parties recognizes that all too seldom do we spend time being informed about the factual background of the issues of the day, and debating these issues openly. The party as a discussion forum is something we have lost sight of recently. If we do anything at all, we are preoccupied at the local level with organizational strategy, personality conflicts, planning for social occasions, training in campaign techniques, and the collection of signatures for petition campaigns. We need to see the organization as a place where issues are debated, by the rank and file as well as by the top leadership. Broder has suggested the "two conventions" idea, "if we want to get more content into our politics" at the national level. He proposes in the presidential year to have one convention for nominations, and the second, later in the year, would "thresh out, with the nominees, the program on which

the party would run." He proposes that the second convention should include a good proportion of the sitting senators, representatives, governors, mayors, and all other party office holders who should have direct responsibility for the party program.[34]

3. Parties have to develop *better means of communicating* effectively with the public. The public images of parties are less positive than ever, and this may be due to what parties communicate, as well as *how* they communicate. American parties are notoriously weak in this regard, compared to British and European parties. Our national parties do only a limited amount of direct comunication with the voters between elections. But, more important, it is what the party tells the voters in its canvassing contacts, and what party leaders running for office or in office tell the voters in their mailings or speeches which influences considerably what the public thinks of the parties.

4. *The local organization* needs to be strengthened and made more societally relevant. There is much organizational slack at the grass roots, where politics comes home to people. There is no evidence really of a decline in the efforts of our local organizations. But the meaning and relevance of what the parties do at the local level appears to have changed. We need well-trained activists at the local level participating democratically in the local organization's decisions; discussing and debating and adopting the policy positions of the party; helping select candidates for local office; and communicating upward to party leaders, and downward to the public. In short, we need to implement the concept of the local organization as consisting of activists with rights, responsibilities, and meaningful roles, communicating to the mass public the primacy of parties for their lives. If party politics could be made interesting, exciting, socially attractive to citizens *and*, more important, if citizens could see party politics as relevant for their lives through the local organization, then we could reverse the negative and apathetic images of parties which now are "the pictures in their heads."

These are goal directions in which we could and should move, without expecting to change the party system completely. They are proposals which move us toward more policy coherence and organizational responsibility. If there is a weakness in our system today, it is not that we have too much organizational control and leadership, but too little. There are obviously other reforms which should be sought—for which this book has argued at other points—in Congress, party leadership, presidential nominations, state party organization, campaign techniques, and finance. But in all of this our major principles and objectives should be kept firmly in mind. Primarily we seek to make our parties more basic and useful instruments for the popular control of government, for the solution of social problems, and for the achievement of system integration. They have been functionally central for the achievement of these purposes in the past. Despite their defects they continue today to be major instruments for democratic government in this nation. With necessary reforms we can make them even more central to the governmental process and to the lives of American citizens. Eighty years ago Lord James Bryce, after studying our party system, said, "In America the great moving forces are the parties. The government counts for less than in Europe, the parties count for more...."[35] If our citizens and their leaders wish it, American parties, will still be the "great moving forces" of our system.

NOTES

Chapter 1

1. Elmer E. Schattschneider, *Party Government* (New York: Rinehart, 1942), p. 1.
2. Samuel Huntington, *Political Order in Changing Societies* (New Haven: Yale University Press, 1968), pp. 89, 91–92.
3. Avery Leiserson, *Parties and Politics* (New York: Alfred A. Knopf, 1958), p. 35. For the most recent discussion of linkage see Kay Lawson ed., *Political Parties and Linkage* (New Haven: Yale University Press, 1980).
4. Jeff Fishel, ed., *Parties and Elections in an Anti-Party Age* (Bloomington: Indiana University Press, 1978), p. xvi.
5. Kenneth Janda, *A Conceptual Framework for the Comparative Analysis of Political Parties* (Beverly Hills: Sage, 1970), p. 83.
6. Frank Sorauf, *Party Politics in America* (Boston: Little, Brown, 1967), p. 18.
7. See, for example, Thomas Hodgkin, *African Political Parties* (London: Penguin, 1961), p. 146; and David E. Apter, *The Politics of Modernization* (Chicago: University of Chicago Press, 1965), p. 183.
8. Max Weber, *From Max Weber: Essays in Sociology*, trans. Hans Gerth and C. W. Mills (New York: Oxford University Press, 1946), pp. 194–95.
9. Charles Merriam and Harold F. Gosnell, *The American Party System* (New York: Macmillan, 1922), p. 3.
10. Gabriel Almond and G. B. Powell, Jr., *Comparative Politics: System, Process, and Policy,* 2nd ed. (Boston: Little, Brown, 1978), pp. 198–205.
11. V. O. Key, Jr., *Southern Politics* (New York: Knopf, 1949), p. 15.
12. See Anthony Downs, *An Economic Theory of Democracy* (New York: Harper & Row, 1965), pp.24–31, for the basic model of parties.
13. V. O. Key, Jr., *Politics, Parties and Pressure Groups*, 5th ed. (New York: T. Y. Crowell, 1964), pp. 222–25.
14. Schattschneider, *Party Government*, p. 1.
15. Leon D. Epstein, *Political Parties in Western Democracies* (New York: Praeger, 1967), p. 315.
16. Aristotle, *Politics* (quoted in Robert Dahl, *A Preface to Democratic Theory* [Chicago: University of Chicago Press, 1956]), p. 34.
17. Alexis de Toqueville, *Democracy in America* (cited in Dahl, *Preface*, p. 35).
18. See introduction by Seymour M. Lipset to M. Ostrogorski, *Democracy and the Organization of Political Parties* (New York: Doubleday, Anchor, 1964), p. xxii.
19. J. A. Schumpeter, *Capitalism, Socialism, and Democracy* (New York: Harper, 1950), p. 269.
20. Dahl, *Preface*, p. 137.
21. Ibid., p. 145.
22. Peter Bachrach, *The Theory of Democratic Elitism* (Boston: Little, Brown, 1967), p. 101.
23. Huntington, *Political Order*, p. 401.
24. Ibid.
25. Robert A. Dahl, *Pluralist Democracy in the U.S.* (Chicago: Rand McNally, 1967), p. 244.
26. *Ibid.*, p. 24.
27. Seymour M. Lipset, *Political Man* (New York: Doubleday, 1960), p. 24.
28. Dahl, *Preface*, p. 132.

29. Huntington, *Political Order*, pp. 90–91.

30. James Bryce, *The American Commonwealth* (New York: Macmillan, 1916), p. 3.

31. Key, *Parties*, p. 9.

32. Samuel Huntington and Barrington Moore, *Authoritarian Politics in Modern Society* (New York: Basic Books, 1970), p. 11.

33. W. D. Burnham, *Critical Elections and the Mainsprings of American Politics* (New York: Norton, 1970), pp. 130–133.

34. William Chambers, *Political Parties in a New Nation* (New York: Oxford University Press, 1963), p. 14.

35. Apter, *Modernization*, p. 179.

Chapter 2

1. A valuable review of the arguments pro and con is presented in Ronald P. Formisano, "Deferential-Participant Politics: The Early Republic's Political Culture, 1789–1840," *The American Political Science Review* 68 (June 1974), pp. 473–87. Formisano argues that early events and activities "did not constitute purposive party building" (p. 476) and the evidence of activity in these early days was "incipient party-like behavior" which "Burnham correctly characterized . . . as 'pre-party' " (p. 486). Other scholars have been somewhat more inclined to see 1790–1800 as the formative party era.

2. *The Federalist*, no. 10.

3. Richard Hofstadter, *The Idea of a Party System* (Berkeley: University of California Press, 1969). Franklin is quoted on p. 2.

4. Ibid., pp. 1–2.

5. William Chambers, *Political Parties in a New Nation: The American Experience 1776–1809* (New York: Oxford University Press, 1963), p. 32.

6. See particularly Ibid., chs. 1–3, for a description of these developments. See also Joseph Charles, *The Origins of the American Party System* (New York: Harper & Row, 1956); and Hofstadter, *Party System*, chs. 1–3.

7. Chambers, *Political Parties*, pp. 64–65.

8. Ibid., p. 93.

9. Ibid., p. 75.

10. Hofstadter, *Party System*, pp. 88–89.

11. Chambers, *Political Parties*, p. 32.

12. Samuel Huntington, *Political Order in Changing Societies* (New Haven: Yale University Press, 1968), pp. 412–20.

13. Gabriel Almond, "Comparative Political Systems," *Journal of Politics* 18 (1956): 391–409; Sidney Verba, "Comparative Political Culture," in Lucian W. Pye and Sidney Verba, eds., *Political Culture and Political Development* (Princeton: Princeton University Press, 1965), p. 518.

14. Chambers, *Political Parties*, p. 145. I have relied heavily on the analysis of Chambers in his lucid discussion of this early period.

15. Robert A. Dahl, ed., *Political Oppositions in Western Democracies* (New Haven: Yale University Press, 1966), p. 333 (quoted in Hofstadter, *Party System*, pp. 7–8).

16. Chambers, *Political Parties*, p. 149.

17. Quoted in Ibid., p. 4.

18. Ibid., p. 89.

19. Ibid., p. 157.

20. Ibid., p. 155.

21. Ibid., p. 165.

22. Ibid., pp. 32–33.

23. William Chambers and Walter D. Burnham, *The American Party Systems* (New York: Oxford University Press, 1967). They also suggest there may be a "cyclic" characteristic to these party eras—that each lasts thirty years or so, each ends in a crisis of realignment, each period accomplishes certain goals, and then a new period seems to be necessary to meet the needs of American society. See pp. 29–30, 288–289 for a discussion of these patterns.

24. Elmer E. Schattschneider, *Party Government* (New York: Rinehart, 1942), pp. 93–96. He speaks of the equilibrium of the two-party system and the "recuperative power of the second major party."

25. Donald E. Stokes and G. R. Iversen, "On the Existence of Forces Restoring Party Competition," *Public Opinion Quarterly*, 26 (Summer 1962).

26. Of course, as Joseph Schlesinger has pointed out, when a party wins narrowly there are also many groups of supporters who claim to be responsible for the victory, and who may be hard to satisfy. See "The Primary Goals of Political Parties: A Clarification of Positive Theory," *The American Political Science Review* 69, no. 3 (1975): 840–49.

27. Angus Campbell, "Surge and Decline: A Study of Electoral Change," *Public Opinion Quarterly* 24 (1960): 397–418.

28. A. W. Dunn, *From Harrison to Harding* (New York, Putnam, 1922), p. 104. Quoted in V. O. Key, Jr., *Politics, Parties and Pressure Groups*, 5th ed. (New York: T. Y. Crowell, 1964), p. 170.

29. See V. O. Key, Jr., *Parties*, 170–73, for these observations.

30. See Chambers and Burnham, *Party Systems*, for a discussion of this same problem, particularly p. 280; Morton Grodzins, to whom they refer, also saw this paradox, suggesting our parties are "anti-parties" in "American Political Parties and the American System," *Western Political Quarterly* 13 (1960): 974–98.

Chapter 3

1. William Chambers, *Political Parties in a New Nation* (New York: Oxford University Press, 1963), p. 149.

2. Morris Janowitz, *Social Control of the Welfare State* (Chicago: University of Chicago Press, 1976), p. 90.

3. See particularly Adam Przeworski, "Institutionalization of Voting Patterns, or Is Mobilization the Source of Decay?", *American Political Science Review* 69 (1975): 49–67; David Cameron, "Post-Industrial Change and Secular Realignment," Ph.D dissertation, University of Michigan, 1975, explores this matter in comparative perspective very carefully. I have relied heavily here on the data presented by Cameron, although my volatility measures differ from his. If the vote (or seats) of Congress is used as a basis for measuring volatility, the United States percentages would be a bit lower but would still rank high.

4. See Douglas Rae, *The Political Consequences of Electoral Laws* (New Haven: Yale University Press, 1967), pp. 100–102 for an argument that proportional representation systems are more stable while ours is likely to "magnify changes in" popular support.

5. Angus Campbell, "Surge and Decline: A Study of Electoral Change," *Public Opinion Quarterly* 24 (1960): 397–418.

6. Based on the National Election Survey (1980) of the Center for Political Surveys, University of Michigan; and, for the earlier years, see Everett C. Ladd, *American Political Parties: Social Change and Political Response* (New York: Norton, 1970), p. 306.

7. "Electing Congress," *Congressional Quarterly* (April 1978): 90–91.

8. Walter DeVries and V. Lance Tarrance, *The Ticket-Splitter: A New Force in American Politics* (Grand Rapids, Mich.: Eerdmans, 1972), p. 30; and "Electing Congress," p. 149.

9. See the retrospective calculation of Norman H. Nie, Sidney Verba, and John R. Petrocik, *The Changing American Voter* (Cambridge: Harvard University Press, 1976), p. 83.

10. See Philip Converse's interesting theory concerning this in "Of Time and Partisan Stability," *Comparative Political Studies* 2, no. 2 (1969): 142–145.

11. W. Phillips Shiveley argues that party identification in Britain is more linked to immediate voting behavior than in the United States, and thus, that identification with parties is "not a lasting attachment transcending particular elections. . . ." See his "Party Identification, Party Choice, and Voting Stability: The Weimar Case," *American Political Science Review* 66 (1972): 1206.

12. Quoted in Chambers, *Political Parties*, p. 149.

13. Seymour M. Lipset and Stein Rokkan, "Cleavage Structures, Party Systems, and

Voter Alignments: An Introduction," in Seymour M. Lipset and Stein Rokkan, eds., *Party Systems and Voter Alignments: Cross National Perspectives* (New York: Free Press, 1967), pp. 26–50.

14. Leon D. Epstein, *Political Parties in Western Democracies* (New York: Praeger, 1967), p. 19.

15. Ibid., pp. 20, 21.

16. Scholars differ somewhat in their dating of suffrage extensions. Perhaps the most careful analysis is in Stein Rokkan and Seymour M. Lipset, *Citizens, Elections, Parties* (New York: David McKay, and Oslo: Universitetsforlager, 1970), pp. 84–85.

17. For an extremely lucid discussion of this argument see Seymour M. Lipset, "Political Cleavages in 'Developed' and 'Emerging' Polities," in Erik Allardt and Stein Rokkan, eds., *Mass Politics* (New York: Free Press, 1970), pp. 23–44.

18. See for example, Maurice Duverger, *Political Parties: Their Organization and Activity in the Modern State* (New York: Methuen, 1951), pp. 204–5.

19. See Converse, "Partisan Stability," *Comparative Political Studies* 2, no. 2 (July 1969): 142–45.

Chapter 4

1. Samuel J. Eldersveld, *Political Affiliation in Metropolitan Detroit* (Ann Arbor: University of Michigan, Bureau of Government, 1957), pp. 127–29.

2. Jack Dennis, "Support for the Party System by the Mass Public," *American Political Science Review* 60 (1966): 606.

3. The 1980 data come from the National Election Survey (1980) of the University of Michigan Center for Political Studies.

4. Samuel J. Eldersveld, *Political Parties: A Behavioral Analysis.* (Chicago: Rand McNally, 1964), p. 20.

5. Quoted by Austin Ranney, *Curing the Mischiefs of Faction* (Berkeley: University of California Press, 1975), p. 153 (reported initially in *The Milwaukee Journal*, July 13, 1973, p. 5); see also "American Ambivalence About Political Parties," in *Curing the Mischiefs of Faction* for Ranney's careful study of the problem; see also Eldersveld, *Political Parties*, p. 440.

6. Jack Dennis, "Trends in Public Support for the American Party System," in Jeff Fishel, ed., *Parties and Elections in an Anti-Party Age* (Bloomington: Indiana University Press, 1978), pp. 3–21.

7. Ibid., p. 13.

8. Walter De Vries and V. Lance Tarrance, *The Ticket-Splitters: A New Force in American Politics* (Grand Rapids, Mich.: Eerdmans, 1972), pp. 30–33; see also William Keefe, *Congress and the American People* (Englewood Cliffs, N.J.: Prentice Hall, 1980), p. 50; also Milton C. Cummings, *Congressmen and the Electorate* (New York: Macmillan, 1966).

9. See Herbert Asher, *Presidential Elections and American Politics* (Homewood, Ill.: Dorsey, 1976), p. 68; Norman H. Nie, Sidney Verba, and John R. Petrocik, *The Changing American Voter* (Cambridge: Harvard University Press, 1976), p. 51; and University of Michigan Center for Political Studies, National Election Survey, 1980.

10. For a recent study of this see Samuel H. Barnes and Max Kaase, *Political Action: Mass Participation in Five Western Democracies* (Beverly Hills: Sage, 1979), p. 580.

11. See Angus Campbell et al., *The American Voter* (New York: Wiley, 1964), pp. 124–44.

12. Merle Black and George B. Rabinowitz, "American Electoral Change: 1952–1972" (with a note on 1976), in William Crotty, ed., *The Party Symbol* (San Francisco: W. J. Freeman, 1980), p. 241. For a presentation of these data, see also Martin Wattenberg, "The Decline of Political Partisanship in America: Negativity or Neutrality," *American Political Science Review* 75, no. 4 (December 1981): 941–50.

13. Warren Miller and Teresa Levitin, *Leadership and Change* (Cambridge, Mass.: Winthrop, 1976), p. 60.

14. In Fishel, ed., *Parties and Elections*, p. 13.

15. Barnes and Kaase, eds., *Political Action*, p. 169.

16. Michael Wolfe, "Personal Contact Compaigning in Presidential Elections" (a paper

delivered at the Annual Meeting of the Midwest Political Science Association, Chicago, April 1979). The paper was based on University of Michigan Center for Political Studies surveys, in which the question was: "Did anyone call you up or come around to talk with you about the election?"

Chapter 5

1. Jeane Kirkpatrick, *Dismantling the Parties* (Washington, D.C.: American Enterprise Institute, 1978), pp. 2, 3.

2. James Q. Wilson, *Political Organizations* (New York: Basic Books, 1973), p. 95.

3. Samuel Huntington, *Political Order in Changing Societies* (New Haven: Yale University Press, 1968), p. 90.

4. Leon D. Epstein, *Political Parties in Western Democracies* (New York: Praeger, 1967), pp. 98–166.

5. See Samuel J. Eldersveld, *Political Parties: A Behavioral Analysis* (Chicago: Rand McNally, 1964), pp. 9–10, 98–117.

6. V. O. Key, Jr., *Politics, Parties and Pressure Groups*, 4th ed. (New York: T. Y. Crowell, 1958), p. 347.

Chapter 6

1. Associated Press dispatch, reported in the *Ann Arbor News*, May 9, 1981.

2. Charles Merriam and Harold F. Gosnell, *The American Party System* (New York: Macmillan, 1922), p. 62.

3. Quoted in Hugh A. Bone, *American Politics and the Party System*, 3rd ed. (New York: McGraw Hill, 1965), p. 208.

4. Harold Lasswell and Abraham Kaplan, *Power and Society* (New Haven: Yale University Press, 1950), p. 204.

5. Democratic National Convention, *Proceedings, 1948*, pp. 548–49, quoted in V. O. Key, Jr., *Politics, Parties and Pressure Groups*, 4th ed. (New York: T. Y. Crowell, 1958), p. 356.

6. Key, *Politics, Parties and Pressure Groups*, p. 346.

7. Charles Jones, *The Republican Party in American Politics* (New York: Macmillan, 1965), p. 103.

8. Donald R. Matthews, *U. S. Senators and Their World* (New York: Norton, 1973), pp. 124–26.

9. Ibid., p. 124.

10. Walter Lippman, *A Preface to Politics* (New York: Macmillan, 1933), p. 249.

11. See Randall B. Ripley, *Party Leaders in the House of Representatives* (Washington, D.C.: Brookings Institution, 1967), pp. 95–98.

12. Cited in Howard R. Penniman, *American Parties and Elections* (New York: Appleton Century, 1948), p. 317.

13. V. O. Key, Jr., *Politics, Parties and Pressure Groups*, 5th ed. (New York: T. Y. Crowell, 1964), pp. 674–75. See also Clarence Berdahl, "Some Notes on Party Membership in Congress," *American Political Science Review* 43 (1949): 309–21, 494–508.

14. Bone, *American Politics*, p. 251.

15. Theodore H. White, *The Making of the President 1972* (New York: Atheneum, 1973), pp. 253–54.

16. Bone, *American Politics*, p. 190.

17. Referred to by William Crotty, ed., in *The Party Symbol* (San Francisco: W. H. Freeman, 1980), p. 40.

18. Cited in Bone, *American Politics*, p. 202, From his syndicated column in *The Chicago Sun-Times*, August 9, 1949.

19. Cornelius P. Cotter and Bernard C. Hennessey, *Politics Without Power* (New York: Atherton, 1964), pp. 22–23.

20. Theodore H. White, *The Making of the President 1964* (New York: New American Library, 1966), pp. 414–17.

21. An excellent source relied on here is Ripley, *Party Leaders.*

22. Ibid., pp. 42, 95–96.

23. Key, *Parties and Pressure Groups,* 5th ed., p. 396.

24. Actually in 1976 thirty-three states had some type of presidential primary, but only thirty used it for the direct election of delegates.

25. The Russian scholar M. Ostrogorski called the conventions a "colossal travesty of popular institutions," among other criticisms. See his *Democracy and the Organization of Political Parties* (Garden City, N.Y.: Doubleday, 1964), p. 143.

26. The fight at the convention over the Illinois delegation is also famous. The issue there was whether Mayor Richard J. Daley's "unrepresentative" state could be seated as a unit. The decision was that it could not be seated. See Theodore H. White's detailed account of this episode in *The Making of the President 1972,* pp. 214–33.

27. See Ibid., for a fascinating account of these events, especially pp. 20–45.

28. *U.S. News and World Report,* August 23, 1976; Jeane Kirkpatrick, *The New Presidential Elite* (New York: Russell Sage, 1976), pp. 84, 86.

29. Sources for these data are John S. Jackson et al., "Recruitment, Representation, and Political Values: The 1976 Democratic Convention Delegates," *American Politics Quarterly* 6, no. 1 (1978): 187–221; Thomas H. Roback, "Recruitment and Motives for National Convention Activism: Republican Delegates in 1972 and 1976," in William Crotty, ed., *The Party Symbol* (San Francisco: W. H. Freeman, 1980), p. 194.

30. Gerald Pomper, "New Rules and New Games in the National Conventions" (a paper presented at the Annual Meeting of American Political Science Association, Washington, D.C., September 1977), p. 31.

Chapter 7

1. David S. Broder, "The Case for Responsible Party Government," in Jeff Fishel, ed., *Parties and Elections in an Anti-Party Age* (Bloomington: Indiana University Press, 1978), p. 26.

2. Frank Sorauf, *Party Politics in America,* 3rd ed. (Boston: Little, Brown, 1976), pp. 76, 84.

3. Cornelius P. Cotter, et al., "State Party Organizations and the Thesis of Party Decline" (a paper presented at the Annual Meeting of the American Political Science Association, Washington, D.C., August 1980).

4. See Edward C. Banfield, *Political Influence* (New York: Free Press, 1965).

5. Malcolm E. Jewell and David M. Olson, *American State Political Parties and Elections* (Homewood, Ill.: Dorsey, 1978), p. 56.

6. Elmer E. Schattschneider, *Party Government* (New York: Rinehart, 1942), p. 147.

7. Cotter, "State Party Organization"; see also Robert J. Huckshorn, *Party Leadership in the States* (Amherst: University of Massachusetts Press, 1976).

8. Jewell and Olson, *State Political Parties,* pp. 67–70. California limits the tenure of state chairpersons to two years. Our discussion here relies on their research.

9. Ibid., p. 69.

10. Ibid., pp. 134–36.

11. F. Munger and J. Blackhurst, "Factionalism in the National Conventions, 1940–1964: An Analysis of Ideological Consistency in State Delegation Voting," *Journal of Politics* 27 (1965): 375–94; see also David C. Nice, "Party Ideology and Policy Outcomes in the American States" (unpublished paper, submitted to *Journal of Politics*).

12. Samuel J. Eldersveld, *Political Parties: A Behavioral Analysis* (Chicago: Rand McNally, 1964), pp. 74–75.

13. Huckshorn, *Party Leadership,* p. 234; also, Robert J. Huckshorn, "The Role Orientations of State Party Chairmen," in William J. Crotty, ed., *The Party Symbol* (San Francisco: W. H. Freeman, 1980), pp. 50–62. See the discussion in Jewell and Olson, *State Political Parties,* pp. 69–70.

14. There is a great deal of literature on the club movement. See Leon D. Epstein, *Politics in Wisconsin* (Madison: University of Wisconsin Press, 1958); Francis Carney, *The Rise of the Democratic Clubs in California* (New York: Holt, Eagleton Institute of Politics, 1958); James Q. Wilson, *The Amateur Democrat: Club Politics in Three Cities* (Chicago: Uni-

versity of Chicago Press, 1962); Hugh A. Bone, "New Party Associations in the West," *American Political Science Review* 45 (1951): 1115–25. See also Jewell and Olson, *State Political Parties*, pp. 83–84.

15. Eldersveld, *Political Parties*, p. 534.

16. Mike Royko, *Boss: Richard J. Daley of Chicago* (New York: New American Library, 1971); also Sorauf, *Party Politics*, pp. 74–75.

17. M. Margaret Conway and Frank B. Feigert, "Motivation, Incentive Systems, and the Political Party Organization," *American Political Science Review* 62, no. 4 (1968): 151.

18. Eldersveld, *Political Parties*, p. 350.

19. Ibid., p. 349.

20. The author's own experience in running for major in Ann Arbor years ago (1957) has brought home to him the potentiality of the party's power. By systematically and meticulously preparing lists of probable supporters in each precinct and then organizing a 100 percent canvass (both by door-to-door and by telephone) a 62 percent increase in the vote was secured and the mayoralty was won for the first time in over thirty years.

21. *Time*, March 12, 1979, p. 22.

22. James Bryce, *The American Commonwealth* (New York: Macmillan, 1916), p. 118.

23. Royko, *Boss*, pp. 60–61.

24. Ibid.

25. Milton L. Rakove, *Don't Make No Waves, Don't Back No Losers* (Bloomington: University of Indiana Press, 1975), p. 115.

26. Len O'Connor, *Clout: Mayor Daley and His City* (Chicago: Henry Regnery, 1975), p. 156. In illustration of this same point there is an interesting report of an interview at the funeral of Boss Frank Hague of Jersey City. A reporter asked an aide why there were so few flowers. The aide shrugged, "When the Big Boy goes, it means we can no longer do anything for anybody." "Political Machines," *American Heritage* (June 1969): 46.

27. Rakove, *No Waves*, pp. 112–14.

28. Much of this summary was based on Ibid., ch. 4. pp. 106–31.

29. Ibid.

30. Ibid., pp. 119–20.

31. Ibid., p. 123.

32. Ibid., pp. 129–30.

33. Ibid., pp. 3–4.

34. See Raymond Wolfinger, "Why Political Machines Have Not Withered Away and Other Revisionist Thoughts," *Journal of Politics* 34 (1972): 365–98. The dimensions and types of machines used here were stimulated by this article although the two-dimensional scheme is not the same.

35. *Time*, March 12, 1979, p. 27.

36. See Leon D. Epstein, *Political Parties in Western Democracies* (New York: Praeger, 1967), pp. 111–18.

Chapter 8

1. Robert Michels, *Political Parties* (New York: Free Press, 1966), pp. 32, 35, 401.

2. James H. Meisel, *The Myth of the Ruling Class* (Ann Arbor: University of Michigan Press, 1958), p. 4.

3. Michels, *Political Parties*, p. 366.

4. See Seymour M. Lipset's Introduction to *Political Parties* (New York: Free Press, 1962), pp. 25–39, for a summary of many of these criticisms.

5. These quotations are taken from Lenin's pamphlet, "What Is to Be Done?" *Sochinenixa* 4: 452–58. See Merle Fainsod; *How Russia Is Ruled* (Cambridge: Harvard University Press, 1963) for an excellent discussion of these early origins of the concept of party in Lenin's thinking, particularly ch. 3.

6. As quoted in Maurice Duverger, *Political Parties: Their Organization and Activity in the Modern State* (London: Methuen, 1954), p. 155.

7. Fainsod, *Russia*, p. 456.

8. Leon Trotsky, as quoted in Fainsod, *Russia*, p. 42.

9. Duverger, *Political Parties.*

10. James Q. Wilson, *The Amateur Democrat: Club Politics in Three Cities* (Chicago: University of Chicago Press, 1962); Robert S. Hirshfield, Bert E. Swanson, and Blanche D. Blank, "A Profile of Political Activists in Manhattan," *Western Political Quarterly* 15 (1962): 489–506; Francis Carney, *The Rise of the Democratic Clubs in California*, Eagleton Foundation Case Studies in Practical Politics (New York: Henry Holt, 1958).

11. Very interesting theoretical and empirical work has been done on the amateur-professional distinctions: See Peter B. Clark and James Q. Wilson, "Incentive Systems: A Theory of Organization," *Administrative Science Quarterly* 6 (1961): 129–66; C. Richard Hofstetter, "The Amateur Politician: A Problem in Construct Validation," *Midwest Journal of Political Science* 15 (1971): 31–56; John W. Soule and James W. Clarke, "Amateurs and Professionals: A Study of Delegates to the 1968 Democratic Convention," *American Political Science Review* 64 (1970): 888–98. The specific items used to test the existence of amateurism and professionalism can be found in these studies.

12. Wilson, *Amateur Democrat*, pp. 222–23.

13. Milton L. Rakove, *Don't Make No Waves, Don't Back No Losers* (Bloomington: Indiana University Press, 1975), pp. 118–19.

14. Joseph Schlesinger, *Ambition and Politics* (Chicago: Rand McNally, 1966), pp. 10, 125–33.

15. This is adapted from William Wright, ed., *Studies in Comparative Party Organization.* Wright develops in greater detail an elaborate schema to distinguish his two polar types. We have here presented only a few of his differentia, but critical ones in our opinion, in order to indicate the nature of the contrasts.

16. Quoted by Rudolf Heberle, "Ferdinand Tonnies's Contributions to the Sociology of Political Parties," *American Journal of Sociology* 61, no. 3 (1955): 216, 217.

Chapter 9

1. Harold F. Gosnell, *Machine Politics: Chicago Model* (Chicago: University of Chicago Press, 1937), pp. 64–66.

2. Samuel J. Eldersveld, *Political Parties: A Behavioral Analysis* (Chicago: Rand McNally, 1964), pp. 124–26.

3. The Detroit study indicates that ideology seemed to be relatively salient for only 17 percent of the Democratic precinct leaders and 29 percent of the Republicans. It did appear to be more important for those higher up in the structure. See Eldersveld, p. 196.

4. From the 1956 Detroit study, Eldersveld, *Political Parties*, p. 254.

5. Peter H. Rossi and Phillips Cutwright, "The Impact of Party Organization in an Industrial Setting," in M. Janowitz, ed., *Community Political Systems* (New York: Free Press, 1961), pp. 90–94.

6. Richard T. Frost, "Stability and Change in Local Party Politics," *Public Opinion Quarterly* 25 (1961): 221–35.

7. Eldersveld, *Political Parties*, p. 103.

8. William J. Crotty, "The Party Organization and Its Activities," in William J. Crotty, ed., *Approaches to the Study of Party Organization*, pp. 247–306.

9. See such studies as C. Richard Hofstetter, "The Amateur Politician: A Problem in Construct Validation," *Midwest Journal of Political Science* 15 (1971): 31–56; John W. Soule and James W. Clark "Amateurs and Professionals: A Study of Delegates to the 1968 Democratic Convention," *American Political Science Review* 64 (1970): 888–98; James Q. Wilson, *The Amateur Democrat: Club Politics in Three Cities* (Chicago: University of Chicago Press, 1962).

10. Soule and Clarke, "Amateurs and Professionals," p. 890.

11. In Detroit 51 percent of the Democrats and 62 percent of the Republicans were aspirers. This is similar to the finding in the Massachusetts and North Carolina studies where from 60 percent to 89 percent of the precinct officials planned to continue in party work. L. Bowman et al., "Incentives for the Maintenance of Grass Roots Political Activism," *Midwest Journal of Political Science* 13 (1969): 126–39.

12. James Canfield, "The Wallace Campaign Worker in Wayne County," Ph.D. dissertation, University of Michigan, 1971.

Chapter 10

1. See Robert Putnam, *The Comparative Study of Political Elites* (Englewood Cliffs, N. J.: Prentice Hall, 1976), pp. 46–70, for an excellent summary of country differences in recruitment.

2. Quoted in James D. Barber, *The Lawmakers* (New Haven: Yale University Press, 1965), p. 4.

3. Lester Seligman, et al., *Patterns of Recruitment: A State Chooses Its Law-Makers* (Chicago: Rand McNally, 1974), p. 191.

4. H. Dewey Anderson, "The Educational Occupational Attainments of Our National Rulers," *The Scientific Monthly* 40 (1935): 511–18. Cited in Putnam, *Political Elites*, p. 23.

5. See Putnam, *Political Elites*, p. 188.

6. Seligman, *Patterns of Recruitment*, p. 191.

7. Leo M. Snowiss, "Congressional Recruitment and Representation," *American Political Science Review* 60 (1966): 627–39.

8. John C. Wahlke et al., *The Legislative System* (New York: Wiley, 1962), pp. 300–308; Leon D. Epstein, *Politics in Wisconsin* (Madison: University of Wisconsin Press, 1958), p. 96; and Frank Sorauf, *Party Politics in America* (Boston: Little, Brown, 1967), pp. 149–50. Cited in Seligman, *Patterns of Recruitment*, p. 5.

9. Barbara Greenberg, "New York Congressmen and Local Party Organization," Ph.D. dissertation, University of Michigan, 1972.

10. David M. Olson, "The Electoral Relationship Between Congressmen and Their District Parties" (a paper presented at the Annual Meeting of the American Political Science Association, Washington, D.C., September 1977).

11. The Comparative Elite Project, University of Michigan, based on interviews conducted 1970–73.

Chapter 11

1. Lester Milbrath and M. L. Goel, *Political Participation*, 2nd ed. (Chicago: Rand McNally, 1977), p. 22.

2. See Robert A. Dahl, *Who Governs?* (New Haven: Yale University Press, 1961), p. 290. See also James D. Barber, *The Lawmakers* (New Haven: Yale University Press, 1965), p. 288. The Dahl study of New Haven, for example, found a low prestige rating for public jobs among college-educated, high social status persons.

3. Samuel J. Eldersveld, *Political Parties: A Behavioral Analysis* (Chicago: Rand McNally, 1964), p. 440. The Detroit study found that only 13 percent of the adult sample would encourage their sons to go into politics.

4. V. O. Key, Jr., *American State Politics* (New York: Alfred A. Knopf, 1956), p. 271.

5. The restrictive time limits used previously by Illinois (twenty-three months), and in New Jersey and Rhode Island (which required the voter to miss one or two primaries before shifting parties) were declared unconstitutional in 1972 because they disenfranchised voters. The six states requiring six months are: Illinois, New Jersey, Maine, Maryland, Pennsylvania, and Kentucky. See Malcolm E. Jewell and David M. Olson, *American State Political Parties and Elections* (Homewood, Ill.: Dorsey, 1978), p. 143.

6. This is similar to, but an expansion of, the classification employed by Ibid., p. 130.

7. Derived from Ibid., p. 143.

8. See Austin Ranney in Herbert Jacob and Kenneth N. Vines, eds., *Politics in the American States*, 3rd ed. (Boston: Little, Brown, 1976), p. 72. V. O. Key, Jr., uses the figure 35 percent (1926–1952).

9. Ibid., p. 71.

10. Jewell and Olson, *American State Political Parties*, p. 144.

11. If the four factors utilized here are combined the contrast in turnout for those states fulfilling all the conditions for high turnout and those states fulfilling the conditions for low turnout (contested primaries, number of candidates, and so forth) is 36 percent for the first group and 26.1 percent for the latter group. Only three and five states respectively, however, are "pure types."

12. V. O. Key, Jr., *Politics, Parties and Pressure Groups*, 4th ed. (New York: T. Y. Crowell, 1958), pp. 417–18, 478–79, 488.

13. Key, *Politics*, 5th ed., p. 437.

14. Jewell and Olson, *State Political Parties*, p. 132.

15. A recent study by Craig H. Grau, "Competition in State Legislative Primaries," *Legislative Studies Quarterly* 6, no. 1 (1981), presents data for primaries for state legislatures in fifteen states from 1972 to 1978. He found that a median of only 29 percent of seats with incumbents were contested (p. 48) and that there were sharp differences for the parties in primary competition overall—a mean of 17 percent were contested by Republicans, but 47 percent by Democrats (p. 40).

16. Jewell and Olson, *State Political Parties*, p. 136.

17. Julius Turner, "Primary Elections as the Alternative to Party Competition in 'Safe' Districts," *Journal of Politics* 15 (1953): 198.

18. Harvey L. Schantz, "Julius Turner Revisited: Primary Elections as the Alternative to Party Competition in 'Safe' Districts" (Communications) *American Political Science Review* 90, no. 2 (1976): 541–45.

19. Ibid, p. 545.

20. Based on Jewell and Olson, *State Political Parties*, pp. 98, 143.

21. Based on Ibid., p. 146.

22. Ibid., p. 174. They cite two studies to sustain this conclusion.

23. Ibid. Calculations are based on data from pp. 146, 333.

24. V. O. Key, Jr., *American State Politics: An Introduction* (New York: Knopf, 1956), pp. 145, 152.

25. Austin Ranney and Leon D. Epstein, "The Two Electorates: Voters and Non-Voters in a Wisconsin Primary," *The Journal of Politics* 28, no. 3 (1966): 602. I have recalculated their data for these purposes.

26. These are based on the University of Michigan Survey Research Center data.

27. Ranney and Epstein, "The Two Electorates," p. 610. Their data were recalculated for our purposes here.

28. Austin Ranney, "The Representativeness of Primary Electorates," *Midwest Journal of Political Science* 12, no. 2 (1968): 229.

29. Ranney and Epstein, "The Two Electorates," p. 612.

30. Ranney, "Representativeness," p. 233.

31. Ronald D. Hedlund, "Crossover Voting in a 1976 Open Presidential Primary," *Public Opinion Quarterly* 41, no. 4 (1977–78): 498–514.

32. David Adamany, "Crossover Voting and the Democratic Party's Reform Rules" (Communications), *American Political Science Review* 70, no. 2 (1976): 536–41. See also the studies by Daniel M. Ogden, Jr., and Hugh A. Bone, *Washington Politics* (New York: New York University Press, 1960), and Ogden's articles on the blanket primary in Washington, "The Blanket Primary and Party Regularity in Washington," *Pacific Northwest Quarterly* 39 (1948): 33–38, and "Washington's Popular Primary," *Research Studies of the State College of Washington* 19 (1951): 146–47. In the latter he presents data from a Washington survey that 37 percent of the respondents said they would cross over into the opposite party's primary when their own party's primary was unopposed (p. 147).

33. Adamany, "Crossover Voting," pp. 539, 541.

34. D. B. Johnson and J. R. Gibson, "The Divisive Primary Revisited: Party Activists in Iowa," *American Political Science Review* 68, no. 1 (March 1974): 67–77.

35. See Sarah M. Morehouse, "The Effects of Preprimary Endorsements on State Party Strength," paper presented at the 1980 Annual Meeting of the American Political Science Association, Washington, D. C., August, 1980. See also her book, *State Politics, Parties and Policy* (Holt, Rinehart, and Winston, 1981).

Chapter 12

1. Theodore H. White, *The Making of the President 1960* (New York: Atheneum, 1980), p. 328.

2. Denis G. Sullivan, Jeffrey L. Pressman, F. Christopher Arterton, *Explorations in Con-*

vention Decision-Making: The Democratic Party in the 1970's (San Francisco: W. H. Freeman, 1976), pp. 122–24.

3. M. Ostrogorski, *Democracy and the Organization of Political Parties* (New York: Doubleday, 1964), pp. 133–37.

4. James Bryce, *The American Commonwealth* (New York: Macmillan, 1916), p. 187.

5. Theodore H. White, *The Making of the President 1972* (New York: Atheneum, 1973), p. 209.

6. Ibid.

7. Jeane Kirkpatrick, *Dismantling the Parties: Reflections on Party Reform and Party Decomposition* (Washington, D.C.: American Enterprise Institute for Public Policy Research, 1978), p. 2.

8. See Sullivan, *Convention Decision-making*, pp. 122–24, for observations elaborating this formulation.

9. See Gary R. Orren, in Seymour M. Lipset, ed., *Emerging Coalitions in American Politics* (San Francisco: Institute for Contemporary Politics, 1978), pp. 130–34 for an elaboration of these explanations.

10. Stephen Hess, *The Presidential Campaign*, (Washington, D.C.: The Brookings Institution, 1978), pp. 27–38.

11. Hedrick Smith in *The New York Times*, March 20, 1980, p. A1. Quoted in Gerald Pomper, et al., *The Election of 1980* (Chatham, N.J.: Chatham House, 1981), p. 15.

12. The history of the adoption of the primary has been recorded by several scholars. See William Crotty, *Political Reform and the American Experiment* (New York: T. Y. Crowell, 1977), pp. 204–18 for a succinct summary of this development.

13. Jerome S. Burnstein and Larry N. Gerston, "Representation Theory and Presidential Primaries: An Examination of the 1976 Nominations" (a paper presented to the Annual Meeting of the Midwest Political Science Association, Chicago, April 1979); "Elections '80," *Congressional Quarterly* (Washington, D.C., 1980), pp. 68–96.

14. Democratic National Committee, "Delegate Selection Rules for the 1980 Democratic National Convention" (June 9, 1978).

15. Based on University of Michigan Center for Political Studies, National Election Survey 1980.

16. Ranney, *Participation in Presidential Nominations*, p. 20.

17. Ibid. for 1976. The 1980 data are reported in Pomper, *The Election of 1980*.

18. Ranney, *Participation in Presidential Nominations*, p. 22.

19. Richard L. Rubin, "Presidential Primaries: Continuities, Dimensions of Change, and Political Implications" (a paper presented at the Annual Meeting of the American Political Science Association, Washington, D.C., September 1977), p. 18. See also Harvey Zeidenstein, "Presidential Primaries—Reflections of 'The People's Choice'?" *Journal of Politics* 32, no. 4 (1979): 856–74.

20. Ranney, *Participation in Presidential Nominations*, pp. 7–12.

21. Ibid., p. 30.

22. Based on reports in the *New York Times*, and reported in Thomas R. Marshall, "Caucuses versus Primaries: How Much Do Delegate Selection Institutions Really Matter?" (a paper presented at the Annual Meeting of the American Political Science Association, Washington, D.C., September 1977).

23. Crotty, *Political Reform*, pp. 223–27.

24. Austin Ranney, "Turnout and Representation in Presidential Primary Elections," *American Political Science Review* 66 (1972): 21–37.

25. Ibid.

26. Burnstein and Gerston, "Representation Theory and Presidential Primaries."

27. Richard L. Rubin, *Party Dynamics* (New York: Oxford University Press, 1976), p. 150. See also Harvey Zeidenstein, "Presidential Primaries," pp. 856–74, for an analysis of competitive primaries during the 1948 to 1968 period. The 1976 and 1980 data were added using the same criteria as for earlier years.

28. William R. Keech, "Presidential Nominating Politics: Problems of Popular Choice" (a paper presented to the Annual Meeting of the American Political Science Association, Washington, D.C., September 1972).

29. *Congressional Quarterly*, June 26, 1976.

30. See Pomper, *Election 1980*, for these 1980 calculations, pp. 16, 26.

31. Keech, "Nominating Politics," p. 5.

32. An Associated Press release said both chairmen intended to set up committees to study the problem. *Ann Arbor News*, April 29, 1981.

33. Gerald M. Pomper, *Elections in America: Control and Influence in Democratic Politics* (New York: Dodd, Mead, 1968), p. 178.

34. Pendleton Herring, *The Politics of Democracy* (New York: Norton, 1940), p. 229.

35. Ibid., p. 238.

36. Lock K. Johnson and Harlan Hahn, "Delegate Turnover at National Party Conventions," in Donald R. Matthews, ed., *Perspectives on Presidential Selection* (Washington, D.C.: The Brookings Institution, 1973), pp. 143–71.

37. Jeane Kirkpatrick, *The New Presidential Elite* (New York: Russell Sage, 1976), p. 7; also, Thomas H. Roback, "Recruitment and Motives for National Convention Activism: Republican Delegates in 1972 and 1976," in William Crotty, ed., *The Party Symbol* (San Francisco: W. H. Freeman, 1980), p. 194.

38. Ibid., p. 330.

39. See David Broder's column, "Presidential Nominating Process Plagues Parties," *The Detroit News*, October 31, 1981, p. 15A.

40. See Paul David, Ralph Goldman, and Richard Bain, *The Politics of National Party Conventions* (Washington, D.C.: The Brookings Institution, 1960) for a discussion of these patterns in the nominating process, p. 117.

41. See Louis Maisel and Joseph Cooper, *The Impact of the Electoral Process* (Beverly Hills: Sage, 1977). Also Sullivan, *Convention Decision-Making*.

42. Quoted by Theodore H. White, *The Making of the President 1964* (New York: Atheneum, 1965), pp. 231–32.

Chapter 13

1. Austin Ranney and W. Kendall, *Democracy and the American Party System* (New York: Harcourt Brace, 1956), p. 339.

2. Quoted in Dan Nimmo, *The Political Persuaders: The Techniques of Modern Election Campaigns* (Englewood Cliffs, N.J.: Prentice Hall, 1970).

3. David A. Leuthold, *Electioneering in a Democracy: Campaign for Congress* (New York: Wiley, 1968), p. 1.

4. Dan Nimmo, *Persuaders*, pp. 9–10.

5. Karl A. Lamb and Paul A. Smith, *Campaign Decisionmaking: The Presidential Election of 1964* (Belmont, Calif.: Wadsworth, 1968). They describe the contrasting 1964 campaigns of Goldwater and Johnson, the former fixed and comprehensive, the latter "incremental."

6. L. Froman, in M. Kent Jennings and Harmon Zeigler, eds., *The Electoral Process* (Englewood Cliffs, N.J.: Prentice Hall, 1966).

7. Elmer E. Schattschneider, *Party Government* (New York: Rinehart, 1942), p. 33.

8. Anthony Downs, *An Economic Theory of Democracy* (New York: Harper & Row, 1965), pp. 114–41.

9. Many scholars have analyzed Downs's theory critically from these perspectives, including Otto Davis et al., "An Expository Development of a Mathematical Model of the Electoral Process," *American Political Science Review* 64 (1970): 426–48. See also Donald Stokes, "Spatial Models of Party Competition," *American Political Science Review* 57 (June 1963): 57.

10. Nimmo, *Persuaders*, pp. 180–81.

11. Ibid., p. 181.

12. Schattschneider, *Party Government*, p. 45.

13. Quoted in Theodore H. White, *The Making of the President 1968* (New York: Atheneum, 1970), pp. 394–95.

14. Lamb and Smith, *Decisionmaking*, argue that in 1964 Johnson used an incremental model successfully while Goldwater used a comprehensive-ideal model, and very unsuccessfully.

15. Herbert M. Baus and William B. Ross, *Politics Battle Plan* (New York: Macmillan, 1968), p. 212. Also see Nimmo, *Persuaders*, p. 61.

16. White, *Making of the President 1968*, pp. 405–10.

17. Nelson Polsby and Aaron Wildavsky, *Presidential Elections: Strategies of American Electoral Politics* (New York: Scribners, 1976), pp. 159–63.

18. See Nimmo, *Persuaders*, pp. 54–55, for a discussion of these themes; also Stanley Kelley, Jr., *Professional Public Relations and Political Power* (Englewood Cliffs, N.J.: Prentice Hall, 1970).

19. Nimmo, *Persuaders*, p. 55.

20. Samuel P. Huntington, "A Revised Theory of American Politics," *American Political Science Review* 44 (1950): 669–77.

21. See Theodore H. White, *The Making of the President 1964* (New York: Atheneum, 1965), ch. 10.

22. Nimmo, *Persuaders*, p. 43.

23. Ibid., p. 47. See also Murray B. Levin, *Kennedy Campaigning* (Boston: Beacon Press, 1966).

24. Theodore H. White, *The Making of the President 1960* (New York: New American Library, 1967) p. 384.

25. Nimmo, *Persuaders*, p. 153.

26. Ibid., p. 57.

27. Ibid., p. 59; also White, *The Making of the President 1968*, p. 99.

28. Thomas W. Benham, "Polling for a Presidential Candidate," *Public Opinion Quarterly* 39 (1965): 192.

29. Quoted in Nimmo, *Persuaders*, p. 63, based on White, *The Making of the President 1964*, p. 379; and White, *The Making of the President 1968*, p. 417.

30. A good discussion of the mushrooming of these firms and the services they perform is found in Nimmo, *Persuaders*, ch. 2.

31. Ibid., p. 86.

32. Ibid., pp. 42–45. Nimmo describes these aspects of their involvement and how one specialist picked Nixon in 1944.

33. See Jules Witcover, *85 Days: The Last Campaign of Robert F. Kennedy* (New York: Putnam, 1969); also David Halberstam, *The Unfinished Odyssey of Robert Kennedy* (New York: Random House, 1969). Cited in Nimmo, *Persuaders*, p. 90.

34. Ithiel de Sola Pool, Robert P. Abelson, and Samuel Popkin, *Candidates, Issues and Strategies*, (Cambridge: M.I.T. Press, 1964). This is a report on the use of surveys and computer simulation in the 1960 Kennedy campaign.

35. Paul Lazarsfeld, et al., *The People's Choice* (New York: Duell, Sloan, and Pearce, 1944).

36. Angus Campbell et al., *The American Voter* (New York: Wiley, 1964), p. 51.

37. See Norman H. Nie, Sidney Verba, and John B. Petrocik, *The Changing American Voter* (Cambridge: Harvard University Press, 1976) for a discussion of these trends in the context of political involvement, pp. 275–76.

38. *ISR Newsletter* 6, no. 1 (1978): 5.

39. Ibid.

40. Richard S. Salant, "The Television Debates: A Revolution that Deserves A Future," *Public Opinion Quarterly* (Fall 1962): 341. See also Stanley Kelly, Jr., "Campaign Debates: Some Facts and Issues" *Public Opinion Quarterly* (Fall 1962): 351–66.

41. See Gerald Pomper, et al., *The Election of 1980* (Chatham, N.J.: Chatham, 1981), pp. 80–81. In 1976 the NBC Survey revealed that 3 percent of the sample said that its final voting decision was based on the Carter-Ford debates. See John P. Robinson, in Sidney Kraus, ed., *The Great Debates: Carter vs Ford 1976* (Bloomington: Indiana University Press, 1979), pp. 262–63.

42. Reported in the *Detroit Free Press*, November 27, 1976. The research was done by Lloyd Sloan, assistant professor of psychology at Notre Dame.

43. Michael M. Wolfe, "Personal Contact Campaigning in Presidential Elections" (a paper presented at the Annual Meeting of the Midwest Political Science Association, Chicago, April 1979). The data for 1980 are from the University of Michigan Center for Political Studies National Election Survey.

44. Daniel Katz and Samuel J. Eldersveld, "The Impact of Local Party Activity upon the Electorate," *Public Opinion Quarterly* 25 (1961): 1–24.

45. William Crotty, "The Party Organization and Its Activities," in Crotty, ed., *Approaches to the Study of Party Organization* (Boston: Allyn, 1968), pp. 247–306. See also

Gerald Kramer, "The Effects of Precinct Level Canvassing on Voter Behavior," *Public Opinion Quarterly* 34 (1970–71): 560–72.

46. Samuel J. Eldersveld, "Experimental Propaganda Techniques and Voting Behavior," *American Political Science Review* 50 (1956): 154–65.

47. Lazarsfeld, *The People's Choice*, pp. 58, 68.

48. Janowitz and Marvick, *Competitive Pressure*, p. 77.

49. Peter W. Sperlich, *Conflict and Harmony in Human Affairs: A Study of Cross Pressures and Political Behavior* (Chicago: Rand McNally, 1971).

50. Robert Schoenberger, "Campaign Strategy and Party Loyalty: The Electoral Relevance of Candidate Decision-Making in the 1964 Congressional Elections," *American Political Science Review* 63 (1969): 515–20.

51. Nimmo, *Persuaders*, pp. 167–68.

52. V. O. Key, Jr., *The Responsible Electorate: Rationality in Presidential Voting, 1936–1960* (Cambridge: Harvard University Press, 1966), pp. 4–8.

Chapter 14

1. David S. Broder, syndicated column, *Washington Post*, 1975.

2. Louise Overacker, *Money in Elections* (New York: Macmillan, 1932), p. 71n.

3. Ibid., p. 73; Louise Overacker, *Presidential Campaign Funds* (Boston: Boston University Press, 1946), p. 32; *Financing Presidential Campaigns*, Report of the President's Commission on Campaign Costs (Washington, D.C.: April 1962), p. 10; Herbert E. Alexander, *Financing the 1972 Election* (Lexington, Mass.: D.C. Heath, 1976). The 1972 data are from *Dollar Politics* 2, (Washington, D.C.: Congressional Quarterly, 1974), p. 72.

4. Herbert E. Alexander, *Financing the 1976 Election* (Washington, D.C.: *Congressional Quarterly Weekly Report*, 1979), pp. 166–67.

5. *Congressional Quarterly Weekly Report*, September 29, 1979.

6. Alexander, *Financing 1972*, pp. 77–78. See also Alexander Heard, *The Costs of Democracy* (Chapel Hill: University of North Carolina Press, 1960), pp. 7–8.

7. Herbert E. Alexander, *Financing the 1972 Election* (Lexington, Mass.: D. C. Heath, 1976).

8. *Congressional Quarterly Weekly Report*, September 29, 1979, p. 2151.

9. Ibid.

10. *Congressional Quarterly Weekly Report*, September 29, 1979.

11. University of Michigan Survey Research Center, cited in Alexander, *Financing Politics*, p. 82.

12. Ibid., p. 81.

13. *Congressional Quarterly Weekly Report*, September 29, 1979, p. 2153.

14. See Alexander, *Financing Politics*, pp. 74, and 84 for these data.

15. Ibid., pp. 87–90, 229–30, and ch. 5, "Special Interests."

16. Ibid., pp. 114–16.

17. CBS television interview, April 27, 1972, reported in M. Margaret Conway and Frank B. Feigert, *Politics and Parties in America* (Boston: Allyn, 1976), p. 262.

18. Data is from University of Michigan Center for Political Studies National Election Survey (1964). Interesting analyses have been made of the motivations of those who contribute to campaigns, suggesting that there is a strong issue-oriented basis for such contributions. See Roman B. Hedges, "Reasons for Political Involvement: A Study of Contributors to the 1972 Presidential Campaign" (a paper presented to the Annual Meeting of the Midwest Political Science Association, Chicago, 1979). Also, see Lynda W. Powell, "A Study of Financial Contributors in Congressional Elections" (a paper presented at the Annual Meeting of the American Political Science Association, Washington, D.C., 1979).

19. Alexander, *Financing Politics*, p. 251. Thirteen states also use a checkoff system, and on the average one-fifth of the citizens contribute this way. See Ruth S. Jones, "State Public Campaign Finance: Implications for Partisan Politics," *American Journal of Political Science* 25, no. 2 (1981): 348.

20. Heard, *Costs of Democracy*, pp. 100–102.

21. *Congressional Quarterly Weekly Report*, March 17, 1973, pp. 577–87.

22. Federal Election Commission, *Record 7*, no. 3 (1981): 11.

23. *Electing Congress* (Washington, D.C.: *Congressional Quarterly Weekly Report*, April 1978), p. 26.

24. Ibid.

25. Ibid., p. 27.

26. Ibid., p. 29.

27. Ibid., p. 22.

28. Ibid.

29. Federal Elections Commission press release, May 10, 1979.

30. Federal Election Commission, *Record 7*, no. 3 (1981).

31. See *Congressional Quarterly Weekly Report*, November 15, 1981, p. 3, for a review of these arguments.

32. *Los Angeles Herald-Examiner*, February 15, 1981.

33. Heard, *Costs of Democracy*, pp. 396–97.

34. *Congressional Quarterly Weekly Report*, September 29, 1979, p. 2151.

35. Edie N. Goldenberg and Michael W. Traugott, "Resource Allocations and Broadcast Expenditures in Congressional Campaigns" (a paper presented at the Annual Meeting of the American Political Science Association, Washington, D.C., September 1979).

36. Ibid., pp. 11–13.

37. The review of the early legislation is based in part on the very useful summary of this period found in Alexander, *Financing Politics*, pp. 61–69.

38. Originally quoted in Eugene H. Roseboom, *A History of Presidential Elections* (New York: Macmillan, 1957), p. 316. Cited by Alexander, *Financing Politics*, pp. 67–68. The three men were Belmont, Morgan, and Ryan.

39. *Newberry v. the U.S.*, 256 U.S. 232 (1921).

40. *U.S. v. Classic*, 313 U.S. 299 (1941).

41. See Alexander Heard, *The Costs of Democracy*, pp. 347–50, for an analysis of the effects of the Hatch Acts.

42. Federal Election Commission, *Record 6*, no. 3 (1980).

43. It is estimated, for example, that in 1976 if George Wallace and the American Independent Party had gotten its 13 percent of the popular vote (and the average Republican and Democratic vote was 43 percent) that Wallace's party would have received then about 30 percent of the average Republican and Democratic vote and thus would have been entitled to receive approximately $6.5 million (or 30 percent of $21.8 million).

44. See Alexander, *Financing Politics*, p. 162.

45. *Buckley v. Valeo*, 424 U.S. 1 (1976).

46. A good discussion is found in Alexander, "Regulation of Political Finance: The States Experience," *Financing Politics*, pp. 169–91; see also Jones, "Campaign Finance," for a careful analysis of the laws in the seventeen states that use public funding.

47. See Richard Reeves's column in the *Detroit Free Press*, April 6, 1979, p. 9A.

48. Quoted in Jon Nordheimer, *New York Times*, October 28, 1976.

49. Neil Staebler, quoted in Robert Shogan's column in the *Detroit Free Press*, February 1, 1976.

50. "How Money Talks in Congress," *Common Cause*, October 19, 1978, p. 1.

51. The Socialist Workers party and the American Civil Liberties Union did in September 1974 file a suit in federal district court in Washington, D.C., alleging infringement of free speech and association. They won a similar suit in Minnesota.

Chapter 15

1. See Robert A. Dahl, *A Preface to Democratic Theory* (Chicago: University of Chicago Press, 1956) and Joseph Schumpeter, *Capitalism, Socialism, and Democracy* (New York: Harper & Row, 1950) for elaborations of this position.

2. *Newsweek*, August 16, 1965, p. 15. Cited in William R. Keech, "Some Conditions of Negro Influences Over Public Policy Through Voting," in William Crotty, Donald Freeman, and Douglas Gatlin, eds., *Political Parties and Political Behavior* (Boston: Allyn & Bacon, 1971), p. 534.

3. Quoted from George Bernard Shaw by Walter Lippmann in *The Phantom Public* (New York: Macmillan, 1930), p. 59.

4. Schumpeter, *Capitalism, Socialism*, p. 269.

5. *Pravda*, February 27, 1955, section A.

6. See Lester Milbrath and M. L. Goel, *Political Participation* 2nd ed. (Chicago: Rand McNally, 1977), pp. 22–23; Sidney Verba, et al., *Participation and Political Equality* (New York: Cambridge University Press, 1978), pp. 58–59; David Butler and Donald Stokes, *Political Change in Britain*, 2nd ed. (New York: St. Martin's, 1969), p. 25.

7. For an analysis see Lester Milbrath, "Political Participation in the States," in Herbert Jacob and Kenneth N. Vines, eds., *Politics in the American States* (Boston: Little, Brown, 1965). These data for 1960 are from p. 36.

8. See the excellent analysis of Thomas E. Cavanaugh, "Changes in American Electoral Turnout, 1964–1976" (a paper presented to the Midwest Political Science Association in Chicago, April 1979), p. 9.

9. Angus Campbell, et al., *The American Voter* (Chicago: University of Chicago Press, 1960), pp. 277–82.

10. James E. Zinser and Paul A. Dawson, "Encouraging Voter Participation," in H. Alexander, ed., *Political Finance*, Electoral Studies Yearbook, vol. 5 (Beverly Hills: Sage, 1979), p. 230.

11. Ibid., p.,236.

12. For example, see William G. Andrews, "American Voting Participation," *Western Political Quarterly* 19 (1966): 639–52. He argues that the effective turnout rate in 1960 was 80 percent, much higher than the official rate. See also Herbert Asher, *Presidential Elections and American Politics* (Homewood, Ill.: Dorsey, 1976), pp. 42–48, for an excellent review of the turnout question in relation to election system requirements.

13. Herbert H. Hyman, *Political Socialization* (1959) (New York: Free Press, 1969), p. 12.

14. Gabriel Almond and Sidney Verba, *The Civic Culture* (Boston: Little, Brown, 1965), pp. 348–49.

15. M. Kent Jennings and Richard G. Niemi, *The Political Character of Adolescence: The Influence of Family and Schools* (Princeton: Princeton University Press, 1974). See also Robert D. Hess and Judith V. Torney, *The Development of Political Attitudes in Children* (Chicago: Aldine, 1967) and Fred I. Greenstein, *Children and Politics* (New Haven: Yale University Press, 1965).

16. See Bruce Campbell, *The American Electorate* (New York: Holt, Rinehart & Winston, 1979), p. 238.

17. Angus Campbell, et al., *The Voter Decides* (Evanston, Ill.: Row, Peterson, 1954), pp. 202–203.

18. Butler and Stokes, *Political Change in Britain*, p. 46.

19. Morris Janowitz and Dwaine Marvick, *Competitive Pressure and Democratic Consent* (Chicago: Quadrangle, 1956), p. 77.

20. University of Michigan Center for Political Studies, National Election Surveys, 1980.

21. Philip Converse and Richard Niemi, "Nonvoting Among Young Adults in the U.S.," in Crotty, *Political Parties*, pp. 464–65.

22. Cavanaugh, *Changes*, p. 12, argues that "elderly southern blacks are at present virtually the only demographic group in the entire population whose turnout is rising." In the short run, 1972 to 1976, southern whites in the upper age categories have also shown slight increases, and elderly northern blacks have also not declined in turnout. Data for 1980 is from 1980 U.S. Bureau of the Census advance report, "Voting and Registration in the Election of November 1980," issued January 1981.

23. Bureau of Census data. See William Crotty and G. Jacobson, *American Parties in Decline* (Boston: Little, Brown, 1980), p. 23.

24. Norman H. Nie, Sidney Verba, and John R. Petrocik, *The Changing American Voter* (Cambridge: Harvard University Press, 1976), p. 280.

25. Campbell, *The American Voter*, pp. 103–106. This early study based on the 1956 presidential election found the following:

*Differentials in Nonvoting Among
Attitude Groups (as a percentage)*

	Percentage Not Voting
A. Very interested	13
Somewhat interested	28
Not much interested	42
B. Concerned about election Outcome—very much	16
—don't care at all	48

26. As further support for this position see Milbrath, *Political Participation*, p. 72.

27. This summary is based on data from the University of Michigan Survey Research Center and Center for Political Studies. See Asher, *Presidential Elections*, pp. 222–29, for a good summary of these data.

28. A careful analysis of these data from University of Michigan Survey Research Center and Center for Political Studies is presented in Michael M. Wolfe, "Personal-Contact Campaigning in Presidential Elections" (a paper presented at the Annual Meeting of the Midwest Political Science Association in Chicago, April 1979). The data for 1980 come from the CBS/NES Surveys.

29. Wolfe, "Personal-Contact Campaigning."

30. Michael Robinson, "Public Affairs Television and the Growth of Political Malaise: The Case of the Selling of the Pentagon," Ph.D. dissertation, University of Michigan, 1972. For the quote used here see his article (same title) in *American Political Science Review* 70 (1976): 429.

31. Gary L. Wamsley and Richard A. Pride, "Television Network News: Rethinking the Iceberg Problem," *Western Political Quarterly* 25 (1972): 449–50.

32. Asher, *Presidential Elections*, p. 235. See his review of this literature and his excellent discussion of it, pp. 238–43.

33. Janowitz and Marvick, *Competitive Pressure*, p. 67.

34. See Samuel J. Eldersveld, *Political Parties: A Behavioral Analysis* (Chicago: Rand McNally, 1964), p. 464.

35. Janowitz and Marvick, *Competitive Pressure*, pp. 77, 84.

36. Philip Converse, "Information Flow and the Stability of Partisan Attitudes," *Public Opinion Quarterly* 26 (1962): 581.

37. Based on University of Michigan Center for Political Studies, National Election Surveys.

38. Martin Wattenberg. "The Decline of Political Partisanship in America: Negativity or Neutrality?" *American Political Science Review* 75, no. 4 (December 1981): 941–50.

39. Nie, Verba, and Petrocik, *American Voter*, p. 171.

40. See Milbrath, *Political Participation*, p. 72, for data relevant to this point.

41. King also said the biggest step Negroes can take is in "the direction of the voting booths." See "Civil Right No. 1—the Right to Vote," *New York Times Magazine*, March 14, 1965, p. 26ff. Quoted in Donald R. Matthews and James W. Prothro, *Negroes and the New Southern Politics* (New York: Harcourt, Brace and World, 1966) p. 11.

42. Quoted in *The Federalist*, no. 53.

43. Warren E. Miller and Donald E. Stokes, "Constituency Influence in Congress," *American Political Science Review* 57 (1963): 48.

44. John Kingdon, *Congressmen's Voting Decisions* (New York: Harper & Row, 1973), pp. 59–60.

45. James H. Kuklinski, "Representativeness and Elections: A Policy Analysis," *American Political Science Review* 72 (1978): 173. See also Duncan McCrae for his early pioneering work suggesting this thesis, *Dimensions of Congressional Voting* (Berkeley: University of California Press, 1958).

46. Sidney Verba and Norman H. Nie, *Participation in America: Political Democracy and Social Equality* (New York: Harper & Row, 1972), p. 335.

47. See Paul A. Beck, "The Systemic Consequences of Election Types: The Electoral Cycle and Patterns of American Politics" (a paper presented at the Annual Meeting of the American Political Science Association, Washington, D.C., September 1979); for a provocative essay on this problem see Cavanaugh, *Changes.*

48. Beck, "Systemic Consequences," p. 22.

Chapter 16

1. V. O. Key, Jr., *Politics, Parties and Pressure Groups*, 4th ed. (New York: T. Y. Crowell, 1958), p. 702.

2. William J. Keefe, *Congress and the American People* (Englewood Cliffs, N.J.: Prentice Hall, 1980), p. 101.

3. Ibid., p. 105.

4. Thomas E. Cronin, *The State of the Presidency* (Boston: Little, Brown, 1975), p. 107.

5. Edward R. Tufte, *Political Control of the Economy* (Princeton: Princeton University Press, 1980), p. 71.

6. Ibid., pp. 101–102.

7. Douglas Hibbs, "Political Parties and Macroeconomic Policy," *American Political Science Review* 71 (1977): 1486. Other scholars disagree with this position in part, at least the implication of presidential manipulation of the economy for electoral gain. See Thad A. Brown and Arthur A. Stein, "The Political Economy of National Elections," unpublished paper, University of California at Los Angeles, November, 1980.

8. Benjamin Ginsberg, "Elections and Public Policy," *The American Political Science Review* 70, no. 1 (1976): 49.

9. Keefe, *Congress*, p. 89.

10. See Julius Turner, *Party and Constituency: Pressures on Congress* (Baltimore: Johns Hopkins University Press, 1951), and the revision of this study by Edward V. Schneier in 1970.

11. Keefe, *Congress*, p. 91.

12. Ibid., p. 94. The session used here was the 94th Congress, 2nd Session, and the data are based on the *Congressional Quarterly Weekly Report*, February 5, 1977, p. 222.

13. Keefe, *Congress*, p. 95.

14. In the average cohesion score calculations (The Rice Index) perfect cohesion would be a score of 100; zero cohesion is when a party is split 50–50. See David W. Brady et al., "The Decline of Party in the U.S. House of Representatives 1887–1968," *Legislative Studies Quarterly* 4, no. 3 (1979): 384.

15. See Roger H. Davidson, *The Role of the Congressman* (New York: Pegasus, 1969), p. 145.

16. John Kingdon, *Congressmen's Voting Decisions* (New York: Harper & Row, 1973), p. 135.

17. Ibid., p. 120.

18. Randall Ripley, *Party Leadership in the House of Representatives* (Washington, D.C.: Brookings, 1967).

19. Kingdon, *Decisions*, p. 21.

20. Ibid., p. 109.

21. Ibid.

22. Morris P. Fiorina, *Congress: Keystone of the Washington Establishment* (New Haven: Yale University Press, 1977), p. 58.

23. Commission on Administrative Review, U.S. House of Representatives, *Scheduling the Work of the House* (1976), p. vii. See Keefe, *Congress*, for a discussion of the implications of this, p. 97.

24. Warren Miller and Donald Stokes, "Party Government and the Saliency of Congress," *Public Opinion Quarterly* 26 (Winter 1962): 541, table 4.

25. Warren Miller and Donald Stokes, "Constituency Influence in Congress," *The American Political Science Review* 57 (1963): 54, 56.

26. Jack Dennis's research since 1964 indicates a decline in party support on some measures. He also sees an increase in nonpartisan orientations. See "Trends in Public Support for the American Party System" (a paper presented at the Annual Meeting of the American Political Science Association in Chicago, September 1974).

27. Richard Neustadt, *Presidential Power* (New York: Wiley, 1960), p. 181.

28. Ibid., p. 33.

29. See William Keefe, *Congress*, p. 50.

30. Everett C. Ladd, *American Political Parties: Social Change and Political Response* (New York: Norton, 1970), pp. 50–52.

31. Speech to the National Press Club, January 14, 1960. Quoted in Robert H. Blank, *Political Parties: An Introduction* (Englewood Cliffs, N.J.: Prentice Hall, 1980), p. 183.

32. Press conference, May 31, 1955. The *New York Times*, June 1, 1955. Quoted in Neustadt, *Presidential Power*, p. 166.

33. James D. Barber, "The Interplay of Presidential Character and Style: A Paradigm and Five Illustrations," in F. Greenstein and M. Lerner, eds., *A Source Book for the Study of Personality and Politics* (Chicago: Markham, 1971), p. 390.

34. Keefe, *Congress*, p. 108.

35. *Congressional Quarterly Weekly Report*, April 16, 1977, p. 691, quoted in Keefe, *Congress*, p. 113.

36. Kingdon, *Decisions*, pp. 18–19, 183.

37. Allen Barton, "Consensus and Conflict Among American Leaders," *Public Opinion Quarterly* (Winter 1974–75): 512n.

38. As quoted by Louis W. Koenig, *The Chief Executive* (New York: Harcourt Brace Jovanovich, 1975), p. 125. Used by Keefe, *Congress*, p. 112.

39. V. O. Key, Jr., *Southern Politics* (New York: Knopf, 1949), ch. 14, p. 309.

40. See David Nice's summary of Key's argument in "The Impact of Barriers to Party Government in the American States," Ph.D. dissertation, University of Michigan, 1979, pp. 2–11.

41. See, for example, Richard Dawson and James Robinson, "Interparty Competition, Economic Variables, and Welfare Policies in the American States," *Journal of Politics* 25 (1963): 265–89; Charles Cnudde and Donald McCrone, "Party Competition and Welfare Policies in the American States," *American Political Science Review* 63 (1969): 858–66; Thomas Dye, *Politics, Economics, and the Public* (Chicago: Rand McNally, 1966); Ira Sharkansky and Richard Hofferbert, "Dimensions of State Politics, Economics, and Public Policy," *American Political Science Review* 63 (1969): 867–79; Brian Fry and Richard Winters, "The Politics of Redistribution," *American Political Science Review* 64 (1970): 508–22; Bernard Booms and James Halldorson, "The Politics of Redistribution: A Reformulation," *American Political Science Review* 67 (1973): 924–33; for a recent analysis see Edward T. Jennings, Jr., "Competition, Constituencies, and Welfare Policies in American States," *American Political Science Review* 73, no. 2 (1979): 414–29.

42. Duane Lockard, *New England State Politics* (Princeton: Princeton University Press, 1959), ch. 12, pp. 320–40.

43. Robert Albritton, "Welfare Policy," in Herbert Jacob and Kenneth N. Vines, eds., *Politics in the American States* (Boston: Little, Brown, 1976), p. 366.

44. Virginia Gray, "Innovation in the States: A Diffusion Study," *American Political Science Review* 67 (1973): 1174–85. An earlier study by Jack Walker pioneered the study of innovation in the states: "The Diffusion of Innovation Among the American States," *American Political Science Review* 63 (1969): 880–99.

45. Thomas Dye, *Politics, Economics, and the Public: Policy Outcomes in the American States* (Chicago: Rand McNally, 1966), p. 107. See also Ira Sharkansky, *The Politics of Taxing and Spending* (Indianapolis: Bobbs Merrill, 1969), pp. 192–94.

46. See Nice, "Barriers," p. 38.

47. Richard Hofferbert, *Socioeconomic, Political and Public Policy Data, 1890–1960*, Inter-University Consortium for Political Research, University of Michigan, mimeographed paper.

48. Nice, "Barriers," p. 139.

49. James Maxwell and J. Richard Aronson, *Financing State and Local Governments* (Washington, D.C.: The Brookings Institution, 1977), p. 89.

50. Walter Burnham, "The End of American Party Politics," *Transaction* 7 (1969): 20.

Chapter 17

1. Walter Burnham, *Critical Elections and the Mainsprings of American Politics* (New York: Norton, 1970), pp. 130–31, 135.

2. David Broder, *Ann Arbor News*, November 20, 1980.

3. Norman H. Nie, Sidney Verba, and John R. Petrocik, *The Changing American Voter* (Cambridge: Harvard University Press, 1976), pp. 241, 354.

4. James Sundquist, *Dynamics of the Party System* (Washington, D.C.: The Brookings Institution, 1973), p. 373.

5. This description is drawn largely from Burnham and Sundquist's treatment of the subject. See also John R. Petrocik, *Party Coalitions—Realignments and the Decline of the New Deal Party System* (Chicago: University of Chicago Press, 1981); see also Kristi Anderson, *The Creation of a Democratic Majority 1928–1936* (Chicago: University of Chicago Press, 1979).

6. V. O. Key, Jr., "A Theory of Critical Elections," *Journal of Politics* 17 (1955): 4, 16.

7. See Philip E. Converse, *The Dynamics of Party Support* (Beverly Hills: Sage, 1976), pp. 103–19.

8. Nie, *American Voter*, p. 350.

9. Ibid., p. 241. The summary presented here rests on the argument (and to some extent on the data) found in ch. 13.

10. Everett C. Ladd, Jr., "The Shifting Party Coalitions—1932–1976," in Seymour M. Lipset, ed., *Emerging Coalitions in American Politics* (San Francisco: Institute for Contemporary Studies, 1978), pp. 92–94.

11. Arthur H. Miller, et al., "A Majority Party in Disarray: Policy Polarization in the 1972 Election," *American Political Science Review* 70 (1976): 753–78.

12. See Angus Campbell et al., *American Voter*, for this interpretation of the 1952 and 1956 presidential elections.

13. Warren Miller and Teresa Levitin, *Leadership and Change* (Cambridge, Mass.: Winthrop, 1976), pp. 63–91, 191–240.

14. Nie, *American Voter*, p. 142.

15. Ibid., p. 245.

16. Ibid, p. 197.

17. For an excellent review of the research on the role of issues in voting see Herbert Asher, "The Issue Voting Controversy," *Presidential Elections and American Politics* (Homewood, Ill.: Dorsey, 1976), ch. 4.

18. Key, "A Theory," *Journal of Politics* and Burnham, *Critical Elections*, support the first theory. For the second see Adam Prezeworski, "Institutionalization of Voting Patterns, or Is Mobilization the Source of Decay," *American Political Science Review* 69 (1975): 49–67.

19. See Nie, *American Voter*, pp. 270–88 for considerable data on this question.

20. Miller, "Majority Party in Disarray."

21. Cited by Peter D. Hart, "The Democrats' Road to Recovery," *Chicago Tribune*, February 8, 1981.

22. For a discussion of these matters on issues and ideology see the analysis by Arthur Miller and others in the *Institute for Social Research Newsletter* (Spring 1981).

23. Gerald Pomper, et al., *The Election of 1980* (Chatham, N.J.: Chatham, 1981), p. 80.

24. Ibid., p. 75.

25. Ibid., pp. 86–87.

26. David Broder, "The Parties Trading Places," *Ann Arbor News*, June 28, 1981.

27. Nie, *American Voter*, p. 166.

28. Philip E. Converse and Gregory B. Markus, "Plus ça change—: The New CPS Election Study Panel," *American Political Science Review* 73, no. 1 (1979): 32–49; see also Edward G. Carmines and James A. Stimson, "Issue Evolution, Population Replacement and Normal Partisan Change," *American Political Science Review* 75 (1981): 107–118.

Chapter 18

1. James Q. Wilson, *Political Organizations* (New York: Basic, 1973), p. 95.

2. Jeane Kirkpatrick, *Dismantling the Parties* (Washington, D.C.: American Enterprise Institute, 1978), pp. 2–3.

3. The controversy between Converse and Burnham over how to interpret the high voting turnouts in American history, particularly before 1900, which were discussed in ch. 15, are related to the concern expressed here.

4. Robert Agranoff, "The New Style of Campaigning: The Decline of Party and the Rise of Candidate-Centered Technology," in Jeff Fishel, ed., *Parties and Elections in An Anti-Party Age* (Bloomington: Indiana University Press, 1978) p. 232.

5. Kirkpatrick, *Dismantling*, p. 10. She cites the *Washington Post* delegate survey reported July 11, 1976.

6. David Broder, *Ann Arbor News*, June 15, 1980.

7. Gerald Pomper et al., *The Election of 1980* (Chatham, N.J.: Chatham, 1981), p. 92.

8. Cornelius P. Cotter et al., "State Party Organizations and the Thesis of Party Decline" (a paper presented at the Annual Meeting of the American Political Science Association, Washington, D.C., August 1980), p. 36.

9. See also ch. 15 for a discussion of the role of party evaluations as linked to voting and nonvoting. Martin Wattenberg has reanalyzed much of the Survey Research Center, Center for Political Studies data in "The Decline of Political Partisanship in America: Negativity or Neutrality," *American Political Science Review* 75, no. 4 (December 1981): 941–50.

10. See Angus Campbell, *The American Voter*, abridged ed. (New York: Wiley, 1964), ch. 7, especially p. 106.

11. Michael M. Wolfe, "Personal-Contact Campaigning in Presidential Elections" (a paper presented at the Midwest Political Science Association Annual Meeting in Chicago, April 1979), pp. 13–14.

12. See Morris Janowitz and Dwaine Marvick, *Competitive Pressure and Democratic Consent* (Chicago: Quadrangle Books, 1964), p. 82.

13. Samuel J. Eldersveld, *Political Parties: A Behavioral Analysis* (Chicago: Rand McNally, 1964), pp. 442–3, 461, 471.

14. Ibid., pp. 460, 469.

15. Ibid., pp. 132, 278.

16. Ibid., p. 223.

17. Michael J. Robinson, "Public Affairs Television and the Growth of Political Malaise: The Case of the 'Selling of the Pentagon,'" *American Political Science Review* 70 (1976): 409–32.

18. Michael J. Robinson, "Media Coverage in the Primary Campaign of 1976: Implications for Voters, Candidates, and Parties," in William Crotty, ed., *The Party Symbol* (San Francisco: W. J. Freeman, 1980), pp. 178–91. Quotation from p. 187.

19. Ibid., pp. 420, 426, 430.

20. This summary is taken from "The Role of the Mass Media in Presidential Campaigns: The Lessons of the 1976 Election," *ITEMS*, Social Science Research Council: 34, no. 2 (1980): 25–30. See Thomas E. Patterson, *The Mass Media Election: How Americans Choose Their President* (New York: Praeger, 1980).

21. Ibid., p. 30.

22. Arthur H. Miller, Edie N. Goldenberg, and Lutz Erbring, "Type-Set Politics: Impact of Newspapers on Public Confidence," *American Political Science Review* 73 (1979): 67–84 (see pp. 80–81 for concluding quote).

23. Austin Ranney, *Curing the Mischiefs of Faction: Party Reform in America* (Berkeley: University of California Press, 1975); see also William Crotty, *Political Reform and the American Experiment* (New York: T. Y. Crowell, 1977).

24. See Crotty, *Political Reform*, pp. 252–55 for details of these provisions of the charter.

25. Ibid., pp. 255–60.

26. See, for example, Charles Longley, "Party Reform and Party Nationalization: The Case of the Democrats," in William Crotty, ed., *The Party Symbol*, pp. 359–78.

27. David S. Broder, "The Case for Responsible Party Government," in Jeff Fishel, ed., *Parties and Elections in An Anti-Party Age* (Bloomington: Indiana University Press, 1978), p. 27.

28. Kirkpatrick, *Dismantling*, p. 2.

29. "Toward a More Responsible Two-Party System," (a Report of the Committee of Political Parties). *American Political Science Review* (Supplement) 44, no. 3, pt. 2 (1950).

30. See Ranney, *Curing the Mischiefs of Faction*, p. 45.

31. Evron Kirkpatrick, "Toward a More Responsible Party System: Political Science, Policy Science, or Pseudoscience?" in Fishel, *Parties and Elections*, pp. 33–54.

32. David S. Broder, "The Case for Responsible Party Government," in Fishel, *Parties and Elections*, p. 25.

33. Anthony King, "Political Parties in Western Democracies," *Polity* 2 (1969): 111–41.

34. Broder, in Fishel, *Parties and Elections*, p. 29.

35. James Bryce, *The American Commonweath* (New York: Macmillan, 1916), p. 5.

INDEX